GODS ON

GODS ON EARTH

THE MANAGEMENT OF RELIGIOUS EXPERIENCE AND IDENTITY IN A NORTH INDIAN PILGRIMAGE CENTRE

PETER VAN DER VEER

LONDON SCHOOL OF ECONOMICS MONOGRAPHS ON SOCIAL ANTHROPOLOGY

Volume 59

Routledge
Taylor & Francis Group

LONDON AND NEW YORK

First published 2004 by Berg Publishers

Published 2020 by Routledge
2 Park Square, Milton Park, Abingdon, Oxon OX14 4RN
605 Third Avenue, New York, NY 10017

First issued in paperback 2021

Routledge is an imprint of the Taylor & Francis Group, an informa business

ISBN 13: 978-0-367-71688-2 (pbk)
ISBN 13: 978-1-8452-0302-3 (hbk)

Contents

Acknowledgements   vii

Note on transliteration   viii

Maps   ix

Preface   xi

I Ayodhya: Time and Place   1

1 Introduction   1
2 Sarayu and the ghats   9
3 The presence of Ram   18
4 The conjunction of time and place   28
5 Ayodhya in history   34

II Problems and Perspectives   44

1 The study of meaning   44
2 Hinduism: the orientalist perspective   52
3 The study of a pilgrimage centre   58

III Devotion and Ascetisicm   66

1 Introduction   66
2 Tradition and Identity   85
3 Tyagis   107
4 Nagas   130
5 Rasiks   159
6 Conclusion: The Ramanandis, an open category   172

IV The sacred as a profession   183

1 Introduction   183
2 The ideal Brahman as an ideological construct   189
3 The formation of professional identities   211
4 Competition and Violence   241
5 Conclusion: Values and Existence   259

Contents

V   Conclusion   268

*Appendix 1   Kanak Bhavan, an example of a temple
  built by a raja*   273

Appendix 2   Caste temples   275

Appendix 3   Rules and regulations of Hanumangarhi   277

Notes   281

Bibliography   296

Glossary   304

Index   306

Acknowledgements

This book is the result of a long interest in Hindu pilgrimage which was encouraged during my study of Sanskrit and Hinduism at the University of Groningen. J. Ensink helped me to find my way to Lucknow and, finally, to Ayodhya. The research was made possible by the Departments of Anthropology of the Free University of Amsterdam and the University of Utrecht. Arie de Ruijter of the latter institution especially kept me on the track with diligence. Three of my field trips were financially supported by the Netherlands Foundation for the Advancement of Tropical Research.

In Ayodhya I received the invaluable help of Ram Raksha Tripathi who acted as my guide, interpreter, teacher, informant and what not. My wife and I were accepted as members of his family and, what is more, we feel like that. Thanks to the Tripathi family Ayodhya has become our second home. It will be clear that a study like this could not have been sustained without the willingness and sometimes even encouragement of the religious specialists whose life and history I had come to record. Although my study may show a rather bleak picture of the pilgrimage system, in which these specialists have to work, their friendliness towards me cannot be overestimated.

I have received great help in preparing the book and in developing and shaping the argument. I am grateful to Mart Bax, Alan Entwistle, Matthew Schoffeleers and Bonno Thoden van Velzen for their valuable comments and suggestions. By inviting me as an academic visitor in the summer term of 1986 the Department of Anthropology of the London School of Economics enabled me to discuss my work with many colleagues. I have especially benefited from the critical comments of Christopher Fuller and Jonathan Parry. I am much indebted to Michael Sallnow for editing my attempts at writing English.

Finally, I want to dedicate this book to my shakti, Jacobien de Boer.

Note on transliteration

A number of problems arise in dealing with the transliteration of Indian languages in a monograph which is written for both Indianists and general anthropologists. I have tried to convey Hindi pronunciation rather than Sanskrit orthography. That means that I have in general dropped the final "a" in, for example, "Ram(a)" and "Shiv(a)". Inconsistency seems, however, the unavoidable price for these decisions. Only the words in italics have been given diacritical marks.

Map of Uttar Pradesh

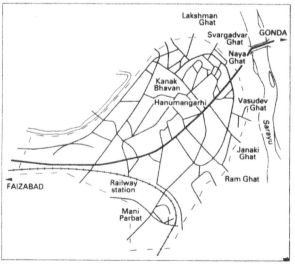

Map of Ayodhya

Preface

This study deals with Ayodhya, a Hindu pilgrimage centre in the North Indian state of Uttar Pradesh.[1] Its subject is not, however, pilgrimage or pilgrims. My research focuses on those who reside in Ayodhya rather than its visitors. By offering an interpretative description of the way religious specialists – monks and priests – live and of the institutions that tie them together, I intend to analyse the main forces that mould religious identity and experience.

The web of relationships among the various groups of specialists to a large extent decides their social position and their leverage over laymen. To understand the way religious specialists are organized, and the beliefs that they hold, it is necessary to understand their interaction and competition between them. Relationships within this arena – the pilgrimage centre – are in their turn affected by large-scale political and economic processes. That all these relations are in a state of flux and that beliefs, values and religious experiences change accordingly, is the keystone of my argument: none of these religious phenomena is fixed in a static system of meaning, nor can they be directly deduced from the sacred tenets of Hinduism.

In the following chapter I attempt to present an 'inside' view of Ayodhya as a place of pilgrimage.[2] This will be supplemented by some broad historical observations relevant to the study. The second chapter will set out the principal theoretical problems and perspectives. Chapters III and IV form the core of the book. Both chapters consider the two chief groups of religious specialists, the Ramanandi monks and the Brahman priests. Central to my investigation is the question of how, and to what extent, their social identity is formed by forces operating within these groups and forces impinging on them from without. Both identity formation and the shaping of religious experiences will be shown to be heavily influenced by political processes, through the interplay and competition of political actors who constantly define and redefine their position in the pilgrimage arena. The priests and monks are depicted as political actors who articulate, underplay or stress their identities, depending on how they perceive conditions in the local arena and how they assess strategic processes in the wider North Indian society. This argument leads inevitably to a critique of dominant 'orientalist' and 'symbolic' approaches to the phenomena of caste and sect, and hence to a reconsideration of certain ideas generally received in the study of Hinduism and of Indian society.

It is necessary to introduce at this stage some of the themes which will be treated in detail in chapters III and IV concerning the Ramanandis and the Ayodhya pandas.

Ramanandis

The Ramanandis are divided into two sections: a monastic order of religious specialists (*sādhus*) and a community of laymen. We are concerned here with the monastic order. The social organization of this order is loosely structured and based on spiritual lineages of gurus and their initiates. Some sadhus have a position of authority when they act as gurus for other sadhus as well as for laymen. The fundamental difference between sadhus and laymen is based upon two qualities the sadhus possess: their specialization in a religious method (*sādhanā*) and their celibacy.

There is much diversity in religious and social attitudes among the Ramanandi sadhus. We can distinguish three sections among them: *tyāgis, nāgās* and *rasiks*. Tyagis follow a relatively radical path of asceticism and renunciation. They lead a peripatetic life in itinerant groups. Nagas are fighting sadhus who are trained in the use of violence and live in fortified temples. Rasiks are sadhus specialized in a kind of 'sweet devotion' which centres on the worship of images in temples. They emphasize the emotional relation between the devotee, who is envisaged as being female, and the deity.

These subdivisions of the Ramanandi order relate to a historical process of sedentarization. Tyagis are still to a great extent ascetics who roam in the jungle, while the nagas are already to some degree sedentarized as a result of their military organization. The rasiks, however, are unambiguously temple-dwellers (*asthānadhārīs*), living in sacred centres. The tyagi may be called a 'world renouncer' and, as such, may be opposed to the lay householder who remains in the caste society. We should, however, be careful not to push this opposition too far, as Dumont (1970) did when he argued that renunciation and caste were two structurally opposed institutions. The social origin of a renouncer is never unimportant for his status among other sadhus, and a renouncer is never a man outside the world, since his religious and economic transactions bind him to the world. Asceticism and renunciation, then, form a tendency in the process of identity formation of Ramanandi sadhus, but the other tendency is that of sedentarization.

The social origin of a sadhu tends to play a larger role in a settled life among householders than in a peripatetic life. One of my arguments will be that the process of sedentarization among the Ramanandi sadhus, which is a correlate of the loss of functional autonomy of sadhus in Indian society, brings about a relatively stronger emphasis on social origin in the determination of a sadhu's status. The latter development is linked to the process of articulating exclusive caste identities in North India during the British period.

My general argument will be that the Ramanandis form an *open category* of sadhus. Their origin is unknown, just as their alleged founder Ramanand is a completely legendary figure. There is no clear theological core to their teaching, or in their methods of reaching spiritual perfection. Moreover, the Ramanandis combine religious ideas and practices which are otherwise found in entirely separate traditions. The tyagis are organized in much the same way as the Shivaite Tantric Gorakhnath Jogis, with whom they share many ascetic practices. The nagas seem to have copied their military organization from the Shivaite Dashanamis. Finally, the rasiks worship Ram in a way which is strikingly similar to the way of other groups who worship Krishna. An important festival in Ayodhya, *Jhūlā*, seems to be a copy of the festival celebrated in Krishna's Braj. Possibly because of their 'openness' in terms of organization and identity, the Ramanandis have become probably the largest monastic order of North India.

Pandas

The Brahman priest is a god on earth. He is the acme of purity and superior to every other being in this life. This is part of Hindu ideology as laid down in the Sanskrit texts written, not surprisingly, by Brahmans themselves. This ideology is taken as the basis of Dumont's interpretation of the caste system, in which the purity of the Brahman priests gives them the highest social status (Dumont, 1972). Both the ideology and Dumont's interpretations are, however, contradicted by social reality. *Paṇḍās* are Brahman priests who work in sacred centres (*tīrthas*). Their position is highly equivocal. They act as sacrificial vessels by accepting gifts (*dān*) of all kinds. Sacrificers (*jajmāns*) try to get rid of sin (*pāp*) and illness (*rog*) by giving donations to these pandas, who become tainted as a result. Another aspect of their ambiguous status is the nature of their relationship with patrons. On the one hand, the Brahman priest is ideologically of superior status, while on the other hand he is economically dependent on the patrons.

Almost the entire discussion of the position of the Brahman priest focuses on value orientations. While Dumont (1972) argues that the Brahman priest has the highest status in Hindu society, because of the importance of the value of purity, Marriott and Inden (1975) go as far as to say that the caste system is organized to enable the Brahman priest to retain his purity. Heesterman (1971), Parry (1980) and Fuller (1984) argue that there is a contradiction in the Brahman's priesthood. The 'ideal Brahman' renounces the priesthood and the dependence on donations. I shall argue that instead of limiting our research to values we should look at behaviour. Pandaship is an occupational identity of Brahmans which is chosen in circumstances that favour such a choice and which can be discarded in other circumstances. There was a time when many Brahmans in Ayodhya were attracted to becoming pandas, but nowadays some of these families try to quit the profession. The social significance of the acceptance of gifts is critically dependent on the changing nature of the social configuration, of which both priest and patrons are part. Moreover, it is important to realize that this configuration is not an isolated entity, but is related to other, more comprehensive configurations. Fundamental to an understanding of the changing interdependence of priest and patrons is the role of state formation in North India.

When the pilgrimage system began to expand in the late eighteenth and early nineteenth centuries, the pandas of Ayodhya started to contract enduring so-called *jajmānī* (patronage) relations not only with élite patrons, but also with pilgrims belonging to middle and lower groups. In that period a professional group of local Brahmans with caste-like boundaries, called the Gangaputras, was formed. Simultaneously, a group of Bhareriya outsiders, known as 'spurious Brahmans' in the contemporary British literature, tried to enter the panda profession. The British attempt to settle 'traditional' rights in the pilgrimage system had a great impact on both the process of identity formation of these groups and on the growing competition between them.

Due to structural change in the pilgrimage system during the twentieth century, the ritual theatre of pilgrimage has become an arena of violent competition not only between the Gangaputras and the Bhareriyas, but also between various individual entrepreneurs within these groups. I shall describe the factors determining the transformation of pilgrimage from a system defined by long-term, personal jajmani relations with a limited role of money-exchange, to a system characterized by short-term, impersonal market relations between a seller of ritual services and a buyer who uses money as his means of paying. Subsequently, I want to measure the effects of these changes on the position of the pandas and to show how after a war of all against all, one entrepreneur with his private army has come to control most of the pilgrimage market.

On the most general and abstract level, my argument is that concepts of sin, greed, purity and independence may have different meanings in different social and historical settings. As I attempt to show, they do not depend only on an elusive 'Hindu tradition', but as much on social interaction in changing circumstances.

I Ayodhya: Time and Place

1. Introduction

Some 120 kilometres from Lucknow, the capital of Uttar Pradesh, India's largest state, lies the rather unimpressive and dusty town of Ayodhya. Coming from Lucknow by rail one first passes Faizabad, an important junction, where many passengers leave or board the train. Only ten minutes after leaving Faizabad the train arrives in Ayodhya. It is a large station, but usually only a few people get out here. The need for such a large station becomes apparent only on those occasions when whole trainloads of passengers have Ayodhya as their destination. Ayodhya is a *tīrtha*, a Sanskrit word we usually translate as 'place of pilgrimage.' Most visitors are pilgrims, who make the journey to Ayodhya, and often also to other tirthas, for religious reasons; a *tīrth yātrā* as they say in India. On some occasions hundreds of thousands of them arrive together in Ayodhya, but in general they come in small parties with their own means of conveyance – a hired bus, a reserved compartment in the train, or, if they are rich enough, a car. The vast majority of the pilgrims are Hindus and the reason for their visit becomes clear as soon as one looks at the architecture of the station. It has been built in the form of a Hindu temple, and over the entrance is a depiction of the divine couple, Ram and Sita, together with Ram's brother Lakshman. Ayodhya is the birthplace of the Hindu god Ram and the place where he spent an important part of his earthly life. It is therefore a place where his presence can be constantly felt, a sacred environment.

But it is not only Hindus who come to Ayodhya on pilgrimage. It is also sacred to Jains, who believe that Rishabdev, the first of their preceptors (*tīrthankaras*), was born here. The Jains have some important temples in Ayodhya which are regularly visited by pilgrims from all over India. Buddhists may also regard Ayodhya as a sacred place because it is identified by them with Saket, one of the oldest towns mentioned in the Buddhist scriptures and a place where, according to local tradition, the Buddha himself meditated. Even

Muslims may feel that Ayodhya is sacred because of the existence of a grave in which they believe Noah was buried.

Although Ayodhya is clearly a place in which the religious interests of different groups converge, it is primarily a Hindu tīrtha and on this we will concentrate. What is a tīrtha? In the words of Mircea Eliade it is a *hierophany*, a place where heaven touches the earth, where sacred and profane meet. In accordance with its literal meaning in Sanskrit of 'ford', the term *tīrtha* is used for places where a river can be crossed. It is no great wonder that in Hinduism the word for 'sacred place' refers to a place at a riverside. The river is an ancient and complex cultural symbol in Hinduism. India's rivers are seen as originating in heaven and flowing vertically from the celestial lake of divine waters down through the atmosphere, and out on to the face of the earth. This is evident in the well-known myth of the descent of India's most sacred river, 'Mother Ganga', which flowed in heaven until the penance and devotion of Bhagirath induced the god Shiv to command Ganga to descend; the god held her in the coils of his matted hair in order to prevent her from destroying the world in her fall. Every Hindu knows the story and Shiv is often depicted with Ganga flowing in his matted hair. Ayodhya, too, is situated on the bank of a sacred river, the Sarayu, and there is also a legend about her descent from heaven. It is not as famous as the story of the Ganges, but is nevertheless important in the sacred lore of Ayodhya:

> In the beginning of creation a lotus sprang from the navel of Narayana, which gave birth to Brahma. Then Brahma worshipped Narayana, and when he had worshipped for a thousand years, Vishnu, gratified by such devotion, blessed him, with tears of affection in his eyes. The adoring Brahma caught the dropping tears in the hollow of his palm, and stored them in a wooden vessel, which he kept next to his heart. Ages after, Manu, the first of the solar race, was king in Ayodhya. His son Ikswaku was so studious in his devotions, that the great Brahma, pleased, told him to ask a boon. Ikswaku asked for a holy river, and Brahma gave him the treasured tears of Narayana which thenceforward flowed as the Sarayu. (Carnegy 1870: app. B: I)

It is clear that the local priests used to relate this story to the pilgrims in order to stress the divine origin and therefore the great power (*mahimā*) of the river. Sarayu is a goddess, just like Ganga and many other great rivers in India; she is therefore worshipped and asked for boons. Her water also has a purifying strength and is therefore of great importance for the Hindu pilgrim who wants to get rid of all kinds of impurity. When we follow a pilgrim who arrives in Ayodhya we find that one of his first ritual acts is to take a bath in the river Sarayu, worship it, and perform other rituals for which the bank of a sacred river is considered to be the most suitable location.

Ayodhya then is a tirtha in the literal sense of ford, a place to cross the sacred river Sarayu. One of the oldest holy spots on the banks of the Sarayu in the sacred area (*kshetra*) of Ayodhya has the telling name of Gopratara, literally 'oxen-ford'. The word tirtha also has a metaphorical meaning since, like the related verb *tr/tarati*, it is traditionally related to crossing in a ritual and a spiritual sense (Eck, 1981). In the ritual context it is connected with sacrifice (cf. Ensink, 1974), the crossing of the sacrificer to heaven, while in the spiritual context it is the crossing from the realm of birth and death to immortality.

The river is, then, part of a ritual context. It is connected with heaven and the sacrificer crosses over to heaven at the tirtha by, for example, making contact with the world of his ancestors. Rivers and death are also clearly associated. The riverside is an appropriate place for cremation, one of the rituals which comes readily to mind when one thinks of crossing over to the other world. Benaras is, of course, India's most famous cremation ground and consequently a complete death industry has grown up there; but Ayodhya on the Sarayu also functions, at least at district level, as a place for the performance of the ritual of cremation. A telling example of the connection between rivers and death is also the Vaitarani ritual. There is an ancient idea that after dying one has to cross the terrible river of death, Vaitarani, which stinks of blood and bones. The cow will help the dead to cross by allowing them to grasp its tail so as to be taken to the far shore. This ritual is symbolically 'acted out' on the bank of the river by a ceremony in which the cow-saviour is worshipped. Going to the tirtha not only has the performance of rituals as its aim, but is also a ritual in itself. Like every other ritual it starts with a declaration of intent (*saṃkalp*) and, depending on what kind of pilgrimage is intended, the pilgrim has to make all kinds of ritual preparations, such as putting on a pilgrim's dress of yellow-brownish colour as if going to renounce the world. The tirth yatra replaces other rites and sacrifices and is in itself a sacrifice. During the journey the pilgrim has to behave like an ascetic by fasting and observing sexual abstinence. Going to a tirtha has a good effect, as stated in the *Vishnudharmottara-purāṇa* 111.273, 7 (quoted in Kane, 1953, IV: 563): 'When resort is made to a tirtha, it removes the sins of the sinful and tends to the increase of merit in the case of the good.'

Ayodhya is, however, not only and not even primarily a tirtha in the ritual sense, but also in the spiritual sense. It is first and foremost the place of Lord Ram. It is not easy to summarize the story of Ram, since it is the subject of an immense literature in Sanskrit and Hindi, as well as in all other Indian languages. Central to this literature are the *Rāmāyaṇa* written in Sanskrit by Valmiki, and a seventeenth-century version by Tulsidas, *Rāmcharitmānas*. The latter was often called 'the bible of the Hindus' by administrators and missionaries in the British period – an inappropriate comparison, but one that indicates its immense popularity in Hindi-speaking North India. Not only is it difficult to give a concise impression of the content of these works, but the task is further complicated by the different theological interpretations given to the Ram story. I will, however, begin with a bare outline (rendered at length in Basham, 1975: 414–15). Dashrath, member of the solar clan which ruled the kingdom of Koshala in Ayodhya, had by his three wives four sons named Ram, Bharat, Lakshman and Shatrughna. The four attended the court of King Janak of Videha, where an archery contest was held for the hand of Janak's daughter Sita. Ram won this contest and brought his wife to the court of his father to whose throne he should succeed as the oldest son. The second queen, Kaikeyi, however, contrived to have her own son Bharat installed as heir apparent and to have Ram banished from Ayodhya. Although both Dashrath and Bharat opposed Kaikeyi's intrigue, Ram went into voluntary exile together with his wife Sita and his brother Lakshman. When Dashrath died Bharat took over the kingdom, but he made it clear to everyone that he was only waiting for the return of Ram. During their exile in the forest, Ram, Sita and Lakshman regularly came into conflict with demons. The king of demons, Ravan, who resided on Lanka, decided to fight these intruders. He succeeded in abducting Sita to Lanka. The two brothers sought the help of the king of monkeys,

Sugriv, and his loyal minister, Hanuman. With their help they succeeded in reaching Ravan's palace on Lanka. After a fierce battle Ravan and the other demons were slain and Sita was rescued. They all returned to Ayodhya where Ram was installed on the throne of Koshala. He ruled as a virtuous king (*dharmarājā*) and brought happiness to all. The story ends with Ram deciding to return to heaven together with the rest of the population of Ayodhya. In heaven Ram resumes the form of Vishnu. In the Sanskrit *Ramayana* Sita, whose name means 'furrow', is swallowed by her mother, the earth.

A common theological interpretation of this story is that Ram is the incarnation (*avatār*) of Vishnu. The latter is, with Shiv, one of the two great male gods of present-day Hinduism. His name means 'pervader', since he is manifest everywhere, pervading everything. He appears in the phenomenal world at all crucial moments in its history in order to guide the evolution of creation. In Hinduism the conception of world history is extremely complicated. According to Hindu cosmogony the cosmos passes through cycles within cycles, for eternity.

The basic cycle is the *kalpa*, a 'day of Brahma' or 4,320 million earthly years. His night is of equal length. 360 days and nights constitute 'a year of Brahma' and his life lasts for 100 such years. The largest cycle is therefore 311,040,000 million years long, after which the whole universe returns to the ineffable world-spirit, until another creator-god is evolved. In each cosmic day the god creates the universe and again absorbs it. During the cosmic night he sleeps, and the whole universe is gathered up into his body, where it remains as a potentiality. Within each kalpa are fourteen *manvantaras*, or secondary cycles, each lasting 306,720,000 years, with long intervals between them. In these periods the world is recreated, and a new Manu appears, as the progenitor of the human race. We are now in the seventh manvantara of the kalpa of which the Manu is known as Manu Vaivasvata. Each manvantara contains seventy-one *Mahāyugas*, or aeons, of which a thousand form the kalpa. Each Mahayuga is in turn divided into four *yugas*, called *Krita, Tretā, Dvāpara* and *Kali*. Each yuga represents a progressive decline in piety, morality, strength, stature, longevity and happiness. We are at present in the Kali-yuga.

This passage, which is quoted from Basham (1975: 323), makes at least one thing clear: the Hindu conception of time and history makes human existence on earth seem insignificant in the extreme. Although the basic outline of this cosmology is known to many Hindus, I have met only one theological specialist in Ayodhya who really could work with it and even succeeded in complicating it further. It has the same impact on most Hindus I have spoken with as it has on me, namely that we seem to be in the worst period of a cycle and are waiting for the world's dissolution. *Dharma*, the order of the world and of society, is disintegrating and only devotion (*bhakti*) to the saviour-god can save us.

The theory of Vishnu's avataras is connected with this cosmology. When the cosmos in a certain yuga is threatened by the powers of darkness, the demons, then Vishnu incarnates to sustain it. In the Krita-yuga he incarnates as a fish, as a tortoise, as a boar, and as half-man, half-lion. In the Treta-yuga he incarnates as a dwarf, as Ram-with-the Axe, and as Ram. In the Dvapara-yuga he incarnates as Krishna. In the Kali-yuga he is incarnated as Buddha and finally as Kalki, who is yet to come. He will re-establish a golden age, punish the evil-doers, comfort the virtuous, and then destroy the world. Later, from the ruins of the earth, a new mankind will arise (Daniélou, 1964: 181).

According to indological interpretations Vishnu has, thanks to this doctrine of avataras, absorbed many formerly separate divine beings. Most important in modern Hinduism are the two great human incarnations, Ram and Krishna, and, as we will see later, Ram has even eclipsed Vishnu in some theological circles. Many pilgrims therefore come to Ayodhya because it is the place where Lord Ram lived on earth. They come for *darshan*, for 'seeing'.

Pilgrimage in Hinduism is to a great extent 'sacred sight-seeing' (Eck, 1982: 20). If we follow the pilgrim who has taken his bath in the Sarayu on his visits to the temples of Ayodhya and ask him his reasons for going, then he will certainly answer that he is going for darshan. He enters the temple, folds his hands and looks at the image of the deity. He may do all kinds of other things, like ringing the temple bell, prostrating, calling out loudly 'Hail Sita and Ram', but the central act is that of beholding the divine image. Going for darshan is done at those times of the day when the god is awake and can be worshipped with offerings of flowers and fruit or sweets.

These offerings are consecrated by the contact with the divine and part of them is returned to the worshipper as *prasād*, the 'grace' of the god.

The pilgrims prefer to go for darshan at particular times and on special occasions. A good time is in the evening or in the morning when *ārati* is performed. Arati is a 'lamp-offering' in which the priest sways an oil lamp with five wicks before the image. This is a colourful event, which concludes with the lamp being taken to the onlookers so that they can put their hands above the flame and bring them to their heads. Special occasions are the birthday celebrations or other important days in the life of the deity. On these occasions the images of the deities are decked with flowers and are specially adorned with even richer clothes and jewellery than normal. Some temples are also more famous than others for the sight of the divine (*jhānki*) that they offer. There is a magic belief connected with darshan: the richer the scene presented, the greater its lustre and attraction for the mortal eye, the stronger also is its beneficial effect. Darshan is not only gratifying for the worshipper, it has all kinds of instrumental effects besides. It is believed, for example, that it has the power to cure illnesses, help barren women to get male progeny, enable businessmen to succeed in their enterprises and students to pass their exams. The manuals written by the local priests promise to a sophisticated audience even higher fruits, such as the liberation of the soul from the cycle of birth and death. The pilgrims not only go for darshan and prasad, they also hear the sacred lore of the temples and other places recited by the priests, or stay for some time in a temple to hear a sermon (*kathā*) based upon theological interpretations of parts of the Ram story. They also can go for darshan of one of the many saints of Ayodhya who live in the temples. To see a saint who is a representative of the divine on earth has the same edifying effect on the worshipper as the sight of an image. It is therefore not surprising that in religious talks in Ayodhya the word for 'image' (*mūrti*) is also used to refer to a saint.

Besides its many temples, a striking feature of Ayodhya is the constant encounter with sadhus. The word *sādhu* is not easy to translate. We may render it as 'saint' in the same way as Gellner (1969) did when dealing with the religious specialists of the Atlas. When, however, a Hindu recommends in English a particular sadhu with the words 'He is a real saint', 'A true saint', then it becomes apparent that to call the thousands of sadhus in Ayodhya saints gives the impression that it is something like a Christian heaven. To call them ascetics is very common in accounts of Hinduism in English, but it obscures the important fact that many sadhus do not live, or even profess to live, an ascetic life. I would opt for the term 'monk' which, according to the *Oxford English Dictionary*, refers to a member of a community of men living apart from the world under religious vows and according to a rule. Already in the train or in the bus the pilgrim will have encountered sadhus who are also on their way to Ayodhya. Many sadhus are mendicants who constantly travel from one tirtha to another. They can be easily recognized by their clothes or relative lack of clothing, as well as by their hair-do and the markings on their forehead. The character of Ayodhya as a tirtha was, more than anything else, determined by the large number of sadhus to be seen in the markets, shops, streets, at the riverside – in short, everywhere.

There are many notable secular features of Ayodhya, of which the most striking is the national highway and the large bridge over the holy river Sarayu. Every day hundreds of trucks and other vehicles use this thoroughfare on their secular journeys and seem to make Ayodhya just another dusty provincial town on the road from Faizabad to Gonda. It is, however, the many temples, and even more the many sadhus, that make Ayodhya what it is to the visiting pilgrim: the place of Ram.

To summarize, Ayodhya can be called a tirtha in both a spiritual and a ritual sense (Van der Veer, 1984). It combines a Brahmanical ritual complex, centred on the sacred river Sarayu, with a Ramanandi spiritual complex, centred on the places connected with Ram's life. The specialists of the ritual complex are, of course, the Brahman pandas (pilgrimage priests) of Ayodhya, while the spiritual complex is dominated by the Ramanandi sadhus. While this distinction is helpful in describing the social and symbolic organiza-tion of Ayodhya as a tirtha, we should note that the pilgrims do not make this distinction themselves. Indeed, as Hocart (1969: 28) remarks: 'How can we make any progress in the understanding of cultures, ancient or modern, if we persist in dividing what the people join and in joining what they keep apart?' This is certainly true, but we should add that what one section of the people tends to join, another section may tend to divide. The analytic distinction made here is clearly relevant to the pandas and sadhus themselves who are, as religious specialists, the ones with great interests at stake. The history, organization and religious content of the two complexes is clearly very different, though pilgrims may unite them on their pilgrimage. What is perhaps surprising is that the two complexes coexist as peacefully as they do. In fact, they are almost completely non-competitive, both safely occupying their respective niches in the pilgrimage system. This situation is certainly a far cry from what has been reported about a somewhat similar configuration of parish priests and monastic clergy in the Roman Catholic Church (Bax, 1983, 1985), in which the competition between the two types of specialists is seen as one of the main factors in religious change.

It is, of course, impossible for an outsider to see Ayodhya, with its sacred geography and its history, through the eyes of a devout Hindu. We can, however, gain something of the atmosphere of the place by following the pilgrims on their tour through Ayodhya using two modern pilgrim guides in Hindi (Sitaram, 1930; Sharma, 1971) and an annotated edition of the *Ayodhyāmā hātmya*, a Sanskrit eulogy of Ayodhya (Bakker, 1986). We will start, like most pilgrims, at the riverside, proceed to the places where Ram's presence is most strongly felt, and finally discuss the seasons and times for the visit to Ayodhya. To conclude, we will take leave from 'the pilgrim's view' and try to summarize some major historical developments which have made Ayodhya what it is today.

2. Sarayu and the ghats

The bank of the Sarayu at Ayodhya is divided into a great number of bathing-places (*ghāṭs*). Some of them are called *pakkā*, which means that they have flights of steps leading down to the river, while others are called *kacchā*, meaning that there is a river bank. We will start our journey from a kaccha ghat called Vasudeva Ghat. A pilgrim who comes to Ayodhya does not, of course, know all of its sacred lore. Moreover, he will not be able to find the sacred spots on his own. He needs a guide, whom he can find among the community of pilgrimage priests, known as either *paṇḍās* or *tīrth purohits*. They are the Brahman priests of the tirtha Ayodhya. One community calls itself *Gaṇgā putras*, sons of the sacred river (*gaṇgā*). Another community also acting as Ayodhya's priests is that of the *Bhareriyas* who prefer to call themselves pandas. These people, whether they are Gangaputras or Bhareriyas, are specialists in the history, geography and rituals of the tirtha Ayodhya. It is to them that a pilgrim must turn if he wants to know where to do what in Ayodhya.

The story the panda will tell while bringing the pilgrims to Vasudeva Ghat is that when Manu lived here in the first yuga, before the first deluge, he encountered a fish whom he recognized as the incarnation of Vishnu. The god informed Manu of the approaching deluge and directed him to build a ship to carry all the sages, plants and animals. When the ship was ready, Manu fastened the vessel to the fish's horn and was thus conducted to safety. Part of the ship was fastened to the soil on Vasudeva Ghat and, although the world has been destroyed several times since, this ship was preserved. In our yuga it was found by King Vikramaditya who restored the city to the glory it had known in the third yuga when Ram was king of Ayodhya. He built a temple on it for Lord Manu, but it was afterwards lost, in the time of the Muslims. A platform or stoop of it can be still seen and is referred to by Muslims as the grave of Noah.

The description of this ghat must be baffling to a western reader: a strange myth about the deluge which resembles the well-known Judaeo-Christian myth, a seemingly historical tale about a king who rebuilt the city and, as a final effort of too fertile an imagination, the mention of a grave of Noah that is sacred for Muslims. To the Hindu pilgrim, however, there is nothing especially amazing in the panda's story. As far as he is concerned, an important creation of the world began at Ayodhya, where the first man lived, and when he hears similar claims made at other tirthas he will not doubt the information given to him in Ayodhya, because he knows that there are so many yugas that if it was not this one then it must have been another. The story of the fish incarnation is well known and there is no reason to doubt that the event took place in Ayodhya, which is already a well-known sacred place thanks to the fact that Ram once lived here. Moreover, it is an enjoyable and edifying story to hear and reinforces the idea that Ayodhya is indeed a centre of a sacred world, a real tirtha.

A second typical element of the story is that a king of our age with the name Vikramaditya restored Ayodhya to its old glory. This story will be retold at several places in Ayodhya and it always has the same structure: Ram's Ayodhya was a city in the Treta-yuga, but the place was rediscovered in our Kali-yuga by King Vikramaditya. After his death the town was destroyed in the time of the Muslims, and only comparatively recently, during the reign of the nawabs of Awadh in the eighteenth century, has the Hindu character of Ram's Ayodhya again been restored. This local legend is partially confirmed by recent historical research. Bakker (1986) argues convincingly that the fictional Ayodhya of the sacred saga *Rāmāyaṇa* became identified with the important North Indian town of Saketa during the reign of the Guptas in the fifth century AD. The Guptas removed their capital from Pataliputra to Saketa, which they decided to name Ayodhya. The Gupta kings Kumaragupta and Skandagupta styled themselves as devotees of Vishnu, and Skandagupta bore as a title the name Vikramaditya. He liked to compare himself with Ram and a dominant theme at the court of the Guptas was that they continued the glory of Ram's dynasty and had restored his ancient capital to its old glory. After the reign of the Guptas the town fell into insignificance, but not into total oblivion, thanks to its successful recognition as the place of Ram. On the eve of Muslim rule Ayodhya contained a number of holy places and sanctuaries, partly of Vishnuite provenance, partly belonging to Shivaite or other creeds. Only in the time of the nawabs did the place become what it is today: the centre of a cult of Ram, controlled by the Ramanandi order.

Little more than a broad outline is given in official historical writing, and this is what is also given in the legend told by the pandas. The legend seems therefore to be proven, or at least not falsified, by historical accounts. The Hindu would welcome this, but at the same time his interest in it would be disappointing to the historical researcher. The pilgrim, at least, is not interested in proofs. He comes for only a few days to Ayodhya and wants to hear its *mahimā* – its greatness, its power – and not its 'real history'. Similarly the pandas are only interested in the claim that Ayodhya is a place beyond time and history. It has been there in all yugas and with their help we can have darshan of it in our yuga. But they have one difficulty: most of the buildings, temples and installations are of rather recent date, yet they are supposed to be the original places of the time of Ram. The pandas therefore refer to the date of the restoration or rebuilding of the temples, if they mention it at all, rather than to the date of their foundation.

The theory generally held in Ayodhya is that when in the eighteenth century the nawabs left Ayodhya for their newly built capital of Faizabad, and later for Lucknow, the Hindus were able to take the opportunity of restoring the places of Vikramaditya's time. Although the temples and pakka ghats appear therefore to have been built rather recently, they are in fact the places of yore. Finally, the fact that Muslims incorporate the Hindu myth about the deluge and the first man into their interpretation of Ayodhya as the place of Noah is not surprising, at least to the older Hindu, who will easily remember that Hindus and Muslims visited one another's sacred places, each with their own modes of interpretation. It is to be expected that the situation has changed and will become even more different for the present and coming generations. Not surprising in itself will be the Muslim effort to incorporate the Hindu tradition, something quite common in Hinduism, as we have already seen in the doctrine of Vishnu's incarnations. What will be different is that the worlds of both groups will increasingly drift further apart due to their current political antagonism. The grave of Noah lies neglected in present-day Ayodhya and it will receive more and more emphasis in the stories of the pandas as a proof of the usurpation of Ayodhya by the Muslims, before the Hindus regained control.

Having seen all this, our walk on Vasudeva Ghat is not necessarily finished. The panda can also bring us to one of several temples dominating the ghat. The pilgrim who is interested in asceticism may urge his panda to take him to a temple where a silent ascetic (*mauni*) lives; another pilgrim may wish to visit a temple founded by a monk called Madhurali. This name means 'bee' (devotee) 'seeking the nectar (of the presence of the lord)', so we may surmise that the temple concerned belongs to the so-called school of 'sweet devotion' (*Rasik Sampradāy*). The panda might also be encouraged to conduct his pilgrims to a temple for altogether different motives, as when, for example, he gets a share of the offerings made by the pilgrims to the deity in the temple. Finally, there is also a temple here built by a petty ruler (*rājā*) from a district in Bihar. Pilgrims from that district or, more restrictedly, from the raja's particular state, might like to visit or even stay here when living for some time in Ayodhya.

Leaving Vasudeva Ghat we walk in a westerly direction and reach what has been called Naya Ghat (the new ghat) since the railway was built here in the second half of the nineteenth century. The old name of this ghat is Dharmaraj Ghat, called after the important temple of Dharmahari here. It is important not because of the interest shown by pilgrims, but because it seems to be one of the oldest holy places of Ayodhya (Bakker, 1986: 102). The present temple contains an idol of the Lord of Death, Dharmaraja, and his scribe, Citragupta. It was built sometime in the nineteenth century by a Kayasth named Narsimhdas. At the beginning of the twentieth century the assembly (*sabhā*) of the Kayasth caste decided to maintain the temple and to build a pilgrims' rest house (*dharmshālā*) for the convenience of caste members visiting Ayodhya. It is one of many dharmshalas in Ayodhya, specifically restricted to only one caste or a few castes. On Naya Ghat is also the main road with the main bazaar of Ayodhya. This road leads to the large bridge built in 1964 and all day long a continual stream of trucks disturbs the religious construction of Ayodhya as a place outside time. Of course it also serves as the main road for the pilgrim traffic. The pilgrim buses use it and all pilgrims who want to take a bath come via this road; they follow it almost to the middle until they leave it for one of the pakka or kaccha ghats. The pandas who have their houses on this road have therefore a strategic advantage over those whose houses are at a distance from it.

On the road and near the ghat are some temples and other places of interest. First there is Gurusadanvihari, the temple founded in the nineteenth century by the celebrated Brahman scholar Umapati Tripathi. He was famous for his knowledge of grammar and for his devotion to Ram and Sita. There is a legend about him in Ayodhya that is told by pandas who conduct their pilgrims to this place. Tripathi had considered himself the spiritual preceptor (*guru*) of the divine couple. It is a well-known devotional procedure in the sweet devotion for the devotee to imagine himself as having a special relation with the gods. Mostly one thinks oneself to be the servant of the gods, but Tripathi had higher aspirations. To imagine oneself as the guru of the gods – and thus worthy of being worshipped by the gods, instead of worshipping them – was a kind of hubris that the contemporaries of Tripathi could not really appreciate. Other sadhus of the place were outraged by this attitude, which also implied that Tripathi was a greater saint than all those sadhus who believed themselves to be just servants of the gods. They took action and forced Tripathi to abandon his practice. When he did so, the legend goes, the images in the most important temple of the sweet devotion, Kanak Bhavan, started to make a terrible noise in the night. The next day a rumour spread among the sadhus that all this hubbub was created because Tripathi was no longer allowed to act as the guru of Sita and Ram. They decided to take the images to Tripathi's temple and see what would happen. When the images were brought and Tripathi appeared on the doorstep of his temple, the idols came forward as if to touch his feet – the traditional reverential way of greeting one's guru. From that miracle onwards Tripathi's fame was almost boundless and the temple he founded, though rather neglected nowadays, is one of the largest in Ayodhya.

Another important place near this road is the so-called *chaunī* (camp) of Raghunathdas, where the *pādukā* (sandal) of Ramanand, the founder of the Ramanandi monastic order, are installed. Here the panda will tell some legends about Ramanand, who saved many Hindus from violent conversion to Islam. Again a temple of a raja can be found here. This time it is a magnificent building, financed by the raja of Rusi, a state in the district of Chapra in Bihar. Nearby is Tulsidas's park, called Victoria Park at the time when Sitaram (1930) wrote his guide. Sitaram tells a charming story about Victoria Park which serves as a good example of the Hindu imagination. In his time a statue of Queen Victoria stood in the middle of the park; it has since been removed to the back yard of the local police station and replaced with an image of Tulsidas. I have never witnessed the worship of the Hindu saint Tulsidas in this park, but Sitaram reports that people used to worship the statue of Queen Victoria. He describes how the police had to prevent the pilgrims from climbing the pedestal to offer flowers, etc. The reason for this is contained in a legend telling how Nal, one of Ram's generals, fell in love here with a local girl. Ram prophesied that this girl's children would become famous, and that in the Kali-yuga they would rule the whole world. This is how Queen Victoria came to be incorporated in the Hindu pantheon.

Approaching the river we come across a Shivaite place that, according to local tradition, is one of the oldest places of Ayodhya: the *mathiya* (monastery) of Siddhigiri. The present *mahant* (abbot) showed me a stone on which the dates of the succeeding abbots from the time of its foundation were inscribed. It is a large institution, but nowadays it does not attract much interest. The abbot can maintain himself only with difficulty because he does not have many lay disciples. This is a typical case for Ayodhya. The Shivaite institutions are old, but they have lost their importance. Some of them have even been transformed into Vishnuite temples. The reason why will be dealt with in another chapter. In the meantime it is interesting to relate a story connected with this temple. In the 1920s the abbot Mahipatigiri decided to remove the old *samādhis* (graves of saints) from the temple. In the night the saints appeared and gave him a horrible punishment, which proves that it is not so easy to change a sacred place in accordance with religious fashions. Only by praying for a long time was Mahipatigiri able to save his life. Although the Shivaite orders have beaten a retreat in Ayodhya, the god Shiv is still of great importance on the ghats. Walking along the river one encounters in one sanctuary after another the *liṅga*, a phallic symbol of the god.

Just in front of Siddhigiri's mathiya we find a few rather modern ghats: Divyakala Ghat and Rupkala Ghat. The first-mentioned is not so much a ghat as an attempt to build one; heaps of stones and bricks lie there, awaiting the building of steps to a river which has already receded from the place, so that the attempt is doomed to remain abortive. The situation here is somewhat strange. When the modern bridge was built the holy Sarayu had to be diverted from the pakka ghats. A long range of ghats, in fact all the important pakka ghats connecting Ayodhya's city to the river, have fallen dry as a result. The government has built new ghats just in front of the old ones, starting from the bridge. Between the old and the new ghats a wasteland about 500 metres broad has been created. The pilgrims still go along the old ghats, but when they want to take a bath in the river they have to cross the wasteland to reach the new ghats, where the pandas help them in their rituals. The second ghat, Rupkala's, has been built but is as functionless at present as the unbuilt Divyakala Ghat. Rupkala and Divyakala were both important leaders of the sweet devotion in the beginning of this century. Their lay disciples gave money to build a temple and a ghat for them. Going onwards along the ghats we come to the temple and ghat built by Ahilyabai Holkar, a queen of Indore. She is very famous in North India because in the late eighteenth century she also rebuilt Vishvanath, the most important temple of Benaras.

Next we come across a very interesting place: the ruins of a mosque and, next to it, a big temple. Local tradition has it that the temple was destroyed by the Moghul emperor Aurangzeb (1658–1707) and that a mosque was built in its place with the material of the old temple. It is obvious that times have changed. Nowadays the mosque is ruined and the adjacent temple of Vishnu Tretanath was rebuilt in the time of Nawab Saadat Ali Khan. The old temple, which was, according to the legend, destroyed in the time of Aurangzeb, had been built by the raja of Kulu. The well-known legend is that an inhabitant of Kulu, a peasant who had visited Ayodhya, came to the court to offer the raja some prasad from Ayodhya as a customary gift. When the king heard that he had been in Ayodhya, the city of Ram, he called out: 'You are fortunate to have seen the heaven-made earth and the jewel-clad buildings of Ayodhya.' The peasant answered: 'O great king, you have only read the books and never been there. I have seen with my own eyes that the earth is the same as here; it is no heaven.' The king ordered him to go back to Ayodhya and fetch a stone from there without looking at it on his way back to Kulu. The peasant did as ordered and when he came back to the court he opened the bag in which he had kept the stone from Ayodhya. To his great surprise the stone turned out to be a diamond. Now the peasant came to have faith in Ayodhya and the king was so happy that he gave orders for a temple to be built in Ayodhya. This story might strike us as a fairy tale, too childish to have anything to do with the depths of the great Hindu religion. We should keep in mind, however, that the tone and style of religion in a Hindu tirtha are different from what is to be found in theological works. These stories are in part recent inventions and in part reworkings of ancient myths. To the mind of the pilgrim there is no difference between the two. He will not make an analytic distinction between the stories about Ram, the myths about the creation of the world on Vasudeva Ghat, and the stories about the king of Kulu. All these stories effect a total idea of the greatness of Ayodhya in all times.

Further along the ghats we come across two important Shiv temples. The first is Nagnath, which has an old Shiv linga. In the time of Sitaram a Ramanandi ascetic lived here, who worshipped Shiv and bathed the linga with water from the Sarayu at three in the morning. When he did so a heavenly light is said to have emanated from the linga. It might surprise us that a Vishnuite ascetic worshipped Shiv, but we will come to this remarkable fact later. The Shiv linga of the second temple, Nageshvarnath, is also very old. The legend of its origin is as follows: Kush, the son of Ram, was bathing in the Sarayu. Kamudti, the sister of a *nāg*, a serpent, who lived in the Sarayu, fell in love with Kush and took his bracelet as a love-token. When Kush drew his bow, the nag and his sister prayed for mercy. The nag was a worshipper of Shiv who duly came to help his devotee. He promised Kush a boon, should he forgive the nag. Kush asked Shiv to come to Ayodhya and to take up residence here under the name Nageshvarnath (Lord of the Serpents). Kush promised Shiv that any pilgrim who failed to worship this linga would not reap the full benefit of his pilgrimage. Whatever the interpretation of this story, nowadays many pilgrims still come first to Nageshvarnath after taking a bath in the Sarayu. They bring water in a small vessel (*loṭā*) as a libation to bathe the linga.

The ghats between Nageshvarnath and Sahasradhara are referred to collectively as Svargadvar (the door to heaven). The pandas have strong claims for the extraordinary power of Svargadvar. According to them there is no tirtha like it in the whole of creation. Some say it is the place from which Ram went to heaven (we will later encounter another place with the same claim). Most of the ghats were built by raja Darshan Singh (1827–51), who also built a temple called Gangamahal on one of them. Nageshvarnath and a temple dedicated to Sarayu were built by a minister of the nawabs, Nawal Ray. There is another Shiv temple on this stretch of ghats which is called Chandrahari and has a linga capable of curing women. Next to it are Chaturbhuji and Videhi, two important institutions of the Ramanandis. Finally we come to Sahasradhara, which is mostly called Lakshman Ghat. In former times the courts of Awadh brought accused persons to the large temple that dominates this ghat and made them swear before the image of Ram's brother Lakshman.

Leaving Svargadvar, but proceeding along the riverside, we arrive at Lakshmankila Ghat. This fortress of Lakshman was built by Mubarak Ali Khan and was at that time called Qila Mubarak. In the time of Wajid Ali Shah, the last king of Awadh, it was given to the saint Yugalananyasharan, a leader of the sweet devotion. It is now one of the most important temples of Ayodhya, built by Dinbandhu, a minister of the raja of Rewan. From this temple there is a wide vista of the riverside. Early in the morning when the sun rises on the river and the city of Ayodhya becomes visible, even a sceptical observer will be touched by the serenity of Ram's birthplace.

Continuing our journey, we come to Rinamochan Ghat and Papmochan Ghat. To bathe at the first of these will free us from our debts (*rina*) to the ancestors and our gurus, while the second will free us from pap, which is usually translated with one of the most problematic terms of Judeo-Christian tradition: sin. On Rinamochan Ghat are the ruins of an old Shiva temple where we find reminders of an active ascetic life in a place called Siddhashram. Nath yogis, Shaiva Sannyasis, Ramanandis as well as Muslim Sayyids seem to have lived here. From Rinamochan Ghat we follow the course of the river to Kaikeyi Ghat, Kaushalya Ghat and Brahmkund. Temples abound on these ghats and many stories are told about them.

Together the ghats form a sacred field. Each has its own power and its own stories, which vary from panda to panda and through time. The most important of the many temples on the ghats are undoubtedly those dedicated to Shiv, even though Ayodhya is the place of Ram. Moreover, the river is not only an area for bathing and performance of rituals, but is also a place for encounters with monks and their magic powers. The riverside is crowded with men covered in ashes, sitting near fires, wearing strange antique weapons and reciting sacred texts. They contribute as much to the religious atmosphere – and probably more – as do the big temples built of solid brick. Their curative powers are much sought after and their teachings are of interest to those who have the leisure to stay in Ayodhya for some time. The temples are easy to enumerate, but all their names and all the stories told about them will be boring to the outsider. Just as important as the temples are the holy trees and stones on the ghats. They also have all kinds of powers, attributed to them by the pandas, and they are accordingly worshipped. The riverside is of course impressive because of the many magnificent temples, but its atmosphere is dominated by the less imposing trees, stones and holy men.

3. The presence of Ram

To meet Ram in his birthplace we have to go to the centre of the city. Here the rickshaw driver has great difficulty in bringing his passengers to their destinations because it is built on a steep hill. This area is called Ramkot or Ramdurga, the fort of Ram. It is an extensive area, occupied by temples and houses of sadhus. In the time of Ram, the Ramkot was defended by soldiers who stood at its four gates. On the northern gate stood Vibhishana and his son Mattagajendra, on the southern gate Prince Bali with King Sugriva, on the eastern gate Hanuman and on the western gate a host of defenders, one of whom was Lakshman. The story of the defence of Ramkot against intruders will certainly be told to the pilgrim, but there is only one important temple at present built on one of the 'gates'. This is Ayodhya's most famous temple, Hanumangarhi. There is also the story of Shiv as the local deity of Ayodhya and there is a Durgeshvar temple in Ramkot in his honour, but it is not well attended. The central place of Ramkot is Ram Janmabhumi, the birthplace of Ram. It was of course lost at the end of the Treta-yuga, but it was rediscovered in our time by the famous King Vikramaditya.

Legend has it that this was the first place Vikramaditya managed to see when he went out to search for the place of Ram. Initially all he knew about Ayodhya was that it was to be found on the bank of the Sarayu. He made his camp and rode around on his horse. On one of his journeys he came across a man on a black horse. he was dressed like a king, but totally black. Vikramaditya saw the man descending from his horse and taking a bath in the Sarayu. When he emerged from the Sarayu this man had become totally white, to the utter astonishment of Vikramaditya. He drew his horse up in front of the stranger and asked him who he was and how he had changed from black to white. The man answered that he was Prayag, the king of tirthas, and that he had become black by absorbing the sins of so many sinners. By coming here and taking a bath he had become white again. Vikramaditya was naturally surprised that the most important tirtha Prayag could wash his sins in this place and so asked what kind of greatness (*mahimā*) it was that made such a thing happen. Prayag answered that the place where they were standing was Gopratara, where Ram had left the world. Vikramaditya was pleased to hear that he now was near Ayodhya and he asked if Prayag knew more about the city. The king of tirthas then showed him all the sites, beginning with the place where Ram was born. Vikramaditya drew a line around it to make sure he would remember it.

It is clear that this story endorses the power of Ayodhya to wash away the sins of the pilgrims. When even the famous tirtha Prayag comes to take a bath here, what would then be the need to go to

Prayag? The story continues, however, and introduces a new element. Vikramaditya was not able to find the line he had drawn. Dejected by this misfortune, he sought the help of a yogi who was in deep meditation nearby. When this yogi came out of his meditation he told the king that it was not easy to 'realize' the birthplace of Ram. Mere directions as to its geographical position would not suffice. Some special procedure was necessary and that was the reason that Vikramakditya could not find his line again. To understand the secret (*rahasya*) of this place the raja should utter constantly (*jap*) the Ram mantra. He should also let a calf together with other cattle roam in this area. When the calf came across the Janmabhumi, milk would drip immediately from its udders. As a result of such a demonstrative incident no one could ever doubt that this was really the birthplace of Ram. The king did as he was told and at midday on Ram Naumi the calf began to shed milk at a certain place. There Vikramaditya built a temple of *shaligram* stone (black fossils, emblems of Ram) and he installed an image of the infant Ram: Ram Lalji. Brahmans belonging to the Vashistha-gotra and the Atharva-Veda became the temple's *pūjāris* (officiating priests).

As a matter of course this temple – being the birthplace of the god – became one of the most important temples of Ayodhya. It was, however, destroyed by the Moghul emperor Babar at the beginning of the sixteenth century. Local history tells that the place attracted both Hindu and Muslim ascetics. Also lay people of both religions brought their sons to the place in the belief that this visit would extend the life-span of the child, a custom that is observed to this day by pilgrims from all directions. In the sixteenth century a Muslim saint with the name Khwaja Fazal Abbas Ashikhan came to the temple and became a *sādhak shishya* (a disciple who wants to learn some methods for meditation, etc.) of the Hindu sadhu Syamanand. He realized his yogic goals by uttering the Muslim mantra. Another faqir who came here was Jalal Shah. Impressed by the power of the place, he wanted to transform it into a Muslim centre. Both faqirs agreed that the temple should be destroyed and that a mosque should be built. When Babar came to India with the intention of becoming its ruler, he visited Ayodhya and consulted these faqirs, who promised him that when he should destroy the temple and build a mosque his desire would be fulfilled. Babar ordered his general Mir Baqi to carry out these instructions and then went on from

Ayodhya to other places. Mir Baqi destroyed the temple, but his efforts to build a mosque failed because each night everything that had been built during the day fell down again. This continued until Mir Baqi grew desperate and proposed to give up. Then the faqir Khwaja dreamt that the mosque should not be built right over the *garbha* (sanctum) of the temple, but somewhat behind it. Thus the mosque was built in such a way that the garbha of the temple remained open to the Hindus for centuries in the form of a pit into which they could throw flowers. In the time of the nawabs, some two or three centuries later, the pit was given to the Hindus and in 1855 a Kayasth named Lala Gangaprasad who lived in Lucknow, took possession of it and built a wall between it and the mosque. He did not get permission, however, to erect a temple on the pit and therefore built a hut of grass and started a programme of worship there.

The Ram Janmabhumi has been the arena of Hindu-Muslim conflict from the middle of the nineteenth century till the present day. We will describe the development of these conflicts later, but here we may say that, until very recently, the government of India kept the mosque closed to Muslims as well as to Hindus and posted soldiers at the place to prevent people from taking the matter into their own hands. Both groups were prevented from entering the mosque. Hindus had a small place in front of the mosque gate, in which they sang religious songs. Here the pilgrims came to make their offerings. After having visited Ram Janmabhumi many pilgrims go to see Ram Janmasthan, a temple founded by a Hindu sadhu named Ramdas shortly after Babar had destroyed the temple at Janmabhumi. Ramdas was very popular among Muslims, who called him Auliya Benzir. There is a story that the aforementioned Muslim faqir Jalal Shah became jealous of Ramdas and mounted an attack on him magically sitting astride a lion. By the power of Ramdas the hapless faqir was devoured by the lion. The shah was buried and on his grave two pillars from the Janmabhumi were set up, which can still be seen. These stories about Muslims and Hindus being worshippers of Hindu sadhus and going to Hindu places and worship, although historically unverifiable, seem to imply that there was a time when Hindus and Muslims were not as far apart as they are now and that it was only fanatic religious specialists who forced Muslim rulers to pursue a true *jihād* (holy war) against Hindu institutions. This conclusion is suggested not only by this kind of legend, but also by historical research in the field of early Hindu-Muslim relations.

The Janmasthan temple seems to have functioned as a partial replacement for the destroyed temple of Janmabhumi. A place there that is certain to be visited by the pilgrims is Sita's kitchen. A small kitchen can also be found within the outer enclosure of the mosque, but here the arrangements for worship are a little more elaborate. It is supposed to be continually filled with food. The sight (darshan) of it fulfils every need and a daily visit keeps one's house supplied with food. Other places to be visited nearby are a well, where Sita worshipped when she came to Ayodhya after her marriage, Sumitrabhavan, where Lakshman and Shatrughna were born, Kaikeyibhavan, where Bharat was born, and last but not least the temple which, together with Hanumangarhi, dominates the religious life of Ayodhya: Kanak Bhavan, the golden palace of Ram. Only in this temple can one realize what the words darshan (seeing) and *jhāṃkī* (divine vision) really mean.

At the end of the last century it was still a charming little temple, although even at that time the place had a certain fame as the palace where Ram and Sita had spent their happy married life. For that reason it had always been a centre for adherents of the sweet devotion, who stress the emotional bond between the devotees and Sita in terms of her relationship with friends and servants in the palace. At the beginning of this century, when the raja of Orccha decided to buy the temple and embellish it in the manner of a real palace, the importance of Kanak Bhavan began to grow beyond measure. An enormous and richly decorated palatial building was built on the site of the old mud building and the images were decked with precious stones and expensive clothing. Hundreds of people come daily when the curtain before the images is pulled back and arati is performed. In loud voices they shout their praise to the gods, some of them dance before the images, and large groups sing religious songs to the accompaniment of musical instruments. The bright pastel colours of the clothes of the images and the richness of their decoration may seem to us *kitsch* and crude, meant for peasants rather than for intellectuals with a refined taste, but this would be a misleading impression. Members of all status groups in Indian society come to Kanak Bhavan and the jhanki of it is widely recommended. People who gave me the most sophisticated explanation of their beliefs and opinions emphasized that to see the divine couple in their richness in Kanak Bhavan was the most fundamental experience in their devotion. It is therefore too easy to make a distinction between the 'simple, emotional and instrumental' beliefs of the common rural people and the 'sophisticated, intellectual and cognitive' beliefs of the higher status groups of the city. In seeing the decorations of Kanak Bhavan all kinds of Hindus experience the emotion of total surrender and bliss which is theologically central to their devotion.

Kanak Bhavan, like Hanumangarhi, stands in the middle of Ramkot. The presence of the divine couple is most strongly felt in Kanak Bhavan, but, as Sitaram puts it, it is no exaggeration to say that in Ayodhya the monkey god Hanuman is even more revered than Ram-Sita. From the original Hanuman temple built by Vikramaditya only a small image has been preserved, which now stands before the large image that is so decked with flower it can hardly be seen. This small image of Hanuman had always been worshipped under a tree in the period following the destruction of the old temple. In the time of the Nawab Shuja-ud-Daulah the Ramanandi saint Abhayramdas got permission to build a temple on the old Hanuman hill, and the project was finished in the time of Nawab Asaf-ud-Daulah. We will turn later to the history of Hanumangarhi in a discussion of the settlement of the Ramanandi order in Ayodhya, but on this point a few remarks are relevant here. Hanuman is the great magician who can cure, can give children, is immensely strong and will certainly help those who resort to him. His power appeals very much to the imagination and although other gods are also famous for their instrumental powers, especially Shiv and the Mother Goddesses, Hanuman ranks in North India among the most powerful. The temple is immensely crowded on Tuesdays, the day of the week on which Hanuman is especially worshipped. On this day people, especially women and children, tend to observe a fast. Another important thing about Hanumangarhi is that it is a monastic centre of fighting sadhus. It is the largest monastic institution in Ayodhya, with 500 to 600 resident sadhus who are trained in a military fashion. Whereas in Kanak Bhavan the pilgrim encounters a Hindu temple, financed by a raja and ritually organized by Brahman priests, in Hanumangarhi he is confronted with a complete monastic institution of the Ramanandis.

Hanumangarhi is a centre of the nagas, the fighting ascetics in the Ramanandi order. On Ramkot there is also a centre of the sadhus who belong to the sweet devotion. It is called Bara Asthana (the big institution) and, like Hanumangarhi, it is a product of the eighteenth century. It was founded by a sadhu named Ramprasad, who was also the founder of the sweet devotion in Ayodhya. His followers wear as their forehead-marking a *bindī*, the dot generally put on by Indian women. Ramanandi history has it that when Ramprasad was in a hurry to attend a meeting of sadhus he forgot to put the customary red line, representing the goddess Lakshmi or Sita, on his forehead. Sita herself appeared and put a bindi on his forehead. When the other sadhus saw Ramprasad with this bindi they asked him to remove it, but this proved to be impossible. When they saw that they could not remove the bindi they began to believe that it really had been applied by Sita. Ramprasad became very famous and attracted many followers. Many marvellous stories are told about his life and his special relationship with Ram and Sita. Up to the present day Bara Asthana is, with Lakshmankila, the central institution of the sweet devotion.

When we leave Ramkot, we do not leave the presence of Ram. There are several places throughout the city of Ayodhya and its immediate environment which have a claim to some special association with Ram and Sita. First we come to Dantadavanakund, a tank where Ram used to brush his teeth. It is a large tank which is used on some festival days, such as *Rām Vivāh*, the marriage festival of the divine couple, when a boat is floated on it in which are seated some young Brahman boys who impersonate the gods and thus present a jhanki. Near it is Tulsi Chaura, the place where Tulsidas started to write his *Rāmcharitmānas*, where there is a temple containing an image of him. A rather long walk from here is Maniparvat, also known as Ratnachal. It is regarded as the place where the Lord plays with Sita and her friends and as the representative of Bhudevi, Mother Earth. It is a rather steep hill, densely overgrown with shrubs and trees. Its importance becomes clear at the beginning of the *Jhūlā* festival when idols from all temples are brought here and placed on swings (*jhūlās*), hanging from the trees. This place has also been an arena for conflicts between Muslims and Hindus. According to local history, a large temple containing an image of Lord Vishnu lying on Shesh, the World

Snake, was destroyed by Muslims, but when they tried to turn it into a Muslim sanctuary they were killed by the huge king cobras on the hill. At the foot of the hill are a few important graves of Muslim *pirs*, Sufi mystics, which are still visited and worshipped by Muslims.

Apart from these places there are several water-tanks in Ayodhya, like Sitakund and Vashishtakund, which are of importance in the Ram story. Depending on their promotion by priests, sadhus or influential laymen, they can become important places of interest for the pilgrim who visits Ayodhya. In some periods they have been neglected, because no-one took the initiative in spending money on decoration, building a temple or dharmshala, or encouraging pandas to bring pilgrims and tell stories connected with the place. In other periods they may flourish, thanks to an active promotion.

There are also several places outside Ayodhya associated with the Ram story. First of all I shall mention the old tirtha Gopratara, a ghat on the Sarayu within the city boundaries of Faizabad, near the military cantonment. Its importance derives from the legend that Ram left his earthly existence here and took the citizens of Ayodhya with him. This is therefore the place where one can bathe to earn the liberation of one's soul after death, and it is considered to be a good place for dying. According to Bakker (1986), it is a very old tirtha but its importance diminished for two reasons. First, a tirtha within the boundaries of Ayodhya, the aforementioned Svargadvar, has the same claims to *mahimā* (greatness) as this place, and secondly, the British decided to build the cantonment here in the second half of the last century, and after that religious festivals became impossible until the departure of the British troops after Independence in 1947.

Another important tirtha outside Ayodhya is Bharatkund in the village of Nandigram. The story goes that Bharat agreed to be king instead of Ram only after much hesitation and deliberation. When he was ordered by Ram to carry out what had been achieved by the intrigues of his mother, he agreed on condition that he would abdicate as soon as Ram returned from the forest. While Ram and Sita were in exile Bharat did not really occupy the royal throne in Ayodhya, but lived near a water-tank, which is therefore called Bharatkund. There he worshipped the *pādukā* (sandals) of Ram until the moment when Ram came here to meet him, described as a very emotional episode in the Ram story. Pilgrims mostly come here when they do not restrict their pilgrimage to Ayodhya but follow what is a very common pilgrimage route: from Ayodhya, via Bharatkund, to Benaras, Gaya, Puri and then back to the place where they have come from, sometimes via another, less well-known tirtha.

The presence of Ram is not only felt in places connected with his earthly existence. Central to it are the many institutions of the Ramanandi order. We have already met individual sadhus of this order preaching on the ghats and we have seen that there are at least two important centres in Ramkot: Hanumangarhi and Bara Asthana. But throughout the city there are numerous *maths* (monasteries), *mandirs* (temples), *chaunīs* (literally army camps) and *akhāṛās* (literally fortified camps) as well as buildings which appear to be normal houses but contain groups of sadhus. Historically they have made Ayodhya into what it is and they still dominate its religious climate. I will mention two of these institutions in this connection. One of them, Vidyakund near Maniparvat, was the first settlement of the so-called *lashkarī* Ramanandis in Ayodhya. This group of sadhus was founded in the eighteenth century by Balanand as a military organization. One of his disciples went to Ayodhya and founded Vidyakund, a second went to Janakpur, the birthplace of Sita, to establish temples there and a third went to South India. The area around Vidyakund is looked upon by the inhabitants of Ayodhya as a mystic area, full of esoteric secrets (*rahasyabhūmi*), and people say that in former times the sadhus came here to play with Ram and Sita.

The second institution is Bari Chauni, the big camp. It was founded by Raghunathdas, a disciple of a mahant of Vidyakund, and is an enormous place, covering a large area. In it are registers of names of hundreds of thousands of devotees from all over India. In the area enclosed by its high walls there are seven temples and lodgings for hundreds of sadhus. Since it was founded at the end of the last century it has been one of the central monastic institutions of Ayodhya, where sadhus as well as laymen are welcome to eat and sleep. These two institutions are famous among sadhus and laymen, but they are only examples of the dominance of the Ramanandi order in Ayodhya. Sadhus of all persuasions in this order have founded institutions at the birthplace of their personal Lord (*ishtadevatā*).

This is not to say that there are no representatives of other Hindu orders in Ayodhya. I have come across many Shivaite institutions on my journeys through Ayodhya, and in some of these institutions have met sadhus who spoke of the decline of their order and the expansion of the Ramanandis in Ayodhya. I also have encountered sadhus who adhere to the principles of South Indian Shri-Vaishnavism, calling themselves Ramanujis. The history of these two groups is intertwined with the history of the Ramanandis, as we shall see later, but there are also groups with a rather more independent history, for example the Sikhs who have a *gurdwārā* beside the river at Brahmakund. For them, the place is important because it was visited by the founder of their religion, Guru Nanak. Other groups, such as the Udasis, Kabirpanthis, Pustimargis and Satsangis, also have prominent institutions in Ayodhya. The last group deserves special mention because it was founded by a Brahman, Swami Narayan, born in Chappia near Ayodhya at the end of the eighteenth century. It has attracted much attention from western scholars because it has become one of the prominent religions among Gujaratis who migrated from India to East Africa and later to Britain and America (cf. Williams, 1984). This group has become rather wealthy thanks to foreign donations and to a rather modern, business-like outlook, with the result that a prosperous temple has been built in Ayodhya for the convenience of Gujarati pilgrims on their way to Chappia, the birthplace of Swami Narayan.

It is not only Hindus who are attracted to Ayodhya as a tirtha; there are other groups, some of which have been there longer than the Hindus. In the first place there are the Jains, who have some big temples in Ayodhya which are regularly visited by pilgrims and sadhus from all over India. The first, second, fourth and fifth of their *tīrthaṅkaras* were born in Ayodhya, as well as the fourteenth. There are temples of the Digambara sect of Jainism dedicated to all these tirthankaras. The other sect in this religion, the Svetambara, is represented by a temple devoted to the first tirthankara. The other ancient non-Hindu religion, Buddhism, is represented by an ancient *stūpa* on Maniparvat which reminds us of the fact that Ayodhya was once the Buddhist place Saketa. I have never seen Buddhist pilgrims here, but people in Ayodhya told me that they come sporadically from Buddhist countries like Japan and Thailand. A religion which was introduced later in Ayodhya was Islam, and on our journey we have seen mosques and graves that have been centres of Hindu–Muslim strife. Nowadays Islam is very much a minor presence in Ayodhya and derives its importance mostly from the political issue of the use and possession of Janmabhumi.

Ayodhya is thus a place sacred to many Hindu and non-Hindu groups, but its importance to all of them derives to some extent from the central place of the Ram cult in Hinduism, India's dominant religion. The reason for most of these groups being represented in Ayodhya is that a market for religion has been created. In order to spread one's message one has to be present at places frequented by many religious-minded people. The presence of Ram is therefore felt by all, most strongly of course by the Hindu pilgrims and sadhus, but to some extent by the members of other religious groups as well.

4. The conjunction of time and place

In the two last sections we have followed the pilgrims, guided by their pandas, to several ghats along the river, and to temples and tanks in the city. This kind of journey can be made at all times, on any day and in every season. Some days and some seasons, however, are more auspicious than others for particular visits and ritual performances. They have a special power. To understand this we have to pay some attention to the complicated way in which the Hindu conceives time. First of all, some times are auspicious and others are not. Astrology is therefore one of the traditional sciences regarded as absolutely indispensable for the ordering of life. Every year Brahman scholars produce a *panchānga*, a rectangular book of newsprint, containing astrological charts, giving details of the relative auspiciousness of certain dates for travel, marriage or any other enterprise. The whole subject is so immensely complicated that most Hindus have to consult a knowledgeable Brahman pandit in order to be able to use it. Although many Hindus may travel or start some business without consultation, almost no one will contract a marriage or perform some important ritual without having done so. An important distinction is made in the panchanga between solar and lunar days (*vara* and *tithi*). The Hindu solar calendar, like the western one, has seven days (*vara*) in a week, each governed by a heavenly power:

Sunday is governed by Ravi (Sun): Ravivar;
Monday is governed by Soma (Moon): Somvar;
Tuesday is governed by Mangala (Mars): Mangalvar;
Wednesday is governed by Budha (Mercury): Budhvar;

Thursday is governed by Brihaspati (Jupiter): Brihaspativar;
Friday is governed by Shukra (Venus): Shukravar;
Saturday is governed by Shani (Saturn): Shanivar.

Some days of the week are more important than others, because
major gods or deities are especially worshipped on them. Monday is
a special day for Shiv, while Tuesday and Saturday are dangerous
days. People may fast on one of these days and visit temples credited
with strong power, like those of Hanuman or the Goddess (Devi or
Durga). Saturday is of course a day for worship of Shani, should a
pandit come to the conclusion that this inauspicious planet will have
some bad influence on your life.

The lunar days follow the monthly cycle of the moon. Each lunar
month consists of two fifteen-day fortnights (*pakshas*). The first is the
waning fortnight, the *krishna-paksh* (dark fortnight) and the other is
the waxing fortnight, the *shukla-paksh* (bright fortnight). Krishna-
paksh moves towards the new-moon night (*amāvasyā*) which is a
highly ambiguous and dangerous time. Someone who is born on
amavasya has a very inauspicious start in life. Usually a dangerous
time is also a very powerful time and so it is good to invoke the god's
power on this day, because then this power is heightened and more
easy to reach (cf. Stanley, 1977: 30). Shukla-paksh moves towards
the full-moon night (*purnimā*), which is unambiguously auspicious
and powerful. The lunar days are of great importance in dating
religious festivals because they are reckoned as being held on, for
example, the second or the third of one of the pakshas of a month.
The two eleventh days of both pakshas (*ekādashis*) are associated with
Vishnu and therefore in our case with Ram. Likewise there are other
lunar days associated with other gods and goddesses.

The lunar calendar has twelve months, just like the solar, but since
it is shorter an extra month is added every two or three years in order
to square it with the solar year. The names of the month are as
follows:

Chaitra	March/April
Vaishākh	April/May
Jyesth	May/June
Ashādh	June/July
Shrāvan	July/August

Bhādrapad	August/September
Āshvin	September/October
Kārttik	October/November
Mārgashīrsh	November/December
Paush	December/January
Māgh	January/February
Phālgun	February/March

The year begins in the spring with the *shukla-paksh* of Chaitra. I will enumerate some of the important festivals in Ayodhya according to season in the same way as Eck (1982) has done for Benaras.

SPRING: CHAITRA

The year begins with a festival which is celebrated in the spring and in the autumn, called *Naurātra* – the 'Nine Nights' for the Goddess. Tirthas exclusively devoted to the Goddess, like the *shaktipithas*, where, according to myth, parts of her limbs fell on earth when they were cut off by Vishnu, are of course the best places for this celebration. In other tirthas like Ayodhya, however, there is a religious infrastructure (religious specialists, temples, ritual material) for the performance of whatever ritual the pilgrim wants to perform. In this way festivals which are not specific to Ayodhya are observed here with a greater intensity and frequency than in secular cities of India. A place like Ayodhya, as a matter of course, specializes in festivals connected with Ram and Sita, but it also has for the Hindu a kind of cosmopolitanism to the extent that the festivals peculiar to different communities in different parts of India are also performed here with added lustre. On the ninth day (*Naumi*) of the shukla-paksh Ayodhya's greatest festival, *Rām Naumi*, the celebration of Ram's birthday, is held. Taking a bath in the Sarayu and doing *pūjā* (worship) of the image of Ram is central to this festival, for which, at a conservative estimate, about half a million pilgrims come to Ayodhya. On the purnima of this month groups of sadhus start a *pradakshin parikram* (clockwise circumambulation) of 84 *kos* (a kos is two miles), which takes 25 days. On this *parikram* around the holy city, which can be seen as a special type of worship, several tirthas are visited in a prescribed order which is laid down in manuals. It is believed that people wanting to have children will have their desire fulfilled if they make a wish before the idol of Ram on the day of the full moon.

THE HOT SEASON: VAISHAKH AND JYESTH

In these months the hot wind of North India, called the *lu*, begins to blow and prevents people from leaving their houses between noon and six in the evening. For this reason there are not many festivals in this period. Special for Ayodhya is the celebration of the birthday of Sita on *Jānakīnaumi*, the ninth day of the shukla-paksh of Vaishakh. It is worth noting that this festival attracts people mostly from East India (eastern Uttar Pradesh and Bihar), where the sweet devotion, in which a special place is given to Sita, has taken root more deeply than in other parts of the country. Another festival special for Ayodhya and mostly celebrated by local people, especially the pandas, occurs at the full moon of Jyesth. It is called *Sarayujayanti*, the birthday of Sarayu or the day on which the river descended to earth.

THE RAINY SEASON: ASHADH, SHRAVAN, BHADRAPAD

In Indian poetry the coming of the rains is often celebrated with what strikes us as exaggerated rhetoric and ebullient imagery. But the thunderous opening of the first monsoon rains, the coming of the clouds to the scorched plains after a long period of almost unbearable heat, is indeed an event without parallel. The full-moon day of the first month of the rains. Ashadh, is the time for worshipping one's guru. It is not surprising that this day falls in the rainy season, since in these months the sadhus observe their customary retreat in religious institutions. They give up their wandering for four months as has been a custom since the time of the Buddha. Since travelling is difficult in the monsoon, many laymen worship their guru simply by posting him some form of present on *guruparva*. The shukla-paksh of Ashadh is also a period in which gods enjoy the rains and the rising of the river Sarayu. They are taken out of the temples and brought to the river where they are placed in boats to enjoy the beginning of the rainy season, a festival called a *rathyātrā* after the cars (*rath*) on which the images are conveyed through the city. Shravan is the month in which one of Ayodhya's largest festivals, attended by some 300,000 to 400,000 people, is held: *Jhūlā*, the Swing Festival. The festival starts with another rathyatra on the third of shukla. The images from all the temples are brought to Maniparvat, where they are put in swings, suspended on the branches of the many trees on and around the hill. Two days later *Nāg Panchamī* is celebrated on the same hill, which is a place inhabited by *nāg* (snakes). They are worshipped because of their holiness to Vishnu and Shiv and yet are feared, because they tend to appear everywhere in the rainy season. The shukla-paksh of Shravan is further celebrated in the temples by placing the images there on swings. Every temple has its own attractions, ranging from the tricks of magicians to performances by religious singers. In Bhadrapada an All-India festival is celebrated in Ayodhya: *Krishnāstami*, the birthday of Krishna on the eighth day of the krishna-paksh. Although Krishna's birthplace, Mathura, is the best place to celebrate his birthday, it is also a festival of importance in Ram's Ayodhya. On ekadashi of the shukla-paksh of this month, an auspicious day for Vishnuites, the images of all temples in Ayodhya are taken for a nightly boat trip to celebrate the festival called *Jalbihārī Ekādashi*.

AUTUMN: ASHVIN, KARTTIK

Ashvin begins with a fortnight for the ancestors, *pitṛpaksh*. In this fortnight pilgrims come to Ayodhya to perform rituals in honour of their ancestors. Often they not only visit Ayodhya, but continue their pilgrimage to Benaras and Gaya. In this period a special attraction in Ayodhya and Benaras is the performance of a series of mystery plays on the life of Ram, called *Rām Līlā*. These are staged at several places in the city and organized by different, often competing groups. Young Brahman boys play the gods and are duly worshipped as such. On the tenth the play reaches its culminating event, the victory of Ram over the demon king Ravan: *Vijay Dashami* or *Dashera*. On the following day one of the most emotional scenes from the *Rām Līlā* is performed, the meeting of Ram with his brother *Bhārat Milap*. The following month, Karttik, is one of the most auspicious in the Hindu year. People come to stay for a month in Ayodhya as so-called *Kalapbāsis*. They vow to follow an ascetic way of life during the month and stay in a temple or with their panda.

All over Ayodhya religious sermons (*katha*) are delivered and pilgrims come to take a bath and have darshan. On amavasya India's great festival of Divali in honour of Lakshmi, the goddess of wealth and happiness, takes place. This is celebrated at home with the family, letting off fire-crackers and arranging rows of lamps in and around the house. In Ayodhya on the day before Divali the birthday of Hanuman is celebrated with great pomp and show in Hanumangarhi. On the ninth of the shukla-paksh another pradakshin parikram is organized, this time for sadhus and laymen alike and covering a distance of 14 kos (28 miles). It is a great event, attended by up to 400,000 pilgrims. It cures illnesses and fulfils all kinds of wishes. The month closes with one of the greatest bathing-fairs of the year held on *Karttik-purnimā* and celebrated at all important tirthas along the Ganges, the Yamuna, the Sarayu and other great sacred rivers of India.

THE COLD SEASON: MARGASHIRSH, PAUSH AND MAGH

On the fifteenth of the bright half of Margashirsh the marriage of Ram and Sita is celebrated: *Rām Vivāh*. This is a festival in which part of the marriage ceremony is performed in the temples, with Brahman boys who play the roles of Ram and Sita. It is a gay festival, just like any Hindu marriage with lavish parties and great wedding processions. The adherents of the sweet devotion are the foremost organizers and performers of the ceremony. The cold season can indeed be quite cold in North India and so Paush is a quiet month, in which people prefer to stay home. In Magh pilgrims come to Ayodhya on their way to the big festival in Prayag (Allahabad) held on *Makar Sankrānti*, when the sun enters the sign of Capricorn (*Makar*). The first signs of spring are celebrated on the fifth of the shukla-paksh in Magh by a festival called *Vasant panchami*.

SPRING: PHALGUN AND CHAITRA

The great festival celebrated in Chaitra is the spring festival connected with Krishna: *Holi*. It is a typical springtime and New Year festival with its rituals of reversal and saturnalia. Although Holi falls on the first day of Chaitra, Phalgun is also part of it, because bonfires and other preparations are already being made in this month.

God is everywhere, a Hindu may easily say. Very important to him on a metaphysical level is that God is in the exterior and in the interior landscape, to use A. K. Ramanujan's words. The identity of these two is emphasized by the well-known quotation from the Upanishads: *Tat Tvam Asi*: That are you. Nevertheless Hindus are prone to believe that this identity is more easily realized at special times, and in special places. Ayodhya is such a place and there are many favourable times to visit it.

5. Ayodhya in history

The pilgrim is not interested in the 'true history' of Ayodhya, merely in its greatness and power and in what are the most auspicious times to partake of those qualities. We have seen that the Ayodhya pandas relate that the tirtha is beyond time and history. Ayodhya has been in existence in three of the so-called 'world-periods' or yugas and by means of our meditation we can 'realize' the period in which Ram was there. As the story of the pandas goes, the world was created in Ayodhya during the Satya era. Ram was born in the second, Treta era. At the end of that period the place was lost until it was miraculously rediscovered by the legendary king Vikramaditya, who lived in the same era in which we are supposed to live: the Kali-yuga. After the reign of Vikramaditya, who had restored the place to its old glory, almost all temples were destroyed by the Muslims who gradually became the most influential power in northern India from the twelfth century onwards. When the Muslims disappeared from Ayodhya in the course of the eighteenth century, the heyday of Hinduism could begin. Those temples from Vikramaditya's time which had been only partly demolished were repaired, while new ones were built at 'old places', traditionally connected with the Ram story. This is in short the 'historical' tale told by Ayodhya's pandas.

Ayodhya's sacred buildings, as seen with the devout eyes of the pilgrims, have therefore various layers. First, the surface: a temple built some time between the eighteenth century and the present. Second, a layer showing that this building is in fact a restoration of a temple built by King Vikramaditya, who was able to rediscover the original locations of Ram's life by means of meditation. Finally, the last and most important layer: the building which is seen at the present time is ultimately a replica of the building in which Ram lived in the Treta-yuga. The relatively recent building is by this process equated with the building described in the sacred lore which the Hindu has heard from childhood. Time and history are made irrelevant in this treatment. It is a religious vision which makes the present transparent. By visiting Ayodhya the pilgrim is able to penetrate visually, in his darshan, into the eternal and supernatural world of Ram. From this point of view 'true history' is entirely irrelevant.

This is also made perfectly clear by Sitaram in the introduction to his Hindi guide to Ayodhya, of which I have already made extensive use (Sitaram, 1930). He argues as follows:

> People keep saying that what was built in this town in modern times is new. And there is a grain of truth in that; but on the other hand no one doubts that the pure stream of the Sarayu and the land of Ayodhya, founded by the first man, are without beginning and that the pure stream of Sarayu is the unworldly fruit of the formidable penance of the son of Brahman, Vashisth.

To Sitaram the western type of historical knowledge is worthless. It is just the placing of events in sequence according to the day and year:

> What conflict and when was it? But by deciding this we do not advance one step. We should accept that Indian time is without beginning and end and goes beyond counting. To call one thing present and another thing past is against the idea that all is permeated by the One. Small and great are equal. What we call one moment is in fact indestructible time and when we cut it into small parts, then there is no end to our cutting. We can only see the divine setting of Ayodhya with an Indian eye. The knowledge of Europe is of no avail to reach the depth of Ancient India.

Sitaram uses this line of argument to legitimize his own writing on Ayodhya:

> That is why I also include all kinds of mythical stories in this book which will strike youth educated by western methods as nonsense.

But the author is not misled by English education. Without the praise of the lives and actions of Saints we would not understand the community of believers (*satsang*).

Sitaram's emphasis on the irrelevance of time and history is evidently motivated by his religious beliefs, and would be fully accepted by Hindu pilgrims. But time and history are not of course irrelevant. The legendary presentation of Ayodhya's history by the pandas not only has a religious background, but also serves their interests. Ayodhya's rise as a supra-regional place of pilgrimage is relatively recent. Only during the eighteenth century did Ramanandi sadhus start to build their institutions here, while many of the buildings we see today were built in the second half of the nineteenth or the first part of the twentieth century. In a civilization in which 'tradition' and 'antiquity' are seen as respectable, these facts do not recommend a sacred place. This problem is evaded by an anti-historical presentation.

This is not to say that the pandas' account is entirely false. From the scholarly account given by Hans Bakker (1986) of what one can glean from scattered archaeological and historical sources for the history of Ayodhya from the seventh century BC to the middle of the eighteenth century AD, it is clear that from the thirteenth until the eighteenth century no Hindu temples of any significance were built. On the eve of Muslim dominance in the region, however, Ayodhya had already established itself as a sacred centre of some importance. As we have already seen, Bakker argues that in the fifth century, Ayodhya (Saketa) already had been successfully identified with the fictional Ayodhya of the Ram story, so that it should be no surprise to us that during the eighteenth century it emerged as one of the central tirthas of the Ramanandis.

The pandas' interpretation that the presence or absence of Muslim rule in Ayodhya is the only explanation for the fall and rise of this Hindu tirtha is, however, much too simple. In fact there seems nothing definite to say about the attitude of Muslim rulers and officials towards Hindu institutions in the Mughal period. Their actions ranged from the outright demolition of temples, as in the case of Babar destroying the temple on Ram's birthplace, to actively supporting their construction, as in the case of the Gauriya temples of Vrindaban, which were given grants by Akbar and Jahangir

(Mukherjee, 1980). To neglect the call of Muslim religious leaders, like the one in the case of the temple on Ram's birthplace, would have been a sheer impossibility for Muslim rulers, since the legitimation of their power and the extent of the support given by several groups to their regimes depended to a great extent on their use of Islamic symbols and rhetoric. There is certainly no evidence of a total suppression of Hinduism in Ayodhya. Hindu worship remained possible in the compound of the newly built Babar mosque and the activities of Brahman pandas are recorded by the first European to visit the place, William Finch, between 1608 and 1611 (Foster, 1921: 176). Actually, as Bayly (1981) argues, the consolidation of the Mughal empire in the seventeenth century and the ensuing expansion of communications had a positive influence on the growth of Hindu pilgrimage. For Ayodhya the expansion of the Ramanandi order in the seventeenth and eighteenth centuries, which we will discuss in the fourth chapter, was clearly the central development.

At the positive pole of the continuum between destruction and support of Hindu institutions stood the regime of the nawabs of Awadh (Oudh), who succeeded the Mughals as the dominant rulers in northern India in the eighteenth century. Awadh is, of course, Ayodhya, and during the rule of the first nawab, Saadat Khan (1722–39), the Hindu sacred place was the centre of this expanding regional realm. His successor, Safdar Jang (1739–54), however, removed the administration from Ayodhya to the newly built Faizabad, and later in the eighteenth century Lucknow was made the capital of Awadh. In the modern literature on Ayodhya Hindu writers tend to interpret the removal of the nawabi administration from Ayodhya as the liberation of a Hindu sacred place from Muslim oppression (see, for example, Sinha, 1957). The idea is that only after this removal could Ayodhya develop as an important pilgrimage centre, a theory that is substantiated by pointing out that most of the older temples in Ayodhya were built in the eighteenth century. There can be no doubt about the fact that Ayodhya became an important pilgrimage centre only in the eighteenth century. This seems not to have been the result of the removal of nawabi interference, but, on the contrary, the effect of patronage of the nawabi court. Richard Barnett makes it very clear in his recent study (1980) that the rule of the nawabs depended to a great extent on the successful collaboration of Hindus and Muslims. The administration was largely in the hands of *Kayasths*, a caste of Hindu scribes, while the military force was dominated by Shivaite nagas. The growing significance and prosperity of Ayodhya in this period seems to be due to the upward mobility of Hindu groups in the expanding realm of nawabi Awadh rather than the result of the removal of Muslim rule from the place. This view is reinforced by documentary evidence found among the Brahman pandas and Ramanandi sadhus. The *dīwān* (chief minister) of Nawab Safdar Jang, the Saksena Kayasth Nawal Ray, built and repaired several temples in Ayodhya, while Safdar Jang himself gave land to Abhayramdas, abbot of the Nirwana *akhāṛā* (fighting ascetics) for building a temple on what is known as Hanuman's hill. Later on, Asaf-ud-Daulah's diwan, the Srivastava Kayasth Tikayat Ray, contributed to the building of the important temple-fortress Hanumangarhi on this land. Moreover, in the documents kept by the pandas, we find evidence of several gifts given by Muslim officials of the nawabi court for rituals performed by these Hindu priests.

There seems, therefore, to have been considerable mutual understanding between Muslim rulers and Hindus in the eighteenth century, but it had its limits. There was no sign of removing the mosque from Ram's birthplace, although Muslims and Hindus continued to worship in the same compound. When the power of the nawabs was gradually eroded due to the growing influence of the British in Awadh's politics, the peaceful coexistence of Hindus and Muslims in what had become one of the most important Hindu pilgrimage centres in North India came to be threatened. During the reign of the last king of Awadh, Wajid Ali Shah (1847–56), who was virtually a puppet in the hands of the British, the Sunni leaders began to assert themselves against the authority of the Shia nawabs. In 1855 Muslims of Ayodhya, led by a Sunni leader, Ghulam Husain, claimed that there had been a mosque within the precincts of Hanumangarhi and that it should be reopened for Muslim worship. The Muslims gathered in the Babar mosque and started to threaten the Ramanandi nagas with an attack on Hanumangarhi. This led to a violent battle, won by the nagas who killed some seventy Muslims. The events caused considerable agitation among Muslims in the whole of Awadh, which the British tried to quell by appointing a commission of both Hindu and Muslim noblemen to investigate the

Muslim claim. Although the commission came to the conclusion that the claim was unjustified, the Sunni preachers continued to incite their followers to start a holy war against the nagas of Hanumangarhi. An army was formed under the leadership of Maulvi Amir-ud-din, *alias* Amir 'Ali, against the explicit orders of the king of Awadh. Before it could reach Ayodhya, however, it was stopped by British troops (Bhatnagar, 1968: 117–41). When the British annexed Awadh in February 1856 they decided to put a railing around the Babar mosque, so that the Muslims could continue to worship inside it, while the Hindus were forced to make their offerings on a platform which they raised outside the fence (Carnegy, 1870: 21).

The configuration in the eighteenth century, in which the co-operation of Hindu groups was essential for the expansion of the realm of the Shia nawabs, had also been important for the rise of Ayodhya as a pilgrimage centre. The British rule did not have a negative influence on this development but it did change its character. Patronage of Muslim rulers and officials was no longer necessary. Petty rajas and *zamīndārs* (landholders) of the region started to invest money in Ayodhya's temples on an enormous scale, probably because of the greater security of property which they enjoyed in the British period (cf. Metcalf, 1979: 352). As one of the descendants of a great builder once explained to me: 'We (the rajas) did not have to fight any more. We could spend all our resources and time on religion.' And indeed they did. They built temples, pakka bathing wharves and pilgrim lodges. In this way they tried to acquire merit (*puṇya*) and fame (*kīrti*). Generally they did not give these temples to Ramanandis as the patrons in the nawabi period tended to do, but appointed their own Brahman priest (pūjāri), together with other staff to manage the temple. When on pilgrimage to Ayodhya they could therefore stay in their own temples. Carnegy (1870) gives an extensive list of the buildings which were erected between, say, 1850 and 1870, while from my own research I can report that the building activities of these élite groups continued till the 1920s. The position of these élite groups, however, started to change considerably in the 1920s and 1930s. The decline of their influence is clearly shown by the Congress Party's defeat of the landlords' parties in the 1930s (cf. Reeves, 1968). The aftermath of this decline was the abolition of 'royal' privileges after Independence in 1947 for those who were recognized as rajas, while the final blow to all large landholders came with the abolishment of zamindari in the 1950s. Due to these economic and political processes, rajas who had become great patrons of religion in the course of the nineteenth century lost that position again in the twentieth. The results of this change can be clearly seen in Ayodhya. Most of the temples built by rajas and zamindars in their heydays are now in decay because their owners can no longer afford to manage them. The ruins which in the eyes of the pilgrims seem to date from Ram's days on earth are therefore in fact mostly very recent. Only a few of the great buildings erected by the royal patrons have survived the onslaught on their builders' exalted and protected position. The most important of these is, of course, the aforementioned Kanak Bhavan, of which some details are given in appendix 1.

The buildings in Ayodhya as well as the position of its religious specialists, as we will see in chapters III and IV, reflect neatly the processes of state formation and socio-economic change which have affected North Indian society at large. Ayodhya is no different from other places in North India in that it was affected by the so-called Cow Protection Movement, and there is evidence of riots on a great scale during the Muslim festival of *Bakr-Id* in 1912 and 1934. In both cases the Hindus launched an attack on the Babar mosque. In 1934 hundreds of Muslims seem to have been massacred and the army had to intervene. After this explosion of violence the British imposed a punitive tax of a few hundred thousand rupees on the Hindu citizens of Ayodhya. Nevertheless Ayodhya does not seem to have been a centre of Hindu-Muslim communal strife, but rather to have followed the general pattern of deteriorating Hindu–Muslim relations in the national polity in the first half of the twentieth century.

A fundamental change in the status quo concerning the Babar mosque on Ram's birthplace took place in the years following the Partition of 1947. On the night of 22 to 23 December 1949 an image of Ram suddenly appeared in the mosque, protected by an armed guard to prevent any breach of the peace. The news spread very quickly the following morning. For the Hindus Ram had appeared, while the Muslims interpreted the events as an attempt to defile their mosque. The ensuing riots were quelled only with great difficulty by police and army, while both religious groups were prevented from entering the mosque. Leaders of both parties started litigation to assert their right of entrance, but the case is still pending, illustrating the capacity of the Indian judiciary not to decide 'unsolvable' cases. In the meantime, the commissioner of Faizabad, Shyam Sundarlal Dar, ordered the district magistrate, K. K. K. Nair, to remove the image from the mosque, but this official refused by arguing that such an action would mean the rekindling of communal violence. Nair was a supporter of the Hindu communalist movement, *Rāshtriya Swayamsewak Sangh* (RSS), and was forced to retire from his post together with his assistant Gurudatt Singh because of his role in the Hindu–Muslim conflict. Gurudatt Singh continued to play a prominent role in communal politics in Faizabad (cf. Gould, 1966). Ram's image remained in the mosque and, since an image has to be worshipped, a committee was formed for this purpose. From 1950 the members of the Ram Janmabhumi Seva Committee obtained permission to worship Ram's image once a year on the night of 22 to 23 December. In addition, the committee organized a so-called uninterrupted devotional singing (*akhand kīrtan*) in front of the mosque to last as long as the birthplace was not liberated. The organization of this activity was given into the hands of a sadhu, Ram Lakhan Saran, who was succeeded by Ram Dayal Saran in the 1960s.

The new situation had therefore become one in which both Muslims and Hindus were refused entrance to the mosque, while Hindus had organized an activist devotional practice in front of it. Both parties were engaged in legal procedures, which gave the government the opportunity to remain neutral pending the decision of the court. The persons who had contrived to put the image in the mosque had tried to use the changed configuration in North India after partition to the advantage of the Hindus, but they did not really succeed. Till 1984 the mosque remained guarded by the police, but nothing much happened.

In 1984, however, the *Vishva Hindu Parishad*, a Hindu communalist movement, organized a procession 'to liberate the spot on which Ram was born': *Rām Janmabhūmi Mukti Yajna*. The implication is clear: the Hindus wanted the government to remove the Babar mosque and to give them permission to build a temple for Ram in that place. An explanation of this sudden attempt is not given here, since it would imply an analysis of complex changes in the national political arena, in which attention should be given to the fear of the international 'revival' of Islam as well as to the success of regional movements in Assam, Andhra Pradesh and Panjab. Although the movement was not particularly successful at the local level in Ayodhya (cf. Van der Veer, 1987b), it met with considerable enthusiasm in other parts of Uttar Pradesh. It is impossible to predict what would have been its political implications at the national level had not the murder of Mrs Gandhi diverted attention away from the competition between Muslims and Hindus and on to the 'Sikh controversy'.[1]

Events in Ayodhya not only reflect communalist processes but also, for example, the new emphasis on caste identities in the British period. Since the beginning of the twentieth century there has been a considerable increase in the number of temples and pilgrims' lodges for the exclusive use of the members of one caste (see appendix 2). This development can be understood in the context of a much broader process in which caste identities came to be defined in new ways to serve as vehicles for social and political mobility. On our walk through Ayodhya we have on several occasions encountered these caste temples and lodges. Most of them do not belong to higher castes, like Kayasths or Marwaris, but to low or untouchable castes, like the Chamars, the Dhobis and the Telis. Like other tīrthas, Ayodhya has become an arena for the display of respectablility and therefore the building of caste temples is instrumental for status mobility. From another angle, this development has provided Ramanandi sadhus of low caste with new opportunities; for example, to become priest or manager in an institution of their original community.

An important higher caste which invests on a large scale in religion is that of the Marwari merchants who have gradually taken over the position of landowning élites as the great religious patrons. They operate religious trusts and have rationalized their patronage in a bureaucratic way. They are clearly much less interested in the spread of their fame (*kīrti*) than the rajas were. They have a puritan life-style in which religion plays a dominant role. Many Marwari tycoons withdraw to tīrthas in old age, and leave their business affairs in the hands of their sons. From a sociological point of view it is interesting that the meetings of the religious trusts function as occasions for business contacts and community solidarity in a similar way to such organizations as the Lions clubs in western society.

Ayodhya can therefore at the same time be seen as a place both beyond and within time and history. We shall, of course, attempt to study our subject from the latter perspective, but we should be aware that our informants were both religiously and politically motivated to suppress this perspective. As will be seen from our treatment of the changing position of both the Ramanandis and the pandas, we are forced to approach our subject with great caution. First, however, we have to set out the theory and methodology that inform this study.

II Problems and perspectives

1. The study of meaning

The present monograph intends to give an anthropological description and interpretation of religious organization and experience in a Hindu pilgrimage centre. There is nothing especially strange or new in anthropological research in a peasant society with a complex civilization like India's. Already in the 1930s field studies began to be carried out in Mexico, Guatemala, Canada and Japan by Robert Redfield and his associates. In the 1950s Redfield formulated his project on the 'Comparative Study of Civilizations' which led, for example, to the volume on *Village India* edited by Marriott (1955). While turning their attention to the study of peasant societies, anthropologists retained the traditional tools of their trade such as participant observation and the collection of local history during an extended period of stay in the field. It would be of little profit to review here the development of theoretical paradigms and empirical insights in post-war peasant studies, but it might be justifiable to point out the tendency to emphasize politics and economics rather than religion. Turner (1974: 187) laments the 'almost obsessive emphasis on kinship, law, politics and economics rather than on religion, ritual, metaphor and myth: on pragmatics rather than symbolics'. This statement seems, however, somewhat exaggerated. The important point seems rather to be the general tendency to divorce the study of economics and politics from the study of religion, or, in Turner's words, 'pragmatics' from 'symbolics'. This implies the relative neglect of the politics of religious organization and of the relation between on the one hand changing value-orientations and religious experiences and on the other hand economic and political processes.

A general problem in the anthropological study of meaning is a failure to relate it to social action or to take into consideration structures of power and changing power relations. When anthropologists concern themselves with civilizations, often indicated with adjectives like 'high', 'great' and 'ancient', the problem is intensified. The major cause of this seems to be that anthropologists are in a way 'outsiders' and 'intruders' in a field of civilizational studies which have been dominated for centuries by disciplines like Islamology, indology, in short Oriental studies at large. In what seems to be an attempt to gain respectability, anthropologists have tended to reproduce the static and harmonious image of a *Hochkultur* which had long been maintained by textual scholars. Before turning to the fallacies of what I shall call the orientalist perspective in the study of Hinduism, I would like to criticize the major contribution to the study of religion and culture of complex peasant societies made by Clifford Geertz; I do so to clarify my own theoretical and methodological perspective.

Clifford Geertz is probably one of the most influential anthropologists at present. His work is primarily devoted to the study of religion in the peasant socieites of Indonesia and Morocco, but he has also published on political and economic developments in these 'new nations'. His work appears to be one of the best examples of the tendency to divorce the study of meaning from that of power. His theoretical programme for the study of religion is most carefully expounded in his well-known essay 'Religion as a Cultural System' which was first published in 1966 and reprinted in his widely acclaimed *The Interpretation of Culture* (1973). In this essay he gives a definition of religion which is indicative of his theoretical outlook: religion is 'a system of symbols which act to establish powerful, pervasive and long-lasting moods and motivations in men by formulating conceptions of a general order of existence and clothing these conceptions with such an aura of factuality that the moods and motivations seem uniquely realistic' (1973: 90). Geertz wants to develop 'the cultural dimension of religious analysis' and to him the culture concept 'denotes an historically transmitted pattern of meanings embodied in symbols, a system of inherited conceptions expressed in symbolic forms by means of which men communicate, perpetuate and develop their knowledge about and attitudes toward life' (1973: 89). Finally he sees the anthropological study of religion as 'a two-stage operation: first, an analysis of the system of meanings embodied in the symbols which make up the religion proper, and, second, the relating of these systems to social-structural and psychological processes'. (1973: 125). As the title of the collection of essays from which I have quoted makes clear, Geertz is interested in the interpretation of the meanings embodied in the cultural systems of symbols, of which religion is one of the most important. Geertz's interpretive anthropology is very much akin to Weber's actor-oriented methodology of 'Verstehen', although Geertz uses the more modern idiom of 'symbols' and 'semiotics'.

In an important criticism of Geertz's text Talal Asad (1983) attacks the notion that religion and culture make up an *a priori* system of meaning. According to Asad, Geertz omits the crucial dimension of power by evading the question of how power creates religion: what are the historical conditions (movements, classes, institutions, ideology) necessary for the existence of particular religious practices and discourses (1983: 252). In this way Geertz creates a universal and eternal image of the religion of mankind which is in fact the kind of 'natural religion' that has already been defined in the west since the seventeenth century (1983: 244–5). Asad also criticizes Geertz's presentation of the anthropological study of religion as a two-stage operation:

> How sensible this sounds, yet how mistaken, surely, it is. If religious symbols are understood on the analogy with words, as vehicles for meaning, can such meanings be established independently of the form of life in which they are used? If religious symbols are to be taken as the elements of a sacred text, can we know what they mean without regard to the social disciplines by which their correct reading is secured? If religious symbols are to be thought of as the patterns by which experience is organized, can we say much about that experience without considering how it comes to be formed? Even if it be claimed that what is experienced through religious symbols is not, in essence, the social world, but the spiritual, is it possible to assert that conditions in the social world have nothing to do with making that kind of experiencing accessible? Is the concept of *religious training* vacuous? (Asad, 1983: 250–1)

I entirely concur with Asad's criticism of Geertz's a-historical and to some extent even a-sociological approach to religion, but it seems essential to see to what extent Geertz's theoretical programme affects his empirical studies. Since, as Geertz puts it himself:

In anthropology, or anyway social anthropology, what the practitioners do is ethnography. And it is in understanding what ethnography is, or more exactly *what doing ethnography is*, that a start can be made towards grasping what anthropological analysis amounts to as a form of knowledge. (Geertz, 1973: 5–6).

Geertz believes that it is central to ethnography that 'our formulations of other people's symbol systems must be actor-oriented' and again that 'we begin our interpretations of what our informants are up to, and then systematize those' (1973: 14–15). It is, however, systematization which seems to be Geertz's greatest quality. The reader of his latest monograph, *Negara: The Theatre State in Nineteenth-Century Bali* (1980), will be surprised to read the description of only one 'system of meaning' which, as Geertz would have us believe, is shared by all Balinese. Such a formulation seems to be little 'actor-oriented'. The 'commoners' are merely 'stage-crew and audience' in the drama of the theatre state, in which the gentry lives out its status-aspirations, but the reader is left to guess what kind of interpretations the commoners have themselves. Geertz makes the theatre state a harmonic and aesthetic whole, in which the actors apparently have shared perceptions and ambitions. Whatever conflict or strife there might have been in nineteenth-century Bali it is restricted to the political field without affecting the system of meaning.

In fact, what is basic in Geertz's approach to Balinese culture is the distinction he makes between *cultural ambitions* – the beliefs and values forming the basis of the traditional state – and the *instruments* which one uses to realize these ambitions. This reminds us of Asad's criticism of the anthropological study of religion as a two-stage operation. Geertz does not ask the connected questions of how perceptions of reality relate to constellations of power and how they change with developments in these constellations, nor of how use is made of certain beliefs and values to claim and maintain certain social positions. Although his programme is Weberian, he neglects the *Wahlverwantschaft* between economic, political and religious processes. The major flaw in his description of Balinese reality is that it can be summed up in the notion that Balinese culture is an unchanging harmony, an eternal thing of beauty.

In this way Geertz writes a strange kind of historical ethnography.

In the first chapter of *Negara*, entitled 'Bali and Historical Method', he rejects a history of events, because there are no historical sources available for it. Instead a developmental history should be made on the basis of an appropriate model of socio-cultural process(1980: 5–6). However, Geertz offers us only the model, not the history. His model is based upon interviews made in the 1950s and on secondary literature. It appears to be nothing but the historical image his informants had in the 1950s about the 'traditional state', and that image is systematized with the aid of secondary information into a harmonic whole which Geertz believes not to have changed between 1343 and 1906 (1980: 134). It is at least surprising that Geertz does not enter into the theoretical and methodological difficulties of doing historical research merely on the basis of ethnography. He appears to share the Balinese conception of time and person which he has eloquently described in 'Person, Time and Conduct in Bali' (1973). In this essay he argues that the Balinese have a 'non-durational' concept of time, which is cyclic and means that the Balinese live in a depersonalized and detemporalized present. In *Negara*, time and person also appear to be irrelevant; drama is important, not the actors. Moreover, the Balinese are said to have the idea that history in itself is unimportant, yet it serves as a kind of aesthetic correction of the present: a model for the present. This religious representation of historical reality is *reproduced* by Geertz who does not ask himself the question how and why it is *produced* at a certain point in history.

Although I believe that Geertz does not put his own precepts into practice, I should make it clear that some of these ideas as, for example, the emphasis on the 'native's point of view' and the use of ethnography in writing history, have my full sympathy. I certainly agree with Asad's criticism of Geertz's a-historical views, which are apparent even when Geertz attempts to write history, but he does not seem sufficiently aware of the methodological difficulties involved in writing on the history of value-orientations and religious experience in societies like Indonesia, Morocco and, for that matter, India. The first major problem here is the relation between history and religion. In the preceding chapter we have seen the extent to which history and time are *made* irrelevant by religious specialists. In doing so the specialists make use of a very intricate Hindu conception of time. This is, however, not the only relevant conception of time. Besides this religious conception there exists a universal idea of 'durational time' which, according to Bloch (1977), pertains to political, economical and other pragmatic contexts. Bloch's argument is that there is a universal, durational concept of time which belongs to the infrastructure of economic conditions and actions, and besides that a ritual, non-durational concept of time belonging to a superstructure which serves to maintain the impression of an unalterable social structure. Ritual cognition therefore hides the world, according to Bloch, while it is challenged by non-ritual cognition which reveals the world. I do not, however, feel much attracted to Bloch's argument, with its neat dichotomy between two types of cognition. The obvious rejoinder is that religious cognition often belongs as much to pragmatic contexts like warfare and agriculture as to ritual contexts, while it often challenges vested interests (cf. Bourdillon, 1978).

In Bloch's argument, which follows that of Durkheim, religion is more or less a projection of the social on to the religious plane. It is, however, not at all clear that it is society which is sacralized in the way the Ayodhya pandas present time and history. Rather Ayodhya's sacred time and place are set beyond profane society and history. This is the distinction made by Mircea Eliade, for whom profane is connected with suffering and sacred time is an attempt to deny historical event. Eliade's sacred is to some extent irrelevant for the here-and-now; unbounded by space and time, it is considered to be absolute (cf. Stirrat, 1984). This makes our problems perfectly clear. The tendency in Hindu religion to obliterate historical time and historical person makes it exceedingly difficult to find independent, historical facts.

In this regard, a comment of Sudhir Kakar (1982: 125), who did research among a religious cult in North India, the Radha Soami Satsang, is illuminating:

It is important to note here that for the Satsangis (of whichever persuasion), as indeed for members of all mystical cults, a historical account of the cult's origin that does not read like the unfolding of a divine plan and biographical sketches of their gurus that are not exercises in hagiography are *essentially* false. They feel that historical accounts are misleading, since they reduce the eternal to the temporal and limit what is universal to the confines of a particular geographical region. The spiritual base and mystical regimen of the Radha Soami cult, they claim, are not the products of individuals or of historical movements, nor can they be explained by recourse to any psychological or sociological constructs. To its adherents, the Radha Soami faith is the *real* teaching of *every* saint at *all* times of history.

It is not just nonsense when Geertz claims in *Negara* that the very material on which the history of Bali could be based is to a great extent lacking. The same situation pertains to my research on the early history of the Ramanandis and the pandas. Should the anthropologist then modestly refrain from writing history? To some extent he should and to some extent he should not. To understand the present configuration in Ayodhya it is necessary to understand its development, to use a historical perspective. But what we should emphasize is the debate on the past which we encounter during our fieldwork. Such a debate as a source of legitimation between several power groups in society is the anthropologist's domain and in terms of this debate he should use his historical perspective.

Recently, Arjun Appadurai (1983) made a case for the study of such a debate. He reminds us of Leach's (1954) argument that discourse concerning the past between social groups is an aspect of politics, involving competition, opposition and debate. Appadurai, however, argues that the past is a scarce resource, since it is organized culturally. In his research on the politics of a South Indian temple he locates five norms which provide the cultural framework of the debate of the past:

1) that *textual evidence* for the authority of any charter is superior to any other kind;
2) that the evidence for a charter ought to involve the ratification of a credible *external authoritative figure* (whether sacred or secular) in the past;
3) that the charter should be based on an authoritative document that encodes (in addition to the claims of the group in question) the privileges of a maximum number of *other relevant groups*;
4) that the evidence for the charter in question should be reflected, as far as possible, *continuously* in the documented past; and
5) that the greater the *antiquity* of the referents of the charter in question, the better the case for the rights in question.

Appadurai makes the additional remark that there seems to be an order among these five norms in that the first is least dispensable and the last the most. Appadurai puts these norms, which regulate the debate, outside the debate itself. They are the constraints, the cultural framework of the debate between power groups in the temple, which in his case are the state, Tenkalai Brahmans and non-Brahman worshippers.

A study of temple priests in the same region by Chris Fuller (1984), however, makes Appadurai's notion of cultural restraints at least problematic. Fuller shows convincingly that the state of Tamilnadu forces the temple to perform the rituals according to the so-called *Agamas*, a set of sacred texts believed to have been dictated by Shiv himself. These texts are in every sense authoritative and as such are acknowledged by all interest-groups in the temple. The difficulty is, however, that the Agamic literature is nowadays largely unknown. There are only three priests in the whole of southern Tamilnadu considered to be proficient in the *Agamas*, and even these three do not know the 'real' content of the *Agamas* but are learned only in its ritual method, which, however, is totally different from what has actually been practised for centuries by the families of ritual specialists in the temples. The ritual is in fact preserved by the principle of heredity from father to son, while the texts, whatever their original role may have been, have now become tools in the hands of those demanding changes in the temple. What becomes of Appadurai's framework of the debate in this case, of central importance in temple politics in Tamilnadu today? Everyone in the temple agrees on the unquestionably authoritative status of texts which are either non-existent or irrelevant. We see only that the state can use *the idea of the Agamas* as a tool for penetration in the temple's affairs. This is not to say that Appadurai's norms are worthless in a study of the debate of the past, but to emphasize that our primary attention should be given to the politics of the debate and not to its unchanging cultural framework.

The purpose of our study then, in a general and theoretical sense, is to study the intricate texture of the changing relations between power and religious meaning. Religion is politically organized and its content of religious symbols cannot be divorced from that organization. This is not to follow a reductionist line of reasoning in which religious beliefs and experiences are merely reduced to reflections of the political and material order. They have in a way their own force and pattern of change which affect the organization of those who live by them. There is a dynamic interdependence between power relations and symbolic formations and actions (Cohen, 1974). Furthermore, 'what the actors think they are up to' is as important to me as to Geertz, but in the interpretation of their meaningful actions we have to pay attention to their power and interests. History is a problem in this study. This is not and does not pretend to be the history of Ayodhya as a pilgrimage centre. History is, however, as important to me as to the participants in the social field I studied: it is part of the content of religion and part of its organization. History is studied here in terms of the political debate on the past and as a resource in that debate. As far as a developmental history is given in these pages it is meant to be of help in understanding the present configuration.

2. Hinduism: the orientalist perspective

Indian civilization and its study show a remarkable continuity. Many of the assumptions and interests underlying research carried out on Indian religion and society since the Second World War developed during the preceding two centuries of British dominance in India (cf. Cohn, 1968). It is therefore interesting to trace in broad outline some of these developments.

A clear understanding of India's religion became of vital importance to the British when they established their power during the late eighteenth century. Traditional Hindu law was considered to be especially valuable for the administration of justice. It is not surprising that one of the first serious British students of Sanskrit – 'the sacred language of the Hindus' – was Sir William Jones, a Supreme Court judge on the Calcutta Bench. By observing in 1786 that Greek, Latin and other European languages must have sprung from the same source as Sanskrit, he laid the foundation for a comparative perspective on Indo-European languages and religion, developed among others by Max Müller and, in our times, by Georges Dumézil. The ensuing interest in Sanskrit sources caused an 'oriental renaissance' through the European romantic movement, which, as we know, was deeply influenced by the 'discovery' of

Hindu spiritual wisdom. This interest has remained till the present day and has been institutionalized in several branches of scholarship, which harp on the Wonder that was India (Basham, 1975) before the expansion of Islamic powers (*c.* AD 1200). The related notion that oriental spirituality and occidental materialism are antithetically opposed is also deeply rooted, not only in the works of western scholars such as Edward Conze, but also in those of such leading Indian intellectuals as the former president, Sarvapalli Radhakrishnan.

The orientalist perspective has above all led to a picture of Indian society as static, timeless and spaceless, and dominated by the Brahmans as guardians of the sacred order of society (Cohn, 1968: 7).[1] There can be no doubt that this picture has haunted social research on Indian religion and society from Weber to Dumont. Interestingly, this picture was not seriously challenged by the growing stream of empirical data collected by British administrators in different parts of the country. The overall picture was supplemented by administrative views on the caste system and the 'village community'. Much effort was expended on 'collecting' the customs of castes in various parts of the country and on discussing the merits and demerits of the Indian caste system (cf. O'Malley, 1974). The idea that caste is the basis of the Indian social order and that to be a Hindu is to be a member of a caste became an axiom in the British period. What actually happened during that period was probably a process of caste formation and more rigid systematization due to administrative and ideological pressure from the colonial system which reminds us of the so-called 'secondary tribalization' in Africa. In the chapter on the Ayodhya pandas we can follow this process in some detail.

After the Second World War India gained independence and the investigating administrators were succeeded by 'independent' social scientists. While in the colonial period anthropologists had focused their attention on 'simple' societies living on the frontier of the complex Hindu civilization, like the Todas studied by Rivers, they now turned to the study of Hindu civilization itself. In the 1950s village India became the object of study. The major problem was, of course, how to understand Indian society and civilization from synchronic field studies of particular villages. One answer to this problem was the model of the interaction between great and little traditions devised by Robert Redfield (cf. Redfield, 1956; Singer, 1972). The great tradition was identified with beliefs and practices found in Sanskrit literature and located in 'sacred centres' (cf. Vidyarthi, 1961). The little traditions made up the culture found by the anthropologist in his village study. With few exceptions the major interest of the anthropologists working along these lines was, as we have seen, in the villages, where they thought to find the parochialized representations of the great Sanskrit tradition. According to McKim Marriott, 'parochialization is a process ... of limitation upon the scope of intelligibility, of deprivation of literary form, of reduction to less systematic and less effective dimensions' (Marriott, 1955: 200–1). To put it differently, village culture was backward and limited in comparison with the high and ancient Hindu civilization, as studied by the indologists. In this way there were two worlds in India· the textual civilization, and a meagre derivation of it as found by the anthropologists in their village studies.

It is clear that the orientalist perspective reigns freely here. The textual studies of the indologists provide the anthropologist with a framework to approach his often unruly fieldwork material. As Stirrat (1984: 206) remarks, this is an élitist representation of social reality which is partly caused by the fact that the anthropologists as intellectuals are drawn to the most logical systems of thought available in the societies they study, which are often only produced by the higher strata of that society. Moreover, as 'newcomers' in the field of civilizational studies anthropologists tended to adopt the perspective of the already established humanist disciplines. A telling example of the combination of both these tendencies is Milton Singer's fieldwork in Madras, in which he was guided by a staunch Brahman who was at the same time a respected professor of indology (Singer, 1972).

Another important answer to the problem of the relation between Hindu civilization and village reality was given by Louis Dumont and David Pocock. Their research programme was revealed in a programmatic article in the first number of an influential new journal edited by them, *Contributions to Indian Sociology* (1957) (Dumont, 1970: 2–18). The opening sentence is revealing: 'In our opinion, the first condition for a sound development of a Sociology of India is found in the establishment of the proper relation between it and classical Indology.' According to the authors, that proper relation implies that the sociology of India lies at the point of confluence of sociology and indology. Their programme is to develop a sociology of values and ideas, and for that they need the indological interpretation of those texts in which the Hindu 'system of meaning' is laid down. In Dumont's work this leads to an excessively orientalist perspective which coincides – not to our surprise – with the perspective of the learned Brahmans who were the authors of these texts. Dumont argues that only by understanding the Hindu ideology, which is based upon the hierarchical subordination of two opposites, pure and impure, can one try to grasp the workings of the caste system, the most fundamental Hindu institution, and the actual behaviour of social actors. Pertaining as he does to the tradition of Durkheim and Mauss, Dumont makes no difference between religion and society: 'One might say that all that appears to be social is in fact religious and that all that appears religious is in fact social' (Dumont, 1970: 16). Religion in the sense of, for example, the Hindu belief in gods, he sees as secondary to and derived from the fundamental values of caste.

Dumont's central argument is that the seeming diversity in Indian society and history can be interpreted by paying attention to the underlying ideology of caste:

> unity is found here above all in ideas and values, it is therefore deeper and less easily defined: on the one hand it is social in the strictest sense, and this justifies our sociological perspective, it makes *Indian society as a whole* the true object of our study. On the other hand, this unity consists more in relations than in isolated elements. (Dumont, 1970: 5)

In this way the actual complexity of religious beliefs and actions, as found by the anthropologist in his field, is simplified by the reduction to a unifying ideology. Moreover, change and history also disappear from the scope of interest of the anthropologist, since the ideology of the caste system has already been fixed in the classical period of Indian civilization, before the Islamic invasions. History can only be understood in terms of the mental framework of the Hindu ideology (cf. Biardeau, 1981: 9).

There are several objections to be raised against Dumont's

position, but we will limit outselves to two major ones. The first is similar to the objection we made against Geertz's position. In the work of both authors there is no systematic attention to the changing relation between power and meaning. Dumont does not deny that power exists in society, but it is encompassed by the value of ritual purity. The relations of politico-economic power are of secondary importance and separated from the production of meaning. Dumont, in fact, reproduces the Brahman ideology in which the *dharma* or universal order of the Brahman is considered to be superior to the *artha* or realm of interest or advantage. Asad's criticism of Geertz can directly be extended to Dumont's programme.

The other major objection concerns the use of an ideological model, derived from the indological interpretation of Sanskrit texts. The reference to the textual tradition is extremely problematic. In the first place texts are generally taken from the Vedic and Classical periods of Hindu civilization, i.e. texts dating from about 1000 BC to AD 1200. Let us compare this with the study of modern Christianity. It is perfectly clear that the Bible and the interpretations of men like Augustine are of great importance to modern Christianity, but no one would even attempt to derive models from these texts to interpret the actual behaviour of Calvinists in a Dutch village. Such a method is based upon the assumption that before the arrival of the Europeans, the traditional society was a kind of 'frozen' social reality, in which no changes of any importance occurred. This assumption is, however, entirely mistaken. The study of the textual traditions after AD 1200 shows already considerable changes in Hindu beliefs and practices. In the 1960s the indologist Van Buitenen (1966: 40) observed already that anthropologists who wished to collaborate with textual scholars in their endeavour to understand modern Hinduism, should take the study of much more recent texts as their starting-point.

Secondly, those who want to have recourse to indological materials should pay more attention to the nature of these materials. A text is always a social text, written from a certain point of view which pertains to a certain social group. By selecting texts one may obtain a partial view on the historical situation. Dumont, for example, is often accused of presenting the Brahman ideology without paying attention to other ideologies, in what Edmund Leach has called his 'mixture of Vedic ideas and contemporary facts'. A solution to this specific problem could be the construction of more cultural models, deriving from several native ideologies, as found in the texts. This is proposed by Richard Burghart (1978a, 1983b) who argues that we should study the intra-cultural debate of the ideological representations of Brahmans, kings and ascetics, who are in his view the most important actors in Hindu society.

This solution, however, does not account for what I am tempted to see as the most important problem that arises when anthropologists refer to the textual tradition. The social significance of this tradition in contemporary India is too easily assumed. Following Goody (1968, 1977), a distinction is drawn between pre-literate and literate society. Writing favours historical thinking, makes possible a movement from myth to history and permits public criticism and discussion of social knowledge, while in pre-literate societies history and knowledge are an almost infinitely plastic resource. This assumption, to be short, is incorrect. Those texts which are marked by indologists as important, are often not known or are insufficiently known by the contemporary actors (cf. Fuller, 1984). Moreover, texts do not lay down anything at all, and certainly not beliefs, which are very diverse and are only exceptionally the subject of a debate between theologians in places like Benares. As far as the past is concerned, the most remarkable thing when doing research in India, is its extreme plasticity. In India one finds a mixture of oral and textual tradition which might even be more variable than the oral history of African societies. 'Ancient' texts can be made by the day in India, as I have actually observed in Ayodhya, while traditions can be transformed in accordance with changing social configurations (cf. Parry, 1985b).

The outsider who visits Hindu centres and is bewildered by the great and seemingly incoherent variety of beliefs and practices is often reminded by Hindus that what he sees are only phenomenological images of the One, that the variety is merely an illusion (*maya*), while true knowledge can only be reached by studying the ancient texts. In fact, the anthropologists seem to have adopted this 'emic' view that there is an unchanging, scriptual source for contemporary beliefs and practices. This view is fundamentally a theological one which is highly detrimental to anthropological research.

As we will see in the following chapters, the orientalist perspective, developed by anthropologists in the 1950s and 1960s, is still of importance in the study of Hinduism. It seems necessary therefore in this study of the politics of Hindu religious organization and the production of meaning to take a position which is, repeatedly and consistently, critical of current approaches. As far as I see it, the central problem facing the anthropological study of Hinduism is to get away from the orientalist perspective with the intellectualist and theological overtones that have dominated it from the start. The present study of Hindu monks and priests in Ayodhya is a modest attempt to do so.

3. The study of a pilgrimage centre

The subject of this monograph is not Hindu pilgrimage as such. Although the aims and behaviour of the pilgrims who visit Ayodhya have an important bearing on the subject, they have not been the focus of my research. What I want to present in this study is a descriptive interpretation of the changing social configurations formed by the religious specialists of Ayodhya. The focus therefore is on the sacred centre and the religious specialists, and not on the pilgrim and his journey. Nevertheless, since the sacred centre and its social organization are aspects of the total socio-cultural institution of Hindu pilgrimage, it seems valuable to review here some of the major contributions to the study of pilgrimage in order to clarify our perspective and research problems.

A theory of pilgrimage with universal pretensions has been offered by Victor Turner (1974). Turner argues that social life cannot be fully described in terms of patterned arrangements of role-sets, status-sets and status-sequences, because situations exist in which these social distinctions disappear and 'a direct, immediate and total confrontation of human identities arises which tends to make those experiencing it think of mankind as a homogeneous, unstructured and free community' (1974: 169). This kind of situation he observed first in his study of rites of passage among the Ndembu, a tribe in Zambia, Central Africa. These rites take place in the periphery of the residential area and thus imply a journey from one place to another and back, during which a change in status from boy to adult takes place. The total process can be described in terms of the analytic distinctions developed by Van Gennep (1977): separation, limen, reaggregation. Turner observed that in the place where the rituals were performed during the 'liminal' phase of transition from one status to another, a feeling of oneness arose among the participants in which their structural differences disappeared. This confrontation of 'total' individuals Turner calls *communitas*, and the totality of phenomena in social life which give rise to it he calls *anti-structure*.

Whereas in tribal societies anti-structure is expressed in rites of passage, in more complex societies with historical religions it seems primarily to be expressed in pilgrimage. The place of pilgrimage is 'a centre out there' and the journey to it can be analysed by making use of the distinctions developed by Van Gennep. According to Turner, pilgrimage is 'liminal' in the spatial sense and has the social quality of *communitas*. Turner, however, does not equate pilgrimage with tribal rites of initiation. Voluntarism, free choice, plays a much greater role in the historical religions than in tribal religions. Further he remarks that 'the relationship between social structure and social *communitas* varies within and between societies and in the course of social change' (1974: 202), and 'this quality of *communitas* in long-established pilgrimages becomes articulated in some measure with the environing social structure through their social organization' (166–7). This suggests a dialectical relation between structure and anti-structure, so that in a sense '*communitas* is not structure with its signs reversed, minuses instead of pluses, but rather the *fons et origo* of all structures and, at the same time, their critique. For its very existence puts all social structural rules in question and suggests new possibilities. *Communitas* strains towards universalism and openness' (202). We can easily imagine that this model, in which a dialectical relation is suggested between 'normal' social life in village, town, neighbourhood or family and the process of pilgrimage, is attractive to those who refuse to see in religion a mere reflection of social structure and want to give symbolic action an important place in the study of society.

In a way Turner's contribution is to be seen as an attempt to get away from functionalist arguments about the representation of society by religion, but in fact he perpetuates its difficulties in another form. Several dichotomous oppositions in his work, such as individual and society, free choice and obligation, between the emotion of *communitas* among human beings and structured life, in short between pilgrimage as a ritual process and normal life 'at home', seem to me products of religious ideology rather than of sociological thinking. A simple objection is the observation already made by many fieldworkers, that the divisiveness implicit in everyday social relations is preserved in pilgrimage (Eickelman, 1976; Sallnow, 1981; Van der Veer, 1984). Sallnow, for example, argues that in fact in Andean pilgrimage a new arena is created in which social interactions take place *ex novo*. The regional devotions of the Andes, however, can be characterized by their endemic competition and conflict. In my own article I have argued that in the pilgrimage to Ayodhya the ritualistic pilgrimage of purity and the ancestor rituals reinforce social structure from a functionalist perspective, whereas the spiritual pilgrimage for the liberation of the soul has something like *communitas* as an ideological component, which is not found in practice. What Turner in fact does is to objectivize part of an ideology that is common to universal religions. What should be studied, the sociological meaning of the ideological message that 'everyone is equal before God', is made to form the essence of an important ritual, although this is contradicted by easily observable empirical facts.

The notion that pilgrimage is a ritual of the wider community is, of course, a truism. It is difficult to connect this notion with more penetrating interpretations. Often emphasis is given to the fact that it is not the 'limited moral community of the village' that is reinforced by pilgrimage, but 'the larger moral community of the civilization' (Obeyesekere, 1966). A classical statement of this function is made by Wolf in an article on the Virgin of Guadelupe in Mexico, which 'links together family, politics and religion; colonial past and independent present; Indian and Mexican ... It is, ultimately, a way of talking about Mexico: a collective representation of Mexican society' (1958: 38). Srinivas (1967: 74) argues that the sacred centres are the places in which the great Sanskritic tradition is transmitted to the peasants of the region: 'Every great temple and pilgrim centre was a source of Sanskritization, and the periodic festivals or other occasions when pilgrims gathered together at the centre provided opportunities for the spread of Sanskritic ideas and beliefs.' I have already expressed my doubts about the usefulness of making a dichotomy between great and little traditions, observing that the social actors themselves do not make such a distinction between higher and lower forms of religion. Moreover, the content of what is called the Great Sanskritic tradition is completely unclear. Is it the tradition of the Brahman priests, who are engaged in death rituals and therefore have a very ambiguous status, or is it the tradition of ascetics, who have renounced all ritual activities – or maybe of those ascetics who eat human flesh and are considered to be extremely powerful? There is no Great Sanskritic tradition in Hindu India, but a great many interacting traditions, followed by sometimes local and sometimes regional or national groups, organized on the basis of sect-like networks or family ties, all of them making up the complex civilization of Hindu India. We can only agree with the motto given by Bhardwaj to his book *Hindu Places of Pilgrimage in India* (1973): 'To the countless dedicated pilgrims whose footprints have given meaning to India as a cultural entity', when we immediately add 'and as an arena of cultural diversity'.

The argument that pilgrimage acts to create national identification and thus plays a role in nation-building is succinctly expressed by Mandelbaum (1972: 401):

> There is a traditional basis for the larger national identification. It is the idea, mainly engendered by Hindu religion but shared by those of other religions as well, that there is an entity of India to which all its inhabitants belong. The Hindu epics and legends, in their manifold versions, teach that the stage for the gods was nothing less than the entire land and that the land remains one religious setting for those who dwell in it. That sense was and is continually confirmed through the common practice of pilgrimage.

This is no doubt partly true, but only partly. A notion of *bharatvarsha* as the sacred land of Hindus with Mount Meru as its *axis mundi* is created by religious teaching and by the ritual of pilgrimage, but this is different from the notion of India as an entity to which all its inhabitants belong, which is falsified not only by separatist movements among Muslims and Sikhs, but also by the movement of N. T. Rama Rao's *Telugu Desam* in Andhra Pradesh, using Hindu symbols to enforce a Telugu regional identity. Pilgrimage can and does act as much as a ritual enforcing regional, sectarian or communal identifications, as it does as one that enforces national identifications.

Bhardwaj tries in his book to develop a typology of Hindu places of pilgrimage in a hierarchical scheme which includes five levels: pan-Hindu, supra-regional, regional, sub-regional and local. This is not a ranking that exists in the minds of the responding pilgrims, but is based on the objective determination of the distance travelled by the pilgrim. In this way the catchment area of the place of pilgrimage is determined. Then he combines his findings with a hierarchy among the pilgrims patronizing the shrines. Pilgrims to the highest-level sacred places are generally from the ritually higher castes and higher classes and tend to be on pilgrimage more for spiritual than material reasons. At the middle level, he finds personalized deities propitiated for material gain by mixed groups of pilgrims, while at the local level he finds scheduled caste pilgrims and Mother Goddess shrines. Bhardwaj's empirical findings seem to verify the notion of levels in Indian civilization from high to low which coincides with levels in the social hierarchy in Indian stratification. These findings are, however, not corroborated by the material collected by Morinis (1984) and myself. Morinis states that the highest percentage of Brahman pilgrims was found in what was, by Bhardwaj's criteria, a low-level, sub-regional shrine, Tarapith in West Bengal, whereas the regional shrine of Navadvip had a higher proportion of lower-caste pilgrims (Morinis, 1984: 269). The identification of pan-Hindu centres with non-material pilgrimage is in my opinion untenable, since, as we have seen already, pilgrimage to Ayodhya has clearly material aims, among others; more generally, it has not proved fruitful to separate these aspects from others, just as Hanuman cannot be separated from his master Ram.

A major drawback of all these functionalist, anti-functionalist and typological attempts to understand pilgrimage is that they are highly abstract and a long way from the meanings attached to tirth yatra in the statements of the social actors, pilgrims and specialists. Morinis (1984) develops an alternative to these approaches by investigating the explicit understandings of the participants themselves as well as the implicit meaning given to pilgrimage in Hindu tradition as an encompassing system of belief. The explicit meanings given by participants are summarized and unified in the notion that pilgrimage is seen by the participants as a mechanism for merit accumulation:

The merit (*puṇya*) thus accumulated can be applied to bring about changes in the existential conditions of the life of the pilgrim in the immediate or distant futures, and so in this life or the next, and can be brought to bear on immediate personal problems or general metaphysical conditions. A common idea that journeying to the sacred place where the divine is accessible can (and indeed does) bring about a transformation in the life of the individual underlies all this variety. (1984: 282)

The implicit meaning given to pilgrimage in the wider spectrum of Hindu cosmology and theology is less easy to determine. Morinis is aware of the difficulties encountered by the anthropologist who wants to foray into cultural models which derive from literary sources, but 'foray we must, for it is only in relation to more general patterns of the Hindu religious tradition that the journey and practices of the individual pilgrim in the sacred place make sense. I seek to interpret my fieldwork data by relating it to encompassing systems of belief' (1984: 284). He then continues by giving an implicit model of pilgrimage based upon the Hindu cosmological notion of the homologous structure of all levels of the cosmos. The universe can be found in the structure of the human body, in the structure of the temple and in that of the sacred place. The pilgrimage is a journey of the soul to God's abode 'whether that abode is situated in the spiritual heart of hearts, the bodily heart, the temple, the earthly realm, or the universe' (295).

Although I sympathize with Morinis's attempt to give the concept of meaning a more central place in the analysis of pilgrimage, I must conclude that he also falls into the orientalist trap. He makes an implicit model of pilgrimage of his own by taking ideas from disparate traditions and unifying them to Bengal Hinduism as manifest at different times and places. This strikes me as a theological rather than an anthropological argument since it does not take into account the production and management of meaning by various interest groups involved in pilgrimage. To a certain extent there is no doubt something common in Hindu religious traditions which seems to unify its different rituals and pilgrimages. As we have seen in the first chapter, the concept of tīrtha is a forceful and ancient cultural symbol in Hinduism, which is used in various ways in many Hindu traditions. What seems interesting to me, however, is that the tirtha of Ayodhya, which was formerly a place where Ram had lived in his human form and which was primarily a centre of Brahmanical rituals for a limited region, has gradually, under the influence of Ramanandi theology, become more an esoteric reflection of the heavenly abode of Ram and Sita, the ground for their divine play (*lila*). By emphasizing that there is one 'Hindu model' implicit in pilgrimage one easily skips over these subtle changes in meaning and in their organizational correlates. The *Wahlverwantschaft* between the growth of importance of pilgrimage in North India and political and economical transformations during the last three centuries can also be easily neglected when we formulate a-historical models of Hindu pilgrimage. It is not correct to argue that the meaning of pilgrimage does not alter when it becomes an important ritual for larger groups of Hindus. The content of religion changes when localized forms of religion lose importance and more universal forms become more prominent. This is the type of change broadly indicated by Pocock (1973), in which Shivaite and Mother Goddess forms of Hinduism are more and more replaced by Vishnuite devotional practices. It is often not possible to probe into changes of mentality and meaning because independent historical data are lacking. It will not do, however, systematically to exclude this area of investigation by formulating the kind of models offered by Morinis.

As I have mentioned earlier, my approach focuses on the sacred centre and the relations between specialists and pilgrims. In this area of research two kinds of contributions have to be mentioned. The first is Vidyarthi's research on the Brahman pandas of Gaya, the Gayawals (1961). He shows that the position of these specialists in the rituals of ancestor worship (*shrāddha*) has changed considerably over time. Whereas they were rich and independent in the last part of the nineteenth and the first part of the twentieth centuries, they have since become impoverished and enmeshed in a situation of strong mutual competition. The growth of pilgrimage in the British period is discussed in terms of infra-structural changes, whereas for the modern period of independent India the impact of the abolition of large landholdings is discussed. Although Vidyarthi uses rather unhelpful terms like 'feudalization' and 'proletarianization' to describe these processes, and his comprehensive description of the sacred centre of Gaya is hindered by his adherence to the Redfieldian model, he offers important insights into our subject-matter, which I will try to take a step further. The second approach to be mentioned is that of a group of scholars from the University of Heidelberg, who carried out research on the cult of Jagannath (Vishnu) in Puri, Orissa (Rösel, 1980; Kulke, 1979; Eschmann *et al.*, 1978). The important point stressed here is the relation between kingship and the Jagannath cult in Orissa. The enormous shrine of Jagannath is seen as a focus of regional integration as well as of the ritual enactment of political power. Although Ayodhya does not have a great temple that serves as a cultural institution (see also Appadurai and Breckenridge, 1976) like those found in Orissa and Tamilnadu, the investigation of the position of the secular ruler and the cultural concept of the virtuous king (*dharmarājā*) will also prove important in the case of Ayodhya.

III Devotion and asceticism

1. Introduction

I have already chosen to translate the word *sādhu* with 'monk'. This implies that the Ramanandi sadhus as a whole form a monastic order. My main task in this chapter will be to describe the process by which the Ramanandi sadhus, at least to some extent, evolved into such an order. Before doing so I should remove some of the theoretical and even terminological confusion which hinders any attempt to make an anthropological study in this field. First, the term 'monastic order' is much less often used in describing a religious group like the Ramanandis than the term 'sect'. Dumont (1972: 233) offers a good definition of the Indian sect:

> Indian religious groups which are readily characterized in terms of renunciation are conveniently called 'sects', without prejudging their similarity to what are called by this name in Christianity. The Indian sect is a religious grouping constituted primarily by renouncers, initiates of the same disciplines of salvation, and secondarily by their lay sympathizers any of whom may have one of the renouncers as a spiritual master or guru.

Although Dumont does not want to prejudge the similarity between the Indian and the Christian sect, the western connotations of the term 'sect' make it rather inappropriate to use it in the Indian context. There is a long tradition in which the term 'church' stands for the institutionalized dominant orthodoxy, while the term 'sect' is used as a pejorative label for a heterodox group which attempts to break away from the 'church'. The church–sect dichotomy deriving from the Christian tradition has become standard sociological vocabulary. The use of the term 'sect' in the context of Hinduism may easily obscure the important fact that there is no Hindu church. It is even difficult to speak of Hindu orthodoxy as against Hindu heterodoxy. Some authors (e.g. Staal, 1963) have argued that instead of looking for an orthodoxy–heterodoxy opposition we should look for one between orthopraxy and heteropraxy, since while there are no strict rules in Hinduism about what to think, there are many about what to do. The latter are the rules of the caste system.

Instead of the church–sect dichotomy a number of other dichotomies have been proposed. Dumont has found the opposite of the sect in the institution of caste. Hinduism is the religion of the caste system and its secret can, according to Dumont (1970: 36–7), be found in the dialogue between the renouncer and the man-in-the-world. The latter may have all kinds of folk-beliefs of a polytheistic nature which are connected with caste values. These beliefs are systematized in a speculative theory and a ritualistic practice by the members of the Brahman caste who are, according to their own theory, superior to all other men. Their theory and practice are the orthodoxy of the man-in-the-world. Caste is the most fundamental institution of Hindu society and the theories and ritual actions of the Brahman priests safeguard the *dharma*, the universal order of the caste system. Besides the caste system, however, there is an institution which contradicts it: renunciation.

In renunciation a man becomes dead to the social world, escapes the network of interdependent caste relationship ... and becomes an end for himself, as in western social theory, on the condition that he is cut off from ordinary social life. That is why I have called this person, this renouncer, an individual-outside-the-world. (Dumont, 1972: 230–1)

As we have seen, the Hindu sect in Dumont's view is primarily constituted by renouncers, so that the church–sect dichotomy, common in theories of western religious development, seems to have been translated into a caste–renunciation dichotomy in the Hindu context. On the one hand we have the caste society under the aegis of the Brahman priests and on the other we have the sects guided by the renouncers. The dialectic between these two opposite poles explains the development of both caste values and religious innovations.

Although it cannot be denied that Dumont's abstract theory and definitions are illuminative for the correct interpretation of what is meant by the terms 'sect' and 'renunciation', it is also true that to some extent they tend to obscure important aspects of what is found by empirical investigation. For example: to what extent are Ramanandi sadhus world renouncers? Certainly, they have the ideal of not keeping a wife and having children; in other words they tend to be celibate. This does not mean, however, that they renounce the social world of caste. On the contrary, it remains of great importance for them. In their establishments only members of the three highest *varṇas* (social categories) may enter the sanctum in which the idol of the god is placed; only Brahmans may cook in the temple; and, although this is not a written rule, only Brahmans become abbots of the important temples. Moreover, many Ramanandi sadhus of low or untouchable caste have founded separate institutions for the members of their own caste because they found their attempts at upward mobility blocked within the Ramanandi sadhu group. Besides this, there are many so-called Hindu sects which are completely dominated by a leadership which is hereditary in Brahman families, so that it becomes difficult, or, rather, impossible to speak of a group primarily consisting of renouncers. To define the Ramanandis in terms of the opposition between caste and renuncia-tion creates many conceptual and empirical difficulties. As Richard Burghart (1983c) has pointed out, intra- and inter-sectarian differences cannot be understood in terms of Dumont's structural opposition, and I would like to add that important changes over time in the relationship between sadhus and lay disciples also tend to disappear from view when the researcher attempts to understand change only in terms of conceptual dialectics.

Despite his criticism of Dumont's ideas, however, Burghart seems to perpetuate Dumont's opposition between the man-in-the-world and the man-outside-the-world in his description of the way Ramanandi sadhus conceive of the distinctions between ascetics and non-ascetics. Referring to his field data on the Ramanandis of Janakpur in Nepal he claims (1983c: 634f) that the pursuit of the religious goal of release from the transient world 'conceived as eternal union with Ram' obliges the Ramanandis to separate themselves from householders, for they believe that the houses and hearths of householders are permeated with desire: 'Upon receiving initiation from his *guru*, a Ramanandi no longer sleeps in a house, nor does he accept any cooked food from householders, including his parents, if that food has been cooked upon a householder's hearth.'

There are a few objections to be made against Burghart's

exposition. As we will see in detail later, the religious goal of the Ramanandi sadhus is much more ambiguous than Burghart would have us believe. There is a strong devotional current in Ramanandi theology in which the transient world is represented as the divine play (*līlā*) of Ram and Sita. Eternal union with Ram and Sita and release from the play is not seen as a goal of Ramanandi devotion. On the contrary, the devotee wants to remain in the transient world, to return to it after death in order to serve Ram in his play. Giving pleasure to the god (*tatsukhi*) is seen as the primary object of Ramanandi devotion. It is deemed necessary to realize that the transient world is a divine play, but we should not strive to attain release from it. This point was brought home to me several times in conversations with Ramanandi sadhus, but most forcefully when I witnessed a heated debate between a Shri-Vaishnava (Ramanuji) sadhu, who argued that release (*mukti*) was the religious goal of devotion, and a Ramanandi sadhu, who argued the point of view I have just described. In that discussion Burghart's presentation of Ramanandi theology was thus attacked by a Ramanandi and defended by a sadhu belonging to another religious group. We should, however, be aware of the fact that Ramanandi theology is extremely elastic and that the point of view described by Burghart is perhaps current among certain sections of the Ramanandis which are better represented in Janakpur than in Ayodhya.

This brings us to the observation that we should be wary of attempts at understanding religious phenomena and processes in terms of theology. Burghart's general argument is that Brahman householders and renouncers situate themselves in different conceptual universes (1984: 636). This is not corroborated by the interviews I had with both Ramanandi sadhus and Brahman householders. The difference is rather a matter of degree. Both are participants in the divine play of Ram and Sita, and it was maintained by many sadhus that it was more appropriate to be a householder in this play than a sadhu. The idea behind this is that marriage and the family constitute the highest and most sacred institution in life, which is clearly reflected in the married status of Ram and Sita themselves. The great advantage of the sadhu is, however, that he can devote himself entirely to religious duties, whereas a householder is constantly involved in secular considerations and worries. The opportunity for the sadhu to follow the injunction of *deo vacare* is therefore much greater than for the lay householder, but this is considered to be a matter of degree. As we will see later, the distinction between householder and ascetic cannot in the case of the Ramanandis be interpreted as a static, conceptual opposition, but should be regarded as a changing boundary, affected by a process of sedentarization of sadhus. As regards actual behaviour, the distinction between householders and Ramanandi sadhus also seems less rigid than Burghart argues. In Ayodhya Ramanandi sadhus not only sleep in houses of householders, but may even stay in them. They will, however, decline to eat the food cooked by householders. It would indeed be surprising if sadhus were to accept cooked food from householders, since by doing so they would be acknowledging themselves as socially inferior. The only way sadhus and householders – and for that matter castes of more or less equal rank – can dine together is by engaging a Brahman cook who cooks pure (*pakka*) food in clarified butter (*ghee*). In fact the sadhus follow the same rules of behaviour as are followed in the caste society of the householders, so that it is unconvincing to argue here for different 'conceptual universes'.

Returning to our starting-point, I would argue that analysing our data in terms of questionable dichotomies, like church–sect, orthodoxy–heterodoxy, caste–sect, householder–renouncer, does not help us in our attempt to understand the social position of Ramanandi sadhus. Since we are primarily concerned with a group of religious specialists, Ramanandi sadhus, and only secondarily with their lay followers, I would prefer to speak of a Ramanandi order instead of a Ramanandi sect, evading some of the terminological difficulties discussed above. To use an indigenous word, as McLeod (1978) proposes in the case of the Sikhs, does not seem a good solution, since the only term available, *sampradāya*, refers more to the theological 'tradition' than to the social group which maintains this tradition and alters it in relation to changing social conditions. Instead of ascetics and renouncers it seems better to speak of sadhus or monks, since the place of renunciation and asceticism in Ramanandi values and behaviour is problematic and a major subject in our discussion of the Ramanandi identity.

Thus we find in Ayodhya an order of Ramanandi monks or sadhus. They are visited by pilgrims who seek their advice and teaching and who may become initiated as *shishyas* or lay disciples.

The latter are householders who support by their donations the sadhus who act as their *gurus* or religious preceptors. The whole can be called a religious community with, as its nucleus, an order of sadhus supported by a relatively unorganized group of lay disciples.[1] Central to its organization is the relationship between gurus and disciples, within the community as a whole as well as within the order. A man can become a sadhu by asking a sadhu to become his guru and by subsequently leaving his family for the spiritual family of sadhus. A man can also remain a layman while asking a sadhu to become his guru. The guru-shishya relationship is in both cases the fundamental organizational principle. The difference between a Ramanandi sadhu and a lay Ramanandi is therefore a difference in degree. To see its difference more clearly it might be helpful to look at the initiation ritual.

A man comes to Ayodhya and is impressed by a Ramanandi sadhu. He wants to have this sadhu as his guru, and when the sadhu agrees he is initiated by him in a ceremony (*Pānch Samskār Dīkshā*) consisting of five ritual actions (*samskārs*):[2]

1) *mudra*: the sign (*mudra*) denoting the god Ram is put on the right upper arm. It consists of a bow and arrows and can be applied with a stamp dipped in sandal paste, or by a branding iron (*taptamudra*).

2) *tilak*: whereas the mudra is the same for all Ramanandis, the *tilak*, a symbol painted on the forehead and thus visible to all, varies according to theological differences. Ramanandis who have the same tilak commonly belong to the same subsection.[3]

3) *nām*: a new name is given to the disciple. Most Ramanandis are given a name ending in *dās*, meaning 'slave'. For example Ramdas, 'slave of Ram'. One section of the Ramanandis, which will be discussed later, uses *sharaṇ*, 'refuge', instead of das. For example, Ramsharan, 'he who has his refuge in Ram'.

4) *mantra*: the guru gives the disciple a meditation formula which he should repeat in order to reach the godhead. The guru whispers the mantra in the ear of the disciple below a piece of cloth, but even though they are transmitted in secrecy, the various mantras are well known. The most important is the following: *Rām Rāmāya Namah*, 'I bow to Ram'.

5) *māla*: to conclude the ceremony the disciple is given a necklace of beads from the tulsi plant, which is sacred to Ram. The necklace is called *kanthi*.

Both sadhu and lay initiates have to undergo the same ritual but there is a difference in the naming ceremony. Whereas the lay initiate may also ask his guru for a devotional name, he will retain his own name which was given to him as a child in the *nam-samskar*, one of the rites of passage of a householder. The sadhu initiate, however, loses both his secular name and his clan name (*gotra*). They are replaced with the devotional name and with the gotra of God: *acyut-gotra*.[4] In this way he comes to belong to the spiritual family of Ramanandi sadhus, in which kinship terms are used for expressing the relations among them. Two sadhus initated by the same guru are *guru-bhai* (brothers), while the guru-bhai of one's guru is called *guru-cacha* (uncle). The implication of this replacement of real kinship ties by the putative ones of the spiritual family are of course tremendous. It implies that one is no longer bound by the jurisdiction and obligations of one's family and one's *jāti* (caste). Some Brahman jatis drastically sever all relations with a caste-fellow who decides to become a Ramanandi sadhu. It is extremely difficult for such an ex-Brahman to be readmitted into his caste should he decide to return to normal society. The extent to which it is difficult for a Ramanandi sadhu to 'fall back' to the condition of householder in his own jati depends on 'the boundary maintenance' of the jati in question. Some castes will ask only for a purification ritual, others will make no difficulty at all. Here the factor of history also plays an important role. There is evidence of large Ramanandi castes in Rajasthan, Gujarat and Saurasthra that were formed by Ramanandi sadhus who returned to the state of householders but were rejected by the jatis to which they had belonged. In this way they were forced to form their own castes, resembling the numerous castes of the so-called *gosains*, ex-Shivaite Dashanami sadhus. It is clear that the formation of such castes is directly related to the strictness of caste boundaries in certain periods of history.[5].

Besides the nam-samskar, which is different for sadhus and lay disciples, the mala-samskar is also distinctive. The necklace (*kanthi*) of tulsi beads symbolizes the connection with Ram and is compared with the *yajnopavit-sūtra*, the sacred thread worn by the three highest varnas, the so-called *dvijās* or twice-born. The yajnopavit ceremony marks the second birth of the members of these three varnas and is in fact their central rite of passage. The putting on of the necklace by the guru signifies a new spiritual birth within the Ramanandi fold. The important thing, now, is that there is a tendency within the Ramanandi order to see the tulsi necklace as a replacement for the sacred thread, meaning that the differences between the four varnas are effaced by initiation into the Ramanandi group. An opposite tendency is to make a difference between *sutradhāris* (wearers of the yajnopavit-sutra) and *māladhāris* (wearers of the kanthi) within the order. The mala-samskar part of the initiation ceremony has therefore become a bone of contention. The kanthi is sometimes refused by lay disciples of high-caste provenance, while high-caste sadhus tend to wear both. In some religious groups the wearing of the kanthi or of a thread round the neck with only one bead of tulsi is seen as equivalent to the yajnopavit. This is, for example, the case with the Kabirpanthis, who cater primarily for the religious needs of non-dvija groups. The wearing of the kanthi in North India is therefore a symbol of devotion to Ram, but also a social symbol which tends to devalue the importance of the yajnopavit-sutra of the dvijas. Finally, to make it more complex, sadhus of non-dvija background have, in the last forty years or so, begun to wear the yajnopavit-sutra as well, so that it becomes difficult for the outsider to see the difference between the sutradhari and maladhari sadhus. Only by coming to know them more personally can one work out that those who wear the sacred thread are not always of high caste.

These subtleties of the initiation ritual make it clear that some distinctions are made between sadhus and lay disciples and that these distinctions have social implications. The most critical distinction, however, seems to be the vow of celibacy made by the Ramanandi sadhus. Because the sadhu retains his semen he only founds a spiritual family, being a tradition of gurus and disciples (*guru-shishya-paramparā*). For 'celibacy' the Sanskrit word *brahmacharya* is used. It has as its first meaning the study of the Veda, as its second the state of an unmarried religious student, and finally a state of continence and chastity. This refers to the Brahmanical theory that life has four stages (*chaturashrama*):

1) *brahmachārī*, the state of a chaste student of the Vedas;
2) *grihastha*, the state of founding a family and having male progeny;
3) *vanaprastha*, withdrawal from the family by going into the woods with one's wife;
4) *saṃnyās*, the total renunciation of everything.

In the Brahmanical theory, then, chastity is observed before and after the begetting of male progeny, and as such should be observed at certain periods in the life of a Brahman householder. Actual practice is, however, very different. Many of the sadhus are lifelong celibates (*naisthik brahmacārīs*). Attitudes to this practice are ambiguous. That a man should not be blessed with a son is generally considered to be a curse. Therefore the sadhus are pitied, but also feared, because they roam about freely and may cast a desirous glance on one's wife or daughter.[6] On the other hand the retaining of one's semen is one of the most powerful themes in Indian mythology. To keep one's semen is to keep one's power. Celibacy is therefore a means of acquiring religious, magical power as is clearly illustrated by the many myths relating to the power of a saint's asceticism, which may even threaten the world order. A recurring theme is that of a sage cursing a king with the result that rain does not fall. The only way to end such a drought is to send a prostitute, so that the saint may lose his semen and therefore his curse its power. The tension between asceticism and eroticism is most clearly elaborated in the fascinating mythology of Shiv, the great ascetic god (cf. O'Flaherty, 1973).

Therefore, in the Ramanandi community the most effective boundary between lay disciples and sadhus is the celibacy of the sadhus. Many of the Ramanandi sadhus are lifelong celibates, while some of them follow the Brahmanical doctrine by first marrying and founding a family, postponing celibacy to a later stage in life. The strong emphasis on celibacy as a boundary in the Ramanandi order is, however, somewhat problematic. Generally, the Ramanandis are considered to be a Vishnuite devotional group which focuses on the devotion (*bhakti*) to Ram. The Ramanandis are, however, rather different from many of these groups which are lumped in the same elusive category, since they emphasize celibacy as an organizational principle. Especially in groups which focus on Krishna devotion there is a hereditary guruship which is transmitted within Brahman families.

This makes the Ramanandis in some respects resemble Shivaite ascetic orders. The Shivaite renunciation is a radical one, called *saṃnyās*. Celibacy belongs to the essential core of that type of renunciation and acts as a boundary between laity and ascetic orders in the same way as it performs that function with the Ramanandis. The Shivaites, however, appear to think that renunciation forms a radical path to the attainment of release from the transient world (*moksha*). This is not true for the Ramanandis, as we have already observed. The Ramanandi renunication is called *vairāgya* (literally 'detachment') and it can, in principle, also be followed by a married householder, though it is admitted that such a way of life is not easy for a married man. Celibacy and renunciation are considered to be practical ways of devoting oneself completely to the service (*sevā*) of Ram. In that way vairagya as a method is encompassed by devotional service. It should, however, be clear that there is a structural tension built into the notion that vairagya can be practised by both sadhu and householder. Vairagya as a concept covers many different and sometimes conflicting perceptions of devotion and renunciation. If it implies celibacy, it leads to monasticism, but even within the monastic order there are great differences as to the extent of renunciation and the importance attached to it. As we will see, these differences form a major aspect of the process of identity formation and boundary maintenance which resulted in the present organization and orientation of the Ramanandi order.[7]

To understand this process we should be aware that the Ramanandis are characterized by a great organizational and doctrinal freedom. The only organizational structure which is of importance is the relation between guru and disciples. In fact, this is the common distinction between expert and non-expert which is the basis of all religious organization. Sadhus are specialists and therefore they act as gurus and teachers for laymen. Within the order of Ramanandi sadhus the same distinction pertains: some sadhus are gurus to others. For the rest, the organization of both the Ramanandi collectivity and the Ramanandi order is extremely loose. There is no central authority which decides upon doctrinal and organizational matters. Every sadhu may go and roam throughout India, teaching, within certain limits, his own religious message; and great value is put on that freedom of the sadhu. Moreover, any sadhu can be chosen by any layman as his guru. For the lay disciples the person of the guru is of primal importance, not the doctrinal orthodoxy of his teaching. The guru-disciple relation is a personal one, which gives a great span of freedom in doctrinal and practical matters.

It should therefore not surprise us that the differences between Ramanandi sadhus are often enormous. To illustrate this point I will offer some vignettes.

Ramdas is a stout man in middle age. He wears one piece of white cloth wrapped around his body like a bath-towel; his hair is matted and worn loose. He is an energetic man, always talking and inviting people to his temple. He is very active politically and has often been elected to the municipal council. His electoral advice is sought by many politicians at local and regional level. In his temple there are twenty to thirty sadhus, mostly young men who are trained in the use of weapons and in wrestling. The temple is called an *akhara*, a settlement of a subgroup of the *nagas*, the fighting section of the Ramanandi sadhus. Ramdas is a militant man who does not like to miss an opportunity of venting his disagreement with what he considers to be the anti-Hindu politics of the central Congress (I) government. In the aftermath of the murder of Mahatma Gandhi by Hindu extremists he was sought by the police and had to go underground. This is not to say that he does not have religious interests. On the contrary, all his opinions are corroborated by extensive and often amusing quotes from the sacred scriptures. Most of his lay followers, however, are less interested in learned discourses than in militant political speeches. Ramdas is a staunch believer in the Hindu dharma and therefore believes caste to be a God-given institution. He is proud of being a high-caste Brahman and he prefers their company to any other. From his early youth he had shown interest in religion and came to study in Ayodhya at a traditional Sanskrit school (*pāthshālā*). At the time he was attracted by a naga of this akhara and he decided to take initiation. He still maintains contact with his family in his native village in Bihar. Although he is a strict celibate and likes to censure sadhus who are a bit lax in their celibacy, he loves children and for him it is not sexual desire, but the desire for children, that is the greatest difficulty of his being a sadhu.

Tyagiji is, as his name implies, a real renouncer. *Tyāg* is more an equivalent of the Shivaite *samnyās* than of the Vishnuite *vairāgya*. He is a man of at least fifty, with matted hair, clad in a mere loin cloth and smeared with sacred ashes. Often one can find him near the river Sarayu, where he sits smoking hashish (*ganja*) in his earthenware pipe. Occasionally some younger tyagis are sitting around him, talking idly. Sometimes, however, a group of householders also comes to see him. In such a case he lectures them on *yog* and the power acquired by following ascetic practices. The lay disciples or other pilgrims also come for his advice on problems they face in their personal lives. Some may be pestered by ghosts (*bhūt*) and they ask Tyagiji for powerful formulas (*mantras*) to be uttered to drive them away. Others are ill and ask Tyagiji for herbs to cure them, since they know that he has a great herbal knowledge thanks to his long stay in the woods of the Himalayas. Still others come to ask for the blessing (*ashirvad*) of Tyagiji, which is considered to be very strong thanks to his radical renunciation. In particular, barren women are brought to him for the ashirvad, since it is thought that the blessing of a celibate sadhu will be especially fruitful for begetting male progeny. Although the attitude of the lay Hindus is very respectful, there is little cordiality in their relations with Tyagiji. Rather one can speak of awe mixed with fear. This can be easily understood when we see that the sadhu's behaviour is uncontrolled or rather asocial. He is not at all concerned by social conventions and reminds one very much of the irreverent Diogenes in Greek tradition. He may at any moment walk away when one is talking to him and can be very impolite when he thinks certain questions to be exceedingly stupid. In short, he is a rough and unpredictable type with a very independent character. When he is not at the Sarayu, he may be found in a temple of the tyagis. He does not, however, have any formal position in their organization. Nevertheless, he is treated as a great saint, even more so than the abbot. Matters outside religion do not interest him at all. Time and history are elusive things in his world-view. He reckons events such as conflicts and splits among the tyagis in units derived from the twelve-yearly bathing festival, *Kumbh Mela*: 'three Kumbhs back' or 'before last Kumbh'. He is very reluctant to speak about his private past, but he told me that he had been a celibate from his childhood (*naisthik brahmacāri*). He only lives in Ayodhya during short periods and leads in general an itinerant life, going from one sacred place to another.

Ramvallabhsharan is an ochre-clad abbot of a large temple with some fourteen regular inhabitants. He is a bald-headed, suave-looking man, who is extremely friendly, though with an authoritarian tinge. The temple property is written in his own name. This implies that he is at liberty to choose his own successor and that he can manage the temple affairs without consulting anyone.

When he is not looking after his fields, which are near his temple, he is reading or lecturing to lay disciples. The reverence shown to him is extreme. People enter the room where he sits and prostrate themselves full length, 'like a stick' (*dandavat*) as they say in India. They put their forehead on his feet, push themselves up with their arms and lower themselves again on the feet, an action which is reiterated several times. Ramvallabhsharan's forehead is completely covered by a brownish paint and sometimes he wears a kind of female kerchief wrapped round the head. He is an older man, in his late sixties, and has been married, but became the celibate *mahant* (abbot) of this temple when his son was old enough to take over the family responsibilities. His wife is still living and is looked after by his oldest son. He is a high-caste Brahman, and everyone is aware of it. His disciples are predominantly middle- or high-class Hindus. His fame is largely based upon his great scholarship. He likes to give lectures (*katha*) on the *Rāmcharitmānas*, one of the works he knows by heart. He is also able to speak in Sanskrit, a feat which has given him some reputation in Vishnuite Brahman circles. Although knowledge is therefore the basis for his fame, he teaches that total devotional surrender to Ram and Sita is the only path by which to realize God. He sees himself as a female friend of Sita (*sakhi*) and propagates the sweet devotion (*madhuropāsana*). His method of devotion (*sādhanā*) is esoteric and can only be learnt after initiation.

It is important to see the guru, the only medium through which one may reach God, as a god himself. Ramvallabhsharan has many disciples all over Uttar Pradesh and Bihar and is regularly visited by them. He decides, for example, what names should be given to their children and he may preside over the sacred thread ceremony of the sons of his wealthier disciples. He also goes often on tour in his white Ambassador car with driver and cook. In this way he also collects money for his temple.

Finally, we encounter Ramcharitradas. He is a big, bald-headed man, resembling a Japanese wrestler in the drawings of Hokusai. Indeed, he has been trained as a wrestler in an akhara, but does not practise any more. As a young boy he had come from a village not very far away to study at a Sanskrit school in Ayodhya and to be trained in wrestling. He became the disciple of an abbot of a small temple near the riverside, who had only a few disciples. His guru, before he died, appointed one of his disciples as his successor, but Ramcharitradas, with some of his old wrestler friends, succeeded in capturing the temple by chasing away the appointed sadhu. Court cases were launched, but the appointed successor could not prove his rights, so that Ramcharitradas became the new abbot. After a few affairs with female disciples he began a permanent relationship with the daughter of a panda who worked at the riverside, by whom he has two sons and a daughter. He therefore bought a house separate from his temple and started to live there with his family. He remained abbot of the temple, however, and also succeeded in attracting lay disciples. Some of them know of his double life, but are not interested in it; others are not aware of it, because they live far from Ayodhya and visit the place only once in a few years. In his temple there are still a few sadhus, but they are also content with their abbot, since he is a good fund-raiser and so they are better off than many of their colleagues in other temples. Ramcharitradas is not known for his theological knowledge or ascetic power, but he is an influential and powerful man in Ayodhya. He himself engages in money-lending activities which are highly profitable. He also has consider-able commercial interests in Ayodhya, being the proprietor of several shops and tea-houses. Moreover, thanks to his wife, he has been able to invest in the plots on the riverbank which are let out to pandas for their ritual activities. In all such activities power, based upon the threat of violence, is of importance in India. Therefore Ramcharitradas has a small group of toughs (*goondas*) at his disposal, who may be called into action when his debtors withhold payment or when he needs to defend his rights against intruders. Ramcharitradas's greatest concern is the marriages of his sons and daughter. One of his sons married a woman from a Brahman family far from Ayodhya who did not bother to make a thorough enquiry into the credentials of this 'family from Ayodhya'. To marry your daughter to the son of a sadhu is not a desirable prospect, even when the sadhu in question is a rich and influential man and a Brahman by birth. The other son, who is not yet married, proclaims himself to be the disciple of Ramcharitradas and to be the son of a man from a village near Ayodhya. This man happens to be Ramcharitradas's brother. Except for the moot issue of the marriage of his offspring, nobody is really interested or worried about the double life of Ramcharitradas. This life-style of the 'domesticated' sadhu, to use Michael Carrithers's phrase, is not the ideal of the Ramanandis and tends to be obscured in confrontation with outsiders, but it is shared by many sadhus.

These vignettes show that there are considerable differences between sadhus calling themselves Ramanandi. Behind all this diversity there is, of course, some measure of unity. This can be found in their sacred book. They all recite Tulsidas's *Rāmcharitmānas*, which may be said to constitute the theological core of the Ramanandi teachings. It might therefore be helpful to give a short account of the content of this work.

THE RAM BHAKTI OF TULSIDAS

Tulsidas's works are recited everywhere in North India and his *magnum opus*, the *Rāmcharitmānas*, is often called by outsiders 'the bible of North India' – a misguided comparison, but one that points out well enough the significance of this work. Tulsidas's writings are the main point of reference for the theological thinking in the Ramanandi community, but it is not easy to summarize his views, because they can be characterized by what Gonda (1963: 168) would see as a lack of theological clarity and a tendency to synthesize different views. In fact this is Gonda's comment on the *Adhyatma Ramayana*, a Sanskrit work composed in the fifteenth century, which is commonly seen as an important source for Tulsidas's theological views. The main purpose of this work is to combine the monist (*advaita*) philosophy of the Shivaite philosopher Shankara with devotion towards a personal god (*bhakti*). In Tulsidas's writings we therefore find the monist view that the World Soul (*brahman*) is impersonal and attributeless (*nirguṇa*) and at the same time the *bhakti* view that there is a personal deity (*īshvara*) who has descended to earth as an incarnation (*avatār*) and therefore possesses overt attributes (*saguṇa*) which make personal devotion possible. The essential message in Tulsidas's work seems to be that Ram should be worshipped with devotion and that he has two aspects: nirguna and saguna. The attributeless Ram can only be reached through 'gnostic knowledge' (*jnāna*), but for the common devotee another, easier path is open, that of personal devotion to the Ram with attributes

who lived in Ayodhya and whose exploits are described in the
Rāmcharitmānas. Elsewhere Tulsidas says that nirguna Ram becomes
saguna Ram through the devotion of the worshipper and that both
are equally true, in fact the two aspects are the same. The essence of
Ram is contained in his name (*Rām Nām*). The method to reach the
ultimate truth is the repeated utterance of *Rām Nām*, since Tulsidas
himself says in the *Rāmcharitmānas* (Balakand 23): 'I declare that the
Name is greater than the Absolute and Ram.' Moreover, in the
Vinayapatrika (228.5) he says: 'The achievement of the Name is even
greater than Ram himself.' Theologically this can be seen as a special
form of the doctrine of the phonic body of God or *shabda-brahman*
(Bakker, 1986: 119; De, 1961: 289), which is the basis of the Vedic
use of the syllable *Om* to indicate the Absolute. In the Ramanandi
community the mantra is therefore not *Om Rāmāya Namah*, as it
would be in Vedic usage, but *Rām Rāmāya Namah*. Ram in
Tulsidas's work is thus at least three things:

1. the nirguna Ram, attributeless World Soul;
2. the saguna Ram, divine ruler of the universe, residing in his
   heaven (*saket*);
3. *Ramchandra*, the incarnation (*avatār*) Ram, whose heroic exploits
   are described in the *Ramcharitmanas*.

These three Rams are synthesized in the cult of the *Rām Nām*.
Essential for Tulsidas is the devotion to Ram in whatever aspect. In
the *Rāmcharitmānas* he gives a scheme of the way to lead a
devotional life (Allchin, 1966: 64ff.).

Bharat is the ideal devotee for Tulsidas. He became king when his
elder brother Ram was sent into exile, but rejected the enjoyment of
kingship and devoted his life to the worship of Ram's feet. His
attitude is clearly expressed in the *Ramcharitmanas* (2, 204): 'I desire
not wealth or spiritual gifts or sensual pleasure, nor do I ask for
liberation; only this one boon I crave, devotion to the feet of Ram in
successive lives'. This is the relation of the devotee to God, that of
unrestricted service (*sevā*), as a servant. Besides Bharat, it
is Hanuman who is taken as the ideal servant (*sevak*) of Ram.
He is filled with the love a servant shows for his master. The essence
of this type of bhakti is apparent from the poet's name, which means
the 'slave' (*dās*) of the plant (*tulsi*) that symbolizes Ram. What we

have here is a religious slavery as the dominant mood in the Rambhakti.

The tone of this kind of bhakti is fundamentally moralistic and non-erotic. Ram is the ruler of the universe, preserver and protector of its moral order (*dharma*). He is the paradigm of the good, dutiful ruler (*dharmarāja*) and in this capacity he fights the demons who threaten the dharma. Sita is generally seen as the paradigm of the good, dutiful and bashful Hindu wife, the object not of lust, but of the desire for marital stability. While Ram is the 'virtuous' king (*dharmarāja*), she is the 'virtuous' wife (*dharmapatni*). Theologically she is Ram's creative energy (*shakti*) and therefore also *māyā* (illusion) since, at least according to the monist views of the Shivaites, creation is *maya*, illusion. Ram is the lord of Sita as her husband and thus also the lord of maya, of which there are in fact two kinds. The first is 'good' maya, completely controlled by Ram, who uses it as the source of creation. Epistemologically it is knowledge (*vidyā*) as opposed to lack of knowledge (*avidyā*), which is the result of 'bad' maya and the source of rebirth and pain. Only through *bhakti* (devotion) can one deliver oneself from ignorance and recognize one's true nature as identical to God. The word *bhakti* is feminine, as is the word *maya*, and it is only this feminine method that is not ensnared by the wiles of maya, unlike the masculine methods (wisdom, detachment, austerity and scientific knowledge: *jnanā, virāga, yoga, vijnāna*, all nouns of masculine gender). While one can discern three paths to salvation – correct belief and bhakti, correct knowledge and correct behaviour – it is only the first which is the easiest and the most successful. That is not to say that knowledge and behaviour are unimportant, but bhakti is supreme. The foundation of bhakti is faith (*shraddhā*), and to this faith Ram responds by bestowing his grace. The tone of the Ram story is moralistic and centres on the performance of duty, so the devotee is expected to be dutiful (Hill, 1952: xxx–xxxiii).

The correct attitude for the worshipper is that of Bharat and Hanuman: total surrender to the service of Ram while doing one's duty according to the normal order of the world. Asceticism and yoga as well as gnostic knowledge are not rejected, but brought into the total framework of devotion to Ram. The essential method of reaching Ram is the constant repetition of his name in the company of other devotees and under the guidance of a revered guru.

Since the *Rāmcharitmānas* is the basis of the beliefs of all types of Ramanandis, it may be useful here to follow Gross (1979: 374–88) and give some idea of the allegorical interpretation given by the Ramanandis to this 'bible of the Hindus'. The book is seen primarily as an allegory of the spiritual journey of the soul to God. The story is that of a *lila*, a sport or play of God, in which the central plot concerns the exile of Ram, Sita and Lakshman from their kingdom of Ayodhya, Sita's abduction by the ten-headed demon Ravan, during their stay in the jungle, and finally, after Ravan is slain, the return of Ram, Sita and Lakshman to Ayodhya. Ram is the Universal Being incarnate in human form, while Sita is the Divine Mother, creative power or *māyā-shakti*, who during her abduction is a representation of the *māyā* (illusion) in which the individual soul is trapped during its separation from the Universal Being. Ravan represents the individual soul enmeshed in desire and ignorance and also the hindrances to be conquered on the spiritual path. The book is divided into seven *kandas* (chapters). The first, *Bālakānda*, deals with the birth and childhood of Ram and his three younger brothers – Bharat, Lakshman, Shatrughna – and ends with the marriage of Ram and Sita. Each of the brothers represents important qualities necessary for spiritual development. Ram's father, Dashrath, has three wives, each representing a path to salvation. Dashrath means 'one who is in control of the ten chariots', i.e. the five organs of action and the five senses. He symbolizes the controlled ego, while Ravan symbolizes the uncontrolled ego.

In the second chapter, the *Ayodhyakānda*, Ram is banished for fourteen years. These years of exile represent the cosmic journey of the soul, which begins with spiritual exercises in the jungle, described in the *Aranyakānda*. This chapter is the favourite one of the tyagis, since they interpret it as showing that Ram was really an ascetic, living in the jungle, just like themselves. In the jungle Ram and Lakshman, representing spiritual truth and discriminative wisdom, have to fight with the many demons who threaten spiritual progress. Ravan then succeeds in abducting Sita to his palace on the island of Lanka. Here she represents the individual soul which, because of desire, leaves the protection of the guru and is abducted by the uncontrolled ego. In the next two chapters, *Kishkindhākānda* and *Sundarkānda*, Ram plans to get his beloved back. With the aid of an army of monkeys and bears, representing the community of slave-devotees, an assault is launched against the demons inhabiting Lanka. The *Lankakānda* describes how Ram's most devoted slave, Hanuman, jumps over to Lanka to inquire about Sita's position. Symbolically he jumps over the ocean of worldly existence and, thanks to his non-attachment, conquers all obstacles. This power is given to him because he carries in his mouth a ring with Ram's name inscribed on it, so that *Rām Nām* is constantly on his lips. When all the demons have been killed by Hanuman, who begins to burn down the whole city of Lanka, only Ravan and his inner circle are left to reckon with. Ravan is supported by Kumbhakarna, who represents the pride which remains when all the other demons (attachments) have been destroyed, by his son Meghnad, who represents lust, and by his general Mahodar, who represents greed. A middle position is taken by Vibhishan, the younger brother of Ravan, who is ensnared by pride, lust and greed, but who seeks to liberate himself through devotion to Ram. The battle ends with the death of Ravan at the hands of Ram. Sita is thus reunited with Ram and all return to Ayodhya, which is described in the epilogue, the *Uttarkānd.*

It is clear that Gross's analysis does not exhaust the symbolic levels of this narration, which is constantly repeated by the Ramanandis, and over and over again reinterpreted. One thing should, however, be clear: that below the surface of the text there are other levels of signification which are in fact the basis of the entire belief system of the Ramanandis. This is not at all a closed system: all the different sections of their order derive legitimations of their particular beliefs and actions from the *Rāmcharitmānas.*

The theological vagueness of Tulsidas's work leaves plenty of scope for the doctrinal freedom which characterizes the Ramanandi order. The importance of doctrinal and practical freedom in this order makes it to a great extent an 'open category'. This might be said of all Hindu orders, but the unsolved tension between devotion and asceticism makes it even more strongly felt with the Ramanandis. There are at least three groups within the Ramanandi order, representing three different tendencies. The first is that of the *tyāgis,* who are 'real' ascetics and whose central beliefs and practices centre on a radical type of renunciation (*tyāg*) and on specific ascetic methods (*tapas, yog*) while they tend to lead a peripatetic life. The second is that of the *nāgās,* fighting ascetics who are organized into armies (*anis*). They are the military backbone of Ramanandi organization, and they concentrate more on wrestling and the use of weapons than on strictly religious activities. Finally, there are the *rasiks* who are, more or less, the 'real' representatives of devotion in the Ramanandi order. They consider asceticism to be irrelevant while emphasizing devotion (*bhakti*) and emotional surrender (*prapatti*).

A long-term historical process of sedentarization has led to members of the order settling in holy places like Ayodhya. Contrary to what one might expect, however, this process has not had as its corollary the unification and centralization of the order. As we have seen in the vignettes, the differences between tyagis, nagas and rasiks persist. My major objective in this chapter will therefore be to bring these differences in organization and beliefs into the light as well as to describe the way they have been affected by the process of domestication and sedentarization. Before I do so, it might be profitable to start with some ethnohistorical observations on the rather mysterious origin and historical development of the group of sadhus which calls itself Ramanandi at present.

2. Tradition and identity

Commonly the Ramanandi order presents itself to the outsider as a Vishnuite devotional group, comparable to many other groups as they are found in Bengal and the Braj area as well as in South India. On closer investigation the picture becomes somewhat obscured by several difficulties. One of these is the alleged link of the Ramanandi order with the Shri-Vaishnavas of South India. Some of the Ramanandis hold the theory that they are in fact Shri-Vaishnavas, others vehemently reject this theory and claim that the Ramanandis are a separate community. Another difficulty is the apparent incompatibility of the two major strands in the community's theology and organization. On the one hand we have seen that there is a strong ascetic current in the Ramanandi community which emphasizes renunciation as well as peripatetic life. This current is known as that of the tyagis. It seems to have been organized militarily at the end of the seventeenth century or the beginning of the eighteenth century into regiments or *akhāṛās*. In their military guise the tyagis came to be known as *nāgās*, fighting sadhus. On the other hand we have seen a strong current in the Ramanandi order which strongly emphasizes a sweet surrender to the god and which transforms reality into a *lila* or divine play of Ram and Sita, in which the devotee acts as a female friend or *sakhī*. This is not to say that all the Ramanandi sadhu are either of the tyagi type or of the rasik type. A long process of sedentarization has simply turned many sadhus of both types into citizens of Ayodhya, and this has the implication that besides the distinct tyagi and rasik types there is, let us say, a silent majority which has a kind of theological and practical cocktail to offer on the religious market. The traditional affiliation of many sadhu groups to one of the two major strands remains, however, mostly recognizable in the particular cocktail offered.

As I have argued before, an anthropological study as such cannot uncover the historical past of the Ramanandi community, its origin and transformation. What can be done, and what is in fact one of the aims of this study, is to uncover the ways in which the community changes its view of the past strategically in the present. Moreover, an anthropologist may also have something to say about the reasons for the use of these strategies. In this way he may have an independent and valuable contribution to the field of historical reconstruction, in which textual scholars play a predominant role. In order to explain the use of traditions in the process of identity formation in the Ramanandi community, I will first offer a general, broad reconstruction of the community's history on the basis of my field notes on its present organization and beliefs, as well as a summary of the results of textual research on the poetry and religious literature of the probable period of origin.

THE ORIGIN OF THE RAMANANDI ORDER

The Ramanandi order was founded by the religious teacher Ramanand who lived some time between AD 1300 and 1500. We do not know anything about his exact dates, life or work. The only information we have is Ramanandi history, which, however, is not unanimous, to say the least. Richard Burghart (1978c) therefore comes to the conclusion that Ramanand did not actually found the Ramanandi order and that his having done so was rather a product of the imagination of his followers. Although I agree with Burghart that one of the most important facts about Ramanand is the very scarcity of information, and in general agree with most of his factual remarks in his paper, I am of the opinion that the question whether Ramanand founded the Ramanandi community or not is misguided. Burghart argues that we know much more about the lives of Gorakhnath and Shankaracharya, founders of other religious orders, but this is actually not the case. We cannot do better than refer to Kakar's statement that 'a historical account of the cult's origin that does not read like the unfolding of a divine plan and biographical sketches of their gurus that are not exercises in hagiography are essentially false ... Instead of being individuals with distinctive names and personal histories, the gurus become "the embodiment of the same Supreme Spirit" and in a sense flow into each other' (Kakar, 1982: 125). This makes the study of religious history a frustrating affair in India. Ramanand is not so much an exception to this rule as an exceptionally good example of it, because we really do not know anything of him besides the Ramanandi hagiographical legend. Another important aspect of our problem, which seems to be neglected by Burghart, is what we should mean by the 'founding' of a religious order. None of the great religious leaders of India seems to have done such a thing as to found a formal organization, an order of celibate sadhus. It is better to speak of a gradual evolution as McLeod (1975) does in his admirable study of the Sikhs. As we will see in our description of the tyagis, even today it is difficult to speak of a formally organized ascetic order with a central authority and it not likely that this situation was very different in the fifteenth or sixteenth centuries.

The framework of the legend of Ramanand as told by Ramanandis at present and as recounted in their literature contains the following elements:

> Ramanand was born from a Kanyakubja Brahman family of Prayag (Allahabad) in North India. He was initiated as *saṃnyāsī* in a monastery in Benares, which monastery had been founded by members of the Shri-Vaishnava community from South India. This community had been established by Ramanuja, one of the most influential Vishnuite philosophers of all time. When Ramanand came to the monastery, he was initiated by the then incumbent Raghavanand. After completing a long pilgrimage to the country, during which he had failed to observe the rules of

purity enjoined by the Shri-Vaishnavas, he was on his return to his monastery in Benares denied commensality by his guru and the other Shri-Vaishnava sadhus. Therefore Ramanand founded his own community in which he spread the doctrine of Ram and Sita and in which caste restrictions were removed. Everyone could become a member of his community, including women, and members of the low and untouchable castes, as well as Muslims. The last group is important since, according to some Ramanandi sources, Ramanand came to Ayodhya to convert those who had become Muslims back to Hinduism and this was said to have been exactly the meaning of his message. One important verse is always attributed to Ramanand, 'Do not ask about caste or community; he who worships Vishnu belongs to Vishnu.' This quotation hangs, for example, above the entrance of Hanumangarhi in Ayodhya. Important disciples of Ramanand are, according to the same legend, people like North India's greatest poet, the *julaha* (Muslim weaver) Kabir, the *chamar* (cobbler) Ravidas, the barber Sena, and a woman Padmavati.

The story of Kabir's initiation is often repeated and is very remarkable: Kabir wanted to be initiated by Ramanand in Benares, but he did not dare to ask because he was of low caste. Therefore he waited for Ramanand to pass on a narrow street and let him fall over him in the darkness. Ramanand exclaimed 'Ram' and with that mantra Kabir was initiated.

This is the general framework of the story, of which there are naturally many slightly different versions. For example, some say that it was Raghavanand who had been expelled from the Shri-Vaishnava community, because of his Tantric leanings, after a visit to North India.[8] In that case Raghavanand would have belonged originally to South India. An altogether different story was told to me by a rasik abbot:

In the Shri-Vaishnava community there are two mantras. The first is the so-called Narayan mantra: *Om Narāyanāya Namah*. This one is generally known by Shri-Vaishnavas. The second is the so-called Ram mantra: *Rām Ramāya Namah*. This one is only given to those who are near to the guru. It is a *rahasyamantra*, an esoteric mantra. This Ram mantra was transmitted from guru to disciple till Purushottamachari's turn came. He went to the Himalaya for meditation and was in Amarnath, the *Shivaite* place of pilgrimage, persuaded to give the Ram mantra to everyone in the world. This Purushottamachari belonged to the Shri-Vaishnava community one could say, but at the same time he was thirteen guru-disciple generations before the appearance of Ramanuja. Purushottamachari went back to the South and found there in Totadri a temple built by a raja for Ram. This temple had been captured by believers in Tantra, but Purushottamachari chased them away. In the lifetime of Ramanuja the temple was again captured by such sadhus, but this time Ramanuja was able to drive them out. The disciples of Purushottamachari were so pleased with Ramanuja's action that they revered him as a guru and started to accept him as their leader. This was also done by their followers till the twentieth century.

The factual historical content of these legends cannot be retrieved and is as such less important than what these stories seem to tell us, in terms of meaning. In the first place, there is emphasis that the Ram mantra was given to all, that is to people of all castes and creeds. Sociologically speaking the community had an open recruitment and this was frowned upon by the strict Brahman Shri-Vaishnava community. In this way a link is suggested with the Shri-Vaishnava community, but on the other hand the separation of the two communities is also emphasized, the basis of the separation being the Brahman exclusiveness of the Narayan mantra and the inclusiveness of the Ram mantra. This opposition is also couched in terms of North (open) and South (restricted).

In the second rasik version it is interesting to see that there is a Tantric enemy which is expelled by Ramanuja or, as I would prefer, by force of the suggested link with Ramanuja and the Shri-Vaishnava community founded by him. This is interesting since we will see that at least the tyagis in the Ramanandi community are deeply influenced by the Tantric community of the Nath yogis. It seems possible to say that the Tantric elements were probably more the enemy within than the enemy without, although the one does not exclude the other, as we shall see.

In a long introduction to the poems of Kabir, Vaudeville (1974) gives a coherent picture of the religious situation in the time of the poet, who is said to be a disciple of Ramanand, despite the curious way in which he was initiated. From the sixth or seventh century AD it seems clear that Shivaism was the dominant religion in northern and central India, while Jainism and Buddhism were on the wane. This Shivaism had clear Tantric overtones in the sense that it propagated Tantric yoga methods for realizing God within oneself. Those who had realized godhead were a kind of self-made gods, real saints who should be revered as such. These perfect yogis or *siddhas* (accomplished ones) could also work wonders, because of their great magical knowledge, and were as such resorted to by the common people. The most important order of the time seems to have been that of the Nath yogis or Kanphata yogis. They are called Nath yogis after their first and foremost guru, Gorakhnath. In the legends of the community itself the great god Shiv is the first Nath (the *Ādināth*) and the second is Macchendra, who is also identified in Tantric Buddhist circles (for example, in Tibetan Buddhism) with Avalokiteshvar, the ancient protector of Nepal. Macchendra initiated Gorakhnath, the founder of the Gorakhnath yogis. These yogis were ascetics emphasizing yoga and having a system of open recruitment, because of their Tantric contempt for purity regulations.

In this period we also have to acknowledge the influence of Islam and more particularly of the Sufis. They brought a strongly monotheistic religion to India's countryside, but as they emphasized the personal charisma of holy men, called *pirs*, they could easily interact with the Nath yogis, who also had a cult of self-made gods. In this respect it is telling that the abbots of the Nath yogis were also called *pirs*. In fact we find here a strong form of syncretism in which folk magic and social therapy by living or dead saints seem to be the central elements. At the same time sufis and yogis remained organized into different ascetic orders roaming the countryside.

From the fourteenth century AD there was an efflorescence of mystical poets in northern and central India who propagated *bhakti* which Vaudeville (1974: 97) defines as 'a religious attitude which implies a "participation" in the deity and a love relationship between the individual soul, the *jīva*, and the Supreme Lord, *Bhagavān*, the "adorable one"'. These saint-poets are generally seen as Vishnuite, but Vaudeville shows that Shivaite bhakti has greatly influenced them. They are called *sants*, free enterprising saint-poets whose devotion centres on the unborn, formless, all-pervading godhead, who is essentially conceived of as *nirguṇa*, devoid of qualities. Within themselves they hear the *Satguru*, the all-pervading reality. In the exterior, they recognize only two manifestations of the godhead: the 'name', which may be uttered by mouth or meditated upon, and the 'saint', who himself has merged into God and is also conceived of as a human guru. According to Vaudeville these sants formed loose confraternities of mostly low-caste laymen of which there was no historical founder, although the Ramanandis appear to have incorporated the saints within their order.

It is Vaudeville's opinion that the northern Vishnuite devotional communities which developed from the fifteenth century onwards were a completely northern innovative development, owing nothing to the old Vishnuite bhakti of the so-called *Pancarātra-Saṃhitās* of *c.* AD 600–800. She thinks that there is a large hiatus between this Pancaratra faith and the new northern Vishnuite bhakti sects. This claim is disputed by Bakker who, on the basis of his study of the twelfth-century *Agastya Saṃhitā*, comes to the conclusion that the cult of Ram gradually arose from the Pancaratra type of worship (Bakker, 1986: passim). In this devotional work there is already a strong emphasis on the power of the Ram mantra. It might be of some help for understanding this mantra theory to quote Bakker at length on this point:

The highest reality has two aspects: it is supreme light (*parajyotis*) which is homologised with the sound RA, and it is the essentia of all phaenomena (*prapancātman*), homologised with the sound MA. These together form the highest reality, RAMA. This transcendent reality manifests itself in the form of a phonic body comprised of the fifty syllables of the Nagari alphabet (including ksha), and out of this 'body' all phenomenal realities evolve. All deities, powers and realities are thus homologised with a particular combination of sounds. *Mantras* are therefore not merely formulae that refer to a particular god or force but are in fact this god or force itself. To utter a mantra in the proper way is to manipulate a particular divine cosmic force. Because all sounds directly evolve from Ram, Ramaite *mantras* constitute the most important and powerful of divine and cosmic realities and forces. Worship of Rama is thought to be the most effective since it makes use of such *mantras*. (Bakker, 1986: 72)

In the *Agastya Saṃhitā* we find also the important distinction between saguna and nirguna. It teaches two roads to salvation:

1) yoga and meditation on God's nirguna mode;
2) worship (including meditation) of God's saguna mode (Bakker, 1986: 71).

To us it is of minor importance whether the worship of the name of Ram and the nirguna view of Ram's reality is of Shivaite provenance (as Vaudeville claims) or a continuation of ancient Vishnuite theology (as Bakker claims). What seems very clear is that in the fifteenth century, the era of the origin of what was later to become the Ramanandi order, there were several developments that contributed to the formation of a 'Ramanandi identity' which are recognizable today. In the first place there is the strong resemblance between ideas and practices of the Nath yogis and those of the Ramanandi tyagis. The cult of Hanuman is common to Nath yogis as a form of Shiv. Hanuman is also represented in their *tilak* (the mark on the forehead indicating the religious community). We find the same kind of beliefs concerning Hanuman in both communities. He is a *mahāyogi*, a great yogi, and as such possesses the qualities necessary to cure people. He is a magical therapist, specialized in curing mental diseases. Moreover, the Ramanandis also believe that he is actually the *avatār* (incarnation) of Shiv. The only emendation they make is that Shiv is the greatest devotee of Lord Ram and that as such it should not surprise us that Hanuman is regarded not only as a great yogi (*mahāyogi*), but at the same time as a great devotee (*mahā-bhakta*), just as the Ramanandi tyagis themselves are yogis and devotees simultaneously.

Another striking similarity between Nath yogis and Ramanandi tyagis is the importance they attach to the ascetic life-style as a means to attain the godhead within, 'to realize God'. Like the Nath yogis the tyagis smear themselves with ashes, an ascetic practice commonly associated with Shiv, the great ascetic god. Likewise, they follow the Nath yogis in making sacred fires, *dhunis*, in accordance with a common ascetic doctrine of magical heat, *tapas*. Finally, they hold liberal social opinions similar to those of the Nath yogis. Several low-caste tyagis told me confidentially that, while they were travelling, caste restrictions were not followed in cooking and eating. Only when they settled in a sacred place did these restrictions emerge again under the vigilant eye of lay patrons. The low-caste tyagis felt that they were effectively kept out of positions of authority, like that of abbot, but that in general the peripatetic life was individualistic, democratic and socially relaxed.

In the second place there is the strong influence of the sants or nirguni bhaktas. This influence is again most strongly felt among the itinerant Ramanandi sadhus. Like the sants the tyagis emphasized nirguna bhakti. They often told me that they thought the Ultimate Reality to be nirguna, 'devoid of qualities' or 'transcendent'. Since it was difficult for their lay followers to grasp this, they felt compelled to worship images of Ram in his saguna or 'phenomenal' aspect. In fact, the tyagis often worship non-anthropomorphic objects like the *shālāgrām* stones that symbolize Ram.[9]

It is striking that nirguna bhakti is generally identified with low-caste practices. Sadhus of low-caste provenance were not allowed to be officiating priests (*pūjāri*) of the images Ram and Sita, but were said to restrict themselves to the worship of non-anthropomorphic objects, like the shalagram stones. The sants are also often of low-caste. Kabir was a weaver and Ravidas was even an untouchable leather-worker as we have seen. Their doctrine emphasizes that the meditation and repetition of the name of Ram is open to all, irrespective of caste or community.

The disregard of caste or religious affiliation (Shivaite, Vishnuite or even Muslim) in the nirguna bhakti is echoed in the famous verse, attributed to Ramanand: 'Do not ask about caste or community; he who worships Vishnu belongs to Vishnu.' It does, however, have a definite Vishnuite overtone. It should therefore not surprise us that Ramanand is generally regarded as the founder of a Vishnuite order which absorbed the sants. Although this is probably no more than a product of the imagination of members of the Ramanandi order, it highlights some important aspects of their beliefs and practices, such as the emphasis on nirguna Ram among the tyagis and the related liberal attitude towards caste. We should, however, be aware that this attitude is a far cry from an active religious protest against caste discrimination, as has often been assumed.[10] Rather, it is a studied disregard of caste distinctions in the religious field which is quite feasible in the peripatetic life of the tyagis, but is problematic in an existence that has become sedentary. It is important to acknowledge that other inheritors of the sant tradition, like the Kabirpanthis and Sikhs, have followed a much more open recruitment policy than the Ramanandis. The Ramanandis have always kept this policy rather vague and flexible. Their abbots and important gurus are almost always Brahmans of high caste, whereas they allow the three highest *varṇas* (social categories) to enter the sanctum as *pūjārī* (officiating priest). In the peripatetic life of the tyagis, however, there seems to have been a strong tendency towards equality. This flexibility may account for the fact that the Ramanandis have become the largest ascetic order with a very large and diverse following of lay disciples in North India, while the Kabirpanthis have become identified with lower castes and the Sikhs with one caste specifically, that of the Jats.

Finally, there is the expansion of the Vishnuite devotional movement in North India, which gained momentum in the sixteenth century. This has proved to be the most lasting influence on the Ramanandi 'Identity'. Temple worship of images clearly implies saguna bhakti, which in devotion to Krishna acquired strong emotional and even erotic features. As we will try to show later, the Ramanandis adopted much of the Krishnaite theology and methods of worship. In this way they developed into the kind of Vishnuite bhakti community which they profess to be at present. By claiming that they belonged to an ancient Vishnuite community, that of the South Indian Shri-Vaishnavas, the Ramanandi ascetics were able to affiliate themselves with the expanding Vishnuite devotional movement. We will trace this development in the next section of this chapter.

From the results of textual research, which are corroborated by those of fieldwork, we can come to the provisional conclusion that the tyagis have remained most faithful to the original identity of the Ramanandi order. They belong to a period in the religious history of North India in which Tantric yoga and nirguna bhakti were the most important religious currents. According to the tyagis, Ram is essentially a nirguna reality. In worshipping this reality one may use shalagram stones, but more important is a system which focuses on techniques of the body, like heating (*tapas*). The Ram mantra is seen as essential for the attainment of the godhead: it was the 'saving mantra', *tāraka-mantra*, and in this sense it is still commonly used by the Hindu masses when they go to the burning ghats to cremate a body – *Rām Nām Satya Hai* (The Name of Ram is truth). To die with the name of Ram on your lips, as Mahatma Gandhi did, is the only way to reach salvation. The saguna meaning of Ram as Ramchandra, the avatar who came to the world as the Saviour, is important among the tyagis, but primarily in their contacts with laymen when teaching the *Rāmbhakti* of Tulsidas. Their ascetic practices seem to have been reinterpreted in terms of Tulsidas's theology, which leaves enough room for reinterpretation without necessitating any alteration in their life-style. To say that Ramanand 'must have been a Shaiva and a partisan of Advaita' or that the Ramanandis are a yogi sect, as Vaudeville (1974: 113–14) is willing to assert, is claiming too much knowledge of dark times. It could be expected that a different thesis, as that of Bakker who interprets the Ram cult as a continuation of earlier Vishnuism, would arise as a counterpoint to such assertions. However, from the anthropological point of view it seems clear that the Ramanandi tyagis are the inheritors of the developments sketched by Vaudeville, and that they could hardly be distinguished from the Nath yogis in appearance and practice, as is still the case even today- a fact they themselves readily admit.

RAMANANDIS AS SHRI-VAISHNAVAS

In the important Ramanandi hagiographical text *Bhaktamāl*, written in the late sixteenth or early seventeenth century, the author Nabhaji names Ramanuja, Nimbarka, Vishnuswami and Madhvacharya as the founders of the so-called *Chatuh Sampradāya*, the four Vishnuite communities. These communities do conform to the criteria for an Indian sect as proposed by the indologist Renou (1968: 91–5):

1) adherence to a particular sacred text and to a specific deity;
2) adoption of a unique philosophical orientation;
3) a charismatic ascetic founder.

Community	Sampradāya	Founder
Shri-Vaishnava	Shri	Nathamuni, Ramanuja
Nimbarki	Sanakadi	Nimbarka
Vishnuswami	Rudra	Vishnuswami
Madhva	Brahma	Madhva

The Nimbarkis worship Radha and Krishna. Their founder was a philosopher who hailed from the Telugu area of South India, but lived in Vrindaban, the tirtha of Krishna. The Vishnuswamis were founded by a philosopher of whose work we know virtually nothing except that it also concentrated on the worship of Radha and Krishna. As far as we know, he also belonged to South India. The Madhvas were founded by a well-known philosopher born in Udipi in Kanara, South India. There is still an important Madhva community in Karnataka, in which Madhva's theological system is propagated. The worship is here centred on Vishnu, and on Krishna as his incarnation (*avatār*).

The Madhvas and Vishnuswamis are thus both South Indian communities, while the Nimbarkis were founded by a South Indian philosopher who came to live in North India. The Madhvas belong exclusively to the south. They neither have nor claim any link with North India. The Vishnuswamis as such are extinct in North as well as South India, but the community founded by Vallabhacharya, the *Pustimārg*, claims to be the inheritor of the Vishnuswamite tradition.

Vallabha was an important philosopher whose commentaries on the sacred books are still referred to by his community. The Nimbarkis are the only original, ancient community among the four sampradayas, which is found in North India before the sixteenth century. They are a predominantly Krishnaite ascetic order, also known as Harivyasis.

Because we are mainly concerned here with the Shri-Vaishnava community they have to be treated more extensively. Ramanuja (*c.* 1050–1137) is one of the most important philosophers in the Indian tradition. He was the greatest Vishnuite opponent of the doctrines of the famous philosopher, Shankara, the alleged founder of the Shivaite order of ascetics, the Dashanami Samnyasis. An important aspect of his doctrines is that a less prominent place is given to what is central in Shankara's view, the attainment of 'gnostic knowledge', necessary for breaking through the veil of illusion (*māyā*). Ramanuja gives preference to religious feeling and emotional surrender to a personal god – in short, bhakti. While Shankara stressed absolute monism (*advaita*) and the identity of the individual soul (*ātman*) with the Absolute (*Brahman*), Ramanuja stressed a 'qualified monism' (*vishishtadvaita*), indicating a persistent difference between the individual soul and the personal god who is worshipped. Liberation of the soul (*mukti*) is also considered to be the goal, but it implies an eternal life in the presence of the Lord.

It would not do to give a crude summary of the extremely complicated theology of Ramanuja. For us it is important to know that he propagated Vishnuism in a philosophically sophisticated and socially successful way, defending it against the rival doctrine of the Shivaite Shankara. Ramanuja belonged to the spiritual lineage of Nathamuni (*c.* 900). As theologians they were greatly influenced by a succession of saint-poets, the Alvars, who wrote mystical devotional poetry of high quality. Over the exact place of this tradition of poetry (*prabandham*) within the Shri-Vaishnava community there has been considerable dispute (cf. Hardy, 1983). It was democratic in the sense that it was written not in the language of the Brahman theologians, but in the vernacular Tamil. Its democratic character was even clearer from the fact that the Alvar poets included a woman and a Shudra. Moreover, we have epigraphical evidence that Shudras came to play an important part in temple worship from Ramanuja onwards (Stein, 1968). In the fourteenth century, however, an important conflict arose between two types of theo-logical opinions on salvation, leading to the schism between a northern School (*Vatakalai*) and a southern School (*Tenkalai*). The opinion of the Vatakalai is that the human being should make some effort to attain salvation, while the opinion of the Tenkalai is that it is only the grace of God which saves man. The Tenkalai have also more regard for the Tamil prabandham and in social affairs they give more scope for the low-caste participation in worship, while the Vatakalai have more regard for the study of the Sanskrit scriptures by the Brahmans as exclusive specialists (cf. Stein, 1968; Appadurai, 1981a).

Sociologically it is clear that the Shri-Vaishnavas are a Vishnuite community, dominated by Brahmans. The priests in the temple cult as well as their religious preceptors are Brahmans who resemble strongly the socially strict caste of Smarta Brahmans in South India. Although the Tenkalai are at least in theory somewhat less restrictive in social matters than the Vatakalai, the above is true for both sections. Asceticism is found with them, but only as a stage in life, which follows marriage and having children. They adhere to the Brahmanical theory of *varnāshrama*, in which society is divided into four categories (*varnas*) and life into four stages (*āshrama*). They do admit non-Brahmans into their community, but allow them only a distinctively inferior position (cf. Rangachari, 1931; Appadurai, 1981b).

These are the 'traditional' four sampradayas as mentioned in Nabhaji's *Bhaktamāl*. According to Nabhaji Ramanand, the alleged founder of the Ramanandis belonged to the spiritual genealogy of Ramanuja.[11] This meant that the followers of Ramanand were 'really' Shri-Vaishnavas. A North Indian group of devotees of Ram was thus connected with an important South Indian Vishnuite sampradaya, the devotees of Shri (Lakshmi) and Vishnu (Narayan).[12] A similar connection was also made by two other North Indian religious groups. The community founded by Vallabhacharya, Pustimarg, claimed to be the inheritor of the Vishnuswamite tradition which was extinct in South as well as North India. Vallabhacharya is said to have been a disciple in the spiritual lineage of Vishnuswami, but this cannot be verified since we know almost nothing about Vishnuswami or his sampradaya. The Gauriya community founded by the Bengali saint Chaitanya claimed, though probably not before their leader Baladeva Vidyabhusana in the eighteenth century (Dimock, 1966: 41), that they belonged originally to the Madhva sampradaya. Three major North Indian religious communities were related in this hypothetical way to three much older South Indian Vishnuite sampradayas which conformed to traditional criteria for Indian sects.

This search for respectability of the North Indians was greatly stimulated in the early eighteenth century by the ruler of Jaipur, Jai Singh II (1688–1743). He convoked a conference of religious leaders in 1726 to decide upon a greater unity of the North Indian communities by bringing them strictly under the scheme of the four sampradayas (Mital, 1968: 218, 358). Somewhat later, around 1734, another conference organized the North Indian communities in what was called a *Chatuhsampradāya Khālsā* (Mital, 1968: 359). This *khālsā* or 'order' had fifty-two 'doors' or spiritual clans through which a Vishnuite ascetic could claim admittance. These doors were said to be founded by spiritual descendants of the founders of the four sampradayas. The importance of the Ramanandis in this khalsa is clear from the fact that thirty-six of these clans were Ramanandi, while there were twelve belonging to the Nimbarkis, two to the (Madhva) Gauriyas and two to the (Vishnuswami) Pustimargis. It shows that the Ramanandis were the only important full-fledged ascetic order in the Vishnuite fold. As we will see in the section on the nagas, the khalsa had also been organized to enable the Vishnuites to defend themselves in a military way against the Shaivites. In this military organization the Ramanandis were also going to play a central role.

There is clear evidence that traditional links between North Indian communities and older, allegedly 'original' South Indian ones were invented for strategic reasons. No doubt, there are certain resemblances between, for example, the Ramanandis and the Shri-Vaishnavas. Both have the *pānchsamskāra* initiation which I have already described; both use the so-called *urdhva-pundra*, two vertical lines with a red one in the centre, as their community mark (*tilak*). The differences are, however, greater than the similarities. For the Shri-Vaishnavas there are essentially two caste groups, both of the Brahman category, important in religious organization: the temple priests (*archakas*) and the devotional community of Brahman Shri-Vaishnavas. Outside that there are the non-Brahmans who play a very minor role in their religious organization. The Ramanandis are essentially a monastic order in which the three highest castes (*varnas*), the twice-born (*dvijās*), can attain the important positions of priest and guru. They perpetuate their existence not by biological reproduction, but by co-optation in spiritual lineages. In short, the varnashrama theory is not adhered to by the Ramanandis.

This in itself does not exclude the possibility that a sadhu with the name of Ramanand or Raghavanand went to North India and was expelled from his community because of his unorthodox social behaviour and then founded his own order. This becomes, however, rather improbable when we find no mention of these gurus in either the Tenkalai or the Vatakalai guru-disciple successions. In fact there seems to have been almost no institutional relations between South Indian Shri-Vaishnavas and North India before the nineteenth century, when a Shri-Vaishnava temple was founded in Vrindaban.[13] What appears to have happened, therefore, is that the Ramanandis whose origin I have discussed in the previous section, decided at a certain point in their history to claim a link with the far away Shri-Vaishnava community.

Likewise, the new communities of the Gauriyas and Pustimargis thought it better not to capitalize upon their originality, but on their traditionalism. Why did they follow this strategy? According to Burghart (1978c), these interpretations of the past enabled a community to compete more effectively for three limited resources: devotees and disciples, pilgrimage routes and pilgrimage centres, and political patronage. Since respectability is very much connected with antiquity it should not surprise us that tradition is invented on a large scale. Certainly of great importance is the aspect of political patronage. There can be no doubt that Jai Singh II wanted the North Indian devotees of Ram and Krishna to follow the rules of Vishnuite religion which endorsed caste regulations, the supremacy of Brahmans and the postponement of celibacy to the last stages of life or the strict adherence to the vow of celibacy. According to correspondence between Jai Singh and the leaders of various religious groups, found in the Kapaddwara records of Jaipur, Jai Singh had not only the right to install abbots but also to abolish entire sampradayas (Thiel-Horstmann, n.d.). Roy (1978: 23ff.) found an undated bond (no. 1520) in which the incumbent abbot of the Ramanandi monastery at Galta, Madhuracharya, agreed to follow strictly the rules of the caste system and that of the stages of life, while forcing every young monk to marry at the age of fifteen, unless he explicitly wanted to remain a lifelong celibate. The connection with the 'original' four sampradayas was therefore not only a strategy on the part of the religious communities, but also a model of behaviour forced upon them.

Compared with the Pustimarg of Vallabhacharya and the Gauriyas of Chaitanya the Ramanandis are a special case. While the first two have a hereditary leadership, transmitted in Brahman families, the Ramanandis are a monastic order. Moreover, the first two have a definite devotional theology developed in the formative phase of their communities, in which the devotee surrenders to the grace of Krishna. The Ramanandis, however, are the inheritors of an immensely complex tradition, of which I have given an outline. Nevertheless, the Ramanandis have been subsumed within the 'official' Vishnuite fold in the course of their history. In their bid for respectability they had to get rid of low-caste connections. As Burghart (1978c) shows, they did this by accepting only 'doors' or spiritual clans founded by high-caste descendants of Ramanand. Saints like Kabir or Ravidas, though in the early sixteenth-century

Bhaktamal mentioned as descendants of Ramanand, were not included in the eighteenth century as founders of 'doors'.[14]

While Vallabhacharya had connected his community with the extinct Vishnuswamis and the Gauriyas had related themselves to the Madhvas who either did not know or ignored this claim, the Ramanandis had forged a link with the Shri-Vaishanavas who developed an interest in it in the course of the eighteenth and nineteenth centuries. The history of the development of South Indian Shri-Vaishnava interest in North Indian religious affairs is still almost completely in the dark. We have therefore to take an immense leap in history from the first half of the eighteenth century in which the conferences sponsored by Jay Singh II took place, to the early twentieth century. During the Kumbh Mela of 1921 the Ramanandis agreed upon the fact that Ramanand was not a descendant of Ramanuja and in that way they denied the earlier claim that they belonged to the Shri-Vaishnava community as a North Indian branch. Subsequently a spiritual genealogy of Ramanand was published from which the name of Ramanuja had been removed. Since I have been able to collect documents and to interview several informants who have witnessed the events leading to this momentous decision I will summarize them in the following section.

BHAGAVADACHARYA AND THE SHRI-VAISHNAVAS

At the beginning of this century there arose a conflict within the Ramanandi order between those sadhus who adhered to the idea that Ramanand, and therefore the Ramanandis, belonged to the lineage of Ramanuja, and those who disowned this tradition. A central role in this conflict was played by Bhagavaddas or Bhagavadacharya. His life-story is told in his autobiography and in the introduction to the *Vaishnavamatābjabhāskar*, edited together with the *Shrirāmarchanapaddhati* by Bhagavadacharya's opponents.

Bhagavadacharya was an orphan whose caste remains unclear, since he himself claimed to be a Brahman, while his opponents, typically, were sure that he was of low caste. He was brought up in an Arya Samaj orphanage in Dhanapur, Bihar. This is interesting, since the *Ārya Samāj* is a neo-Hindu reformist movement which proclaims a 'return to the Vedas' and consequently endorses neither image worship nor caste distinctions. In this way it can be seen as 'traditional' in religious matters and modern in social outlook. Nevertheless, according to his opponents, Bhagavadacharya was taught Sanskrit at the orphanage till the Brahman teacher came to know that he was of low caste and refused to teach him further. The son of the pandit continued the lessons, however, and Bhagavadacharya, being a bright boy, could already speak in Sanskrit at a young age. He also learnt English and after finishing school went to the Arya Samaj headquarters in Calcutta where he studied the commentary on the Veda by Dayanand Saraswati, the founder of the Arya Samaj. Later he came to Ayodhya, where he started to study the Ramanandi teachings and became a Ramanandi. He wanted to take initiation with a visiting Shri-Vaishnava guru in Ayodhya, the leader of the Tenkalai monastery (*math*), Totadri, in South India, Anantachari, but was persuaded by his friend Raghuvardas not to do so. His friend told him that those who were initiated by South Indian Shri-Vaishnavas would deny commensality with Ramanandis initiated by Ramanandi gurus. In that way they would not be able to eat together in the future and so he advised Bhagavadacharya to take initiation with the abbot of Bara Asthana, Rammanoharprasad.

In his autobiography Bhagavadacharya describes the visit of the leader of Totadrimath, Anantachari, to Ayodhya. This guru did not prostrate before the images of Kanak Bhavan and Bara Asthana, which means that he did not show respect for the tutelary deity of the Ramanandis, Ram, nor did he accept *charanamrit* ('the nectar of the feet', the water with which the feet of the idol are washed and which is distributed among the devotees as *prasād*, a mark of grace, to drink). Moreover, in his sermons he insulted the Ramanandi beliefs by declaring them to be inferior. Theologically and socially he behaved like a strict Brahman who thought the Ramanandis an inferior community without clearly disowning the claim that Ramanand or Raghavanand had ever belonged to the Shri-Vaishnava community. His behaviour created some tension among the Ramanandis. Some of them threw away their *kanthi*, the necklace which is peculiar to the Ramanandi initiation; others felt insulted and began to think of revenge. The visit of Anantachari of Totadrimath was followed by a visit of Sudarshanachari of the Vatakalai institution, Prakalmath, in Mysore. He was somewhat more relaxed in religious matters, so that he accepted the charanamrit of Ram and also prostrated before the images, but socially he refused all commensality with Ramanandis.

The atmosphere in Ayodhya was further made more tense by the behaviour of the Sanskrit teacher in the *Chatuhsampradāy Vedānta Vidyālaya*, the school for Vedanta philosophy and study for the four Vishnuite communities (*sampradāyas*). This man was a Shri-Vaishnava of South India who refused to teach others than those who were branded with the Shri-Vaishnava markings, a disc and conch, the Ramanandi markings being a bow and arrow. Moreover, this Balramachari gave *katha*, sermons, in which he claimed that the mantra given by the Shri-Vaishnavas was stronger than that of the Ramanandis. This provoked a great deal of discussion among the public, in which some tyagis in particular attacked his views. Bhagavadacharya and Balakram Vinayak, both intelligent Sanskrit scholars, decided to do something about the arrogance of the Ramanujis, the Shri-Vaishnava followers of Ramanuja. They called a meeting of Ramanandis in Hanumangarhi and, against the opposition of his guru, Rammanoharprasad of Bara Asthana, Bhagavadacharya became the founder of an organization of Ramanandi sadhus, the *Shri Rāmānandi Vaishnava Mahāmandal*. In this attempt to organize the Ramanandis he was helped by the abbot of Hanumangarhi, Sitaramdas, and by the abbot of the Barabhai Dariyam tyagis, Ramdas. Together with Balakram Vinayak he decided to forge a new genealogy of Ramanand in which there was no longer a mention of Ramanuja. This forged document was 'found' by Raghuvardas as the wrapping of a book that he bought in Ayodhya and was said to have been written by Agardas, a direct disciple of Ramanand. The interesting thing is that in his biography Bhagavadacharya freely acknowledged his forgeries, considering them to have been made in a good cause, since he believed he had won his case.

As I have already remarked, the Kumbh Melas are the only occasions in which the Ramanandis come together in a big assembly and decide upon their community policies. The first Kumbh Mela following the conflicts in Ayodhya was held at Ujjain in 1921. The new genealogy had to be acknowledged at this event. According to his opponents Bhagavadacharya had already created a suitable atmosphere for the split between Ramanujis and Ramanandis by publishing books under the names of Ramanujis in which the devotion to Ram and the Ram mantra were ridiculed. A heated debate had already emerged between Bhagavadacharya and his guru Rammanoharprasad, but Bhagavadacharya could not be defeated by his opponents, since he knew all the tricks of such a religious debate. At the Kumbh Mela he invited the Ramanujis to a *shāstrārtha* ('debate on religious interpretation'), a real verbal contest and as such an old method of defeating opponents in India. The contest was to be held in Sanskrit and on the side of the Ramanujis Shriramprapannaramanujadas put forward the thesis that there was no insult to Ram or Krishna in the Shri-Vaishnava books. Bhagavadacharya opposed him with the counter thesis that there might be no insult to Ram, our god, in those books, but there was also no special praise of him. The Ramanujis asked for an adjournment, but did not return in time for an answer. The jury of the contest was strategically composed with the chief abbots (*shrī mahants*) of the three armies of fighting ascetics and the abbot of the Barabhai Dariyam tyagis. These radical men decided to declare Bhagavadacharya the victor and stated that the Ramanandis were from then on independent of the Shri-Vaishnavas.

This had important implications for the procession to the river at the Kumbh Melas. Till that time the great preceptors of the South Indian Shri-Vaishnava community had always been carried to the river on *pālkhis* (palanquins), by Ramanandi sadhus of Brahman birth as a token of their superiority. This custom was no longer followed and the Ramanujis were no longer allowed to walk with the Ramanandis and be protected by their armies. Bhagavadacharya devoted the rest of his life to the organization of the Ramanandis and the dispute with the Ramanujis. Since the Ramanujis as a token of their learning always put *achārya* (preceptor) after their names, whereas Ramanandis use the humble suffix *dās* (slave), he decided to alter his name, until then Bhagavaddas, to Bhagavadacharya. Moreover, he started to follow the custom of Ramanuji samnyasins who wore an ochre robe (*kashavavashtra*), while the Ramanandis had traditionally worn white (*sītāpadris*). Bhagavadacharya was a political man, an excellent orator and agitator who by changing the tradition succeeded in his life's ambition of giving the Ramanandis a proud identity.

Although the decision of the Ujjain Kumbh was a major success for those who wanted to sever the link with the Shri-Vaishnavas, it was not the end of the story. During the 1920s and 1930s there were regular discussions in Ayodhya between the two parties and the topic is still an emotional one. This can be easily understood when we learn the personal histories of those Ramanandis who suffered under the arrogance of the Ramanujis. Here, for example, is the story of Lakshmandas, the abbot of a small temple belonging to the lashkari section of the Ramanandis, founded by Balanand:

Lakshmandas was born in a high-caste Brahman family in Uttar Pradesh and joined the Ramanandis under the influence of a famous preacher who became his guru. When he was a young man of twenty he studied Sanskrit and philosophy with a guru who was a householder and a member of the Ramanuji community. He never got anything to drink or eat in his guru's house, but one time when he was very thirsty he asked for some water to drink. The guru gave him a water pot, but when he came outside and walked to the well he saw that it was the pot used when going to the latrine, which was never cleaned. The guru knew that he was of high-caste birth, but since he was a Ramanandi he thought him so low that he did not give him the brass water pot normally used for guests. Without making a quarrel Lakshmandas left his guru and took another Sanskrit teacher of his own Ramanandi community. This happened in 1943, but he is still very emotional when he tells this story. This is all the more striking because Lakshmandas is a strict sadhu who still keeps a distance from sadhus of non-Brahman birth. In his temple there are three water pots: *Bhagvanpātra*, only to be used by the pujari for the worship of the image; *Svapātra*, only for Brahman sadhus who live in the temple; and *Parpātra*, for Brahmans from outside the temple. In the bhandaras of the sadhus he eats separately from other sadhus. This implies that even a sadhu of high caste was seen by Ramanujis as inferior, simply because he belonged to the Ramanandi community.

In Ayodhya different positions were possible in the conflict. First there were the followers of Bhagavadacharya, who flatly denied any link with the lineage of Ramanuja. They became the 'pure' Ramanandis. This attitude is almost always found among the tyagis

and nagas. Then, at the other end of the continuum, there were the
'pure' Ramanujis. These sadhus said that they were not Ramanandis
but pure Shri-Vaishnavas, belonging to South Indian monasteries.
Most of them have in fact relatively little connection with South
Indian Shri-Vaishnavism, because they do not understand Tamil.
They almost always have a relation with the Shri-Vaishnava
institution in Vrindaban, which was founded at the beginning of the
nineteenth century and is still the only really important Shri-
Vaishnava institution in this part of India. There is only one Shri-
Vaishnava institution of older date in Ayodhya, dating from the
beginning of the nineteenth century: a small family in Yajnavedi,
who are Telugu immigrants of an endogamous Shri-Vaishnava
caste, and who have no social relations with the sadhus of Ayodhya.
Finally there is the institution of Dantadhavanakund which is
probably an old one, but, as we shall see, it originally belonged to the
Ramanandi community. However, its present abbot claims that it
was the only Shri-Vaishnava institution in North India and that his
ancestors, when they were threatened by the Shivaites, invoked the
help of the Ramanandis. This claim is, however, yet another
reinterpretation of the past which is made acceptable by the antiquity
of the institution. Except for the Shri-Vaishnava family of Yajnavedi
therefore, there were no 'pure' Shri-Vaishnavas in Ayodhya, but
some Ramanandi communities have taken sides with the Ramanujis
and consequently became Shri-Vaishnava. Surprisingly this choice
is not made simply on the basis of caste. Even abbots of Kurmi and
Barhai castes chose to become Ramanuji.

Between the opposite poles of 'pure' Ramanandi and 'pure'
Ramanuji there is enough room to move. In particular some high-
caste Brahman abbots of rasik institutions, who might secretly have
preferred to be Ramanuji, did not disown their Ramanandi
affiliation, since that would have incurred considerable disadvantages
in North India, where only the Ramanandis are strong. At the same
time they have maintained friendly relations with those abbots who
became 'pure' Ramanujis. This is the case with the successors of
Rammanoharprasad, the mahant of Bara Asthana and the greatest
opponent of Bhagavadacharya. In public they will never disown their
Ramanandi affiliation, but in secret they still adhere to the position of
Rammanoharprasad. These ambiguities are possible because of the
vagueness of the tradition, with the result that ordinary lay devotees

will in general never inquire deeply into these matters. The vehement debate between the sadhus has ebbed away and nowadays comfortable positions in the middle are increasingly acceptable.

Having given these ethnohistorical observations on the strategic ways in which the Ramanandis have altered their views of their past at different stages of a long-term process of identity formation, I now come to the description of the three major groups within the Ramanandi order which represent the important strands in their religious views and practices: the tyagis, the nagas and the rasiks.

3. Tyagis

Asceticism has a very long and extremely complex history in India. It has been traced back to the period of the Vedas, i.e. the beginning of the Aryan civilization in India (*c.* 1500–500BC), and, according to some archaeologists, even to the pre-Aryan civilizations of Mohenjo-Daro and Harappa. Moreover, anthropologists and historians of religion have discovered aspects of the phenomenon in many of the shamanistic practices of India's tribal population. Wherever the phenomenon may have originated, it has continued to play a central role in India's religious history. In the context of Hindu discourses and practices asceticism is a common translation of the Sanskrit word *tapas*, meaning heat and power. When we use the word asceticism here, it is in the sense of 'accumulating heat in order to acquire power'.

Asceticism is a major strand in Ramanandi beliefs and practice. It is represented most clearly in the life-style of the so-called tyagis. *Tyāg* is a Sanskrit word, meaning 'leaving' or 'abandoning'. It therefore seems to be equivalent to the common Sanskrit word for renunciation, *saṃnyās*, which is used in the Brahmanical varnashrama doctrine as well as by Shivaite ascetics. A tyagi is a Ramanandi sadhu who is strictly celibate, leads a peripatetic life and believes that tyag is the best way to realize God. Tyagis 'leave' the comfort of clothing, food, housing and sexual gratification, in short everything that constitutes a 'happy married life'. Besides leaving behind the comfort offered by settled life as a householder, they follow all kinds of ascetic practices which induce certain types of religious experience and result in the obtaining of magical powers (*siddhis*).

Although ascetic renunciation can be considered to be an attempt at liberating oneself from the demands of the physical and social body (Eliade, 1973), it cannot lead to absolute freedom. Freedom is no doubt one of the most important aspects in the life-style of the tyagis, but several constraints on that freedom need to be mentioned.

First of all, the tyagi may 'leave' ordinary society, but only for another type of society. He is never the 'world renouncer' who is the subject of Dumont's abstract theories. Tyagis tend to be organized into families (*parivār*), itinerant groups (*jamāt* and *khālsā*), and regional circles (*mandals*). No doubt, these are extremely loosely organized groups, but there is at least one strong social relation on which they are based: that between guru and disciple. There are two types of guru. One is the mantra guru who gives the disciple a mantra, mostly the common Ramanandi mantra *Rām Rāmāya Namah*, and teaches him how to meditate upon it. The mantra guru is the sadhu who has initiated the disciple into the Ramanandi order. He remains one's life-long guru and a spiritual family (*parivār*) is formed by the disciples of one guru. This is not to say that the initiated tyagi remains with his family for the rest of his life. He may roam on his own accord or join up with other sadhus.

Moreover, he may take a second guru: the sadhak guru or siddha guru, by whom he is given a secondary initiation. This guru teaches a specific practice or method (*sādhanā*) of reaching God. Mantra guru and sadhak guru may be the same person, or may be two different people. A sadhu who has been initiated by a Ramanandi guru who does not really belong in a direct way to either the tyagis, nagas or rasiks, may, after his mantra initiation, choose to take a second initiation from a guru who is famous because of his tyagi, naga or rasik teachings. For some time this sadhu will therefore either remain with his sadhak guru before returning to the group of his mantra guru, or go around on his own accord or with followers of his second guru. By choosing a specific method of ascetic or devotional practices one becomes, of course, constrained by that choice to follow that method and the traditions pertaining to it. This makes it to some extent not too difficult for an outsider to distinguish between tyagis, nagas and rasiks, since their behaviour shows that they follow different methods (*sādhanā*). One could say that the guru-disciple relation is a major force 'from within' that encourages sadhus to accept a certain group identity. This force acts to create what we may call spiritual kin-groups which serve as vehicles for the maintenance of certain religious traditions.

A major force 'from without' in the process of identity formation is the dependence on the support of householders who act as lay disciples. Although it is possible in principle to 'withdraw to the Himalayas', which is an important theme in Indian asceticism, the institution of renunciation is in fact dependent on the support of non-experts, who live their secular lives in India's towns and villages and give part of their surplus to the sadhus, to enable them to follow their religious calling. The renouncing monk in the Buddhist tradition is therefore called *bhikkhu* (one who begs). A sadhu who wants to sustain his way of life has therefore to be successful in attracting the support of laymen. The more support he attracts, the more he will also attract sadhu disciples, since he has food enough to give them. There is, however, a contradiction in all this. A tyagi will become a successful sadhu who attracts many lay people, when he has endured an extreme form of asceticism and accordingly has become liberated. The more liberated he is from the restraints of the physical and societal bodies, the more he will be surrounded socially by ascetic and lay followers.

Since beliefs are extremely elastic among Ramanandi sadhus, differences among them are either methodical, based upon differences in religious methods (*sādhanā*), or personalistic, based upon the differential success of sadhus in attracting followers. These two types of difference tend to blend, since methodical differences are used as a boundary-maintaining mechanism to distinguish one group from another. To illustrate this it may be useful to make some empirical observations of group formation among the tyagis of Ayodhya.

GROUP FORMATION AND IDENTITY AMONG TYAGIS

Richard Burghart (1983a: 365) reports that whenever he 'tendentiously asked a wandering Renouncer for his "fixed address", he invariably replied, "Khak Cauk, Shri Ayodhya-ji"'. Maybe the tyagis he interviewed answered his question as tendentiously as he asked it, for there are in fact several fixed centres (*chaunis, kutis*) in Ayodhya of various groups of tyagis, among which there is only one called Khak Cauk, located near the river Sarayu.

In Ayodhya we find, first of all, three important centres of the so-called *Barabhai Dāriyām* ('stick-holders who are twelve brothers'): Bhaktamali ka mandir, Maniram ki chauni and Tapasviji ki chauni. 'Brothers' here of course means *guru-bhai*, disciples of the same guru Jagannathdas who founded this *khālsā* (order of itinerant tyagis). The sadhus of the Bhaktamali temple say that they have separated themselves from the Barabhai Dariyam and have formed a separate Bhaktamali or Saket khalsa. To outsiders, however, they still belong to the Barabhai Dariyam. Generally acknowledged is the separation from the former khalsa by the so-called *Terabhai Tyāgī* ('renouncers who are thirteen brothers'), under guru Siyaramdas. This khalsa has as its main centre in Ayodhya the aforementioned Khak Cauk, which was founded by one of Siyaramdas's guru-bhai, Arjundas, *c.* 1935. From the Terabhai Tyagi two groups separated themselves: the *Caudabhai Mahātyāgi* ('great renouncers who are fourteen brothers') under Prayagdas and the *Mahātyāgi Kamp* under Suniramdas. Both of these latter groups have big temples in Ayodhya. The Mahatyagi further split into several groups: *Saptarishi*, *Sankadhik Cārbhai* and the *Mahāvirakta.* During my last visit to Ayodhya, the Saptarishi were building a temple, but, as far as I know, the others have no separate establishments in Ayodhya.

The differences between the khalsas are often couched in symbolic terms. The Barabhai Dariyam are regarded as *vastradhari*, wearers of cotton garments, while the Terabhai Tyagi are regarded as *vibhūtidhari*, wearers of ashes, and the several groups of *mahātyāgi*, 'great renouncers', are regarded as wearers of nothing but a *langoti*, a loin cloth made from a special type of grass (*munj*). I deliberately write 'are regarded as', since these differences are not strictly maintained in practice, for reasons to be discussed later. These differences may have been important at the time of separation of the khalsas, but one can hardly be sure of this, since it seems impossible to describe the development of the khalsas. It is clear that the symbolic differences in fact mark differential grades of austerity: wearing clothes, ashes or next to nothing. They mark differences which may have arisen from status conflicts, but they also have a religious value. Gross (1979) mentions a distinction between sadhus who wear a wooden (*kāthiya*) belt (*arbandh*), a belt made of *kela* (banana-tree bark) or *munj* (a type of grass), or a belt made of *loha* (metal: iron, steel). My informants told me that the distinction between kathiya and kela (or munj) also marked an organizational difference between the Indore Khalsa and the Ratlam Khalsa, both deriving from the important Dakor Khalsa, founded by Mangaldas. The Indore Khalsa was the most successful and from it all the later groups originated, beginning with the Barabhai Dariyam. Historically, the Dakor Khalsa seems, therefore, to be the first independent khalsa. According to my informants it was founded by Mangaldas at the end of the nineteenth century, and before that there had been only a great organization of all Vishnuite sadhus, called the *Chatuhsampradāya Khālsā*. All the informants concurred in claiming that Mangaldas must have lived not more than a century ago. This, however, is proved to be incorrect by the historical evidence that Mangaldas Munjiya, the founder of the Dakor Khalsa, was one of the signatories of an agreement reached at the court of the Peshwas, dated 1813, to the effect that the Shivaite and Vishnuite sadhus should bathe at different places during the Kumbh Mela of Nasik (Burghart, 1983a: 374). Oral tradition is in this rare case clearly contradicted by the independent written sources. The reason for this is that the tyagis of all the different groups are almost completely uninterested in history unless it has some use in the present.

In this connection Sudhir Kakar (1982: 125) is again illuminating:

The attempt at *universalization* and *eternalization* (and hence at achieving permanence) of the sect's theory and practice is also extended to the personage of its gurus. Instead of being individuals with distinctive names and personal histories, the gurus become the 'embodiment of the Supreme Spirit' and in a sense flow into each other. They receive respectful appellations that seem so totally familiar – Swamiji, Maharajji, Perfect Master and so on – which differ from each other only marginally. In fact, these appellations seem to be interchangeable not only within the same sect but even between different mystical cults. Indeed, ... the negation of human finitude, the denial of human limits and the claim to transcend history and time are perhaps the distinctive therapeutic levers of all mystical cults and comprise the essential building blocks of their theory and practice.

Because of this tendency in Hinduism to obliterate time and person, it is often hard to find historical facts. Leaving historical questions aside for the moment, we may turn to sociological questions, like those concerning the implications of membership of tyagi groups and their social functions.

It is not easy to understand what the membership of *khālsās* (orders of itinerant sadhus) implies. It is no doubt a very loose type of organization, since informants were often very embarrassed by questions about the organizational structure and type of leadership. They were often unable to answer questions on the history of the group and the reason for its separation from other khalsas. Ad hoc answers were often given to the question of why they had separated: such as 'Because they ate rice and we did not', said without the respondent's being able to elucidate the significance of eating rice or declining to eat it. Only at the time of the twelve-yearly Kumbh Mela or of other great gatherings of sadhus did the distinctions seem to acquire some significance. On these occasions the sadhus are grouped together and given a separate place near the river according to their affiliation. Moreover, all the fissions mentioned above have occurred during these bathing festivals and, according to old informants who happened to be there at the time, they all arose from rather petty issues. For example some sadhus were not given enough respect in the *bhandārās* (large feasts, in which sadhus eat together in long rows), which were financed partly by their own funds. The decisive point seems to be whether a sadhu is able to command enough independent resources to bind so many sadhus to him that he can found an independent khalsa. It is therefore a question of honour and status, which can be understood as follows. A disciple of a guru has finished his apprenticeship and goes wandering on his own through the country and starts raising funds for his own livelihood. If he is successful, he will also acquire more and more sadhu disciples who start raising funds and give at least a part of them to their guru. In this way he will have a successful group of itinerant sadhus, a *jamāt*. At the big meals, however, his jamat will go into the khalsa of his guru or his guru's guru, in other words to the khalsa with which he is affiliated. On that occasion he has to give part of his resources to the leader of the khalsa, who is called the chief Abbot, *Shrī Mahant*. These resources will be used in the feeding of the sadhus of the khalsa and in the reciprocal feasting of the different khalsas which are gathered at the festival. A sensitive matter is then, for example, the place given to a leader of a jamat in the bhandaras and other honours distributed by the Shri Mahant of the khalsa. If a successful leader of a *jamāt* feels insulted by the behaviour of the Shri Mahant or by other sadhus of the khalsa he may try his best to become independent. To do so he must be supported by leaders of other jamats and this support is only given when the sadhu in question is known as a good fund-raiser, who will be able to sustain an independent khalsa in difficult times, and who will give opulent bhandaras during festivals. In this way independent khalsas are founded.

From the point of view of influential tyagis, leaders of jamats or khalsas, the great gatherings of sadhus at religious festivals like the Kumbh Melas serve as arenas for status competition. This is certainly an important factor in the constant fission of tyagi groups. Besides providing channels for status mobility the jamats and khalsas also serve other functions. Group affiliation provides solidarity when events require it. Sadhus surrounded by hostile neighbours may need help from their brethren and may receive this through their affiliation with a khalsa. A khalsa may pool resources for a project such as the building of a temple in, for example, Ayodhya, as I have witnessed a few times. It is, however, important to realize that these are occasions which require ad hoc solutions, not structural ones. They may occur once a year, or only once in a tyagi's lifetime. As far as I have been able to see in Ayodhya, the khalsas' only function for the tyagis was when there were great gatherings of sadhus.

Very similar to the khalsa is the institution of *maṇḍals* (regional circles) of Ramanandi sadhus. In Ayodhya a mahant of an important temple may invite other 'abbots' for a big feast and ask them to make him the *maṇḍaleshvar*, master of their regional circle. This is done only among the tyagis. The other sadhus of Ayodhya have an institution rather similar to it. I gained a strong impression that the institution of a mandal with a mandaleshvar, who is addressed as 'Shri Mahant', has the same limited functions as the khalsa. The only solidarity ritual of the mandal is the *bhandārā*, the feast which is paid for by the host and which is used as a show of conspicuous consumption. This is not to say that mandals have only this limited function at all times and places. Burghart (1976) informs us that mandals are commonly found in the Bhojpur and Mithila regions of

India and Nepal. Also in these cases 'the *mandal* only exists in so far as the local *bairāgis* take an interest in maintaining it'. In a few cases described by Burghart the mandal really functions as an institution for regulating internal and external affairs.

However, all date from the beginning of this century or earlier. Burghart concludes his article with the remark: 'In sum, what one might call the honorary functions of the mandal still exist although these functions are constrained by the financial resources of the *sthāns* and *kutis*. The regulatory functions of the mandal, however, have more or less ceased to exist' (1976: 98). From Burghart's work on the mandals in and near Janakpur we may derive the suggestion that the mandals have lost their function due to the emergence of other state-controlled institutions like the courts and the government offices, which control religious affairs and endowments.

During my fieldwork I came to the conclusion that mandals have hardly any significance for the tyagis of Ayodhya. In comparison with the spiritual family (*parivār*), the affiliation with more embracing social groups like khalsas and mandals appears to be of minor importance.[15]

A DISCIPLINED LIFE: BELIEFS AND RITUALS

The tyagi sadhus do not have a clearly demarcated, coherent system of beliefs. They have, however, clusters of ascetic practices which define their life-style and which are to some extent theologically underpinned. They do not value theology highly, since they do not consider knowledge an intellectual asset, but rather have the practical aim of realizing God through the transformation of the body and mind. I will try to describe their way of disciplining their lives by focusing on some clusters of beliefs and practices.

Fire and Ashes

A tyagi may have taken his primary initiation from any Ramanandi sadhu, but to become a tyagi he should take secondary initiation from a tyagi guru. Central to that secondary initiation is the application of ashes (*vibhūti*, *khāk* or *bhasma*) on several parts of the body: forehead, throat, breast, navel, both sides of the body, left forearm, left upper arm, right forearm, right upper arm, back of the neck and small of the back. The ashes are applied by the guru, who first takes some ash and smears it over the hands of the disciple to write subsequently with his finger the mantra *Om* on the disciple's left hand. After the application of ashes the guru gives his disciple a secret (*gupt*) mantra. The disciple is instructed to meditate on this mantra every morning when he applies the ashes to his body.

Ashes thus play an important role in the initiation of tyagis and in their ascetic life. Every morning a sacred fire (*agni*, *dhuni*) is kindled from which the ashes are taken. The fire is the focus of the tyagis' life. It is simultaneously regarded as the god Fire, Agni, and as the Ultimate Reality, Brahman or Ram. A unity between the fire and the body is created by the smearing of ashes, which is seen as symbolizing the unity between the individual soul and the Ultimate Reality. Ashes are also symbolic of death. In Hindu India the dead are cremated and thus reduced to ashes. By applying ashes to one's body one is constantly reminded of the perishability of the body: *Bhasmāntam Sharīram*, 'the end of the body is ashes'.[16]

By giving the sacred fire a central place, the ritual life of the tyagis resembles that of the Brahman householder, which focuses on the Vedic fire-sacrifice. A common interpretation of asceticism in Hinduism, however, has it that the ascetic interiorizes the Vedic sacrifice and goes beyond it. The ascetic can renounce ritual activities and concentrate on himself. In this way he comes to be called *anagni* (without fire), in early Sanskrit writings on asceticism (cf. Olivelle, 1975, 1981). This might also explain why many sadhus of ascetic persuasion do not want to be cremated after death, since the cremation itself is seen as an important sacrifice (cf. Parry, 1982). After death these ascetics are thrown in the river, their bodies weighed down by stones. I witnessed this only once when an important tyagi leader died. However, tyagis *are* often cremated, just like laymen and many of their Ramanandi sadhu brethren. The Shivaite ascetics sometimes bury their dead. These graves (*samādhis*) are thought to emanate power and are accordingly worshipped. This is, however, never the case with Ramanandi tyagis.

The renunciation of the sacred fire by interiorizing it characterizes the ascetic life-style of the Ramanandi tyagis only in a limited sense. They constantly need fire for all their ritual activities and, most significantly, some of these activities are clearly Brahmanical. Tyagis are famous for the large 'Vedic' sacrifices (*havans, yajnas*) they stage.

Brahman priests also take part in these sacrifices, so it would be incorrect to suggest an opposition between asceticism and Brahmanism here. The way fire is usually used by the tyagis, however, differs significantly from the way Brahmans use it. The tyagis kindle the fire in order to accumulate *tapas*, which might be translated as 'magical heat'. Fire creates heat which is full of power and energy. This power (*shakti*) is ambiguous and dangerous, so that it takes great effort to contain it. In fact a great deal of the tyagis' ascetic method is directed towards accumulating heat and therewith magical power. Since the theme of *tapas* is one of the most elaborate in Hindu tradition, it would take us too far to treat it even in broad outline. What is of importance to us at present is the way tyagis use fire as a method of accumulating heat.

The common idea is that tyagis acquire heat and thus become *tapasvin* over a period of twelve years, in which the initiate begins with five fires round his body, eventually has an endless number around him and finally places fire on his head. The exact succession is the following:

1. *panchdhuni* (5), symbolizing the five essences of creation (*panchatattva*: fire, earth, water, wind and space);
2. *saptadhuni* (7), symbolizing the seven skins of the body;
3. *dvadashadhuni* (12), symbolizing the twelve suns of creation;
4. *chaurasidhuni* (84), symbolizing the 84 creations;
5. *kot dhuni* (endless);
6. *shiragni* (fire is put on the head).

Although I have observed the first three phases of this sequence in Ayodhya, since it is a daily practice of some tyagis, I doubt whether the rest will be found in reality. The meaning, however, is sufficiently clear. Heating of the body is increased over a long period of ascetic training until finally it is necessary to put fire on the head to prevent the body from being consumed by heat from inside.

The placing of fires is restricted to a certain period of the religious year. It starts at *Basantpanchami* (the fifth lunar day of the bright fortnight of *Magh*, February–March) and ends at *Gangadassehra* (the tenth lunar day of the bright fortnight of *Jyesth*, May–June). From then until *Vijaydashami* (the tenth lunar day of the bright fortnight of *Ashvin*, September–October) the ascetics stay outside, and from *Vijaydashami* until *Basantpanchami* they stay up to their neck in water. In this way the year is completed. I have not been able to check if this rule was really followed by anyone. A special feature of the programme is that they have to stay outside in the rainy season, contrary to an ancient injunction in ascetic life, already existing in the time of the Buddha, that in this period ascetics should stay *inside* their monasteries for four months (*chaturmās*) (*pace* Burghart, 1983a: 363). According to my informants the retreat of four months is only observed after the initiatory tapas of twelve years. It is also interesting that there is a period for standing in water, for then the heat is contained in water, its opposite. There is an ancient tradition that the ascetic comes out of the water rejuvenated and that creation in general starts from water (cf. O'Flaherty, 1973). A few times in my fieldwork I saw a tyagi enter the Sarayu in the evening and remain there for the rest of the night. In the morning crowds of people, especially barren women, would come to ask for the tyagi's blessing (*ashīrvād*), a clear manifestation of the traditional idea of the (pro-)creative power acquired by standing in the water, being 'heated'.

It is clear, in sum, that the fire and its ashes form an important symbolic cluster in the life-style of Ramanandi tyagis. The smearing of ashes on the body distinguishes the tyagi clearly from other Ramanandi sadhus, but on the other hand it obfuscates the difference between him and other non-Ramanandi renouncers. The placing of fires is also a major item in the ritualized life of the Tantric Shivaite Nath yogis, and in general ashes are symbolic of Shiv, the great ascetic god, and not of Vishnu. Ramanandi tyagis will readily admit that their tradition is in the first place an ancient ascetic one and that for this reason there is great resemblance between their life-style and that of Shivaite ascetics. The important difference lies in their mantra, in which Ram, not Shiv, is seen as the Ultimate Being. In their opinion Shiv is the most important god after Ram and at the same time his greatest devotee. In this connection it is easy for them to quote from Tulsidas's *Rāmcharitmānas*, in which this position is clearly expressed.

Another theological point which differentiates Ramanandi tyagis from other ascetics is that they regard the reaching of Ram as the goal of their methods. This goal of reaching the lord (*Bhagwān prāpti*) is held to be the fifth goal in human life, an addition to the four traditional goals of man (*purushārtha*) in Brahmanical doctrine: *kāma* (desire), *artha* (wealth), *dharma* (religious rules) and *moksha* (liberation of the soul). Since Hindus generally hold that liberation is the goal of asceticism, this is an admittedly vague, but significant addition. In this way asceticism is encompassed by devotion to God. The tyagis can thus be seen as the inheritors of an ancient tradition of asceticism. That is the reason for their common epithet '*tapasvi*', meaning 'one who has *tapas*'. In their case asceticism is, however, subsumed in the devotion to Ram. Moreover, it is not a radical break with Brahmanism, since they use the fire also for quasi-Vedic sacrifices.

Vows

While the cluster of fire and ashes is discriminative within the Ramanandi order, the taking of austerities is not. The meaning given to the austerities, however, is. The most important austerity is, of course, that of celibacy (*brahmacharya*). This is, for sure, a common austerity among Ramanandi monks, since it is the basis of monastic life, but the tyagis give a special meaning to it. According to them the tyagi retains his seed (*urdhvaretas*) and therefore his heat, energy, power. Contact with women is therefore seen as highly dangerous, because it may cause the spilling of semen even involuntarily. What the tyagi tries to accomplish by taking vows is the killing of his desires (*kāma*), just as in the well-known myth the great ascetic god Shiv kills the Hindu Cupid, Kama, god of sensual love. Desire is, of course, not only directed at women, although they are its primal object; it is also directed at food. Therefore several types of fasting (*upavas*) belong to the common stock of ascetic austerities. In the first place all Ramanandi sadhus are strict vegetarians, for they will not eat meat, fish or eggs.[17] They connect this with the ancient Hindu idea of *ahiṃsā* (non-violence). The simple fact of being vegetarian does not distinguish them from a large number of householders. Sadhus, however, tend to be more strict in their diet and are in general more particular in their observance of complete fasting on important religious days dedicated to certain gods. Many tyagis fast completely on Tuesdays, which are sacred to Hanuman, and also on *ekadashis* (the eleventh lunar day of the bright fortnight), which are sacred to Vishnu. However, strict householders and especially their wives and daughters may also observe these days. Some tyagis go even further. They seek fame by proclaiming the vow that they will take only milk or fruit juice (*dudhahari, payohari*), as one of the most famous tyagis of North India, Deoriya Baba, is doing. Others will proclaim that they will not eat anything cooked, but only what they find growing wild in the jungle. They live predominantly on fruits. The greater the austerity, the greater the bid for fame among householders and fellow-sadhus. In some cases dietary restrictions do not seem to be sufficient, since I met a famous sadhu who was called Baluiya Baba, because, according to the legend, he had for a few years eaten nothing but sand from the banks of the Sarayu. Others may even proclaim a vow to eat absolutely nothing for days, weeks, or even months.

In such a diet, the opposition between nature and culture, raw and cooked, is of importance, for the tyagis claim that they eat only uncooked things from the jungle. In this way an opposition is created between the jungle and life in sedentarized villages and towns. The same is also true for ways of dressing. Although there seem to be naked tyagis, as is already suggested by the use of the word *nāgā* (naked) to refer to fighting ascetics, I have never met any of them in Ayodhya. They will stay in the jungle and put a loin cloth on when they enter settled areas. However, there is in Ayodhya a noticeable tendency among tyagis to use grass, or the bark of a tree, or metal for their loin cloth and belt. To some extent these ways of dressing serve as markers of group boundaries, but they also serve as symbols of the 'raw' jungle. In this way there is a clear distinction between relatively naked tyagis and the sadhus who wear clothes (*vastradhari*) of woven cotton.[18] Another symbol of nature is the skin of a deer or leopard for sitting on. In principle a sadhu will either sit on the bare ground, or on a skin, which is a sign of his ascetic accomplishments. This seems to be inconsistent with his vow of non-violence (*ahiṃsā*), since on the other hand he will not wear leather shoes. It was therefore always embarrassing for my informants to be confronted with questions about it.

A further well-known vow is the keeping of silence (*mauna*). This is commonly done by all Ramanandi sadhus, often for a fixed period which may last up to a couple of years. They communicate with the outside world by writing on a slab. This is done as a means of avoiding idle talk and thus enabling them to concentrate on their inner experiences. Another aspect of it, of course, is that it makes communication something special by giving it an extra, sacred aura. It is a form of austerity that is easily recognizable and readily respected by lay disciples.

Rather more controversial are such vows as standing on one leg for days or even years or holding one arm up until it is atrophied. Another is to keep the fist closed until the nails enter the flesh of the palm and come out the other side. These are some of the austerities I have witnessed, but there are endless variations. It is clear that these actions are specific exercises in self-control, but they are controversial among tyagis as well as among laymen, since they are considered as a spectacular display of asceticism, but not as signs of any spiritual progress. Such tyagis, however, are able to attract offerings from many pilgrims who acknowledge their outward signs of extreme austerity as proof of their ascetic power. The pilgrims come to see them, to have *darshan*, just as they come to see the images of the gods. Others may, however, dismiss them casually as false ascetics, just as the Buddha is said to have done in the Buddhist scriptures.

In sum, we can say that the taking of vows is a way of disciplining one's life. The reason for it is to enhance self-control and to quench desire. Seen in a slightly different way, it is also a positive activity that aims not to suppress, but to acquire special religious experiences and thereby to obtain power. The latter is not always explicitly claimed by tyagis, but is certainly ascribed to them by their lay followers, who seek their magical blessings and their therapeutical advice. The tyagis are often seen as especially effective in exorcising demons, since they have conquered the world of desire, a clear allusion to the fact that demons arise from that world.

However, tyagis never fail to stress the point that attaining a vision of God (*Bhagwān prāpti*) is more important than acquiring powers. In these different methods of disciplining the body and the extreme cases of mortification, the goal, as with the North American Indians of the Plains, is to obtain mental experiences. These experiences, which are clearly hallucinatory and different from common-sense experiences, are interpreted with the help of the symbolical vocabulary offered by the guru.

The beliefs of the tyagis may be said to become true by the consequent disciplining of their bodily and mental sensations. This method of restraining the body is complemented in an interesting way by the method of indulging in intoxicating substances. The tyagis are, most of them, accustomed to smoking and drinking large quantities of hashish (*ganja* or *bhang*).[19] It is difficult to write about inner states, but there is no denying the fact that the constant intake of this drug must have lasting effects on the way they experience the world as *ephemeral*. Just as in the case of the extreme austerities, indulgence in drugs is highly controversial among both sadhus and lay followers, since it is seen as the opposite of self-control. It is, however, very important to notice that the taking of vows is couched in a very radical and violent language by the tyagis themselves. They speak of breaking of the mind (*man-tor*), so that the illusions of normal secular life are broken and its attractions warded off. One can go even further by also performing *tang-tor*, actual physical castration. In this way the greatest danger for ascetics, sexual intercourse, is effectively made impossible. Gross (1979) gives an account of the ritual of tang-tor based on descriptions by his informants, but he has not been able to witness it. During my fieldwork I have met three tyagis who had been sterilized for ascetic reasons, but they had all had it done in hospital.

Generally speaking, the taking of vows as such is not a boundary which distinguishes sadhus from householders, or tyagis from other sadhus. Rather it is individual extremism or radicalism in taking vows and living according to them that makes some tyagis different from others.

Yog

The word *yog* is etymologically related to 'yoke' and means 'discipline'. It can be taken to refer to a complex philosophy and methodology which was classically systematized in a Sanskrit treatise by Patanjali, called the *Yoga Sutras*. The problem we are facing here is that there is an extensive primary and secondary literature on yog which suggests that it is one of the most important aspects of an ascetic life-style, while during my fieldwork I found only fragmentary traces of knowledge about it among the tyagis. Although almost all tyagis, when asked, answered that they performed yogic exercises, only very few of them were actually able to show more than a few positions.

Contrary to expectation therefore, yog does not seem to play an important role in the life-style of tyagis.

As far as some tyagis practise yog they emphasize the so-called *Hatha-yog* which accords great importance to the body. In this system much attention is given to various kinds of purification. I have witnessed a few times the so-called *basti*, the 'cleansing of the large intestine and the rectum, which is performed by anal suction', and the so-called *nauli*, 'energetic and complex movements of the stomach and intestines' (Eliade, 1973: 230–1). The tyagis stress that these purifications are helpful in preserving health. Besides these purifications the bodily postures (*āsan*) are of importance. The best-known posture is of course the so-called *padmāsan* or lotus posture. These asans are also regarded as healthy exercises, but their main purpose is to enable one to sit fixed in meditation for a considerable length of time without being disturbed by fatigue or imbalance. The bodily postures are also important for the rate of respiration and control of breathing in general. Control of breathing is the main object of the so-called pranayam exercises (cf. Eliade, 1973: 233–49). Much could be said on this subject, but it would amount to a summary of textual research. The statements of my informants were altogether very disappointing on the subject. What seems more important, however, is their assertion that pranayam helps to retain sexual energy in the body. This ties up with our observation that it is absolutely necessary for the tyagis to prevent the loss of semen.

My interviews with tyagis led to the conclusion that yog can be useful for retaining health and for building up and preserving energy, but it does not seem to be essential to their life-style.

Mantra and puja

The most important method of reaching God is continually to repeat his name, Ram. This monosyllabic word is commonly seen as the bridge between the devotee and the Absolute. This in itself is nothing special for the tyagis, since it is an example of the ancient Indian tradition of *mantras*, the mystical sounds or meditation formulas. Of central importance in the Indian tradition is the sound *Om*, which is identified with the ultimate reality, the Brahman. Eliade (1973: 212–16) interprets the use of mantras in the first place as 'supports' for concentration. Mostly they are unintelligible syllables, such as *Hrim, Hram, Hrum,* to be used as instruments of concentration during meditation. They are often secret and not uttered in normal parlance. Their 'real value' or power becomes clear, however, only through practice (*sādhanā*) under the guidance of the guru. This might imply the use of a secret language (*sandha-bhāshā*), which can only be understood by the initiate.

By uttering the mantra in the correct way one can realize God. In addition the mantra has also all kinds of therapeutical and magical powers. The constant repetition (*jap*) of the name of Ram is extolled as highly efficient for all practical and spiritual purposes by the Ramanandi sadhus. Mantras play a central role especially in the Tantric tradition, and the Ramanandis seem to have inherited much from that tradition, since it would be no exaggeration to say that their special message is that of the power of *Rām Nām.* The Name of Ram is considered to be a *bīja-mantra* (a seed), containing the essence of Ram. The stories of the Ramanandis abound with examples of the special force of the Name of Ram in all kinds of cases. Most significant, in their initiation the Vedic mantra *Om,* symbolizing the Ultimate Reality, has been replaced by Ram. While most initiation mantras begin with *Om,* the Ramanandi mantra starts with Ram: *Rām Rāmāya Namah.*

Besides the constant repetition of the Name of Ram and other mantras the daily recitation of Tantric invocations, like the *Hanumat Kavachan,* the armour of Hanuman, or the *Rām Rakshā Stotra,* the praise of the protection of Ram, is of importance. These invocations have the same kind of value as the mantras: they cure, protect and lead to salvation. They are often used by the sadhus to help laymen who seek protection from evil spirits or cure for diseases. Once I witnessed a householder come to ask a tyagi for help because he had heard noises all night and had dreamed that his house was going to be burned. The tyagi promised to come and with a few disciples recite Tantric invocations in his house. In this case, at least, no investigation of the circumstances was made by the tyagi. It was taken for granted that the man was right in believing that his house was threatened by evil spirits (*bhūts* and *prets*) and that a ritual should be performed to ward them off.

Mantras and invocations are also used in what can be called the central ritual complex in the whole of Hinduism: the worship of God through an image of him (*mūrti-pūjā*). It is clear that the tyagis who wander hither and thither cannot carry heavy idols of Ram, Sita and Lakshman with them. As we have seen, their centre of worship is the fire, but since *dhuni-pūjā* does not differentiate them from other ascetic orders, Ramanandi tyagis also carry small images about with them, especially of Ram and Hanuman. The worship is essentially the same as the temple worship, which we described in the first chapter. The idols are fed, washed, in short treated as human beings of high status. In the puja proper the *ārati* is the central ritual act. A lamp with five wicks is swayed before the image(s): fourteen times before different parts of it; three times before the mouth; and seven times before the whole image. It is interesting to note that often the tyagis do not actually carry images with them, but a special black stone (*shālāgrām*), which is said to represent Ram. The image of Hanuman also resembles a stone smeared with red paste. The general opinion of the tyagis I met was that murti-puja is in itself irrelevant, but that it is done because the lay people cannot understand worship without these attributes. According to them the essence of Ram is without attributes (*nirguna*) and therefore the worship of him as having attributes (*saguna*) is of minor importance. Murti-puja was, however, indispensable for establishing contact with the supporting cast of villagers and other donors. In murti-puja there is a clear preference for Hanuman and Ram when compared with the common trio of Ram, Sita, and Lakshman.

As we have observed before, the shalagram stone is a non-anthropomorphic representation of the Ultimate Reality and it is important to note that its worship is considered to be socially unrestricted. The worship of anthropomorphic images (*mūrti-pūjā*), however, is restricted to the twice-born castes.

Bhandārā

The final ritual activity which is of importance in the life of tyagis is the *bhandārā*, the ritual feasting of a group of sadhus. This is a way in which group solidarity is reinforced among the tyagis of a jamat or a khalsa, since mostly only affiliated sadhus are invited. They are often sponsored by wealthy laymen who derive spiritual merit from this feeding of sadhus. In this way it resembles the feeding of gods and Brahmans. The sadhus sit in long rows (*pangats*) which are indicative of the existence of commensality between types of sadhus. Since interdining is an occasion when hierarchical ranking in Hindu India can be observed with the help of interactional criteria, it is good to summarize our findings on this point.

The bhandara is sometimes offered by a sadhu and sometimes by laymen. In principle sadhus will not accept cooked food from a householder's kitchen, but they will accept grains and other raw foodstuffs to be prepared in their own kitchen. The bhandara is, however, as far as possible a neutral event. The food is cooked by a Brahman and is thus acceptable to everyone, except to some orthodox Brahmans who believe that their status is endangered by accepting food from outside their *biraderi* (marriage circle). The event is not only neutral because of the Brahman cook, but also because of the use of pure, so-called *pakkā* food, which is not cooked in water but prepared in *ghee* (clarified butter).

The ritual neutrality of the event which is thus ensured does not prevent it from being a competitive ritual in which status ranking is reinforced or altered. One can properly speak of the politics of the bhandara. In the first place the relation between householders and sadhus should be considered. When a householder is a lay disciple of a Ramanandi sadhu he may not only sponsor a bhandara, but also take part in it himself. To some extent, he is a spiritual brother (*bhai*) of sadhus who have the same guru. A high-status Brahman will, however, be reluctant to take a place in the same row as Ramanandi sadhus; they can belong to any caste except an untouchable one, and he might therefore lose his purity if he sits down with them. Some sadhus, especially tyagis, will also decline in principle to eat in the same row as householders, whether they are Brahmans or not. In this case the sadhus feel that they belong to a fifth varna, a so-called *shukla varṇa* (pure category), over and above the usual four into which Hindu society is divided. In this way they use the idiom of the caste system to carve out a place for themselves.

In the second place, during a bhandara the internal differences among the Ramanandi sadhus come into the open. Among the tyagis, members of different khalsas may decline to eat with one another. Tyagis may also refuse to dine with non-tyagi sadhus of Ramanandi persuasion. These are formal differences, but there are also personal ones. Some Ramanandi sadhus will always eat apart from the row, because they consider themselves, most often because of their Brahman birth, to be too high to sit next to sadhus from

another social background. In these cases the caste system is simply
reproduced within the ascetic order. Moreover, as observed earlier,
in this way the ritual becomes an event in which status can be
established. In general, we may say that internal caste differences are
not strictly observed among tyagis, especially not when they join
itinerant groups (*jamāt*). One informant of low Shudra provenance
told me that he had even cooked meals for the jamat and that,
contrary to statements often made to outsiders, caste differences
were of no importance among the members of his jamat. For the rest
one cannot but conclude that caste plays a role in determining the
status of the sadhus. The first question asked of a sadhu who comes
to stay in a Ramanandi temple is '*Taksal kyā hai?*', 'What is your
caste?', in order to determine if he can be allowed to enter the
kitchen and to approach the image. The way these caste differences
are observed is, however, a matter of temple policy.

Finally, the bhandara serves to demarcate differences with other
ascetic orders and religious communities. A Ramanandi will not
accept food from a sadhu who belongs to another group, and most
other communities will not accept food from Ramanandis.

The bhandara is often used to stress occasions of importance such
as the *mahanti*, the inauguration of a new *mahant* (abbot). The
mahant-to-be invites other mahants of his khalsa or of the
neighbourhood for a bhandara. If they decline his invitation he may
continue to call himself mahant, but he has lost face within the
community of sadhus. If the other mahants accept the invitation,
they come and place a *māla* (a garland) and a *cādar* (a sheet, more or
less a shawl) over his shoulders and accept his food. When they leave
the bhandara the mahants get a farewell gift (*bidai*), the amount of
which is fixed according to the status accorded to the guest. In
addition, all the uninvited visitors also receive a gift. All this is an
exact copy of ritual feasts in which Brahmans are fed to celebrate
some event or to realize some goal by feeding them.

SEDENTARIZATION AND DOMESTICATION

I wish to close this section on the tyagis with some final remarks,
which will be resumed in the conclusion of this chapter. The tyagis
have 'left' society: they call themselves *alamgi*, 'without a fixed
abode'. For a proper understanding of the tyagis it seems necessary

to stress that they are peripatetic sadhus, since this seems to be a central element in their life-style. On the other hand it is important to observe that most of the tyagis have settled down in some temple, *kuti, chauni* or whatever. An empirical account of their life-style, such as I have tried to give here, cannot but stress the long-term process of what might be called the *sedentarization* of the tyagis, who thus become rather less alamgi than they profess to be. It is clear that there is a contradiction between a central part of the ideology of the tyagis and some empirical facts. The centre of 'ash-clad' tyagis of the Terabhai khalsa in Ayodhya, called *Khak Cauk* ('square of ashes'), which I mentioned above, is in fact inhabited mainly by sadhus clad in cotton clothes (*vastradhāri*) who do not live in the open air but in a palatial building provided with every modern amenity, such as a ceiling fan, refrigerator, mixer, radio and even television. Naturally the question arises as to what kind of renouncers these people are and what *alamgi* means in their present situation.

This problem is addressed by Carrithers (1979, 1984) and Strenski (1983) with reference to a case similar to ours, that of a Buddhist order, the *Sangha*, of Sri Lanka. Carrithers argues that the social history of the Sangha can be described as the consequence of a few enduring principles. First, the Sangha is organized into small face-to-face, kin-like groups. Second, monks and laymen are closely interdependent. Third, the Sangha is dispersed throughout the agrarian countryside, which, along with the first two principles, leads to the gradual abandonment of ascetic practices and the adoption of lay values, a tendency Carrithers calls domestication. In the fourth place, the preservation of the ideals of asceticism has ensured that reforms have continually occurred, and it is the play between ascetic reform and domestication which creates the pattern of Sangha history. Such is the argument given by Carrithers in his own summary (1979: 294). The first three principles are also applicable to our case. Just like the Buddhist Sangha in Sri Lanka, the ascetic orders of Hinduism flourished in a sedentary, agrarian society which supported them. Sadhus are mendicants who depend on the laity for material support in exchange for spiritual guidance and merit. It is clear that, as Carrithers observes, in a sedentary society a monk tends to be dependent not on the populace in general, but on a particular group of people who farm a particular set of fields (1979: 295). This has also been observed in the case of Ramanandi tyagis by Burghart who discusses the situation in the Nepalese Terai (Burghart, 1976). However, on the basis of our material one may add that the concentration of sadhus in a sacred centre such as Ayodhya, which is dependent on large and unspecified groups of laymen spread over an extended area, is also a form of sedentarization which might lead to a related process of domestication. In the ideological sphere Carrithers observes two opposed climates of opinion among Buddhists: forest-dwellers against village-dwellers, meditation versus scholarship. Something similar can be found with the Ramanandis in the opposition between culture/nature, jungle/sedentary life, asceticism/ theological scholarship. These are significant oppositions which inform many of the internal differences within the Ramanandi order.

Sedentarization is clearly a process which has affected the peripatetic tyagis, but what about domestication? In a critical article, Strenski (1983) argues that Carrithers follows Weber in an essentially 'romantic fatalist' view which leads him to consider the domestication of the Sangha as an inevitable result of spiritual decline into routinized settled life. According to him, the domestica-tion of the Sangha should be seen as a natural process by and in which the Sangha and laity enter into a complex variety of relationships: residential, ritual, social, political and economic (1983: 466). The residential aspect is often emphasized, but Strenski is right in observing that domestication may be compatible with peripatetic monasticism:

> Would a monk who maintained elaborate ritual relations with lay communities, who meddled in politics, who conformed to the status system of lay society and who perhaps trafficked in the exchange of goods and services be considered undomesticated simply because he maintained no fixed residence? To be sure, he might be considered *less* domesticated than one who did. But would he be any less so than the travelling salesman is considered less a full-blooded *bourgeois* than his settled counterpart? The answer is obvious. (1983: 469)

I also believe that what Carrithers calls 'domestication' is a natural process which should be described without immediate reference to its ideological rejection within Buddhist or western circles. The interdependence of sadhus and laity in Hinduism may lead to mutual adoption of one another's values, but also to an emphasis on the opposition in life-styles. The sadhu needs the support of the laity and therefore he may stress what he has in common with the group of laymen whose support he seeks, for example by pointing out that he is of the same or a higher caste. On the other hand, he may also choose to stress the aspects of his life-style which differ from those of the laity. This strategy may also provide him with the support he needs, since the layman tends to ascribe special powers to these oppositional features. In general, we may say that sadhu and layman have a cultural idiom in common which patterns their relationship, so that we should not make too much of the so-called structural differences between these social categories. I would like to emphasize that it will indeed not do to regard lay and sadhu values as being simply in mutual opposition, affected by processes of domestication or sadhuization. Our problem is rather the implications sedentarization of itinerant sadhus has for their religious experiences and their organization.

We should start with some empirical observations. The number of itinerant groups (*jamāt*) which traverse the country has rapidly declined within the memory of my informants. Generally this process is reckoned to have begun at the beginning of this century. Between the First and the Second World Wars – to use a clear demarcation – many of all types of khalsa renounced their peripatetic life and settled in Ayodhya. The result of this sedentarization is clearly visible in the Tyagi institution, Tapasviji kicchauni, in which a hundred small images which can now be seen in the sanctum were formerly carried by different jamats. During my fieldwork the leader of one of Ayodhya's last big jamats died. He had told me that it had become very difficult to lead this kind of life in present-day India, since long-distance trade, which was their chief occupation, had been taken over by other agencies. In his lifetime he had specialized in the trade of horses and elephants. In this trade his group, which had consisted of more than fifty sadhus, had been helped by members of the *Chandpolia* tribe of Rajasthan, who were clad as Ramanandi tyagis but were in fact tribal kinsmen who acted as the agents of the sadhus in the villages which were visited for buying and selling.[20] Trade was in his view one of the fundamental aspects of the peripatetic life, but it was of course combined with more strictly religious activities such as preaching and the performance of ascetic rituals. As we have seen, there are only a few important centres of tyagis in Ayodhya, and for a large part they were founded in this century. In this way there seems to be an intimate link between the decline of possibilities of long-distance trade and the growth of the number of temples of formerly peripatetic sadhus.

This does not mean that sedentarization is a phenomenon which is only relatively recent in Ramanandi history. On the contrary, we will see later that the expansion of Ayodhya as a sacred Ramanandi centre from the eighteenth century onwards is directly linked to this phenomenon. The only remarkable thing is that the old possibility of sedentarization has gradually become the all-dominating factor in the Ramanandi order. This cannot be explained in terms of a structural dialectic of life-in-the-world and renunciation, or in terms of the interplay between ascetic reform and domestication It has to be understood in terms of changing social configurations, of which both sadhus and laity are part, or to put it differently in terms of long-term historical transformations such as state formation and the emergence of new patterns of commerce. To understand these processes we must be bold enough to make some broad ethno-historical observations. This we will leave for the conclusion, but here it may suffice to stress that both Carrithers and Strenski seem to imply that it is the mere interdependence of sadhus and laity which leads to the domestication of the sadhus. I would, however, argue that a fundamental change of the position of sadhus in society as a result of larger political and economic transformation of that society results in their sedentarization without prejudging the effects that process has on their religious experiences and values. Certainly, sadhus, whether sedentary or not, always cater for a market which offers changing demands and opportunities. In that way laity and monastic order are interdependent and their life-styles and identities are affected by the same broad transformations. Domestication, however, does not have to be the inevitable outcome of the historical process. To understand the implications better we have to pay more attention to the content of religious identities and experiences.

4. Nagas

The literal meaning of the word *nāgā* is 'naked'. It refers to naked ascetics, but since all ascetics are to some degree scantily dressed, the word has come to refer exclusively to one section of them, the fighting ascetics. The Ramanandi nagas are organized into armies and regiments, live in fortified temples and are trained in wrestling and fighting with weapons. Just as one has to take a secondary initiation to become a tyagi, one has to take a secondary initiation with a siddha-guru of the naga section to become a naga. Many Ramanandi sadhus join the ranks of the nagas because they are attracted by the military training they receive from their siddha-gurus, who are often renowned as wrestlers. The mere fact that Hindu sadhus are trained in a military fashion is rather confusing for those who have western preconceptions about 'eastern spirituality'. Often the Hindu notion of *ahiṃsā*, which can be translated as 'non-injury' or 'non-violence', is considered to be a fundamental aspect of such a spirituality, all the more so since Mahatma Gandhi made it a cornerstone of his political philosophy.

The relation between the institution of nagaship among the Ramanandis and the notion of ahimsa is no doubt very complex. Historically, the notion of ahimsa seems to have originated as a part of Buddhist and Jain propaganda against the Vedic sacrifices which were dominated by Brahmans.[21] The slaughter of animals had always been a central feature in Vedic sacrifice. Although it was originally an anti-Brahmanical notion, ahimsa gradually became incorporated into mainstream Hinduism. It seems to refer primarily to vegetarianism and to be vegetarian is generally regarded as an important status symbol. Vegetarian castes are considered to be of higher status than meat-eating castes. High-status Brahmans are often more or less vegetarian, while untouchables are often (considered to be) meat eaters. This opposition is confused, however, by the fact that some high castes, like that of the warriors (*Kshatriyas*), eat meat as a consequence of the nature of their caste. Since they have to fight and kill, warriors need to eat meat in order to obtain the necessary strength. Their standing is not impaired by their eating meat; on the contrary, it is a symbol of their status. A solution to this particular problem would be to argue that Kshatriya meat-eating is a symbol of their worldly power, while Brahman vegetarianism is a symbol of their religious authority. This is, however, contradicted by the fact that some gods worshipped by Brahman priests are offered meat, while other gods, also worshipped by Brahman priests, are offered vegetarian food. In temples devoted to the Mother Goddesses the sacrifice of goats is a major ritual activity (cf. Preston, 1980: 62–70). It is therefore not possible to solve the problem by relating it to a structural opposition of high and low castes (cf. Dumont, 1970: 20–33) or to an opposition between secular and worldly power.

'Non-injury' has become an important religious injunction, especially in the Vishnuite devotional movements (*bhakti*). Here also it appears to refer primarily to vegetarianism and to the prohibition of animal sacrifice. For Vishnuite sadhus it therefore seems sufficient to be vegetarian and to worship the gods with fruits and flowers, if they want to honour the rule of ahimsa. Nevertheless, the devotional emphasis on sweetness and love does not appear to be designed to prepare sadhus for military action. I would therefore suggest that the militarism of the Ramanandi nagas derives from the ascetic tradition of the tyagis. While in other Vishnuite communities nagaship is at best a marginal phenomenon, it is a major one among the Ramanandis. In this respect they once again resemble the Shivaite ascetics whose military organization they seem to have copied, as we shall see later.

We have already discussed the organization of the tyagis in itinerant groups (*jamāts*). It is not difficult to imagine that these groups had to be able to defend themselves in a violent society in which everyone was armed (Kolff, 1983). In fact, asceticism and organized violence is a historical combination of long standing in India. Lorenzen (1978: 61) quotes an informative poem, written by the fifteenth-century poet Kabir, which attacks the trading and military proclivities of the Shivaite ascetics of his time:

> Never have I seen such yogis, Brother.
> They wander mindless and negligent
> Proclaiming the way of Mahadeva.
> For this they are called great mahants.
> To markets and bazaars they bring their meditation,
> False siddhas, lovers of maya.
>> When did Dattatreya attack a fort?
>> When did Sukadeva join with gunners?
>> When did Narada fire a musket?
>> When did Vyasadeva sound a battle cry?
> These make war, slow-witted.

Are they ascetics or archers?
Become unattached, greed is their mind's resolve.
Wearing gold they shame their profession.
Collecting stallions and mares and
Acquiring villages they go about as tax collectors.

Besides this poem of Kabir, Lorenzen shows from scattered pieces
of evidence that there is a long tradition of organized ascetic violence
in India which began even before the Muslim conquest in the twelfth
century. From the religious point of view there is no reason at all why
this should not be so. *Tapas*, the heating of the body by ascetic
exercise, is a means of acquiring power. From Sanskrit myths we
know that this power can be used in a political way by threatening the
king with calamities like drought. It is a spiritual power over nature
and this power is admired and feared at the same time. As we have
seen in the vignette of Tyagiji, the attitude of the laymen is a mixture
of fear and worship. It is quite common for sadhus to show their
anger uninhibitedly and use abusive language. In short, they are
unpredictable and awe-inspiring. Their physical power is not seen as
contradictory to their spiritual or magical power. Rather they are
complementary. In traditional descriptions of the fights between
different groups of sadhus, magical and physical violence are also
mingled. According to Ramanandi history Krishnadas Payahari, an
important Ramanandi saint, defeated the Kanphata yogi Taranath
and occupied his temple-fortress at Galta at the beginning of the
sixteenth century. The same Taranath is again said to have been
defeated and removed from his temple in Pindori by Krishnadas's
disciple Bhagwanji (Orr, 1940: 86; Goswamy and Grewal, 1969:
5,6). These stories confirm my opinion that in the eyes of Hindus
there has never been anything new or surprising in ascetics using
violence. Ascetics use violence on their own bodies to acquire power
over the microcosm of the body and over the connected macrososm
of nature, and they use violence to acquire power in society.[22]

The necessity for violence was, of course, greatest in times when
the itinerant sadhus had to defend more than their nakedness. It is
hard to say when exactly these sadhu groups began to develop an
interest in long-distance trade, but by the eighteenth century they
had become the principal traders in several parts of North India.
Cohn (1964) points out that Shivaite sadhus were the commercial

leaders of the important North Indian commercial town of Mirzapur. He argues that the ascetics had at least two great advantages as traders. They could pool their resources without being forced to spend them in conspicuous consumption during the great Hindu status ritual of marriage or to divide them up among their inheritors. Moreover, they could use their pilgrimage cycle, which ran from Hardwar in the north through the Gangetic plain to Bengal and Jagannath Puri, as a trading network. Bayly (1983: 143) puts it succinctly:

> Using a combination of military and commercial power, they could link up areas of supply and demand in the stable and productive zones and provide their own protection on the difficult routes between them. Their corporate savings and investment habits enabled them to form and direct the uses of capital with great efficiency. By the 1780s, the ascetic sects seem to have comprised the dominant money-lending and property-owning group in Allahabad, Benares and Mirzapur.

Historians writing about these ascetic 'trader-soldiers' mostly refer only to Shivaite ascetics, perhaps under the false impression that asceticism is limited to the Shivaite persuasion. The historical sources, however, also mention 'byragees', that is Ramanandi sadhus who are acting as traders and military entrepreneurs. Kolff (1971: 215), for example, quotes an account by Tieffenthaler who, writing about Chhatarpur in the 1790s, mentions that outside this town lived Sannyasis and Bairagis who were engaged in commerce and money-changing. In fact, it appears that itinerant ascetic groups of whatever persuasion, Shivaite, Vishnuite, Sikh, Dadupanthi, were engaged in these activities. The most important among them were the Shivaite Dashanami order, the Vishnuite Ramanandi order and the Sikh order. The first two of these orders constantly clashed. Particularly in the eighteenth century several violent disputes occurred between these groups at the great sadhu gatherings at the Kumbh Melas. In the oral tradition of the Ramanandis these fights are always presented as disputes over the order of precedence in taking a bath. This precedence shows the relative status of an ascetic group *vis-à-vis* others and is witnessed by great multitudes of lay Hindus who are actual or potential disciples of the orders.

There is, however, more to these violent disputes than meets the eye. It was clearly of great importance to control the sacred centres which were the nodal points in a system of both pilgrimage and trade. Bayly (1981) argues that Moghul rule, which was at its height before 1720, stimulated the expansion of communications in large parts of India; therefore the connected phenomena of pilgrimage and trade thrived in the eighteenth century. This explains to a great extent the oral accounts of growing competition between Ramanandis and Shivaite Dashanamis in this century. This competition is commonly regarded in these accounts as the reason for the military organization of the Ramanandis, to which we will now turn.

There are very few independent historical sources available on the origin and evolution of the Ramanandi military organization. It is therefore extremely hard to decide upon chronology. We might, however, begin to throw some light on our case by comparing it with that of the Sikhs, which has been admirably described by McLeod (1976). According to Sikh tradition, the Sikh brotherhood (*khālsā*) was founded in 1699 by Guru Gobind Singh, the tenth guru after Nanak, the founder of the community. The same tradition has it that a peaceful religious community, the Panth of disciples (*sikhs*) of Nanak, was forced to form this khalsa, a militant brotherhood. In his critical comments on this tradition McLeod argues that the events of 1699 were not the outcome of any sudden decision of Gobind Singh, but rather the long-term result of the conflict between the expansion of the Jats in the Panjab and the reaction of the Moghul emperors in Delhi. According to McLeod it took almost the entire eighteenth century to organize and centralize power in what was in name a khalsa, but in reality consisted of highly mobile bands of warriors (*jathas* or *misls*). What is relevant to our discussion is McLeod's description of a process of military group formation among the Sikhs which appears to be very similar to what happened in the less documented history of the Ramanandis.

Just like the Sikhs, the Ramanandi tyagis were also travelling in highly mobile bands called *jamāt*. According to Ramanandi sources these bands were combined with other 'Vishnuite' ascetic groups which were actually worshippers of Krishna in a 'Vishnuite' order with a military organization attached to it. In fact there seems to have been an organizing effort in two steps during four successive conferences of religious leaders in the first half of the eighteenth century: in Vrindaban around AD 1713, in Brahmapuri (Jaipur) around 1726, again in Jaipur around 1734, and finally in Galta, east of Jaipur, in 1756 (see Thiel-Horstmann, n.d.).

The notion of a *Chatuhsampradāya* organization is still very much alive among members of all four Vishnuite communities, but its actual existence is doubtful. None of my informants could explain the functions of such an organization in the past or in the present. Though some of my tyagi informants argued that their camps were open to all members of the four sampradayas, I have never seen an ascetic of other than Ramanandi persuasion in these camps, nor could any informant remember when any non-Ramanandi ascetic had last stayed with them. As I have already observed, the main ideological reason for the organization of the *Chatuhsampradāya khālsā* appears to have been a bid for respectability by the North Indian Vishnuites. This is especially clear in the case of the Ramanandis and the Gauriyas who linked their communities with the South Indian communities of Ramanuja and Madhva.

While the Chatuhsampradaya khalsa was probably more a strategic notion than anything else, the second step in the endeavour to organize the Vishnuites was real enough. According to oral history the Vishnuite sadhus were constantly harassed by Shivaite nagas. At that time the Shivaite Dashanami Sannyasins had already founded a military organization of their own community and it was this military organization which had begun to threaten the lives and possessions of the Vishnuites. A typical legend illustrating the situation was that two members of the Giri sub-order of the Dashanamis had taken a vow to kill at least one Ramanandi a day. Because of the attacks by the Shivaites, the Vishnuites agreed to join forces under Balanand, a Ramanandi sadhu. He was already the founder of the military (*lashkari*) section of the Ramanandis. The story of the foundation of the lashkari is that, because of the persistent attacks of the Shivaite Dashanamis, they did not have enough time to put the red and white tilak on their foreheads while preparing for a battle, and so decided to use only white for the tilak. In this way they formed a separate Ramanandi group. It is clear, then, that they were fighting ascetics.

Just like the Sikh tradition, which attributes the formation of a military brotherhood to a decision made in 1699 whereas it was in fact the result of a long-term process, the Ramanandi tradition tends to attribute the formation of their naga armies to the conference of

Galta. Oral tradition, on the other hand, is unanimous in its claim that Balanand and his guru Brijanand were already leaders of an enormous jamat of militant sadhus who were engaged in trading horses and camels. What seems to have happened in the eighteenth century is rather similar to what happened in the case of the Sikhs: an endeavour to centralize and organize the ascetic power of mobile bands of armed Vishnuite ascetics.

The role of Balanand and his relation with the powers that be remains rather obscure. According to some traditions Balanand and his guru were brought to Jaipur by Jai Singh for military reasons, while other traditions have it that Balanand had been the guru of one of Jai Singh's descendants, Madho Singh (r. 1751–68) (Roy, 1978: 191). On the basis of her archival study Thiel-Horstmann (n.d.) argues that Jai Singh had tried to subdue the armed Vishnuite forces, but had failed. In her opinion the official 'establishment' of the naga armies could have happened at the conference at Galta in 1756 during the reign of Madho Singh, who was in need of military support. Whatever might have been the case, it is clear that the early eighteenth century saw the formation of a Ramanandi order, the emergence of a strong idea of North Indian 'orthodox Vishnuism' and the establishment of organized Vishnuite armies. These developments took place in a period of great opportunities for ascetics in worldly matters, such as warfare and long-distance trade.

THE ARMY OF RAM

The new army, allegedly formed by Balanand at the Galta conference, received the name of *Rāmdal*, the army of Ram. This name already indicates the predominance of Ramanandis in an army which was said to be the military arm of the four Vishnuite sampradayas, three of them being Krishna-worshippers. The organization of this army, as laid down by Balanand, is complicated. The following account is based on field notes which were gathered with a great deal of difficulty, since informants were only able to tell something about the group they belonged to without having a picture of the organization as a whole.

There are three *anis* or armies: Nirmohi, Nirvani and Digambar.[23] These anis are again subdivided in *akhāṛās*, a difficult word referring at the same time to a camp and to the band of sadhus camping together. These akharas contain several different groups of Vishnuite nagas. Schematically the division runs like this:

Nirmohi ani

1. *Nirmohi Akhara*:
Ramanandi Nirmohi
Vishnuswami Nirmohi
Maladhari Nirmohi
Radhavallabhi Nirmohi
Jhariya Nirmohi

2. *Mahanirvani Akhara*:
Ramanandi Mahanirvani
Harivyasi Mahanirvani

3. *Santoshi Akhara*:
Ramanandi Santoshi
Harivyasi Santoshi

Note: Sometimes sadhus added a *Dudhadari Nirmohi Akhara*, the military arm of a non-chatuhsampradaya Vishnuite community, the Dadupanthis, famous for its soldiery.

Nirvani ani

1. *Nirvani Akhara*:
Ramanandi Nirvani
Harivyasi Nirvani
Balabhadri Nirvani

2. *Khaki Akhara*:
Ramanandi Khaki
Harivyasi Khaki

3. *Niralambhi Akhara*:
Ramanandi Niralambhi
Tatambari

Digambar ani

1. *Ram Digambar Akhara*
2. *Shyam Digambar Akhara*

Every army has its own banner, all of which feature the sun (*sūrya*), symbol of Vishnu, but there is an interesting difference between the akharas of Ram devotees (i.e. Ramanandis) and those of Krishna devotees.[24] The former have the monkey god Hanuman, Ram's principal ally and servant, on their banners, while the Krishna devotees have Garuda, the bird-vehicle (*vāhan*) of Vishnu. This distinction makes it perfectly clear that after the secondary initiation as a naga, the primary initiation as a Ramanandi (*Rām-upāsak*) or Krishna devotee (*Krishna-upāsak*) retains its importance. In the army of Ram there are seven Ramanandi akharas and eleven Krishnaite akharas.[25] This is caused by the greater divisiveness among the Krishna devotees. The Ramanandis have the organization entirely under their control.

Several times I was told by nagas that the akharas had existed from 'time immemorial', but that Balanand had organized them into armies. The akharas are not only divided according to religious persuasions, there is also a division among the nagas according to the place where their naga initiation has taken place. The nagas are in this way divided into four groups (*selis*): Hardwari, Ujjainiya, Sagariya and Basantiya. Nagas initiated in Hardwar belong to the Hardwari seli, those initiated in Ujjain to the Ujjainiya seli, those initiated in Gangasagar to the Sagariya seli and finally all those initiated in other places in the Basantiya. The different selis tend to have different hairstyles and sometimes even different varieties of mark (*tilak*). In the present time, at least, the distinctions between the selis have no social significance, except in the case of the nagas of Hanumangarhi, to whom we will turn later. Nowadays the naga ceremony is held on the eve of the Kumbh, either in Ayodhya or in Vrindaban. In the ceremony a pledge is taken from the initiate that he will serve the feet of Ramanand. A Brahman priest conducts the ritual of the purifying bath in the river Sarayu when the ceremony takes place in Ayodhya, after which he performs a fire ritual (*hawan*).

Every sadhu initiated by a guru who belongs to the Chatuhsampradāya may become a naga, if he wants to. The naga initiation, however, is a secondary one, as we have already observed, while the mantra initiation remains the primary one.[26] The social significance of this distinction is that by becoming a naga one does not lose one's affiliation to one's spiritual family and community. A Ramanandi remains a Ramanandi and a Madhva Gauriya a Madhva Gauriya, although both can be nagas of the Nirvani akhara and possibly of the same seli. Formerly it was forbidden for nagas to perform primary mantra initiations, but this rule no longer applies. Its function has been clearly to prevent the nagas from forming an independent and separate community. The danger of this possibility is no longer felt, which can be connected with the general loss of function of nagaship in the present century. Although all my informants claimed that members of all the four sampradayas could stay with them (Ramanandi nagas) and could take initiation in their akharas, I have never witnessed such an occurrence. Whatever may have been the case in former times, Ayodhya is nowadays a place for Ramanandi nagas and those who want to worship Krishna have to go to Vrindaban.

Presently the only occasion when the armies (*anis*) come into full existence is at the great Kumbh Melas. At these bathing festivals the akharas combine into armies (*anis*) and lose their separate identities. The great event at the Kumbh Mela is bathing in the river at the auspicious moment. At this time the Vishnuite sadhus unite before they proceed to the river. The armies go in what is called *shahi julus*, 'royal procession'. They are led by the Nirvani ani, followed by the Digambar ani, which goes as a king in the middle, and finally the Nirmohi ani. When they return from the river, the order is reversed, the Digambar ani remaining in the middle. Together with the armies as their protectors go the affiliated khalsas of tyagis. First goes the Chatuhsampradaya khalsa, which has four abbots, one for each sampradaya, and one Shri Mahant, *primus inter pares*, who has to be a Ramanandi. After this comes the Dakor khalsa, which is divided into the Ratlam khalsa and the Indore khalsa. They are all exclusively Ramanandis, just like the other khalsas of tyagis discussed earlier. Together they form the great procession of the Vishnuite sadhus. In order to be allowed to join the procession and to stay in the camp guarded by the armies, a sadhu has to be affiliated with one of them. Abbots of great institutions or of important itinerant groups (*jamats*) now acknowledge, at least for the time being, the superiority and authority of the Shri Mahant of the army with which they are affiliated. They have to ask for permission to go with the army and have to give a parting-gift (*bidai*) when they leave. At the Kumbh important doctrinal decisions can be taken, since it is by far the greatest ascetic gathering. When this has to be done a meeting is called, presided over by Shri Mahants of the anis and other important abbots, such as the Shri Mahant of the Chatuhsampradaya khalsa. Since the last-mentioned as well as the Shri Mahants of the armies all have to be Ramanandis, it is not difficult to imagine the stranglehold which the Ramanandis have on the other Vishnuite communities on these occasions.

On the other hand, I doubt whether any important decisions on matters primarily concerning other communities can be taken at a sadhu meeting dominated by the Ramanandis. From my experience of the loose chain of command in the Ramanandi community itself, and from what I happen to know from the way the Madhva Gauriya community deals with its affairs, it seems very unlikely that the Ramanandis or, for that matter, a gathering of sadhus could intervene in the affairs of one of the Vishnuite communities. We have, however, the important case of the sadhu meeting at the Kumbh Mela of Ujjain in . 1921 in which the Ramanandis took major decisions on their own identity. This case has been discussed fully in an earlier section and shows that the meetings at the Kumbh Melas are important at least for the Ramanandis. I would suggest that this is a result of their being a loosely organized ascetic order which only has this opportunity of making general decisions.

The fact that the formation of armies only takes place at the Kumbh Melas, and that the armies do not appear to have any other important functions apart from protecting the Vishnuite sadhus on these occasions, confirms the Ramanandi version of the origin of the armies as having been occasioned by attacks made by Shivaite Dashanamis, especially at these Kumbh Melas. One informant told me that the important question of status concerning who should precede whom in the procession to the river (*charhao*) was solved by the following agreement: Vishnuites go first in Ujjain and Nasik, while Shivaites go first in Hardwar and Prayag. As far as I can see, the Ramanandis have simply copied many of the names and institutions which were current among the Dashanami nagas who had already been organized in akharas. This points again to the fact that these groups belong to some extent to one and the same tradition: that of asceticism.

THE ARRIVAL OF THE RAMANANDI AKHARAS IN AYODHYA

In the early eighteenth century, Ramanandi akharas started to establish themselves in Ayodhya. The first to come to the city appears to have been the Nirmohi akhara under its abbot Govinddas. At about the same time the Nirvani akhara under Abhayramdas came. Gradually, in the course of the eighteenth century, all the other Ramanandi akharas came to establish themselves in Ayodhya, bringing in their train many other groups of Ramanandi sadhus.

Why was it only in the eighteenth century that the Ramanandis established themselves at Ayodhya, a place that had always been central in their theology, and what was the religious and political situation they found in this sacred centre? As we have already observed, Ayodhya had been a place of some religious importance for centuries. There were at least a few temples, probably maintained by local Brahmans, some of which were destroyed by Muslim rulers. The Ramanandi institutions were, however, all established after the beginning of the eighteenth century.

The Ramanandis seem to have expanded their territory immensely in the eighteenth century. Before then they were apparently operating in a peripatetic manner, primarily in western India and especially Rajasthan. During the eighteenth century they began to spread throughout northern India and to establish monasteries in Uttar Pradesh, in Bihar and in the Terai districts of Nepal. At the same time as the Ramanandis settled in Ayodhya, a similar process occurred in Janakpur, Nepal.

Richard Burghart (1978b: 257–84) describes vividly how the Ramanandis discovered Janakpur, the birthplace of Sita and the site of the marriage between her and Ram, which had disappeared in the Dvapara-yuga. The first ascetic to come to Janakpur was a Dashanami, Chaturbhuj Giri, who dreamed that Ram told him to excavate the divine images of himself and to worship them. At the same time the Ramanandi ascetic Sur Kishor, who had come from the Galta monastery in Jaipur, also arrived and discovered Janakpur. After him many Ramanandi sadhus came and found, in what was then a jungle, the 'lost' places where Sita had lived. Only after these sadhus had established themselves did householders start to settle in the jungle region of Janakpur, according to local history. Archaeological evidence suggests, however, that the region had already been settled and petty kingdoms been formed. A battle for the control of the area had to be fought with the Dashanamis who had settled before the Ramanandis. Gradually the Ramanandis, who appear to have won the struggle, were able to muster the support of the petty kings of the area, and Janakpur became an important Ramanandi centre. This mechanism of expansion of religious orders, in which the (re)discovery of places lost in a former 'world-period' (*yuga*) plays a dominant role, is regularly found in Indian religious history. Vaudeville (1976) shows that similar tactics were used by the Krishnaite community of Madhva Gauriya, when it came from Bengal to the area of Braj in Uttar Pradesh. In both instances the newcomers had to establish their supremacy over traditional forms of worship (of trees and snakes, etc.) and in the case of Janakpur even over an already established order, that of the Dashanamis.

The case of Ayodhya differs from those described by Burghart and Vaudeville. Ayodhya had gained some importance as a sacred centre connected with the Ram story before the Ramanandis came to establish themselves here. Moreover, it was not a place in the jungle, marginal to the core areas of settled agriculture. On the contrary, it had been a centre of Mughal administration for a long time, as is still witnessed by the many ruins of Mughal buildings in the city and, in a different way, by the Babar mosque and the ruins of the mosques which were built in Aurangzeb's time. This is not to say that there was nothing to be 'rediscovered' in Ayodhya. The rediscovery process, however, took the form of 'repair' or restoration of decrepit buildings within the already existing city of Ram. Moreover, the Ramanandis could not limit their attention to the acquisition of Hindu patronage, as in the case of Janakpur, but had to get the support of the rulers of Awadh, who were Muslim. As in the case of Janakpur, however, there was an established Dashanami presence in Ayodhya, with which they had to compete lest their establishment be constantly under threat.

To begin with Muslim patronage, it is clear from documentary evidence that the Ramanandis were successful in obtaining it. A good example is the establishment of the Nirvani Akhara on the so-called *Hanuman tila*, the hill of Hanuman. In my possession is a copy of the original document in which Safdar Jang (r. 1739–54) awarded seven *bīghās* of land to Abhayramdas, the abbot of the Nirvani akhara. During the reign of his successor, Asaf-ud-Daulah

(r. 1775–93), funds were raised by *Dīwān* Tikaitray to construct part of the present fortress-like building on the site. The Khaki akhara also obtained four *bighās* from Shuja-ud-Daulah. Although they do not have documents to prove it, many of the institutions established in the eighteenth century claim to have been supported by the nawabs or their Hindu ministers. The reason for this sudden strong Muslim patronage of Hindu institutions can be found in the process in which Awadh under its nawabs passed from the status of a Mughal province to that of an autonomous regional state, during which it doubled its original size, attained great economic and political power, and began to develop its own cultural and historical identity (Barnett, 1980: 2). The central cultural and political feature in the success of the nawabs' state seems to have been its very liberal attitude towards Hindu participation in military and political arenas. Under the first four nawabs there was hereditary control of the *dīwānī* (chief ministership) by a family of Panjabi Khatris (Hindus): Atma Ram under Saadat Ali Khan; Ram Narayan under Safdar Jang; MahaNarayan under Shuja-ud-Daulah; Raja Jagan Nath under Asaf-ud-Daulah (Barnett, 1980: 28,29). In the reign of Safdar Jang the real administrator of Awadh and Allahabad was a pious Vaishnava, the Kayasth Nawal Rai, 'who transformed Ayodhya from a Muslim town into a Hindu one' (Sitaram, 1933: 11). Even more fascinating than the fact that administrative control of Awadh was in the hands of Hindu Khatri and Kayasth families, is the extent to which the nawabs relied on the military power of regiments of Dashanami nagas in the army. Two of Shuja-ud-Daulah's three most powerful generals were not only Hindus, but Gosain sadhus named Anupgiri and Umraogiri. By 1760 they held in readiness a combined force of 12,000. The two were the chief disciples of Rajendra Giri who had become general in the army of Safdar Jang, the predecessor of Shuja-ud-Daulah (Barnett, 1980: 56). It is not difficult to conclude that in the time of Asaf-ud-Daulah the nawabi Awadh was as much a Hindu state as it was a Muslim one, illustrated by evidence produced by Barnett (1980: 177) stating that eight of the twelve court favourites of Asaf were Hindus who had received enormous *jagirs*.

Barnett's research makes the situation in which the Ramanandis flourished clear enough. A moot question remains, however, as to why it was the Ramanandis who received so much backing. In

Barnett's description it was the great rivals of the Ramanandis, the Dashanami nagas, who were the military support of the nawabs' state. In Ayodhya the Dashanamis seem to have been already well established and they did not appear to have been delighted by the arrival of their competitors. Raghunathprasad describes the situation from the viewpoint of the Ramanandis in his *Shrimaharajacharitra*, which was composed at the beginning of the eighteenth century:

> At the time ... when the occasion of Rama's birth came, people went to Kosalpur and assembled there. Who can describe the enormous crowd? At that place there was an unlimited (number of) strong warriors in samnyasi garb, carrying weapons, with matted hair and ashes smeared on every limb, an unlimited army of soldiers taking pleasure in battle. Fighting with the vairagis broke out. This fight was of no avail (to the vairagis), owing to lack of strategy ... They made a mistake by going there towards them; the vairagi garb became a source of misery. All people dressed in vairagi garb fled – through fear of them (*samnyāsins*). Avadhpur was abandoned. Wherever they (*samnyāsins*) happened to find people in vairagi garb, there they struck great fear into them. Through fear of them everyone was frightened, and wherever they could they took shelter in a secret place and hid themselves. They changed their dress and hid their sectarian markings – no one showed his proper identity. (*Shrīmahārājācharitra*, 42f; translation in Bakker, 1986: 149)

From our knowledge of the political situation in Awadh we would say that the Ramanandi vairagis were at a great disadvantage, compared with the Dashanamis, and the only historical description we have of the fighting in Ayodhya between the groups, quoted above, seems to endorse that impression. Nevertheless we have unquestionable evidence for the establishment of the akharas and other Ramanandi establishments in Ayodhya in the eighteenth century.

Some light might be thrown on what has happened in Ayodhya with the establishment of the Ramanandi akharas by presenting the local history of three important religious institutions.

CASE 1: SIDDHIGIRI'S MATHIYA

The oldest institution of the naga section of the Shivaite Dashanami order in Ayodhya in Siddhigiri's *mathiya* (monastery). According to the present abbot of this institution, which belongs to the Juna akhara of the Dashanami nagas, the Dashanamis were pushed out of Ayodhya by the Ramanandi akharas. The Juna akhara had been the occupants of Hanuman's hill, but had been attacked and defeated by the Ramanandi nagas of the Nirvani akhara under their leader Abhayramdas. According to his version, the Juna akhara had left for Janakpur where they were able to take hold of what is now known as the Ramchandra monastery. The mathiya was the only Dashanami institution which remained in Ayodhya, whereas formerly it had been dominated by Dashanamis. This opinion is supported by all my informants, who emphasize that Ayodhya had been a Shivaite place before the Ramanandis came. As we have seen, Ayodhya's riverside is still Shiv's domain, but the fact remains that Shivaite religious orders have almost entirely disappeared from Ayodhya's religious scene, while there is no clear evidence that Ayodhya has ever been dominated by any of them.

The Dashanamis themselves seem to have superseded an earlier dominance of Kanphata yogis in Ayodhya, which is borne out by the history of Siddhigiri's mathiya. The present abbot of this institution showed me an inscription which had been placed in the temple by his predecessor and was based on oral and written tradition. In this inscription the succession of abbots of the institution is given as follows:

780	Chandranath
840	Kedarnath
984	Brahmanath
1042	Damodarnath
1130	Yamunanath
1216	Kalyananath
1300	Madhuvangiri
1374	Surajgiri
1442	Nirbhayagiri
1500	Bakhtawargiri
1594	Vamsigiri
1664	Jaivahargiri

1722 Gajadhargiri
1782 Siddhigiri (the first to build a brick temple)
1850 Narayanagiri
1912 Mahipatigiri
1960 Maheshvaranandgiri

The present abbot removed the inscription from its place in the temple because he was afraid that Nath yogis would come to demand possession of the temple, which up to 1300 had clearly belonged to them. I am not concerned with the historical truth or falsehood of the given dates, but it is clear from the inscription that the Dashanamis acknowledge in their tradition that they have taken over an institution from the Kanphata (Nath) yogis. Because this tradition might prove to be embarassing in the present era, when the Dashnamis have little or no support whatsoever in Ayodhya, and Ramanandis together with yogis can easily use it to claim the temple, the abbot is understandably afraid and tries to suppress the evidence.

CASE 2: DANTADHAVANAKUND

My informants among the nagas told me that the akharas of the Ramanandis had come to Ayodhya on the invitation of the abbot of Dantadhavan, an old Vishnuite institution which was constantly harassed by the Dashanamis. Nowadays this institution is regarded as a Ramanuji or Shri-Vaishnava institution, related to the Vatakalai subsection. As we have already seen in an earlier section, the distinction between Ramanujis and Ramanandis arose only relatively recently, at the beginning of the twentieth century. Nevertheless, the present abbot of the Dantadhavan temple alleges that the Ramanujis were the first to live in Ayodhya and that the Ramanandis came only later to defend them against the Dashanamis. To prove his claim he showed me the succession of abbots of the institution:

Vishnuprakash
Shatrughna
Gangadhar
Vasudeva
Damodara
Pitambara

Keshava
Purushottam
Kamalanayana
Bhagwan
Jaikrishna
Narayana (the present abbot)

To all these names the suffix *achāri*, characteristic of Shri-Vaishnavas, was attached. The abbot, however, also showed me some landholding documents, in which we found, instead of Kamalanayanachari, the much simpler Kamtadas, and instead of Bhagwanachari, the name Bhagwandas, incorporating the typical suffix attached to Ramanandi names. Moreover, one informant, who was well versed in the affairs of this particular temple, told me that his friend Jaikrishnachari had informed him that Kamtadas and Bhagwandas had been Ramanandi nagas as well as real brothers. Purushottam was a Ramanandi sadhu who had called for the protection of the nagas and who was succeeded as abbot by one of his protectors. Kamtadas had been a Brahman of the Pande subcaste and from his time the temple had remained in the possession of his family – an early case of domestication and sedentarization. The temple was once very rich and I was shown a number of documents proving that akharas had been granted lands from Dantadhavan.

The story that Shri-Vaishnavas (Ramanujis) were the first Vishnuites to settle in Ayodhya and that it was they who had invited the Ramanandis thus appears to be a modern version which was promoted by the schism in the Ramanandi community in 1921.

CASE 3: HANUMAN'S HILL

Hanuman is a strange deity. He is well known from his heroic exploits in the service of Ram, described in the *Ramayana* of Valmiki as well as in the *Ramcharitmanas* of Tulsidas. On the other hand he appears in a completely different tradition, that of the yogis. He is a great yogi (*mahayogi*) who has magical strengths, possesses all the yogic accomplishments (*siddhis*) and consequently is also able to cure people. According to his myth, he is the son of the nymph Anjana and the monkey Kesari. His conception is, however, rather complex. One day, while standing on top of a mountain, Anjana was ravished by Vayu, the god of the winds, to whom Shiv gave his fiery seed for the conception. Hanuman is therefore the son of Kesari and in that sense a monkey, as well as the son of Vayu and the son of Shiv, or rather the incarnation of Shiv as he is represented in Ramanandi theology. There is an interesting myth about how Hanuman got his magical powers. As an infant, he was perpetually hungry. Once he ran after the sun with every intention of swallowing the orb to appease his hunger pangs. This caused great consternation among the gods and their king Indra hurled his thunderbolt at the greedy infant, who fell down on a mountain top, breaking his jaw, or *hanu*; hence his name Hanuman ('who has a jaw'). Vayu picked up his son and in protest went on strike. There was a sudden absence of the ten forms of wind, which thus put a stop to such functions as breathing, digestion, etc. Thrown into panic, the gods came rushing to Vayu, offering to make amends. Each god gave Hanuman a special power, so that in the end he not only became immortal and invincible, but also the personification of all the powers of the gods, including the important power to heal. Because of all these powers he is immensely popular in the whole of North India and receives even more worship than the more aloof figure of Ram. Theologically he is seen as a great powerful yogi who lives a celibate life, but gets his power only thanks to his immense devotion to Ram.

It should not, however, surprise us that this 'incarnation of Shiv', this celibate mahayogi, is also worshipped among Shivaite sadhus. Hanuman is one of the chief deities worshipped by the ancient order of Kanphata yogis. Sometimes he is even represented by the tilak put on the yogi's forehead. Briggs (1938: 17) reports: 'Some Yogis put on the forehead a mark consisting of a black, horizontal line with a black dot above it, representing Bhairom (Bhairav or Shiv); and below it a red circle representing Hanuman.' The Dashanamis also have this type of devotion for Hanuman: 'One such had on his forehead a *tīka* (tilak) consisting of two curved, horizontal marks, both red; with a black dot between them and a black line below them. Hanuman is indicated by the red lines, and the black line and the dot are for Bhairom' (Briggs, 1938: 12, n. 5).

The worship of Hanuman by these orders is evident from the story told about Hanuman's hill in Ayodhya. The legend goes that Hanuman had been worshipped there for centuries by yogis, Dashanamis and even Muslim *faqirs*. The Muslims believed that it was Hathile, one of the five *pirs* or Muslim saints, whom they worshipped there. Elliott (1869: 270) offers the following description: 'He is said to be the sister's son of Ghazi Miyan (popular saint of Muslims and Hindus in Bahraich), and lies buried at Bahraich, near the tomb of that celebrated martyr. Monuments are erected to the memory of Hathile ... and fairs are held at several villages in honour of his name.'

According to local history, Abhayramdas came with his Nirvani akhara to Hanuman's hill, where an image of Hanuman was worshipped under a tree by Shivaites and Muslims. They were not allowed to worship the image and were forced to retire to their camp near the river Sarayu. In the night Abhayramdas dreamt that Hanuman came to him and told him to chase away the Muslims and Shivaites who were defiling his place of worship and to build a temple in his (Hanuman's) honour, because this was the place where he had stayed in the time of Ram. The next day Abhayramdas, given magical power by Hanuman, was able to drive out the Shivaites.

The three cases presented here corroborate our picture of the religious scene prior to the arrival of the akharas in Ayodhya. Dashanamis had to be forcibly removed before the Ramanandis could establish themselves in Ram's birthplace. The success of the Ramanandi expansion is clearly shown by the establishment of many akharas and temples in the eighteenth century and by the gradual disappearance of the Shivaites from the place, a process which only seems to have neared its completion in the present century. There remains, however, the difficult and fascinating question of how it happened that the Dashanamis, who were clearly in favour in the nawab's court, lost their position in what was for some time the nawabi capital and thereafter lay only a short distance from the new capital of Faizabad. Unfortunately, it is not possible to answer this question. It is said that Shuja-ud-Daulah, on his way to the important battle of Baksar in 1764, stopped at the Hanumangarhi to offer his prayers to the image. We also know that his army consisted for a large part of the Dashanami naga regiments. What are we to make of a ruler stopping to worship at a temple from which the community supporting his military expedition had been ousted? The only reasonable guess seems to be that the Dashanami nagas who had entered Shuja's service did not see the Ramanandis as their enemies.

This could have been the case if the Ramanandis did not differ too much from them in a social and religious sense and did not compete with them in the military market, in which Shuja was one of the most important employers. That there was a lack of competition in the military market seems to be evident from Barnett's research, in which the Ramanandis are not even mentioned. The former point is more difficult to prove. I would, however, suggest that the gosains who were in the service of Shuja had, for a greater part, become more like military entrepreneurs than Shivaite sadhus. There is, of course, a continuum at the extremes of which stand purely religious activities and purely military and trading activities; but the career of a naga like Shuja's general Anupgiri, alias Himmat Bahadur (1730–1804), seems to incline more to the secular extreme, to say the least (Sarkar, 1958: 123–261). This is not only evident from Anupgiri's crucial support of his Muslim patron against the Hindu raja of the holy Shivaite tirtha Benares, which can by all means be interpreted as part of his role in the shifting alliances in North India's political system of the time, but much more clearly by his role in an important incident in Shuja's life. The Shivaite naga procured for his master Shuja an unmarried Khatri (Hindu) woman, whom Shuja had seen bathing, by abducting her from her house in Ayodhya for a night of forced intimacy, This incident seriously threatened Shuja's position as a ruler since it outraged the Khatris who, as we have seen, were largely in control of the administration of the state (Barnett, 1980: 44f). What is interesting for us is the cynical role played by Anupgiri, who had deviated a long way from his traditional role of guru for Hindu laymen. It would be no stretch of the imagination to assume that such a man would not have shown much interest in the inter-community strife between Dashanamis and Ramanandis so long as his interests were not harmed.[27]

THE ORGANIZATION OF HANUMANGARHI

To form an idea of the life in a settled akhara in Ayodhya, it would be useful to present in some detail the case of Hanumangarhi, Ayodhya's most important temple. Hanumangarhi, with its 500 to 600 naga inhabitants, is not really typical of Ayodhya's akharas, which have in general no more than thirty naga inhabitants, but it is the most interesting example because of its size and popularity.

Let us start with an individual: naga Lakhandas. According to his
own story he was found as an orphan abandoned near the river
Sarayu. The person who found him brought him to the naga
Narsinghdas who was the head of a subdivision in Hanumangarhi's
organization. When he became older, he took the man who brought
him up, Narsinghdas, as his mantra guru and later as his siddha
guru. In this way the young orphan became a member of the
organization of Hanumangarhi. His co-initiates (*guru-bhai*) were his
brothers, his guru was his father, and all these putative kinship ties
gave him a spiritual family. Lakhandas is now a grown-up naga, who
has been to several parts of India with a jamat and who has attended
the Kumbh Mela. His world is that of Hanumangarhi. He did not
much enjoy the training in wrestling and fighting with weapons, but
turned to the study of languages. Nowadays he is a teacher at the
monastic school of Hanumangarhi (*pāthshālā*) and quite satisfied
with his spacious room in the compound of the temple. His
ambitions do not go much further than being a teacher. He is no
more interested in religion than the average Hindu. He worships
Hanuman every day and believes that the god gives him strength, but
does not like to go into intricate theological questions. This is,
incidentally, an attitude which is quite common among the nagas of
Hanumangarhi; they are practical-minded and are almost entirely
lacking in a philosophical bent of mind.

Another example is Ramcharitradas. Like most sadhus, he does
not like to talk about his life, but since we had been acquainted for
many years he told me at least some details. He comes from Bihar,
where his father died when he was still a young boy. His mother and
the three children (one boy, two girls) came to live with his mother's
brother in the compound where his grandparents and other family
members also lived. From an early age he was attracted by the
seemingly adventurous life of the jamats which from time to time
visited their village to tell the stories of Ram and Hanuman and all
the other stories of Hindu mythology. When he was about ten years
old his family decided that he should get some education beyond the
village school. So when they were on pilgrimage, they brought him to
a Brahman panda of Ayodhya who was patronized by several families
of the village. The panda took care of the boy and sent him to a
temple school for traditional education. After a few years of
religious instruction Ramcharitradas decided to take a naga from

Hanumangarhi as his guru, because the life there appealed to him very much and he had, for reasons unknown to me, fallen out with the panda in whose house he stayed. Now his family started to try to have him back in their village, but his guru persuaded them that he would do well in Hanumangarhi, and so his career as a Ramanandi sadhu began in earnest. Nowadays he holds a rather important position of authority in the temple. He has been officiating priest, *pūjāri*, in his turn and has been able to tap an independent source of income, since he has become the head of a subdivision in Hanumangarhi's organization. In his younger years he went in an itinerant group (*jamāt*), but he is now over fifty and plans to stay for the rest of his life in the temple. Once every few years he is still visited by members of his family or by people from his village, but these contacts have little importance for him.

These are individuals, and there are many more individuals in Hanumangarhi with slightly different careers. But careers they are. Hanumangarhi is a rich temple in a poor agricultural country, offering to boys of a large region a brighter future than they would have at home in their villages. It should not surprise us, then, that boys, especially orphans and those with disadvantages in their family situation, should choose this career. On the other hand we have to avoid the facile idea that they will be economically 'marginal' in a peasant society. Many may choose this esteemed and promising career for very diverse reasons. But it remains hard to choose celibacy in a country in which family life and especially having sons is highly valued.

The channel for status mobility is the organization of the Nirvani akhara. Hanumangarhi is this akhara's central institution (*baithak*), but the akhara has institutions in other tirthas such as Gangasagar, Puri and Prayag. It is, however, clear that Hanumangarhi's naga population is more or less a localized, sedentarized section of the Nirvani akhara with its own interests in the local economy of Ayodhya, and with its subsidiary temples in many places, the most important being that of Kapila Muni in Gangasagar, which is governed from Hanumangarhi.

How is Hanumangarhi organized internally? It is, like all other akharas, governed by *panchāyaṭ* rule, that is by majority vote in the assembly of naga inhabitants. It has a chief abbot (*bara mahant*), who is at the head of the organization, because he is on the throne (*gaddinashīn*). He is appointed for life and is not allowed to leave the temple of his own accord but only with the written permission of the assembly (*panchayat*). Next to the *mahant gaddinashīn* is the *sarpānch*, the chairman of the assembly of nagas. Together they form the central administrative power in spiritual and material affairs. Then the organization is divided in four parts, called *pattis*. They coincide with the seli-division which is the general subdivision of the akharas as we have seen above. In this way there is a Basantiya patti, a Hardwari patti, an Ujjainiya patti and a Sagariya patti. These pattis all have their own abbots and a considerable measure of autonomy. All rights and property are equally divided over the four pattis. The pattis in their turn are each divided into three quasi-itinerant groups or *jamats*: *jhundi*, *khālsā* and *dundi*. These jamats have a segmentary division in two *toks*. The *tok* was said to be a *vamsha*, a lineage. In this lineage there are again several *āsans* or *ghars*, houses or families of nagas who are initiated by the same siddha guru. We can represent the organization graphically in the following way:

Hanumangarhi Panchayat (Gaddinashin, Sarpanch)

(pattis)		Basantiya			
(jamats)		jhundi	khalsa		dundi
(lineages)		tok tok	tok tok		tok tok
('households')		asans asans	asans asans	asans	asans

The other three pattis, Hardwari, Ujjainiya and Sagariya, are likewise divided. All these subdivisions have an abbot, *mahant*, but the only important ones are those of the pattis and the head abbot. They are assisted by a manager (*mukhtār*) who keeps the books, deals with taxes and is in general comparable with an accountant. For the last hundred and fifty years one *Shrivastava Kayasth* family has provided the managers of the institution and has kept its considerable financial secrets. I have only once in my fieldwork met with a flat refusal to answer some questions and that was with the members of this family who are extremely cautious in dealing with outsiders, much more so in fact than the nagas themselves. Besides having managers, the abbots also make use of the services of a *golkhi* or treasurer. Every patti and every jamat has its own treasurer, and the institution also has a few more offices, like those of pujari (priest), cook and *kothāri* (who supervises the distribution of provisions).

The office of officiating priests, *pūjāri*, is very important in Hanumangarhi. Every patti appoints a pujari for a year, so that each year four pujaris are in service. A naga is eligible for pujariship if he is dvija, born into one of the three highest varnas. If he is not, a dvija naga can perform for him vicariously. A naga's coming in line for pujariship depends on his seniority in the asan and the number of asans in a tok. For example, Basantiya has the right to give one pujari a year, and this right alternates among the three jamats. When a jamat's turn has come, the right is given in turn to one of the two toks and within the toks to one of the asans. Within the asan the principle of seniority operates, which is reckoned from the time of secondary initiation into the akhara. Every sadhu initiated as a secondary initiate (*sādhak-shishya*) in Hanumangarhi is entered in the books kept by the manager of the patti. So eventually if he lives long enough his turn will come.

According to some of my informants, every pujari is given one fourth of the income, which according to them amounts in total to 400,000 rupees. This is only the income from offerings given to the deity in daily worship. From this income they pay all the expenses of the temple, including the food-rations allotted to the pattis and the repairs to the temple buildings. Each pujari takes care of his own patti. The weekly allotment to a patti is 37.5 kilos of rice, 6.5 kilos of *dal* (pulses), and 750 grams of salt. This is far too little to feed the members of the pattis, but for the rest the pattis should take care of themselves. A costly expense is also incurred by the material used in worship: from Kashmir saffron (*keshar*) is imported, which is used to make fragrant paste for the image; an oily perfume with the name of *itra* is brought from Kanauj, and from Rameshvaram *janārdhan dhūp*, a special incense for the *ārati* (lamp offering). Some informants who had been pujaris told me that some 300,000 rupees had actually to be spent, so that 100,000 rupees remained, which was the pujaris' private income. It is not difficult to understand that pujariship, by which one can acquire a private income of 25,000 rupees, is a much desired position. Every Tuesday night (the day most auspicious for Hanuman worship) the pujaris come together before the image of

Hanuman and swear that they have not pocketed any money. The next day they pay all the accounts and what is left is theirs.

Despite many efforts it was impossible to inspect the official accounts of Hanumangarhi. Nobody even tried to hide the fact that the temple's income and expenditure should really not be brought into the open. The reason for this is not difficult to guess. First of all, taxes have to be paid to the government and accordingly this is not a subject of public discussion. Second, and also very important, is the fact that an open discussion of income and expenditure would really diminish the ample scope the temple officials have for manipulating powerful and strategic positions such as that of abbot, pujari and manager.

That is why the head manager of the institution, who works for the chief abbot, gave me an official account on the chief abbots's paper, and signed by himself, stating that in the year 1983 the expenditure had been 530,000 rupees while the income had been 410,000. The deficit of 120,000 was paid by subscriptions from the individual nagas. This might be useful when dealing with tax officials, but it does not convince someone who has been given consistent reports by informants who had served as pujaris that they had derived a considerable private income from their position. Another factor that is unclear is the income which is not derived from offerings to the deity. A layman may come and give money, land or whatever to any individual naga. Moreover, the pattis have their own financial policy. They have lands and temples in the name of the patti and not in the name of Hanumangarhi. In the time of intensive trading and money-lending they received a separate income from their jamats and even nowadays there are all kinds of possibilities, such as investing in shops or in several kinds of trade, which do not come under the control of the Hanumangarhi as a whole. Within the pattis even the jamats have their separate *golkhis* (treasurers) and therefore a certain amount of financial autonomy.

Moreover, the individual naga's entrepreneurial activities are almost unrestricted by institutional constraints. He may leave the Hanumangarhi's compound to live in another building in Ayodhya which is owned by Hanumangarhi or by himself. In this way at least a hundred nagas from Hanumangarhi live apart from the temple. They may – and in fact do – start all kinds of secular activities, like money-lending and shopkeeping. When such an entrepreneur dies his property goes to the asan to which he belongs and, if he has taken good and timely measures, to any disciple he names as his heir. Some of the entrepreneurs, however, go further along the path of domestication in the sense that they take a wife and want their children to inherit their property. This is also often the case, and we should be aware that the boundary between celibate naga entrepreneur, whose property goes to his favourite disciple, and 'married' naga is not really clear-cut. We find a lot of ambiguous cases in which nagas keep concubines without being married, having children and disciples of the same age, or call their children disciples. At the same time all this is a subject of much gossip.

The control of the institution's authorities over the individual nagas is therefore limited. When they leave the temple buildings it becomes difficult to exert much authority over them. This, of course, is the reason why at least one naga may never leave the temple without permission: the chief abbot. For the rest, religious sanctions or the fear of God is invoked. That is why the pujaris have to take an oath every Tuesday before Hanuman that they have not secretly pocketed any part of the offerings. Cautionary stories are also told to control the wicked behaviour of those in power. There is, for example, the story of Balakdas who was chief abbot from 1977 to 1981:

In Hanumangarhi there are enormous heaps of fine cloth stitched with gold thread which were given as ceremonial gifts over a long period since the foundation of the institution. These heaps had begun to take up so much space that it became difficult to keep them. When one day a merchant came and asked to buy these antique clothes, Balakdas agreed to sell one of the heaps for 40,000 rupees. The merchant took the clothes with him to Allahabad and started to sort them out. At six o'clock in the evening the merchant threw the worthless pieces into a bonfire and at just the same moment Balakdas fell ill. His neck swelled and swelled until at twelve midnight the fire in Allahabad was extinguished and Balakdas died. When the merchant came the next day to buy more clothes he was just in time to see Balakdas being taken to the river. The rest of the clothes were not sold to him.

The meaning of the story was twofold. Hanuman had become angry because the chief abbot had sold ceremonial gifts which were given to the deity. This interpretation emphasizes the nature of the temple's property: it is not the property of the chief abbot or any other naga, but of the deity. The other meaning was that Balakdas was said to have received much more money for the clothes than he had given account for. He had done this with the connivance of the head of the naga assembly (*sarpānch*) who was his great friend. The plot was proved by the fact that the merchant was able to sell the clothes for more than 200,000 rupees. Balakdas had died after this secret transaction because Hanuman had punished him for acting without the clear permission of the assembly and for his own benefit. The great freedom of individual nagas is given in the nature of sadhuship, as we have seen in the case of the tyagis, but office-bearers should be reminded that they may work only for the communal interest, which is safeguarded by the deity.

We have seen that Hanumangarhi gives much scope for individual careers which are to a great extent unlimited by institutional constraints. There is an age-grade system which every Ramanandi sadhu has to go through if he wants to become a naga. Before he is initiated as a naga in one of the great ceremonies of his akhara already mentioned, he has a rather inferior position and a limited field of action. Once a naga, however, much depends on his own abilities and ambitions. He can become pujari or even abbot, and he may initiate other sadhus. Another course of action would be to devote himself entirely to entrepreneurial activities. His naga connections may give him important advantages above other entrepreneurs, at least in activities like money-lending which are not devoid of violence. When exactly he loses the characteristics of a Ramanandi naga is very difficult to say. Though they are more tightly organized than the tyagi groups from which they have originated, the nagas have a great measure of individual freedom which cannot be controlled due to insufficient centralization of power and authority in their akharas.

As we have seen, Hanumangarhi is organized in a democratic way. It is the assembly of nagas which has the ultimate authority. This is the case in all the akharas of the three Vishnuite armies. However, if a naga feels that he is wronged by the assembly, he may take recourse to the secular courts of law. To be able to defend its policies, the assembly of Hanumangarhi decided to have its rules registered in the 1960s (see appendix). They are basically democratic rules which are intended to keep anarchical tendencies at bay, and clearly lay the authority to govern the institution in the hands of the assembly, while curbing the authority of the chosen officials. This ensures that the chief abbot cannot take all power into his own hands and declare himself the owner of the temple, which is quite often the case in the rasik temples to be discussed in the next section.

5. Rasiks

Finally, there is another group of Ramanandi sadhus in Ayodhya, whose religious life in entirely different in tone and quality from that of the tyagis and nagas. They are the most sedentarized among the Ramanandi sadhus. They do not roam throughout the country in itinerant groups (*jamāt*), nor does their religious practice remind us of the ascetic exercise of the tyagis or the military training of the nagas. Nevertheless, they do not form a separate order nor do they deny that tyagis and nagas are Ramanandis. This section of Ramanandi sadhus is called the *rasik* or *sakhī* community, which practices the 'sweet devotion' (*madhuropāsana*).

Before going into the theological explanation of these intricate terms, some ethnographical details of their way of life should be given. Since the foundation of Bara Asthana, the first rasik institution in Ayodhya, by Ramprasad in the early eighteenth century, the rasik sadhus have gradually come to dominate the religious scene of Ayodhya as a consequence of the high degree of sedentarization in their group.[28] They are the real sadhu inhabitants of Ayodhya. Inhabiting Ayodhya's many temples, they are not *alamgi* (without attachment or residence) like the tyagis, but *asthānadharis*, sadhus living in institutions. In this way they belong to Ayodhya's 'fixed' population, unlike the tyagis and, to some extent, the nagas. They may of course travel to their lay patrons in order to raise money for their temples, but that is fundamentally different from going about in itinerant groups.

At least one distinctive feature of the life of tyagis and nagas is to a great extent lacking in that of the rasiks: personal freedom in doctrinal and personal affairs. The emphasis of their devotional method (*sādhanā*) is on the worship of gurus and gods in temples. The degree of guru worship in their temples is remarkable. In India the guru is generally a person to be respected, not to say venerated, but in the temples of the rasiks this is taken several steps further. We may here speak of a guru worship which is not very different from the way God himself is worshipped. Indeed the rasiks compare and even sometimes equate the guru with God, and in each case he is seen as the path leading to God. The totally uncritical, reverential attitude of the sadhu and lay disciples towards their guru in the rasik temples sets them apart from those in other temples like the akharas, in which an altogether more democratic spirit reigns. Sociologically, the crucial fact seems to be that the abbotship of rasik temples is not decided by election, as in the itinerant groups of the tyagis or in the akharas of the nagas, but by pupillary succession. The inhabitants of a rasik temple commonly form a small community of sadhus, mostly no more than fifteen to twenty persons. The principal guru is the abbot who chooses one of his disciples to become his successor. The abbot actually owns the temple and the disciple is his heir. This makes it possible for some rasik temples to pass into the hands of one family, as when, for example, an abbot makes one of his cousins his disciple and heir. A counterforce is of course the community of sadhus, who may resent such a family solution to Ramanandi succession problems. In my fieldwork I witnessed two such cases in which a rasik abbot tried to make a member of his family his successor and was opposed by other rasik sadhus. At any rate, the fact that he owns the temple makes the position of the abbot-guru in a rasik temple definitely more powerful than that of his tyagi or naga colleagues, which is in a way reflected in the way his religious status is almost equal to that of God. The 'seeing' (*darshan*) of the guru is given a position in the temple worship not very different from that of the image. There is nothing fearful in this type of worship; it is rather different from the mixture of awe and fear which characterizes the disciple's attitude toward the ascetic feats of the tyagi or naga.

Sudhir Kakar isolates two psychological mechanisms in the guru-disciple relation: idealization and identification. The disciple is to a certain extent infantilized because he depends completely on the guru who is idealized as the 'good father', who is omnipotent and omniscient. Kakar attributes this to a 'hankering after absolute mental states free of ambiguity and contradiction in which the onerousness of responsibility is renounced together with the burdens of self-criticism and doubt' (Kakar, 1982: 47). There can be no doubt that guru worship as it is encountered in the rasik group does correspond to a large degree to Kakar's analysis.

The strongest emphasis on guru worship is to be found in the large rasik temple of Golaghat. Here the images have even been removed from the sanctum and instead a portrait of the first guru, who founded the temple, is worshipped. The present abbot Ramsuratsharan describes the spiritual path of the disciple as follows: he begins with natural love for his nurturing mother; the mother shows the way to the father, who becomes the child's first guru; after the father the Brahman purohit becomes the guru; and he is succeeded by the guru of a religious community who gives the community's mantra to the disciple. The mantra guru is what Ramsuratsharan calls the Sat guru, the guru who shows the way to Sat, the Immortal Being. Although the devotion towards the guru is in this temple extreme – every day his feet and hair are washed and the water used is drunk by the disciples as 'grace' (*prasād*) – it has features in common with other temples.

Most significant is the emphasis given to what is called *sringar*, erotic beautification, an entirely unascetic desire to make the temple and the sadhus beautiful with scents and rich cloth. The temple is seen as the place of the Lord. It is clear that it is in the opulent Kanak Bhavan (Golden Palace), a central place of rasik worship, that this idea can be given its highest expression (see appendix). In Kanak Bhavan there is an upper storey on which there are several rooms for the gods: a bedroom, a study-room/library, a *darbār* (court), a shrine and even a toilet. Entrance to this upper storey is restricted to Hindus or even Vishnuites, so that I was not allowed to see it, but I have been told that its splendour is magnificent. It is important to see that much emphasis is given to the beautification of the temple and rituals in the enactment of Ram and Sita's royal life. Everything is done to please the god, which is theologically underpinned by the theory of *Tatsukhī*, 'His happiness'. The god should be pleased by the service of his servants. This is the goal of religious action, not *Svasukhī*, 'one's own happiness'. Although all desires of the gods should be fulfilled, they should be fulfilled by a worshipper who himself is without desire, a somewhat puritan streak in an otherwise rather licentious religious activity.

Besides guru worship and beautification, therefore, the service of god (*sevā*) is also important. This is of course significant in the whole of the Ramanandi community, but it takes a different turn in the rasik tradition. In the common seva of the Ramanandis it is Ram, the Ultimate Being, who is served by the worshipper. In the rasik tradition it is the divine couple, Ram *and* Sita, what they call the *yugal sarkār*, 'the royal couple'. The worship of Ram and Sita together creates a problem. Male sadhus cannot serve Sita; they cannot, for examble, bathe her. Therefore when serving Sita they must think of themselves as women who are female friends (*sakhīs*) of Sita. According to the rasiks this idea originated when Ram and Sita returned from their exile to Ayodhya. Hanuman, among others, had asked to be allowed to serve not only Ram, but also Sita. They became the first sakhis of Sita. As sakhis they also got new names, as follows:

Hanuman	Charushila
Lakshman	Lakshmana
Vibhishan	Padmaganda
Sugriv	Vararoha
Bharat	Subhaga
Jambhavan	Sulochana
Shatrughna	Hema
Angada	Kshema

In this way there are eight sakhis of Sita, corresponding to major characters in the Ram story, but their names are sometimes changed as well as those of people connected with them; for example, the monkey-parents of Hanuman, Kesari and Anjana, become Shatrujita and Chandrakanti. To memorize all these equations of characters in the Ram story with their 'shadow' figures in the rasik version already requires a trained theological mind. I will not enter here into a description of all the theological intricacies, but it is significant to understand that it is extremely complicated and that theological knowledge is therefore much more highly valued among the rasiks than among the other Ramanandis.

Hanuman is given an importance in the rasik tradition equal to that which he enjoys in the rest of the Ramanandi community. In the rasik version, however, he is the intermediary between Sita and the disciple in his/her form of Sita's principal sakhi. The status of Hanuman has in this century been the cause of conflict between two groups of rasiks, which serves as an illustration of the political use of theological intricacies in this community.

In the thirties of this century Ramkishorsharan, an ordinary rasik sadhu, was living in the temple of Hanumatnivas. He had the idea that he should start a new rasik movement and wrote in collaboration with a Sanskrit scholar, pandit Sitaramsharan of the temple Nityaraghavakunj, a doctrinal work with the title of *Lomāshasamhitā*. Instead of stating that they were the authors they claimed that they had found (rediscovered) this ancient book which had been written by the sage Lomasha. The only important deviation in it from accepted rasik theory was that the name Charushila (for Hanuman) was changed to Chandrakala. When this book was published in Ayodhya the mahants of three important rasik institutions in Ayodhya, Lakshmankila, Golaghat and Janakighat, became angry and organized protest meetings against this violation of an old tradition. The two authors acquired, however, the support of an important rasik, Ramvallabhasharan of Satgurusthan, who was the guru of several important rajas in Bihar and therefore an influential man in Ayodhya. The mainstream mahants issued a pamphlet in which Ramvallabhasharan was asked to clarify his support of this innovation, but he died before being able to do so. His successor, a formidable Sanskrit scholar, Vedantiji, could not do otherwise than continue the support given by his deceased guru to the Chandrakala movement, although he could of course produce no other evidence besides the aforementioned. Finally, after fifteen years of rumours and scandals, a meeting of all the rasiks of Ayodhya was held in which the majority decided that the *Lomāshasamhitā* was a forged document and that Charushila was the sakhi incarnation of Hanuman and not Chandrakala. This decision was given on paper and signed by nineteen important rasiks. Only Hanumatnivas, the temple in which Ramkishorsharan lived, and Vedantiji's institution did not comply and to the present day they claim that Hanuman's name as a sakhi is Chandrakala, a tradition also followed by their many subsidiary temples.

No rasik, however, could explain to me the theological significance of that difference in name which had been the source of such heated debate. What was clear to everyone, on the other hand, was the political or, if you wish, the market value of the difference in name. The adherents of the Chandrakala name could argue that the other rasiks did not know the 'real nature' of Hanuman's sakhi transformation, and so emphasize their own knowledge of the correct spiritual path. With Chandrakala they had something new and special to offer to prospective adherents, an important thing on the religious market. This is also the reason why the other rasiks did not acquiesce in this deviation from received knowledge but ardently tried to suppress it. As far as I can see, in this and a few other cases religious entrepreneurs in the rasik movement tried, consciously, to make innovations in order to get a larger share of the religious market.

To give another example, the attempt to offer special religious attractions is also clear in festivals celebrated only in a few rasik temples; for example, *Cārmukhī*, 'four-headed' Hanuman's birthday, which falls on a different day from the normal birthday of Hanuman, and which is primarily celebrated in Hanumangarhi. When asked, the abbots concerned could adduce no textual evidence, either for the existence of 'four-headed' Hanuman or for the date of his birthday. It is only evident that it gives certain temples an opportunity to stage special performances.

As we have seen, the rasiks are theological specialists, who are primarily interested in matters of doctrine and worship. Their ideas and practices fall within Ram devotion and as such they are based on Tulsidas's *Rāmcharitmānas*. We have already observed that this work is the basis of what can generally be called Ramanandi theology. Tyagis and nagas also refer to it when explaining their attitudes. While tyagis emphasize the period when Ram lived in the jungle as a legitimation of their ascetic life-style, the nagas refer to the fights between Ram and Ravan as well as to the role of the monkey armies under Hanuman. The rasiks, however, stress the period when Ram lived with his wife Sita in Ayodhya. This place has a real aspect which can be observed empirically, but beneath it is a layer which can only be observed by esoteric means. As such it is the heavenly Saket, the world in which Ram and Sita perform their divine play (*līlā*). Ayodhya is the theatre of the Ram drama and the living souls (*jīva*) are incarnated only to serve its enactment.

This is the reason why the rasiks give so much emphasis to the dramatic aspects of their worship. This is especially true for the way they celebrate the festival of *Rām Vivāh* (Ram's marriage) in December, in which a great and beautifully decorated procession goes round the town and in several rasik temples marriage ceremonies are staged in which young Brahman boys play the parts of Ram and Sita. It is also true for the way the personal lives of the rasik sadhus are enacted. In the first chapter we saw how Umapati Tripathi, a renowned rasik of the nineteenth century, thought himself to be the guru of Ram and Sita and dramatized this idea in his worship and personal life to an extent which was annoying for his fellow-sadhus. Another example is a queen of a petty state who came to Ayodhya in the nineteenth century to devote her life to the worship of the divine couple. She even brought the images to the toilet and after a couple of minutes removed them and put costly juice and sweets (*laddus*) on this toilet as their waste, eventually removing this and offering it to devotees as 'grace' (*prasād*).

It should be clear by now that we have left the predominantly ascetic and violent life-style of the tyagis and nagas far behind and entered a world of esoteric drama which is to some extent sweet and erotic in tone and quality. To explain the fact that they belong to the same Ramanandi order as the tyagis and nagas, rasiks sometimes interpret the smearing of ashes (*vibhūti*) on the body, as is practised by the tyagis, as an act of beautification (*sringār*) in order to participate in Ram's divine play. Tyagis, however, laugh at this interpretation, which bears no relation to the meaning they attach to these practices. Sweetness (*madhurya*) is important in the rasik worship, and this sweetness may be upheld by nagas, but military training is an area of sadhu activity which is a far cry from the sweetness aspired to by the rasiks.

In fact, the rasiks have gone a long way towards copying religious practices and ideas that have been developed in the context of Krishna devotion. In my opinion we can even speak of a 'Krishnaization' of the Ram devotion by the Ramanandi rasiks.

THE 'KRISHNAIZATION' OF RAM BHAKTI

As we have seen, the story of Ram, first recorded in the Sanskrit *Rāmāyaṇa*, underlies much of the Ramanandi theology. Similarly, the Sanskrit *Bhagavata Purāṇa*, which narrates the life of Krishna, is the principal text of Bengali Krishna devotion. In North India this devotion has been spread by Krishnaite groups like the Pustimargis and the Gauriyas who settled in the Braj area around Vrindaban and Mathura in the course of the sixteenth century (Vaudeville, 1976).

Rup Goswami and his nephew Jiv Goswami were the foremost preceptors (*goswāmi*) of the Madhva Gauriya group which was 'founded' by the Bengali mystic Chaitanya. They developed a highly influential theology in which religious aesthetics and erotic emotionalism were combined. While I do not wish to embark upon a crude summary of their intricate theological system, it seems important to highlight some aspects of it which were adopted in the Ramanandi rasik doctrines. Central in Krishnaite theology is the so-called *ras* theory which was derived from Sanskrit poetics. The literary connoisseur of poetic theory was replaced by the devotee, while the aesthetic enjoyment of literary emotions was replaced by devotional enjoyment of the love of Krishna (cf. De, 1961: 167). The crucial terms in Sanskrit poetics are the almost untranslatable *bhāv* and *ras*. Dimock (1966: 48, 49) writes:

> The term *bhāva* in Sanskrit poetics indicates an intense personal emotion that becomes transformed by the qualities of poetry into a *rasa*, an impersonalized condition of pure aesthetic enjoyment. The Bengal Vaishnavas adapted this poetic theory to their concept of religious realization. To the Bengal Vaishnavas, *bhāva* is the worshipful attitude that the *bhakta* assumes towards Krishna; *rasa* is the experience of the pure bliss of the love relationship between the two ... The *bhāvas* that a *bhakta* can assume are of five basic kinds:
> 1. *Sānta-bhāva*, the emotions a worshipper feels when he considers Krishna as the supreme deity: awe, humbleness, and insignificance.
> 2. *Dāsya-bhāva*, the emotion that a servant feels towards his master: respect, subservience, dedication.
> 3. *Vatsalya-bhāva*, parental or fraternal affection, such as the parents and brother of Krishna feel towards him.
> 4. *Sākhya-bhāva*, the love that a friend feels for a friend, that the cowherd boys felt for Krishna.
> 5. *Madhurya-bhāva*, the highest and most intimate emotion of love, of lover for beloved, the love that the *gopis* felt for Krishna.

The guru helps the devotee to realize the bhava and to raise it to the height of ras. The madhurya-bhava, which is also called sringara-bhava, is the most important one, since it is the bhava felt by the cowgirls (*gopīs*) towards Krishna. Moreover, it is also felt by the principal gopī, Radha, who is Krishna's mistress. It is the king among the different kinds of ras (*ras-rāj*) and is therefore the principal subject of Krishnaite poetry.

Another aspect of Sanskrit poetics which has been adopted into Krishnaite theology is the difference between *svakīyā* women, i.e. those who are one's own, and *parakīyā* women, i.e. those who are unmarried or are married to another man. The *Bhagavata Purāṇa*, the principal text of the movement, describes the gopis as being married to the cowherds (*gopās*). By a kind of 'exegetical gymnastics' (Dimock, 1966: 56) the leading theologians Rup Goswami and Jiv Goswami argued that the gopis were in fact Krishna's svakiya women because the herdsmen had only consummated the marriage with illusory forms of the gopis (cf. De, 1961: 349). Later this theory was replaced by a full-fledged parakiya doctrine. The difference between svakiya and parakiya was considered to have consequences for the kind of love felt by the devotee. For a svakiya woman desires her husband for *kam*, the satisfaction of the self, whereas the parakiya woman wants the satisfaction of the beloved because of her true selfless love (*prem*). Moreover, an important emotion in Sanskrit poetry which was developed in the doctrine was the distress felt at separation (*virāha*), which can only be felt by parakiya women (Dimock 1966: 56).[29]

Not only do the erotic and esoteric meanings of this theology overlap; there is also a large area of interpretation in which what is overtly erotic is 'covered up' by mystical-esoteric interpretations. The yearning of Radha for her beloved Krishna, for example, is interpreted in terms of the yearning for God of the soul that is lost in illusion, and the desire of the union of the flesh as the desire for the *unio mystica*. The theological idea of the separation of the living soul from the World Soul is expressed in terms of *virāha*, love in separation. To my mind, it is true of all mystical 'bride' symbolism that it toys with what is hidden and forbidden in an accepted religious context.

The ideas and practices of the Ramanandi rasik tradition have been profoundly influenced by these Krishnaite theories, as is already evident from the term 'rasik'. Agradas seems to have initiated this current in Ramanandi theology as early as the sixteenth century, and from his time the Ramanandi monastery at Galta remained under the influence of the religious developments in nearby Braj, the Krishnaite centre. According to Sinha (1957: 171) the Ramanandi rasiks went regularly to Braj to learn from Krishnaite teachers before returning to their Ramanandi institutions to promulgate them. This practice was continued even in the eighteenth century, the period of great Ramanandi expansion. The ras theory was adopted in its entirety by the Ramanandis. The Ramanandi sadhus could easily point out that in their devotion the attitude of servitude (*dāsya-bhav*) was foremost, while in the Krishnaite devotion emphasis was laid on the intimate emotion of love (*madhurya-bhāv*). In my interviews with Ramanandi sadhus who are not of the rasik persuasion Ram is often called *Maryāda Purushottam*, the Lord who remains within the realm of propriety. Hawley (1903. 275–6) argues that in the Krishnaite pilgrimage dramas (*ras lilas*), as performed in Vrindaban, the life of maryada is often typified by that of a yogi. The yogic life-style is depicted in structural terms as involving effort. The cowgirls (*gopis*), however, are so much attracted to Krishna that they do not have to make any effort to come near to him. Their life-style belongs to the realm of love (*prem*) that defies structuring. While in Krishna bhakti structural boundaries are negatively valued and transcended in devotion to Krishna, the Ramanandis tend to see these restrictions as positive: Ram is a god of discipline. The difference between rasiks and other Ramanandis is that the former follow the Krishnaites in transcending the boundaries of normal life. They also tend to prefer the emotion of love (*prem*) to that of servitude (*dāsya*).

There are, however, considerable problems in incorporating Krishnaite ideas in devotion to Ram. The first difficulty is that Ram is decently married to Sita, whereas the Krishna story focuses on the relation between Krishna and his mistress Radha. This reminds us of the distinction between *svakīyā*, one's own women, and *parakīyā*, unmarried women or women married to other men. Ram is *ekpatnivrat*, loyal to one woman only who is married to him (*svakīyā*). There can be neither true selfless love (*prem*) nor love in separation (*virāha*) in such a case, at least according to traditional theory.[30]

The next difficulty is the difference between the cowgirls (*gopīs*), in the Krishna story and the *sakhīs* (women friends) in the Ram story.

While Radha is the leader of a troupe of cowgirls who may have an erotic and esoteric relationship with Krishna, the sakhis are simply the female friends of Sita who are only concerned with the happiness of the divine couple and who act as mere spectators of their marital joy.[31] To make the male helpers of Ram, his brother Lakshman and the monkey Hanuman, into the female friends (*sakhīs*) of Sita is already a *tour de force*. However, if one wants to go further than the attitude of a servant by emphasizing the emotion of sweet love with its erotic shades, as the rasiks definitely desire, the story of Ram and Sita has to be interpreted in a very imaginative way. It is, however, certainly true that the rasiks themselves regard their interpretation as perfectly convincing, though some of my other informants, Ramanandi sadhus and laymen alike, sometimes thought them a bit weird. The same could, however, be said about some of the tyagi ideas and activities, which also sometimes met with scepticism in non-tyagi circles.

Nevertheless, rasik practices do take things rather far. The female identification of male devotees is very strong. During the temple worship the sadhu puts on a female dress (*sāri*) and female ornaments. Some of the rasiks even wear these dresses and ornaments in public like transvestites. There are personal differences among the rasiks as to the extent of their identification as well as to the openness with which they behave. An esoteric feature of their life as females is that they sometimes observe the Hindu taboos of the menstruation period. These things are never openly discussed with outsiders, so that it is hard to go deeply into these matters. The relationship between sakhis and Ram is also a matter of esoteric secrecy. Although the rasiks emphasize that they are acting as unmarried innocent girls (*mugdhā*), I found that in at least some temples a part of the Hindu marriage ceremony (*kāragrahan*) was performed as a rasik initiation. In this way the sadhu was symbolically 'taken by the hand' by Ram who was subsequently not officially married with 'her', but could enjoy 'her' body. In this initiation the devotee identifies with one of the sakhis and enters into an erotic parakiya relation with Ram. These practices are, however, kept 'back stage' and could only be found out with considerable difficulty. The common 'front stage' view is that Ramanandi rasiks do not enjoy real erotic love for Ram, but help the divine couple to enjoy it.

In this way Tulsidas's Ram bhakti is 'krishnaized' by the rasik tradition in the Ramanandi community, yet the rasiks will not acknowledge the influence of the Krishna bhakti on their ideas. Ram's incarnation took place before that of Krishna in the Treta yuga and, according to some, he only left the *shringār ras*, the erotic state of bliss, for him. Moreover, in order to stress the absolute antiquity of the notion of ras they quote the *Taittiriya Upanishad* 2.7.1. '*Raso vai sah*' to the effect that he (Ram) is ras itself. It is, however, interesting to see that the Krishnaites use the same quotation as referring to Krishna, as was done by the preceptor of the Pustimarg, Vitthalnath, in his commentary on a work by Vallabha, the founder of the community. It is therefore ironic that the Ramanandi rasiks should use to prove the autonomous growth of their type of devotion a quotation which has been borrowed from the work of Krishnaites (Hawley, 1983: 278). In the context of our study it is not necessary to separate precisely the Krishnaite elements from the Ramaite elements in this rasik tradition. It is my feeling that the Krishnaite writers influenced rasik theology even down to minute details. I cannot prove this without going into a textual comparison of the works of rasik theologians and those of Krishnaite theologians, which would require an altogether different study by a different type of scholar. I must express, however, a feeling of surprise and astonishment that my notes on the theological views of one of the leading contemporary rasik theologians of Ayodhya, one Madhukariya, made during extended interviews, closely corresponded with the summary Edward Dimock gives of the theology of the sixteenth century Gauriya Jiv Goswami (Dimock, 1966: 46–9).

Since the establishment of the Bara Asthana at the beginning of the eighteenth century in Ayodhya the rasiks have spread over the city, and at least three other institutions, Lakshmankila, Golaghat and Janakighat, are leading centres of Ramanandi activity in Ayodhya. Lakshmankila is especially famous as a centre of theological learning. It attracts most of its disciples from Bihar, where the rasiks seem to have more influence than in Uttar Pradesh. Because of their sedentarized status they are, along with the nagas of the important akharas, the leading *magnati*, magnates of Ayodhya's religious and political life. They are the organizers of the great processions during its festivals, they sponsor the *Ram Lila*, the annual drama in which the life of Ram is performed on the streets of Ayodhya for a few days, and finally, as if there were not festivals enough, they compete with each other to invent new ones. They play an important role in the political life of Ayodhya because of their great resources and their influence on disciples spread over a large area of North India. In fact there are only some five or six important sadhu politicians in Ayodhya and of them three are rasiks and two or three are nagas. The rasiks are not only sedentarized, but also domesticated. Most of the rasik abbots have either been married and have children, but left their home when their children were old enough to manage things themselves, or have been lifelong celibates (*naisthik brahmacārīs*) who have taken an illegal wife. One might argue that this is a contradiction caused by the adoption of Krishnaite ideas in a monastic community like that of the Ramanandis. In the Krishnaite communities the abbots are mostly householders of Brahman caste, at least in the case of the Gauriyas and Pustimargis. The position of abbot is in those cases also hereditary. In the Ramanandi community we have on the contrary a democratically organized society of celibates who are related to each other by a putative spiritual kinship. This type of organization is readily compatible with peripatetic ascetic life, but becomes difficult in the context of a sedentarized devotional life, and the tensions in the Ramanandi community between the ideal of celibacy and the common practice of illegal sexual relations are the result of this difficulty.

Apart from the theological influence of the rasik tradition on the Ram bhakti of the Ramanandis, its influence on Ayodhya's festival calendar has also been of great importance. As we have seen, there are three big festivals in Ayodhya, *Rām Naumi*, *Kārttik Mela* and *Jhūlā*, as well as one middle-sized festival, *Rām Vivāh*. *Rām Naumi* is an ancient festival which was held to celebrate the birthday of Ram even before the arrival of the Ramanandis in Ayodhya. *Kārttik* is in fact a religious month full of celebrations throughout India, with slightly more emphasis among Vishnuites. The only thing special to Ayodhya is its big *parikram*, the walk around its sacred area performed by some 300,000 to 500,000 people, but it seems to be an ancient ritual. Relatively recent are the big *Jhūlā* or Swing festival and the celebration of *Ram Vivah*. The *Jhūlā* festival is a borrowing from the Krishna devotion of Braj and received special attention and sponsorship from the raja of Ayodhya at the end of the nineteenth century. The *Rām Vivāh* is also a predominantly rasik affair, a real *līlā* or religious mystery play with a marriage procession and the performance of the marriage ceremony in which Brahman boys impersonate the gods. Only part of the marriage ceremony is performed, otherwise the two boys would really be married to each other. Obviously, drama cannot be sufficiently separated from rituals when it is staged in a temple. Besides these great festivals there is a plethora of minor ones, in which the rasiks especially take great interest, since it is with them that the devotional notions of beautification, celebration and drama have really taken root.

6. Conclusion: the Ramanandis, an open category

My attempts so far have been to bring some understandable order into the historical and organizational flux which has come to be named as the Ramanandi community. We have concentrated on the order of Ramanandi sadhus rather than on the Ramanandi community as a whole, with all its specialists and laymen. Just as there is little order in the 'monastic order' of Ramanandi sadhus, which forms the specialist nucleus of the community, there is not much order in the composition of the multitudes who are either their lay disciples or just worshippers in their temples and around their fires. It is, however, the task of the anthropologist to make the sociocultural reality we have investigated understandable for the outsider. In this 'translation' of the reality of the Ramanandi order there is an almost irresistible urge to pin down the flux to a state of fixedness, to solve problems with paired opposites such as 'caste' and 'sect', or householder and ascetic, or, more central to my endeavour, devotion and asceticism. I am confident that I have not succumbed to these academic temptations, but I am not so sure that I have conveyed a comprehensible picture of who the Ramanandi sadhus are. A major problem is raised by the place of history in this investigation. To bring some system into my data I have been forced to understand 'synchronic' facts by means of 'diachronic' hypotheses. For example, I was faced with the problem of why, in a Vishnuite bhakti community, some specialists had recourse to ascetic methods resembling those of Shivaite Tantrics, while others used a kind of bride-mysticism which bore a much closer resemblance to the practices of other Vishnuite bhakti communities but was evidently somewhat contrary to the moralistic tone of the Ramanandis' basic text, the *Rāmcharitmānas* of Tulsidas. There can be no doubt about the relevance of history when attempting to understand the apparent contradictions of the 'synchronic' facts. But in this case history is the opposite of some inflexible, definite truth accessible to all who are interested. It is a resource in the political strategies of the present and, contrary to what Appadurai proposes, a rather plastic resource at that.

We have seen in at least two cases that the past was reinterpreted or rather reinvented to serve the purposes of the present. The first case was the 'rediscovery' by some rasiks of an ancient text which clearly said that Hanuman was not Charushila in his sakhi form, but Chandrakala. For an outsider it is difficult to understand that the mere changing of fictional names can have a tremendous market value, but for the Ramanandi rasik insiders it was clear enough: they at once started to agitate against this 'forgery'. The second case was the Shri-Vaishnava link claimed by early Ramanandis at the end of the sixteenth century, when the Ramanandi community began to be formed. This claim, based upon a desire to belong to a respectable Vishnuite tradition (*sampradāya*), was withdrawn when contacts with the real South India Shri-Vaishnavas became unpleasant and insulting in an India in which caste and anti-caste feelings had gradually grown in importance and ideological value. These two cases are very striking, but not isolated or exceptional examples of 'historical strategies' in Hindu India. Although India is a literate civilization, there is nothing of the fixed centrality of tradition which is often assumed by anthropologists. Oral traditions are easily written into printed pamphlets and antedated religious books. Printing presses abound in small places like Ayodhya, just as bookshops and opposing religious and social claims can be readily established and then disappear just as easily. In such a society one has to be very careful in trusting the printed word, since one easily makes mistakes on this slippery ground.

Instead of making history of what is essentially the political use of the past in the present we should ask ourselves how this plasticity of the past comes about, and why it has not been used to create a logical, rational myth in which all the contradictions are obliterated. The first important point to observe is that although we have been speaking of a 'Ramanandi community' and a 'Ramanandi order' there are no such things, and thus there can be no creation of *one* logical rational myth. The Ramanandi identity has grown gradually in North India and in this process two developments seem to have been extremely important: the growing popularity of the Ramcharit-manas and the combined expansion of the religious market of pilgrimage and the secular market of trading and soldiering in the eighteenth century. The *Rāmchāritmanas* became a common text for sadhus of diverse spiritual lineages, all of which transmitted the Ram mantra but sometimes had opposite ascetic and devotional methods. Theologically it was clearly an 'open' text on which asceticism and both saguna and nirguna bhakti could be based without difficulty, but as a narration of the adventures of Ram it gave something definite to the followers of the Ram cult. We have already noted that when Tulsidas's contemporary Nabhaji attempted to lump all these followers of Ram together into one community, founded by a saint called Ramanand, they were too numerous and diverse. Only in the eighteenth century do we find more definite accounts of a Ramanandi order, which seems to be organized for the purposes of trading and soldiering. In the same century we find reports of the 'rediscovery' of Janakpur and the 'restoration' of Ayodhya as well as accounts of regular fighting between Dashanami and Ramanandi nagas. This is the period in which the theological development, which began with Tulsidas, acquired an organizational form in the Ramanandi community. Even so, we should not make too much of these developments. It is more a question of common identity than of a formal group, and the reason why is not difficult to guess. Sadhus are free individuals and, if they are organized at all, then it is in a loose and democratic fashion. They are in fact a wild and open category until they are tamed by sedentarization. The only relationship which really counts is that between guru and disciple, and the latter may decide to leave whenever he thinks he can improve his spiritual and worldly prospects. For free-roaming sadhus such a thing as affiliation only becomes important at the twelve-yearly Kumbh Melas. On the other hand, as Carrithers and Strenski rightly observed, their identity is partly defined by their relation with the lay supporters. Freedom is never unstructured by boundaries and the openness of the sadhu's identity is structured by his relations with the society of lay supporters.

Another important observation to be made is the flexibility of theology. This is not in itself a surprising observation, since it is already implicit in remarks of textual scholars that Hinduism is not 'orthodox' but 'inclusivistic'. 'God is one', a Hindu guide will say when a western tourist points out the multitude of gods in the temples. This is a basic attitude among laymen in Hindu civilization, but I have been amazed at the extent to which even religious specialists adhere to this position. Shiv can be worshipped because he himself is the foremost devotee of Lord Ram. Hanuman is worshipped together with Shiv/Bhairav by the Nath yogis, and the same is true for some Ramanandi tyagis. There is no difficulty here, since Hanuman is regarded as an incarnation of Shiv. At the same time this valiant warrior, this mahayogi, is a sweet female friend of Sita and secretly a mistress of Ram. But a tyagi or naga will smile and say this is only a rasik belief. 'Why do they not create a schism?' a desperate Calvinist would ask. The anthropologist would answer that this theological flexibility is in fact a prerequisite of the Ramanandis' open identity. There are few theological restraints, apart from the need to acknowledge the importance of the *Rāmcharitmānas* and the Ram mantra, so that rasiks, nagas and tyagis can live happily together in one tirtha, Ayodhya.

Nevertheless there are a few structural themes and historical trends which may clarify the changing nature of what I have summarily called an 'open category'. Structurally there are the opposite themes of ascetic renunciation and emotional surrender, of an open and peripatetic life-style against a closed and sedentarized one, while historically the trend seems to be that of the taming of the ascetic. First we have the prototypical Hindu ascetic, the tyagi. He is a wild man with matted hair. His body is smeared with ashes of the holy fire in which the perishable body is cremated and from which the cosmos is created. The external fire is internalized through *tapas*, the heating of the body. At the same time sexuality is repressed, in extreme cases even by the violent means of castration. The heating of the body creates magical power (*shakti*), but to retain his vital energy he has to keep his fiery seed drawn up within his body. The life-style of the tyagi requires him to reject the sedentarized life of towns and villages. He has to live in the woods and lead a natural life, naked or clothed in the raw products of nature and eating the fruits of the jungle. *Nihamgi* (without wife or family) and *alamgi* (without residence) are his epithets. As a tyagi he is a

Ramanandi, but as a tyagi he also has much in common with Nath Yogis and Dashanami samnyasis, other sadhus who roam in the jungle. He is not afraid of them because he carries weapons and may call for the help of his trained colleagues, the nagas. Although he may carry images of Ram and Hanuman, he is not really an image worshipper. He believes in the nirguna reality of Ram and that through his tapas he will not only acquire power but also reach godhead within himself. Caste is not important for him, since he has left all that behind. There is democratic brotherhood between him and the other tyagis and the real distinctions are made on the basis of ascetic accomplishments.

However, when our tyagi leaves the jungle with his jamat to collect food and other means of support for his life-style, he has to offer something to the laymen in the villages and towns. In that world caste has become increasingly valued, as has the devotional worship of images. It is not simply that the villagers do not want to have anything to do with the Shivaite type of asceticism. On the contrary, they will still worship the free-moving, powerful and in essence god-like tyagi. Even so, Vishnuite bhakti has swept the countryside. It might be a long-term process, since Vaudeville (1974) points out that it was already widespread in the fifteenth and sixteenth centuries, while Pocock (1973) has shown that at least in some parts of the country it is still going on. Caste gained in strength during the nineteenth century and in our century its closed, exclusive and Brahmanical form, as known to us from ethnographical literature, has probably been on the increase. The tyagi then, who pursues his wild asceticism, is not left alone in the jungle. He has to conform to a certain extent to the changing religious market. In this way the tone and nature of his asceticism are also changed.

Formerly, over a period of several centuries, wild asceticism was an interesting and promising option. The tyagis and nagas wandered in jamats throughout the country and offered not only religious teaching to the villagers and the merchants of the qasba, but also horses, camels, money and many other articles of long-distance trade. Like *naukari* (service as a migrant soldier), tyagiship or nagaship was a career open to all. It should not surprise us to learn that it was places of pilgrimage like Baksar that were important as labour markets for soldiery (Kolff, 1983). The soldiers were not much interested in caste identity anymore, but acquired an open identity of 'Baksariya' or 'Rajput'. Kolff shows that it was especially the Rajput identity which was acquired in soldiery, and that this identity originally had clear ascetic overtones. These mobile bands ruled the countryside between the nodal points in the market-system of the Moghul empire and when they did not have a 'religious' identity, they had a religious background.

This world, which gave great opportunities for 'open categories' like migrant soldiers and ascetic trader-soldiers, disappeared gradually in the nineteenth and twentieth centuries during the *Pax Britannica*. While the eighteenth century was the period which saw its greatest expansion, this era came to a characteristic end in the so-called Sannyasi rebellion, in which ascetics of different orders fought the British in a protracted battle that lasted from 1770 to 1800, and they were finally defeated.[32] This is not to say that the peripatetic life of the tyagis was brought completely to a halt. Soldiering acquired a different form in the British army; for example, in the Bengal army in which Brahmans began to dominate and caste to play an important role.[33] Trading went on, however, although it seems that the sadhus had already lost their dominant position by the beginning of the nineteenth century. Like the *Banjaras*, the gypsy travellers, the jamats of the sadhus still played an important part in long-distance trade in camels and horses, but this role also became less important when railways and other forms of transport which used an improved infrastructure of roads and waterways were stimulated by the British in the last decades of the nineteenth century (cf. Varady, 1980). Gradually the Banjaras disappeared from the stage and were followed, at a somewhat slower pace, by the jamats of the tyagis. We have seen the results in Ayodhya: a hundred portable images were placed in the shrine of the Tyagi institution Tapasviji kicchauni and during my fieldwork the last famous 'peripatetic sadhu' died.

What is characteristic of our prototypical tyagi, then, is his belonging to an 'open category', one which provided enormous opportunities over a long historical period. To leave the civilized world of family life for the wild jungle of asceticism was a promising option. To belong to an open category meant forgetting one's caste identity, or made that ascriptive identity relatively unimportant when compared with the new identity of tyagi. Open recruitment and relaxation of caste rules of commensality clearly belong to a peripatetic life and my low-caste informants have always stressed this aspect. In the jamat there is a kind of brotherhood which is not controlled by the scrutiny of a lay population which follows the caste regulations. The historical trend I have outlined above has limited this option gradually, but never totally. It can best be called a sedentarization or taming of the ascetic.

The nature of the ascetic theme among the Ramanandis is clear enough and does not significantly differ from that among other ascetic orders: gathering heat, vital energy, and not losing it by discharging semen. It is more of a method than a theology, but there is a common theological notion about the ultimate oneness of the microcosm (the body) and the macrocosm. World Soul and Soul (Brahman and Atman) are one and a goal of the method is to realize this oneness. When the World Soul is given the name of a personal god, like Shiv or Vishnu or Ram, the way to devotion is open. The World Soul booomes adorable, is to be worshipped, but that in itself does not imply a change in the life-style of the ascetic, for he may, like Kabir, refuse to worship objects. The World Soul is without attributes or qualities (*nirguna*). He may go a step further and worship natural objects like stones (shalagram), or trees or plants (tulsi), but not images.

To my mind a qualitative change is effected by the worship of immovable, anthropomorphic images which properly belong in temples situated in villages or towns. They are worshipped in a cult which is dominated by 'pure' Brahmans who can act as intermediaries between the god and the impure world. When the followers of the ascetic Chaitanya, the Gauriyas of Bengal, started to find or 'rediscover' images of Krishna in the Braj area, they also started to found temples and abandoned peripatetic life. A 'natural' outcome of this was that guruship became hereditary in Brahman families. Of course the Krishna cult and the Ram cult had already known image worship for a long time, but it had been dominated by Brahman groups who acted as mere priests. A large Krishna temple was built at Mathura, just as there were large Ram temples in Ayodhya, but they probably belonged to Brahman castes and not to the specialists of religious communities. Whatever may have been the exact historical process, it is clear that the great diversity of religious groups which gave the name Ram to the ultimate reality gradually crystallized into two types: those who preferred itinerant ascetic life and those who preferred sedentarized worship of images in temples. Within the open category of Ramanandis both tendencies can be seen throughout their history.

The special character of the Ramanandi order is that it includes both the wild life of the tyagis and the tamed life of the rasiks. What first attracts attention is its openness. Everyone is given the Ram mantra and the necklace of tulsi beads as a replacement of the *yajnopavit* cord which signifies the second birth of the 'twice-born' (*dvijās*). Settled in a tirtha like Ayodhya, however, this openness becomes more closed. The image can only be washed and fed by dvijas who thus monopolize the important function of pujari. In all the important temples the abbots are Brahman. Sadhus of low caste have low positions. The ascriptive caste identity forces itself upon sadhus who live near the watchful householders. Caste plays a role, not only within the order but also in the order's relations with laymen, and this is increasingly so when caste grows in importance as it seems to have done in the course of the later nineteenth century and the beginning of the twentieth century. To be the lay disciple of a guru of lower caste makes the disciple seem inferior. To be a member of the Ramanandi community has to be a respectable affair and it was with this in mind that the Ramanandis first sought fictional affiliation with the ancient community of Shri-Vaishanavas and later rejected it.

The sedentarization of Ramanandi sadhus in temples with image worship had various important implications. Image worship has its own methods which are different from those employed by tyagis. The religious method changed into a mystical eroticism, borrowed from the gurus of the Krishna devotion. Instead of violently disciplining the body – a violence also externalized in the use of weapons – the dominant mood became one of attractively decorating the body, like a female's. Sexuality was no longer suppressed or even terminated by castration, but was played out in religious dramas which could be overtly interpreted in mystical ways, but which also had secret dream-like interpretations. These rasik methods of worship have greatly altered the quality of life in Ayodhya. The rasiks are masters in decorating their temples and have originated some of Ayodhya's greatest festivals. In their temples the democratic character of the free-moving jamat is completely lost. The temples are not owned by the assembly of sadhus, like those of tyagis and nagas, but by the mahants. The mahant can choose a successor, a favourite disciple, and he will inherit the temple. The mahant is worshipped like a god, not because of his magical and ascetic accomplishments, but because he is the necessary intermediary between the disciple and the god (or rather the goddess Sita). He has to be a man of knowledge, a Sanskrit theologian and preferably a Hindi poet.

Celibacy becomes something of a problem with the rasiks. It is the hallmark of Ramanandi sadhuship, but what is the necessity of it when Lord Ram himself was married to Sita and it is this marriage which is celebrated? Moreover, the *vairāgya* of the Vishnuites means 'passionlessness', and this can and should be the tone of married life. Ram himself gave a good example of this in his marriage with Sita. *Kām* (lust) should be removed from marriage and replaced with *prem* (selfless love). In fact these ideas are also found among the Krishna devotees, whose gurus are householders. It seems we have here arrived at a constraint on the flexibility of Ramanandi behaviour, since celibacy is still the only approved way of life. There are of course – especially among the rasiks – compromises with the Brahmanical *varṇāshrama* theory, implying that one can choose celibacy in a later stage of life after having had male progeny, but celibacy should be followed if one wants to be a Ramanandi sadhu. The hidden possibility is, of course, to keep a mistress and this is done surprisingly often. It is remarkable how important caste is for the performance of, for example, pujariship, while celibacy can be transgressed without great difficulty, though never overtly. Once during my fieldwork it transpired that in an important temple a pujari had claimed that he was a dvija, when he was in fact of low caste. He was beaten almost to death and expelled from the temple. At the same time there are several abbots who keep – as everyone knows – a woman or even more than one, yet nothing is done about it. Nevertheless, contrary to reasonable expectation, celibate sadhuship is still a prerequisite for the status of guru in the Ramanandi community. These reasonable expectations, moreover, are not modern, but were already expressed by Nesfield in the middle of the nineteenth century:

There is one celibate order which threatens ere long to become a caste, and by precisely the same process that made the Goshayens (scil. Gosains-Dashanami sannyasis) one. This is the order of Bairagis who hold about the same degree of influence and wealth among the Vishnuite orders that Goshayens hold among the Shivite. Thus far no such thing as marriage is openly recognised among them. But they have acquired vested interests in many of the temples and other places sacred to Vishnu or to deified men and animals who are associated with his history. The great Hanumangarhi at Ayodhya, the fort of the flying monkey-god who aided Rama in the invasion of Lanka, which is visited every day of the year by pilgrims from all parts of India, is in the hands of the Bairagis. In fact the whole of Ayodhya, the city so sacred to the hearts of all Hindus, is overrun by this grasping and mendacious order, who point to one house as the spot where Rama was born, to another as the house in which he played as a child, to another as the courtyard in which his father, Dasharatha, administered justice, and so forth, and they exact a liberal fee for the information. The same kind of fate has attended many of the other cities or temples sacred to Vishnu or his incarnations ...

In another way too Bairagis are following in the footsteps of Goshayens. They have acquired large properties in land given them by pious laymen as offerings to Vishnu and for the benefit of the poor. The boy disciples whom they initiate into their order are often their illegitimate sons, and it is to such disciples that they bequeath the lands given to them for a purpose so entirely different. Probably the day is not far distant when marriage will be openly recognised as one of the customs of the order, and the Bairagis will then have become a caste like the Goshayens. (Nesfield, 1885: 60).

Nesfield's description, in the moralistic tone of his time, of the state of affairs in the nineteenth century is still of interest for the problem we are discussing. The two ultimate options are either caste and marriage or sadhuship and celibacy. The importance of being an open category may have declined during the last century and a half, but evidently it remains important enough to be adhered to. This is not difficult to understand. The only caste which could, with a reasonable prospect of success, emerge from the Ramanandi order is that of the Brahmans who are able to specialize in temple worship. A mixed caste of Bairagis, originating from the fusion of the various dvija castes of which the order is composed, would have as little success as the so-called *gosain* castes. In fact these latter castes have left real religious professions and have become lower land-tilling castes spread over the countryside. In the same way there are also Bairagi castes, but they are regarded by laymen and sadhus alike as 'fallen ascetics', outside of the Ramanandi order. That the Brahmans would be able to take over the organization completely by instituting hereditary guruship within their families is in fact impossible so long as there is an open recruitment of dvijas and to a certain extent also non-dvijas into the order. Therefore we may conclude that the Ramanandi sadhus will probably remain an open category socially as well as theologically, since this gives them the best chance of survival.

IV The sacred as a profession

1. Introduction

Ayodhya is a *tīrtha*, a place of pilgrimage. Its most characteristic religious specialists are the *paṇḍās* or *tīrthpurohits*, and not the Ramanandi sadhus who have only gradually settled in such pilgrimage centres. The title *tīrthpurohit* simply means 'priest of the pilgrimage centre', as distinct from the title *kulpurohit* which means 'priest of the family'. It seems to have a more honorific connotation than the title panda which is used in common parlance. Panda derives from the Sanskrit word *paṇḍita*, which means 'he who has knowledge' and which is commonly used in North India to address Brahmans. Many of the North Indian pilgrimage centres have panda communities. In Hardwar we find Gaur Brahmans working as pandas, in Mathura Chaube Brahmans, while in Allahabad they are called Prayagwals, in Benares Gangaputras, and in Gaya Gayawals. In Ayodhya there are two rival panda communities, called Bhareriya and Gangaputra respectively. They are in constant conflict over the right to practise the panda profession. Both communities claim to be ancient Brahman endogamous castes which have been exclusively devoted to the panda profession since the time of Lord Ram.

The Hindu pilgrim visits Ayodhya for a number of reasons, not all of which are made explicit. The purpose most often mentioned to me was to acquire merit, *puṇya* or *kalyāṇ*, but often a more implicit purpose was to get rid of impurity (*asauca*), sin (*pāp*), or illness (*rog*). In general, the pilgrim will not make a clear distinction between the worship of Ram in the Ramanandi temples and the worship of Brahmans, gods and ancestors on the bank of the river. To some extent, however, an analytic distinction can be made between, on the one hand, a *spiritual* complex, in which the devotion to Ram is central and which is dominated by Ramanandi sadhus who are specialized in a specific theology and mode of worship of Ram, and, on the other hand, a *ritual* complex, which is dominated by Brahman pandas who are specialized in those rituals of Brahmanism for which tirthas are the appropriate places. In fact, this is largely an organizational distinction, which is of greater significance to the specialists themselves than to the average pilgrim, to whom all the ritual acts he performs in Ayodhya have an interconnected meaning. When he wants to worship Lord Ram in a temple he needs the assistance of a Ramanandi sadhu who acts as an officiating priest in the worship (*pūjā*) of Ram. When he wants to worship the river Sarayu or the religious area (*kshetra*) of Ayodhya, or to perform an ancestor ritual, or take a ritual bath in the Sarayu, he needs the assistance of a panda. Although the pandas live in Ram's birthplace, they do not have to be disciples of Ramanandi gurus. Often they are of Smarta or Shivaite persuasion, but this is not at all problematic for the pilgrims.[1] The Hindu needs the ritual guidance of a panda in a number of specific rituals and not his spiritual guidance.

In the first chapter we saw that the literal meaning of the Sanskrit word tirtha is 'ford' or 'crossing-place' and that it is used for places where one might cross the river. Ayodhya is the site of a ford on the bank of the Sarayu, a sacred river, which 'just like the Ganges' is thought to originate in heaven and to flow vertically from the celestial lake of divine waters, down through the atmosphere, and out on to the face of the earth. Sarayu is thus connected with heaven and 'to cross the river' at the tirtha Ayodhya may mean, metaphorically, to come into contact with heaven. Many of the rituals in which the pandas are specialized are therefore performed on the bank of the river Sarayu. The riverbank is parcelled out by the pandas into a great number of plots on which they have erected their stalls, often not much more than a couple of wooden four-posters placed along the riverside in rectangular formation. The word *chowkee* is used for both the plot and the stall. The riverside is further divided into bathing-areas (*ghāṭs*), which sometimes have stone steps (*pakkā*) or are simply the sandy bank of the river (*kacchā*). The boundary between pakka and kaccha ghats is formed by a modern bridge, constructed between 1960 and 1964. The pandas, when they are not engaged in performing rituals, sit at their stalls and wait for pilgrims to come. Their agents are posted at the bus and railway stations to welcome pilgrims and conduct them to these stalls.

The stalls not only bear a sign with the name of the panda, but also a symbol, such as an elephant or a bicycle, so that the illiterate pilgrim will also be able to recognize the stall of his panda. The rituals are, however, not only performed on the bank of the river, but also in the pandas' houses. Often pilgrims stay in houses or lodges (*dharmshālās*) belonging to the pandas, mostly only for a night, but sometimes for a month if they perform the meritorious act of living for a fixed period in a tirtha, *kalpvās*.[2] The Gangaputra pandas live mostly in the ward Svargadvar, the oldest ward of Ayodhya, just behind the central brick wharves. They have eight patrilineages, consisting of some twenty households, closely connected by intermarriage. The Bhareriya pandas, whose community consists of a few hundred families, are spread throughout the city, the more successful among them living near the bus and railway stations. Its social boundaries are difficult to draw for reasons I will discuss later.

Some of the pandas not only wait upon the pilgrims who come to their stalls or houses, but also go themselves on a kind of 'inverted pilgrimage' to those pilgrims with whom they have a more permanent, so-called *jajmānī* (patronage) relationship. In such cases the panda is the hereditary Ayodhya priest of Hindu families living in different parts of – mainly – North India. When visiting his *jajmān* (literally 'patron of the sacrifice') the priest brings sacred articles such as Sarayu water, some red paste which is smeared over Hanuman and distributed among devotees, and *prasād* (literally 'grace') in the form of some food or fruit which has been offered to Ram. Moreover, he himself is the representative of the sacred place and by worshipping him the jajman worships Ayodhya. In this way a jajman can keep in touch with the tirtha without visiting Ayodhya. The jajman can also perform all kind of rituals in which the panda can officiate. Often gifts are given to the panda in a special ritual, but in addition the panda is in each case given some payment in cash or kind for his services.

Having given, by way of introduction, this brief sketch of the pandas and their activities, I would like to come to the theoretical and ethnographical issues with which this chapter is concerned. Often when I tell Indian friends that I am doing research on pandas, they try to warn me about these 'illiterate, dangerous people': 'Peter, beware, they are murderers and thieves, real toughs, *goondas*.' There is no doubt that the general reputation of pandas is very low. What is more, this reputation is partly based on incontrovertible facts. The life of the pandas of Ayodhya is extremely violent. Murders, robberies and large-scale fighting are part of their common experience. The atmosphere reminds one more of the world of the Sicilian Mafia than of the rosy western image of non-violent Hinduism.

Moreover, this situation also contrasts starkly with much of what has been written by anthropologists and indologists about the position of the Brahman priest. In religious ideology, as formulated in the Brahmanical Sanskrit texts, the Brahman is a god on earth. Anthropologists like Dumont, who have taken these texts as their starting point, have developed theories on the status hierarchy of the Hindu caste system, in which the Brahman is shown to be its apex. However, such theories become somewhat problematic when, for example, we become aware of the ill repute in which the Ayodhya pandas are held. This point has been made in recent publications by anthropologists who have been working on Brahman priests in North and South India (Parry, 1980, Fuller, 1984; Van der Veer, 1985). Even so, to my mind much of the discussion on the position of the Brahman priest remains trapped in an orientalist perspective on Hinduism which I am inclined to question.

A moot point in this context is the interpretation of the giving of gifts (*dān*) to Brahmans, one of the major ritual acts in Hinduism. How is this ritual related to the Brahmanical theory of sacrifice and to what extent is the Brahman's pre-eminence threatened by his dependence on the gifts of others? An important tendency in recent anthropological literature on the subject is to explain the relative inferiority of Brahman priests *vis-à-vis* other Brahmans and, more generally, their low reputation as a result of their acceptance of gifts. Part of the argument is that the Brahman priest is negatively valued in comparison with the 'ideal Brahman', the independent world renouncer. We will have to confront this issue from a historical and anthropological angle. Due attention has to be given to the fact that value orientations, which inform Hindu status ranking, tend to be affected by a process of historical change, in which the existence of the priest and the visiting pilgrims is transformed. It is certainly difficult to explain the present behaviour and values of the pandas, as well as their status ranking, by resorting to unchanging textual views of the 'ideal Brahman' as a kind of measure by which to determine the distance between ideal and practice. I hope to show that the circumstances of the pandas have changed dramatically in the last century and a half and that this change has affected their status, behaviour and values.

The major issue in this chapter, therefore, is to clarify the connections between changing social configurations, such as the development of a pilgrimage market, and the field of religious experiences, values and fantasies. Important for this study is an understanding of the change in the configuration of the rival panda communities of Bhareriyas and Gangaputras in the light of more comprehensive transformations in North Indian society, such as the growing importance of pilgrimage and the establishment of the *Pax Britannica* in the course of the last century. A central development to be studied is the transformation of a pilgrimage system, in which Ayodhya pandas contracted hereditary jajmani relations with only a happy few among the North Indian élite who took the trouble to come there on pilgrimage, into a system in which pilgrimage to Ayodhya grew considerably in terms of the number of pilgrims partaking in this status ritual as well as in the variety of social groups to which the pilgrims belong. This development gave rise to bitter conflicts between Gangaputras and Bhareriyas, whereas the interference of the colonial state determined to a great extent its direction and outcome. The emergence of so-called traditional rights to practise the profession of panda in the beginning of the colonial period brings us to an investigation of the social identities of both the Gangaputra and Bhareriya groups. I shall attempt to show that to depict such groups as static, isolated entities, that is as 'castes' in a worn-out anthropological sense, is considerably to misrepresent historical reality. The general proposition here would be that the caste-like identities of both the Gangaputras and the Bhareriyas are the product of forces impinging on the group from within as well as those impinging on them from without (cf. Epstein, 1978: 102). These identities are constructed in what is primarily a political process. The rules of interaction and categorization are defined and redefined according to changing interests (cf. Vincent, 1974).

Finally we will have to discuss the striking contradiction between the present life-style of the pandas and the realities of the pilgrimage market on the one hand and the fact of pilgrimage with its aims of acquiring merit, purification and expiation on the other. It is certainly not easy to understand, for example, the contradiction between the expiatory role of a panda, who acts as the representative of the tirtha Ayodhya in a ritual meant to absolve a man of the sin (*pāp*) of murder, and his own mafia-like activities. This may seem a non-issue in the eyes of cynics who will see it as a matter of course that every religion has a 'front stage' of ritual and theology and a 'back stage' of conflicts over petty interests. To my mind the issue is not simply one of front stage/back stage, but has to be understood in the light of the almost complete breakdown of a pilgrimage system in which jajmani relations between patrons and priest as well as other 'traditional' rights had been central, and the emergence of a totally impersonal pilgrimage market, in which the control of the flow of pilgrims came to be dominated by agents living in the catchment areas; just as at the beginning of the nineteenth century, with the expansion of the scale of pilgrimage, violence was resorted to for acquiring and preserving a share in what indeed may be called a market. The configuration has, however, changed considerably. In the nineteenth century it was the competition between two groups with different identities, Gangaputra and Dhaierlyas, which led to violence. In this century it is the attempt of only a few Brahmans, and finally merely one Gangaputra entrepreneur, to monopolize the entire pilgrimage market which causes the violence.

What I want to present here is therefore a historical-anthropological perspective on the changing social position of Brahman priests in a pilgrimage centre, which can be read as a critique of a-historical orientalist positions. This historical orientation raises certain methodological difficulties, since it is clear that while the change in social configurations can to a certain extent be assessed, the connected change in 'mentalities' and 'identities' is much more difficult to grasp. As in the case of the Ramanandis, the problem is compounded by the fact that the past has a function in the present and consequently we will have to pay much attention to this function. Contrary to Collingwood's famous adage that 'to ask questions you see no prospect of answering is the fundamental sin in science', I would emphasize the necessity of asking some such questions and of partially answering them if we want to go beyond the symbolic reading of religion as a kind of literary text and to introduce an understanding of the changing social conditions in which our informants have to enact their rituals.

In the next section I will try to summarize the current discussion of the status of the Brahman priest with special reference to the theory and practice of the gift-ritual. The third section will deal with the enlargement in the scale of pilgrimage to Ayodhya in the nineteenth century, its consequences for the ritual specialists, and the influence of British administrative measures on the formation of professional identities. The fourth section will highlight the emergence of a money-based, large-scale pilgrimage market, in which agents who bring pilgrims to Ayodhya play a role of growing importance, while some pandas develop entrepreneurial activities. A large part of this section will be devoted to the violent career of one panda who has managed to obtain a major share in the market during the last thirty or forty years. These two historical and ethnographical sections will bring us to the conclusion that to understand the values and the behaviour of the Ayodhya pandas we have to understand their changing conditions of existence.

2. The ideal Brahman as an ideological construct[3]

A GOD ON EARTH

According to an ancient cosmological myth the social organism was the body of Purusha, the primeval Man. This original body was cut up to form four specialized *varna* or social categories. The Brahman varna was born from the mouth of Purusha and had the duty of teaching and studying the Veda, performing sacrifices for two of the lower varnas, and accepting gifts in exchange. The Kshatriya varna was born from the arms of Purusha and had the duty of fighting enemies, protecting the other varnas and offering gifts to the Brahmans. The Vaishya varna sprang from the thighs of the Purusha and had the duty of producing the things to be sacrificed by means of herding cattle and tilling the soil. Finally, the Shudra varna, born of the feet of Purusha, had the duty of serving the others who were engaged in the sacrifice. The first three varnas were called *dvija* or 'twice-born', since they underwent a second ritual birth which enabled them to learn from their Brahman teachers the divine sounds of the Veda. The Shudra varna were forbidden to hear the sacred Veda. In a way, they had to worship the 'twice-born' just as the 'twice-born' had to worship the gods.

McKim Marriott and Ronald Inden (1975) interpret this myth as a first conception of Indian society in terms of genera, each of which is thought to possess a defining coded substance. Every human genus is thought to have as the shared or corporate property of its members

a particular substance embodying its code of conduct. The varna
ideology was linked to the Vedic notion that sacrifice was fundamental for upholding the natural and moral order of the cosmos.
Sacrifice required exchanges between gods and men. Pure food was
fed to the gods by men, while the gods, after eating, returned only
their leavings for the men to eat, which created a ranked relationship
between gods and men. The central human position in the sacrifice
was taken by the Brahmán, who was like a god on earth and acted as
an intermediary between the gods and the other two varnas
partaking in the sacrifice. Post-Vedic Hindu society retained this
general conception of society, but it had come to consist not so much
of four simple categories, but of a multitude of *jātis* or castes.

According to Marriott and Inden the codes of Hindu worship
require the existence of complex local communities of castes:

> The priest must be a male of the highest, most godlike caste
> available – ideally a Brahman skilled by heredity in the mainte-
> nance of ritual boundaries between substances, and empowered
> to transform them. To sponsor the worship there must be a local
> worshipper of means, typically a ruler or man of wealth, who can
> by gifts entreat a priest to mediate with the god. There must be
> specialists of appropriate castes – for example, temple keeper,
> garland-maker, cook, sweet-maker, singer, musician, dancer – to
> feed, attend and entertain the god. Before the worshipper can
> approach the god, he must prepare himself and his caste to be as
> godlike as possible and must remove, as much as possible, from
> his person and his caste any insulting, transmissible bodily
> substance. He does so through bathing and through engaging the
> services practised by other castes, such as those who do the work
> of barber, washerman, midwife, funeral priest, leather-worker,
> scavenger, or sweeper. These castes are by their intimate
> receivings of bodily substance rendered subordinate to the
> worshipper, as a child's receiving of bodily substance renders him
> subordinate to his parents. Each caste contributes in its particular
> way to the worship, directly or indirectly, and each then receives in
> return and in order of rank a share, either in the transvalued
> leavings of the god's food (called *prasāda*, 'favour') or in the
> leavings of those who do receive a share. Hindu worship thus
> greatly ramifies the specialities assigned to the four varnas and

invites specialization by caste. One effect of such worship is a ranking of all participating castes by a pattern of exchanges in which natural substances containing divine benefits pass downwards. Another effect is the establishment of a solidarity of substance among all castes. (Marriott and Inden, 1975: 985).

I have quoted these authors at length, since they articulate an influential line of interpretation which seems to inform much current research in the United States. It appears to have found its first formulation in a lengthy article by Edward Harper on the ritual observances and beliefs about pollution of the Havik Brahmans of South India (Harper, 1964). Harper's argument is that Hindu society 'is organized around the task of caring for its gods, and a division of labor among the castes is necessary to attain this end' (1964: 196). Since gods can only be worshipped by mortals of high ritual purity (i.e. Brahmans), this inherent purity must be preserved by lower castes who remove impurity by taking up defiling activities. Thanks to this social organization all members of the community derive benefit from the worship given by the Brahmans to the gods. The fundamental idea that the gods are more pure than men, that Brahmans are more pure than other men and that the concept of pollution provides the link between gods and caste society has also inspired a recent study of Central India by Lawrence Babb (1975). Babb argues that in Hindu worship (*pūjā*) the devotee's acceptance of the left-over food of the gods indicates a hierarchical relation between the divine and the human.

In the words of Harper, ritual pollution is seen as an integrator of caste and religion, since 'respect-pollution' indicates the hierarchical integration of gods and men and of Brahmans and other men. In the perspective developed by these authors, the position of the Brahman is unequivocally set at the pinnacle of the Hindu caste system; in fact the Brahman is depicted as a god on earth serving as a mediator between the gods in heaven and the men on earth. The basis of the Brahman's position – and, for that matter, of the position of all castes – is to be found in patterns of exchange, which are regulated by concepts of purity and pollution. In Vedic sacrifice and Hindu worship food is offered to the gods by the Brahmans. The left-overs are infused by divine power and taken by the Brahmans who pass on a portion to the other castes. By these exchanges a hierarchical system is founded, in which the Brahman is the purest being on earth, a kind of demi-god between men and gods.

This line of interpretation is in fact at odds on several points with observed reality and even with the Brahmanical texts. In a clear exposition of the Hindu theory of gift, Marcel Mauss (1974: 53–9) shows how ambiguous the position of the Brahman who lives by accepting gifts is. Just as in other pre-market systems of exchange, the gift creates a bond between the donor and the recipient, in which the recipient comes into a state of dependence upon the donor. Mauss argues: 'The gift is thus something that must be given, that must be received and that is, at the same time, dangerous to accept. The gift itself constitutes an irrevocable link especially when it is a gift of food. The recipient depends on the temper of the donor, in fact each depends upon the other' (1974: 58). The ambivalence of the Brahman's position is therefore that he who – divinity among divinities – is superior to every other human being, depends completely on the gifts of his fellow men for his livelihood. According to the Brahmanical rules of giving and receiving (*dānadharma*) a Hindu should regard it as his duty to give to the Brahman. If he performs this duty he will be certain to be rewarded in this life and in the next. On the Brahman rests the obligation to receive; it is one of the functions of his caste. Since, as Mauss rightly observes, the receiver is generally regarded as inferior to the giver, this relation threatens the superiority of the Brahman. Mauss adds that this is *a fortiori* at issue in the traditional gift relation between the Hindu king, the patron of the sacrifice (Sanskrit *yajamāna*, Hindi *jajmān*), and his Brahman priest (*purohit*), the representatives of worldly power and religious authority in the Hindu setting.

The point made by Mauss is taken a step further by the indologist Heesterman who argues, on the basis of his study of the Vedic texts, that in the ancient Indian sacrifice evil was transferred from the king-patron to the Brahman priest through the acceptance of the sacrificer's food and gifts. There are two things involved here. First there is the material dependence of the Brahman priest on the gifts of the king, which results in the Brahman losing 'the transcendent status that formed his literally priceless value' (Heesterman, 1971: 46). Second, there is the transference of evil which makes the Brahman a recipient and remover of evil from the world, which seems even more to threaten his unequivocal social position as the acme of purity, as presented by Harper among others. Heesterman's solution is that the Vedic tradition of the sacrifice contains a process leading to asceticism or world renunciation, in which the Brahman frees himself from his material dependence on the king-jajman. It is Heesterman's suggestion that 'as the representative of transcendence, the ideal Brahman can logically only be a renouncer, as indeed he is in the classical texts' (1971: 46). His conclusion is that at the core of traditional Hindu civilization there is a conflict between, on the one hand, complementarity and interdependence and, on the other, social distance and independence, a conflict which he traces in very diverse historical developments from the Vedic period till the modern period (Heesterman, 1985).

Recent ethnographical evidence seems to support Mauss's and Heesterman's position. This is very clear from the material collected by Jonathan Parry (1980, 1985a) on the Benares funeral priests. These priests, called *Mahābrāhmans*, are specialized in the rituals that are performed from the point of death of a person up to the point at which the transient soul is converted into an ancestor (*pitṛ*). When the Hindu dies he becomes a dangerous disembodied ghost (*pret*) until he enters the world of the ancestors. The Mahabrahman is thus a specialist in the rituals from death up to the rite of passage from pret to pitr, whereafter his priestly role is taken over by the family priest (*kul purohit*) and the pilgrimage priest (*tīrth purohit* or *paṇḍa*). The caste of Mahabrahmans is considered to have the lowest status within the Brahman category because they are involved in handling death pollution. Because of their intimate connection with death and the dead they are commonly avoided, even more than untouchables. In the funeral rites the relatives give gifts (*dāna*) to the Mahabrahman, regarding him symbolically as the representative and personification of the deceased. The idea seems to be that 'the Mahabrahman actually is the deceased at the moment the gift is handed over' (Parry, 1980: 96).

Parry's point is that the status of the Brahman priest is compromised by his calling, and he adds that this is not only the case with the Mahabrahmans, but also with the whole range of priestly specialists represented in Benares. In an interpretation of the symbolism of food and eating in North Indian mortuary rites, Parry argues that in these rites the chief mourner, the Mahabrahmans and the purohits are symbolically eating the deceased. On the one hand these ritual actors eat on behalf of the deceased, impersonate him, while on the other hand there is the idea that in taking part in the funeral meal (*shrāddha*) one eats the dead man or the dead man's sins. Parry's central idea here is that in these rites the metaphor of digestion is used to express the notion that the good part of the deceased which is the source of progeny for his sins is distilled from the bad waste, his sins (Parry, 1985a). The Brahman priest is here presented as a kind of sacrificial vessel (*pātra*) in which gifts and food are put in order to get rid of evil (*dosh*) and sin (*pāp*). In the conclusion of his 1980 paper Parry joins Heesterman in the argument that the social position of the Brahman is contradictory because his pre-eminence, which is put in jeopardy by the jajman's offerings, is of a transcendent nature. According to Parry the highest goal in life for the Mahabrahmans is to renounce the priesthood and the dependence on donations so as to avoid the contradiction inherent in the priesthood. The 'good' Brahman models himself on the world renouncer to solve the contradiction inherent in his priestly calling.

The problem of the priests' status is also discussed at great length by C. J. Fuller in his book on the priests of the Minakshi temple in the South Indian city of Madurai (1984: 49–72). Fuller starts his discussion by stating that the notion of the Brahman priest's relative inferiority is an ideological construct which is more or less universally held by Brahmans themselves, while most non-Brahmans appear to be unaware of or uninterested in it (1984: 50). He therefore chooses to see it as a problem of ranking within the Brahman caste, according to which the Brahman priest is considered to be inferior in comparison to ordinary non-priestly Brahmans. A general explanation of the Brahman priest's relative inferiority is found in the concept of the ideal Brahman as found in textual sources. Fuller does not assert that the texts determine the ideas or behaviour of the Brahmans. In his discussion he carefully evades the problem of the relationship between text and social context (1984: 63). According to Fuller, following Heesterman and others, the ideal Brahman is the world-renouncing Brahman, and he finds this paradigm in the South Indian social setting in the person of the monastic preceptor Shankaracharya of Kanchipuram. The priest's relative inferiority can be defined in terms of the lack of ideal qualities.

This general explanation can be further detailed according to the different configurations in which priestly groups are operating in India. Fuller makes a broad distinction between the position of the Brahman priests who work in the Gangetic region of North India and that of the Tamil priests. The status of the former is endangered by their acceptance of gifts, *dāna*. Fuller suggests that the fact that in North India special Brahman castes have emerged which specialize in funeral rites and alms-taking contributes to the notion that gifts threaten a Brahman's status. These specialized Brahman castes have not emerged in South India, and Fuller suggests here that the relative inferiority of the Tamil priests has to be linked with their deficient learning, their ignorance, when compared with the Brahman gurus of 'sectarian' Brahman castes, which are not found in North India. In the north, therefore, the acceptance of gifts, especially in the context of inauspicious rituals, endangers the Brahman priest's status, while in the south this status is endangered by the priest's lack of Brahmanical learning, when compared with ascetic Brahmans.[4] Both are variants of the general explanation that the ideal Brahman should not be a priest who participates in worship and sacrifice, but an independent learned ascetic.

It is clear that the evidence discussed by Mauss and Heesterman, as well as the ethnographies by Parry and Fuller, make it difficult to regard the Brahman priest as a god on earth, the pinnacle of the caste system. This evidence is therefore problematic for the whole theory of the relation between Hindu worship and caste ranking which we discussed at the beginning of this section. To a great extent it is also damaging for Dumont's influential theory of the Hindu caste system. Central to Dumont's theory is the relation between power and purity: the caste hierarchy is ultimately based upon the structural opposition of pure and impure. Power no doubt exists in society, but only at secondary levels: it is encompassed by the hierarchy of purity. This is clear in the relation between the king-jajman and the Brahman priest. Because of his purity, the status of the Brahman priest is higher than the status of the king, who wields worldly power. The only one who really threatens the superiority of the Brahman priest is the world renouncer, the ascetic who considers the status hierarchy of the caste system, based as it is upon the notion of purity, to be illusory.

In the historical development of the rivalry between Brahman priest and ascetic preceptor, Brahmans adopted a number of ascetic values, such as vegetarianism, and used them as their own status symbols. As a result we find nowadays that the Brahman who behaves like an ascetic (without really renouncing the world) has the highest status within the social category of Brahmans (Dumont, 1970: 33–88; 1972: 114–19). The renouncer is, however, not of this world and Dumont insists that there remains 'a level of social consciousness on which the Brahman has not ceased, for others as well as for himself, to be the foremost *in the world*' (Dumont, 1971: 74–5). It seems difficult to maintain this position in the light of evidence showing that in India priestly activities generally endanger the Brahman's status. This results in the contradiction that the status of the Brahman priest who owes his superiority to a principle of purity – the basis of the caste system – is constantly endangered by his caste's very activities. Dumont's suggestion that the Brahman who accepts the gifts of a king only faces a fall within the category of Brahmans, which is different from a fall from the category or of the category as a whole, is accepted by Fuller who focuses on the relative inferiority of Brahman priests *vis-à-vis* other Brahmans. It is, however, not a solution in terms of Dumont's own theory, since Dumont argues that 'the Brahmans being in principle priests, occupy the supreme rank with respect to the whole set of castes' (Dumont, 1972: 84). The contradiction in the position of the Brahman priest as highlighted by his teacher Mauss cannot be satisfactorily solved by Dumont within the rigid framework of his theory of Hindu society.

The intriguing phenomenon we are facing is that all the authors cited above try to understand the values, ideas and actions of Brahman priests by reference to an ideological construct of the ideal Brahman. Despite their conflicting interpretations there is a shared tendency to start with an unchanging realm of values which forms the ideological unity of India as found in the Sanskrit texts. Fuller is certainly aware of the problems involved in such an interpretation, but he does not go on to suggest an alternative. The general distinctions he draws between South and North India are highly problematic. In Ayodhya knowledge of the tradition is as highly valued as in Madurai and it is interesting to see that the man who was in the nineteenth century regarded as the most knowledgeable and therefore most respected Brahman pandit and *vaidik* (expert on the

Veda) was the abbot of a large temple which he had acquired as a gift from the king of Balrampur. Moreover, he was not an ascetic but a householder whose eldest son inherited the temple, a complete inversion of South India's Shankaracharya as the 'ideal Brahman'. To suggest that the threat to a Brahman's superiority in the north is his acceptance of gifts, while in the south it is his deficiency in knowledge, does not seem to solve our problems. An interesting question is how the Kanchipuram Shankaracharya became a paradigm of 'ideal Brahmanism'. Fuller's work suggests that the answer might be found in new definitions of knowledge engendered by the emerging state bureaucracy. Another very intriguing question is why the Brahman landholders and generally those Brahmans who are not involved in religious activities seem to have a higher status than those who are engaged in hereditary priestly activities. These questions can only be answered when we study the historical relation between changing ideas and values and changing configurations in which Brahman priests have to work. This will inevitably lead to a fragmentation of the notion that Hindu India has an ideological unity, and I cannot see this as a great loss. On the other hand it may give us more insight into the professional difficulties felt by our informants when the material conditions of their life-style change.

THE ACCEPTANCE OF GIFTS: OBLIGATION AND RIGHT

As we have seen in the preceding section, there are two arguments in the anthropological discussion of the position of the Brahman priest. One party argues that the Brahman priest is superior to all other men, that he is a god on earth, while the other maintains that his status is compromised by his priestly calling. In relation to this discussion we will raise here the question whether the Brahman panda of Ayodhya endangers his high status by his professional activities and, if he does, why he does so and to what extent. To answer this question, or rather this set of related questions, we will have to take a closer look at what the panda's activities are.

The Ayodhya panda is primarily a priest who works at the bathing-places. When the pilgrim arrives in Ayodhya he is almost at once brought to the riverside to take a bath in the Sarayu and to perform the appropriate rituals there. The pilgrim chooses one of the stalls (*chowkees*) of the priests, from which he proceeds to take his ritual bath (*snan*). If necessary, the panda instructs the pilgrim in the correct procedure. The main ritual act in taking a bath is a triple immersion. Mostly this is followed by three libations: one to the gods (*devas*), one to the sages (*rishis*) and one to the ancestors (*pitṛis*). These libations (*tarpan*, literally 'satisfying') are offered by cupping one's hands together and casting some water from them in different directions. The panda may help the pilgrim to utter the correct sacred formulas (*mantras*), but quite often high-caste pilgrims know them by heart. The river Sarayu herself is a goddess who should be worshipped. This is generally done by a simple act of worship (*pūjā*) in which the pilgrim throws some flowers into the water. A somewhat more elaborate mode of worship is called Sarayu-*bhent*. This is a gift of a coconut, a typical piece of clothing (*cunri*), which is generally worn by women on festive days, bangles, some red powder (*kumkum*), and some food (*naivedya*). The panda assists in this ritual and instructs the pilgrim in what he should give. The bhent is put in the river. Having finished the worship of the river, the pilgrim takes some water in a brass jug to a nearby temple of Shiv and pours it over the god's *linga*, his divine symbol. The riverside is dotted with large and small temples and shrines of Shiv, so that we may say with the pandas of Ayodhya that while Ayodhya's centre is Ram's area the riverside is Shiv's domain. Then the pilgrim may go on to visit the sacred places and temples connected with the story of Ram. The panda or one of his agents may accompany him on this tour as a religious guide.

The pilgrims may, however, also decide to stay somewhat longer at the riverside to perform a ritual for the worship and propitiation of the ancestors. The riverside is a fitting place to perform rituals connected with death and the ancestors. That Hindu cremations preferably take place at a great cremation-ghat is well known. As we have already seen, a tirtha is a place where heaven and earth meet and is therefore an excellent place for the ritual of liminality *par excellence*: the cremation ritual. As a kind of a *memento mori* the pilgrims generally perform a so-called Vaitarani ritual, in which the panda is the officiating priest. Vaitarani is the name of the terrifying river which has to be crossed after death. It is represented as a rotting river of blood, bones and corpses, infested by vultures. In the ritual a cow is symbolically offered to a panda and the belief is that the cow will help the deceased to cross the Vaitarani. After worshipping the cow by clockwise circumambulation (*parikram*), touching one of its legs and giving it a present, the pilgrim grasps the cow's tail together with some sacred grass (*kush*) and unhusked rice (*akshat*). A sacred formula (*mantra*) is spoken to the effect that the cow should lead the pilgrim safely over the Vaitarani at his time of death.

According to a common belief, the tirtha is also the place where one can always meet one's ancestors. The ancestor ritual to be performed here is the so-called *pindapitriyajna*, or simply the giving of *pinda* (*pindadān*, as it is commonly known). In this ritual small balls of rice or barley (*pinda*) are offered to the ancestors (*pitri*). There is general confusion about the exact significance of this ancestor ritual, since the balls play an important role in a whole series of rituals, beginning with the death of a person. The main significance of the forming and offering of the balls in the beginning of the mortuary rites is to give the dead person a body. A human being has according to general Hindu beliefs two bodies: a gross body (*sthūl sharir*) and a subtle body (*sukshma sharir*). After death the gross body is cremated and the subtle body comes free. This subtle body is seen as a ghost (*pret*) which may turn malevolent if it is not given a kind of intermediate gross body (Monier-Williams, 1883: 276), so that it may be enabled to undertake the long journey to the world of the ancestors (*pitri-lok*). What happens then in the mortuary rites is the offering of pindas to give the ghost a body. When the ghost has reached the heaven of the ancestors there is a special ritual in which a ball, representing the ghost, is cut in three pieces and joined with three balls, representing respectively the deceased's father, grand-father and great-grandfather. The result is that, to put it irreverently, great-grandfather is out and the deceased is in, because in later ancestor rituals three balls are formed representing father, grand-father and great-grandfather. This final ritual is called *sapindikāran* and its main significance seems to be that the ghost of the deceased, which is clearly extremely dangerous in its liminal state between life and afterlife, is made an ancestor. After the completion of the mortuary rites, balls of rice can be given to the ancestors whenever one wants to. The tirtha is believed to be a very good place to come into contact with the ancestors and many pilgrims decide to offer these balls (*pindadān*), especially in the period which is seen as appropriate for ancestor worship: the *pitri-paksh* (dark lunar fortnight) of Ashvin (September–October). In the case of this ritual the object seems not to be the formation of a body of the deceased, but the worship and propitiation of the ancestors.

Except for a few rituals which are done on specific occasions, this is the range of religious action in which the panda offers his services. As a remuneration for his work the panda receives a fee, called a *dakshiṇā*. The minimum fee is customarily Rs 1.25, but depending on the amount of work and the relation between the panda and the pilgrim, it is often more. When the pilgrim stays at the house or lodge of the panda he also pays him a certain fee, which is often called a dakshina as well. These services and the acceptance of a payment for them do not seem to be problematic as far as the Brahman's status is concerned. The difficulty raised in Brahmanical literature as well as in anthropological discussion relates to the acceptance of gifts (*dān*). Indeed, the panda is the specialist in accepting dan on behalf of the ancestors and on behalf of the tirtha as a sacred field (*kshetra*). We have thus to inquire into the nature of these gifts and the extent to which their acceptance influences the panda's status.

Perhaps the most central ritual in the total system of Hindu sacrifice is the gift (*dān*) to the Brahman. In ideological terms the Brahman could best be compared with the sacrificial fire, and indeed this comparison was often made by my informants. 'Brahma (who stands for the supernatural world) has two mouths: Agni (the sacrificial fire) and the Brahman.' In this way fire-sacrifice and gift-giving to a Brahman are equal. Moreover, inside the Brahman – as in other beings – Agni is present in the form of the digestive fire. The analogy with the fire-sacrifice is of course clearest in rituals, in which the Brahman eats what is given to him, but also more generally people conceive of the Brahman's acceptance of even inedible gifts in terms of digestion (cf. Parry, 1985a). Like Agni the Brahman seems a god in his own right as well as an intermediary between the supernatural and society. The sacrificial fire has to be worshipped as the physical presence of Agni, who is the same as Brahma, and in the same way the Brahman also has to be worshipped. These ideas are – and I wish to emphasize this point – not just part of an ancient ideology found in the Sanskrit literature, but part of the ideology and practices of my informants in present-day Ayodhya. Besides being equated with the sacrificial fire, the Brahman is seen as a sacrificial vessel (*pātra*).[5] The word *pātra* is used for the Brahman and has a metaphorical meaning, viz. 'a capable or competent person, an adept in, master of, anyone worthy of or fit for or abounding in' (Monier-Williams, 1899: 613). A more modern comparison is made in equating the Brahman with the mail-box. 'You give something to it and it is brought to its destination.' In this way everything given to the Brahman is brought, unseen, to its destination.

The Hindu who wants to worship the gods can choose between the fire-sacrifice (*yajna, havan*), image worship (*murti-pūjā*) and the gift to the Brahman (*dān*). As we have seen, the first and the last are regarded as similar. Both of these rituals start with the explicit pronouncing of the intention (*saṃkalp*) of the sacrificer (giver). The sacrificer takes some unhusked rice (*akshat*) in his hand, prays to the god he wants to worship, announces the intention of his ritual and, in the case of giving, the name and clan of the Brahman who will accept the gift. In this sense the whole pilgrimage has the character of a sacrifice, since it also starts with the announcement of the intention. There is of course a strong connection between the intention and the result (*phal*) of a ritual. The Brahman who officiates in the ritual has to declare that the ritual has been performed properly and thus 'bears fruit' (*saphal*). It is therefore always perfectly clear with what purpose a ritual is performed. This is, however, not seen by the participants as a kind of mechanical *do ut des* relation with the gods, but as an attempt to build up a kind of communication with the deity – a reciprocal relation no doubt, but one tinged with hierarchy.

There are different supernatural beings to be worshipped and propitiated as well as different intentions with which one undertakes the performance of a ritual. There is, in short, a differentiation in gifts which corresponds with a differentation or specialization among the Brahman priests. The pandas of Ayodhya make a distinction between two types of gifts: auspicious (*mangal* or *vicārini*) and inauspicious (*amangal* or *avicārini*).[6] Auspicious gifts are addressed to gods and ancestors with the intention of acquiring merit (*puṇya*), better karma, well-being, health, prosperity, and all the good things of this life and the next; inauspicious ones are those addressed to the ghost of a deceased person (*pret*), or to the inauspicious planets (*grah*), or to the god with the intention of warding off evil, or to get rid of sin and illness. These gifts are presented within the context of three sorts of ritual sequences. First of all we have the complex of mortuary and ancestral rites, in which the deceased is propitiated. The ghost (*pret*) of the deceased has to be converted into an ancestor (*pitṛ*) in these rites. Rites addressed to the ghost (*pret*) are presided over by a specialized caste of Brahmans called Mahabrahmans or Mahapatras. These rites last thirteen days and during the first eleven days the deceased is a ghost and heavy death pollution afflicts the members of his household. The Mahabrahman is the priest in charge of the rites.

On the twelfth day another Brahman specialist takes over, either the 'priest of the family' (*kul purohit*) or the pilgrimage priest (*tīrth purohit*). The important ritual to be performed is the *sapindikaran*, in which the deceased is united with the ancestors and becomes a *pitṛ* (ancestor). The whole sequence ends with a feast given for Brahmans (*brahmbhoj*). In this complex of mortuary rites the giving of gifts plays a central part. The first sequence, in which the Mahabrahman presides, is concluded with the feeding of the Mahabrahman and, at his departure, the giving of *sajjādān*, a year's supply of such necessities as grains, utensils, bedding and so on. The idea is clearly that what is given to the Brahman is given to the *pret* (ghost). The second sequence, at which the *purohit* (priest) presides, also ends with a *sajjādān* to this priest or another Brahman clearly representing the deceased, who has now become a *pitṛ* (ancestor). The whole complex of mortuary rites ends with the feeding of a group of Brahmans, after which a feast is given for members of the family, relatives and others. This idea of the Brahman representing the ancestor is also present in the feeding of Brahmans (*brahmbhoj*).[7]

Another type of ritual in which gift-giving is important is the worship of the gods (*devadān*). The Brahman priest can represent all kinds of gods. In Ayodhya the pandas receive gifts intended for Lord Ram, for Shiv or for Sarayu, Ayodhya's sacred river. More generally the Ayodhya panda is seen as the human embodiment or representative of Shri Ayodhya-ji, the sacred place itself. The pilgrim makes an offering to the total sacred field (*kshetra*) which he visits: the object of pilgrimage is the object of sacrifice. The worship of the Brahman panda by the pilgrim and the gifts given to him can therefore be interpreted as a total sacrificial act inherent in pilgrimage. The intentions with which people undertake a pilgrimage to a tirtha are very different and accordingly also the gift-giving differs. As we have already seen, a *tīrtha* (sacred centre, mostly near sacred water) is a place where one can address one's ancestors. Gifts to the ancestors are the most common gifts by the Ayodhya pandas. The divine ancestors are expected to have a great influence on the welfare of their descendants. The gifts given are related to the standing of the donor family and may include gold, elephants or horses. Most common are gifts of grain or of a piece of land, the annual harvest of which is given to the panda. The gifts to the gods, ancestors and Ayodhya *in toto* are inextricably intertwined in the perception of the givers, although they may specify them separately in their declaration of intent. This lumping together of the objects of the pilgrimage results from their being generally worshipped with the same end in view, namely religious merit (*punya, kalyān*). The supernatural beings are seen as powerful and as having influence on our mortal well-being; it is important that that influence be favourable, auspicious (*mangal*).

A third category of gift-giving is part of a set of ritual actions to ward off inauspiciousness (*amangal*), and to get rid of sin (*pāp*) and illness (*rog*). Auspiciousness and inauspiciousness are directly connected with certain planetary constellations. Specific conjunctions can be very auspicious (e.g. on the occasion of the twelve-yearly Kumbh Festival) and others highly dangerous (e.g. on the occasion of an eclipse). Moreover, every person has his or her own horoscope according to which some constellations may be very auspicious or inauspicious. Horoscopes play an enormously important role in the life of Hindus. Before starting any important enterprise (marriage, business, religious work, building a house and so on) a devout Hindu will go to a Brahman who is an expert in astrology. The knowledgeable Brahman will then tell him what to do and when to start. In the case of an impending marriage the Brahman will also decide whether the horoscopes of the partners match. Auspicious conjunctions are automatically beneficial and no worship or other human intervention is needed. The effects of ominous conjunctions can, however, be warded off by gifts. Gifts to the planet Shanivar (Saturn) are given to whatever Brahmans accept them. Generally these gifts are accepted by a caste of specialist Brahmans called Bhareriya or Joshi in Uttar Pradesh and Dakhot in Panjab. Miller (1975: 49) gives a description of this type of gift-giving in a Haryana village which he has called Badipur: 'On Saturdays the Dakhot, carrying a brass bucket containing an iron image of Saturn (*sanichār mūrti*), goes from door to door collecting flour, *ghee* and oil.' In this village there was one household of Dakhots. The belief is that the Dakhot takes the inauspiciousness away.

In the same manner a person can also get rid of illness and sin by gift-giving. Illness and sin are thought to be connected. The conception of sin is normative rather than moral. It applies to transgressions of normative rules concerning purity and impurity. Men are considered to be 'tainted' by the transgression of food taboos or other rules pertaining to caste differences and this taint is believed to be a cause of illness. The same is true of such ritual transgressions as the accidental killing of a sacred being, a cow or a Brahman. Of course there is the well-known Hindu idea that the effects of these bad and inauspicious actions adhere to one's transmigrating soul as one's karma and result in a lower rebirth, but this idea is regarded by my informants as rather abstract. It seems to have attracted a philosophical mind like that of Max Weber much more than it attracts the pilgrims and priests in Ayodhya. Much more closely related to immediate experience are the misfortune and illness that befall a person in this life. Bad and inauspicious actions create sin and illness, and the only way to get rid of them is to perform an expiation ritual (*prayashchitt*). It is not always the transgressor who desires to perform such a ritual. Often one is forced by one's community (*biraderi*, a group of clans of one caste connected by affinal relations) to do it, since the transgression affects not only the individual transgressor but the whole community. In some cases, when it is not clear whether someone has 'sinned', a divination takes place. The council of the caste community (*panchāyat*) takes advice from a learned Brahman as to what expiation is needed for a particular transgression. In a village some 50 kilometres from Ayodhya, Bhaimsauna, there is even a family of Brahmans specializing in this kind of advice.

Crucial in these rituals aimed at warding off inauspiciousness and getting rid of sin and illness is the idea that these 'substances' are also given away with the gift. One transfers not only the gift, but also karma in the form of sin and illness; but to what or to whom? Agni, the sacrificial fire, just devours and annihilates what is given to it, but what about the digestive fire of the Brahman? The mere fact that the pandas draw the distinction between auspicious and inauspicious gifts makes it clear that the Brahman's digestive fire is less neutral than sacrificial fire. The Brahman might be tainted by the gifts he accepts and whether this is in fact the case will depend upon the declaration of intent. This is in itself not very difficult to understand.

Parry (1980, 1985a) makes it very clear that Mahabrahmans who officiate in the cremation ritual and in the first sequence of mortuary rites are identified with the deceased. Death is a matter of pollution and danger in India and these Brahmans are handling the liminal phase between life and ancestorship, in which the deceased is a dangerous ghost. It should not surprise us that the Mahabrahman is an equivocal person who is even more avoided than an untouchable. The same is true of the Bhareriya who acts as an intermediary between the highly inauspicious planet Saturn and the Hindu laymen. Often, certain people – generally their enemies in professional competition – doubt whether the Mahabrahmans and the Bhareriyas are in fact Brahmans, and this cynical observation brings to our attention the changing dividing lines between the Brahmanical priestly profession and the non-Brahmanical. Brahmans are not the only priests in village India. There are all kinds of other marginal priests who act as intermediaries with the sacred. Often they are the experts in possession cults, presiding at blood sacrifices for female deities and curing diseases such as smallpox. Pocock (1973) points out that there is a smooth transition from non-Brahmanical priests to Brahmans which correlates with the status aspirations of their clients. We may add that priests, by means of Brahmanical rituals, apparently also handle the same kind of dangerous substances as the non-Brahman priests of low castes and tribes.

It would be helpful if we could say that there is a clear division among Brahman priests between those who accept auspicious gifts and those who do not. We can make some general distinctions, though individual exceptions abound. On the most general level, religious-minded Brahmans living in a traditional environment often do accept invitations to a *brahmbhoj*, a feast for Brahmans. This kind of feast is in fact a sacrifice with a clear purpose of celebration or worship. Often these feasts are organized to worship Brahmans as sacred beings in their own right and generally respected Brahmans partake in them. Those Brahmans would never consider taking any kind of gift on behalf of a ghost, ancestor or planet, nor would they partake in a feast which is held as the conclusion of mortuary rites (*shrāddha*) if they could avoid it. Some high-status Brahmans, however, informed me that they found it hard to refuse an invitation for the latter kind of feast, when they were friends of the inviting family. A respected Brahman would never act as a hereditary priest, but may act as a learned teacher (*guru*) for his pupils and accept gifts in return. People may offer a Brahman some land. This is considered both auspicious and meritorious, and I have never heard of anyone refusing to accept such a gift of *samkalp*-land as it is called in Uttar Pradesh, when the intention (*samkalp*) was to acquire merit. One could argue that such recipients in fact form a category within the Brahman caste which is *economically independent* from priestly income. This category will refuse all types of gifts in rituals in which they act as mere sacrificial vessels (*pātra*), but it is important to keep in mind that this refusal is based upon economic independence.

A second category of Brahmans is formed by those who are hereditary priests (*purohit*) of Hindu families. In terms of the sacrificial idiom they act as priest on behalf of the 'patron of the sacrifice', the *jajmān* (Sanskrit *yajamāna*, he who has the sacrifice performed for his sake). This is a reciprocal relation. The Brahman purohit has an obligation to serve his jajman, while the jajman has a right (*haq*) to give his gifts to the Brahman and an obligation to support him economically (cf. Parry, 1979: 67; Miller, 1975: 131–2). Priest and patron are in this way bound together by hereditary obligations and rights. This relationship implies at least that the priest is obliged to accept auspicious gifts from his jajman. The situation is, however, more complicated when inauspicious gifts are handed over. To a certain extent priests who are bound in a jajmani-relation will have to accept dangerous gifts. Merit and demerit belong to life not as Manichean opposites in a moral universe, but as two related aspects of human action in a normative universe, and a Hindu entertains jajmani-relations with a Brahman priest to handle both categories. This is not to say that a purohit will feel obliged to accept each and every gift. In cases of severe danger, impurity and inauspiciousness he may advise his jajman on the course of action to be taken. If gift-giving is a necessary aspect of an expiation ritual then he may try to find a poor Brahman who will accept it or will send the jajman on pilgrimage in the hope that the pandas will handle the case. The pandas are the hereditary priests of the pilgrimage centres (*tīrth purohit*). They are also bound to their jajmans by reciprocal relations and are as such obliged to take certain types of inauspicious gifts. In the case of a ritual of expiation (*prayashchitt*) they often use the fiction that the gifts are accepted by sacred *kush* grass which symbolizes the Brahmans. It is, however, clear that the pandas act on behalf of the ancestors in accepting gifts given on a riverbank, which is never done by family priests. It is the exclusive right and obligation of pandas to accept this type of gift.

Finally, there is a specialized category of Brahmans who take specific types of gifts no other Brahman will ever accept. The Mahabrahmans take gifts connected with funeral and mortuary rites, while the Bhareriyas take those offered to the planets and often all other kinds of gifts which are considered to be dangerous. The Mahabrahmans form an endogamous priestly group with clearly defined caste boundaries. It is not clear whether they, like purohits, have jajmans. In Benares (Parry, 1980) and Ayodhya they clearly do not have such jajmani relations. They observe a rota system by which a particular Mahabrahman has the right to perform the rituals for all the dead bodies brought to the cremation place during a specific period in the year. Although it is impossible for me to say whether this situation is specific for Mahabrahmans operating in pilgrimage centres and is different for those who operate in villages (see Parry, 1979: 65), the data seem to suggest that the absence of jajmani relations among Mahabrahmans in Benares and Ayodhya implies that reciprocity with Brahmans who impersonate the deceased's *pret* (ghost) is not desired. People try to avoid the Mahabrahman, just as they try to avoid death, and it seems obvious that they do not initiate jajmani relations with him.[8] The Bhareriyas are a much less clearly defined caste than the Mahabrahmans. I will discuss them in detail later, but at this point I would like to argue that these priests aspire after purohitship and jajmani relations with wealthy patrons. However, my impression is that as long as they take the gifts intended to ward off the influences of inauspicious planets they do not entertain jajmani relations.

The last category of Brahmans can clearly be distinguished on the basis of its acceptance of dangerous gifts. The Bhareriyas are caught in a kind of poverty trap, to use a term of Parry's (1979: 66). They seem to be a group of impoverished Brahmans who are forced to accept for their livelihood gifts that no one else is prepared to accept. The Mahabrahmans are somewhat different. They seem to be a caste, defined by its hereditary occupation which clearly connects it with something that might be more dangerous than degrading: death pollution. The other two categories of Brahmans discussed above cannot be easily distinguished on the basis of their acceptance of certain gifts. A dividing line seems, however, to exist between those Brahmans who enter into jajmani relations which are characterized by obligation and right, and those who do not. Those who do not depend on the support of their patrons (*jajmān*) may accept some invitations and refuse others. This is not to say that they have withdrawn from the religious sphere and depend for their status only on their economic position.

In this connection it is useful to point out a difference between three presentations in the chain of sacrificial acts. First there is the gift (*dān*) which is considered to be equal to the sacrifice as such (*yajna*); secondly there is the so-called *saṃgitā*, a small gift which is said to make up for a deficiency in the central gift; and finally the *dakshiṇā*, a gift which my informants interpret as a remuneration, a fee for the priest's services. The idea is that the priest has to be paid for his services, so that he may be free to accept the gift as a sacrificial vessel. The Brahman priest therefore has two separate functions in the ritual: to act as fire or vessel and to act as an officiating priest. In the first function he receives a gift which he has to digest on behalf of a supernatural being, while in the second function he presides over the ritual. This distinction has considerable implications, since some Brahmans may act as ritual specialists (*karmakāndin*) in a gift ritual, while only accepting a *dakshiṇā* (fee) for their services, leaving the *dān* (gift) for those Brahmans who want to accept it. This type of specialist is learned in theory and practice of the ritual and is summoned and paid for specific performances, but is not bound by jajmani relations (cf. Miller, 1975: 131–2 for a distinction between pandit and purohit). But even when the gift-receiving Brahman and the officiating Brahman are the same person a fee (*dakshiṇā*) has to be given to accomplish the fiction of the Brahman being the sacrificial fire. Therefore it is said that 'what is given without *dakshiṇā*, all that remains without fruit' (*adakshinam tu yad dānam, tad sarvam nishphalam bhavet*'; a Sanskrit text in a ritual manual, *Dānachandrika*, used by the Ayodhya pandas).

Dakshina is not given only for priestly services, but also as payment for the services of a Brahman adviser or teacher (*guru-dakshiṇā*). When a Brahman does something for you in the religious sphere he should get some dakshina. There is thus a clear difference between dakshina and dan, which implies that some Brahmans may accept the one but not the other. The local gloss of dakshina as 'payment' seems, incidentally, to support Malamoud's interpretation of the ancient Indian sacrifice *contra* the argument of Heesterman and Gonda that the dakshina is just a particular case of the gift (Malamoud, 1976).[9] Performing some ritual functions for which one is paid a *dakshiṇā* (fee) seems, in the eyes of my informants, altogether different from acting as some *jajmān's purohit* who is obliged to accept some of the *dān* (gifts) of his *jajmān* (patron). Moreover, a Brahman who does not enter into jajmani relations is considered to have a higher status than one who maintains them.

The discussion of the relation between the acceptance of gifts and the status of the Brahman centres therefore on two issues. First of all there is the acceptance of 'bad gifts'. A special category of low-status Brahmans has arisen to cope with inauspiciousness, illness and death. In some aspects they resemble the low-caste specialists of possession cults, but they belong to the Brahman estate (*varṇa*), since their ritual activities belong to the Brahmanical tradition. The second issue concerns the hereditary relation between a patron and a Brahman priest (*purohit*), which is called jajmani in this part of India.[10] The concept of the so-called 'jajmani system' as a system, seen as the 'traditional' or 'natural' economy of North India, is in my view largely a colonial and anthropological construct. It has been discussed in a great number of publications (for references, see Commander, 1983) and I do not intend to cover the same ground yet again. What is important is that the purohit stands somewhat apart from the other service groups which are tied to a caste of patrons (*jajmāns*). As Commander (1983: 296–8) points out, the locus of the 'system' is the possession of *land*: 'For it is land or its produce that provides the crucial "good" disbursed, upwards or downwards, by the *jajmān*.' The service castes (*kamins*) *depend economically* on the caste(s) of landholders and this dependence implies an inferior status. It is, however, a meritorious act to give a Brahman rent-free land and by acceptance of such a donation a Brahman family may come *economically independent*. A Brahman landowner whose father received his land some generations ago as a gift (*saṃkalp, dharmarth, birt*) for some long-forgotten purpose and who has no jajmans but sometimes acts as a guru or a ritual specialist (*karmakāndin*), has a high status. He is an independent religious agent who can only be paid a fee (*dakshiṇā*) for his services, but has no hereditary tie to a patron who may force him to accept gifts he does not wish to accept.

In this case the status of the Brahman seems therefore not to be determined primarily by the nature of the gifts which he accepts, but by his economic position.

There is, however, another side to jajmani relations. Economic dependence might be seen as degrading, but it can also be regarded as providing economic security. Patronage means obligations and rights: the patron is also tied to the specialist. Moreover, there is again a difference here between the purohit and other service castes, since, as Parry (1979: 80) points out, the purohit's service is essential to the patron's status, so that the purohit-jajman relationship tends to be enduring. Even if we infer that economic independence is seen as an ideal, it depends on developments in the economic field whether such an ideal will have implications for the behaviour of Brahmans. Often security might be more highly valued than independence, so that it begs the question to refer to an unchanging concept of the Ideal Brahman when discussing Brahmanical values and behaviour.

In the case of the pilgrimage priest, with whom we are concerned here, we should add one more observation. A central feature of the picture of the so-called 'jajmani system' in the historical and anthropological literature has always been that it is shown to operate in a kind of autarkic village economy, in a 'miniaturized economic universe', and that it falls apart when labour becomes mobile (Commander, 1983: 286–309). Whatever may be the empirical value of this picture, it is clear that pilgrimage priests have always been working in a political and economic universe as large, in principle, as the Indian subcontinent itself. A tirtha like Ayodhya is 'a centre out there', to use Victor Turner's phrase, and its catchment area, though expanding in the last two centuries, has always been regional. This is no doubt significant for the relation between jajman and priest, which is at least much less of a face-to-face relation, in which considerations of relative status play an important role, than is the case in a village setting. Conclusions drawn from studies on jajmani relations in villages cannot therefore be readily applied to the field of pilgrimage. As we will see, there was a great increase in the number of pilgrims contracting jajmani relations with Ayodhya pandas in the nineteenth century, when, according to many studies, jajmani in villages lost its importance.

On the other hand, when jajmani relations started to become less important in pilgrimage during the present century the implications proved to be rather similar to what has been observed in general: money becomes more general than wage in kind, agents who act as middlemen between employers (pilgrims) and workers (priests) attain a dominant position in the new system, the relative security of the jajmani system is replaced by the impoverishment of many priests and the relative success of a few. It is these themes which seem more relevant to the changing social position of the Brahman priest than the transcendental values to which, as we have seen, much of current anthropological discussion is devoted. In the following sections we will discuss them from a historical perspective.

3. The formation of professional identities

THE EXPANSION OF THE PILGRIMAGE SYSTEM

Ayodhya is an old place and is mentioned in Sanskrit texts of considerable antiquity, as we have seen in the first chapter. This is not to say that it is equally ancient as a place of pilgrimage, though we may assume that pilgrims visited Ayodhya centuries before the traveller William Finch gave us the first historical description of it, based upon his experiences during his visit there some time between 1608 and 1611:

> A citie of ancient note, and seate of a Potan king, now much ruined; the castle built foure hundred yeeres agoe. Heere are also the ruines of Ranichand(s) castle and houses, which the Indian acknowled(g)e for the great God, saying that he tooke flesh upon him to see the tamasha of the world. In these ruines remayne certaine Brahmenes, who record the names of all such Indians as wash themselves in the river running thereby, which custome, they say, hath continued foure lackes of yeeres (which is three hundred ninetie foure thousand and five hundred yeeres before the worlds creation). (Foster, 1921: 176)

I have seen only two documents dating from the period in which Finch writes, the first being from the raja of Jodhpur to an Ayodhya panda:

Samvat 1622 Magh Shukla-paksh Dashami (tenth day of the bright half of the moon, in the month January/February, in the year 1565), Ayodhya. Shri Maharajadhiraja, Raja Udayasingh, Maharaja Rao Baladevaji, son of Shri Maharaja Rao Gangaji, grandson of Rathor Juhadji of Jodhpur came to Ayodhya on pilgrimage and acknowledges Shri Raghupande as his tirtha guru. Whoever of my Rathor family of Jodhpur ever comes to Ayodhya on pilgrimage should acknowledge him as guru.

The second is from a leader of the Pustimarg community, one of the leading devotional groups of North India:

Samvat 1699 Ashadh Sudi (bright half of the moon, in the month June/July, in the year 1642) the Reverend Giridhar Mahaprabhu saw the old papers in the house of the tirtha purohit and, writing in his own hand, he wrote that anyone of his family [*atmaja*] who comes should acknowledge him as the tirtha purohit.

It should be clear from both Finch's account and the two documents that as early as the late sixteenth and early seventeenth centuries there were already Brahmans in Ayodhya who acted as tirtha purohit or panda for patrons (*jajmāns*). There are only very few documents extant from the period up to the late eighteenth century, but their number increases rapidly afterwards. These documents can all be found with the Gangaputra pandas. From the beginning of the nineteenth century they are supplemented by large ledgers (*bahis*) in which are entered the names of all pilgrims together with their caste and place of origin. The other group of pandas, the Bhareriyas, possesses no ancient documents and their ledgers date only from the middle of the nineteenth century.

In the few documents dating from around 1600 to 1800 the Brahman pandas are indicated by such terms as 'Brahman', 'tirtha purohit', 'Janaodar' (meaning 'wearing the sacred thread') and a few times by a caste name such as Mishra, Pande, Tripathi or Pathak. It is interesting to see that documents pertaining to an old jajmani relation between some patron and a Brahman panda with the name of, for example, 'Mishra', can be found with a present-day Gangaputra with the name Pande of Chowbe. In my opinion the little evidence that can be gleaned from these documents points only in one direction: there were Brahmans in Ayodhya who acted as pandas for jajmans, but these Brahmans were not yet clearly organized into an occupational caste-like group of Gangaputras. The documents were probably passed from one family to another by sale, or by inheritance through the female line or through adoption, just as happens nowadays, and we have insufficient documentary evidence to trace this process in detail during this period. Not only is the number of old documents in the priests' collection small, but they are increasingly neglected, since they have lost their value in the modern pilgrimage market.

The surviving documents only refer to high-caste jajmans. From this evidence it seems that the rajas and *zamīndārs* (landowners), in short the landed gentry of North India, were the most important patrons. Only in the second half of the eighteenth century do we find from the documents that the scope of jajmani relations between the Brahmans of Ayodhya and the visiting pilgrims expanded from the established élite to new groups which profited from the opportunities offered by the expansion of the regional realm of the nawabs of Awadh. In fact, we can see here the same picture which we have already encountered in the case of the Ramanandis. Both Muslims and Hindus belonging to the court culture of the nawabs of Awadh acted as patrons for Hindu institutions. The Gangaputras not only have a vast collection of official documents (*farmāns*), but also documents recording religious gifts by high Muslim officials at the court of the nawabs. It seems that the Muslim élite followed their Hindu equals in participating in the Hindu gift ritual with various intentions, of which the aspect of status would not have been the least important.

The development suggested by my research into the documentary evidence seems to be that pilgrimage to Ayodhya in order to contract jajmani relations with the Brahmans was primarily a ritual for the élite of the Hindu society which was later imitated by socially mobile groups to emphasize their status aspirations. It is not only evidence from Ayodhya which suggests such a pattern. C. A. Bayly (1981) reports much the same from his research on the three great North Indian tirthas, Benares, Allahabad and Gaya. The majority of the great bathing- and cremation-ghats on the river Ganges in Benares were constructed between 1730 and 1810, while most of the temples and rest houses appear to date from the same period. He shows that pilgrimage was expanding in this period for a number of reasons, the most important being the establishment of British rule. Communications improved thanks to the *Pax Britannica*. Moreover, not only the landed gentry, but also what he calls the 'service gentry', merchant groups and, for example, Bengali government servants, the main beneficiaries of British rule, became important patrons. Between 1780 and 1820 the number of pilgrims who went annually to Allahabad, Gaya and Benares may have trebled. Pilgrimage, in short, was a status ritual which spread from old ruling dynasties via new dynasties and large landowners to emerging service and business classes at the end of the eighteenth and beginning of the nineteenth centuries. This long-term process first had its influence on the greatest pilgrimage centres which are described by Bayly, but soon embraced also a more parochial place like Ayodhya, which was, moreover, somewhat peculiar in that it depended to some extent on the expansion of the Ramanandi order and on the vicissitudes of the realm of Awadh.

It is only from the beginning of the nineteenth century that big ledgers have been used to register the visits of common people to Ayodhya. The names of all kinds of land-tilling castes can be found, with the dates of their visits and their exact places of origin. References in each of these registers specify some 'little kingdom' of a raja and are further subdivided into smaller units, finally giving the village which is divided into castes and families recorded under their caste heading. From this type of registration we can deduce how important the connection with a royal patron was for the panda. When a panda had a ruling dynasty as his jajman then he had the right to have all the subsequent jajmani bonds with the pilgrims from the king's realm. This situation was clearly expressed in the rule, *Us ka rājā, Us ki prajā*, meaning 'Whose king, whose people'. This rule was followed with all new pilgrims visiting Ayodhya for the first time and was enforced by the fact that the same rajas also built temples and rest houses where their people could stay during their visit. When the old status ritual of pilgrimage thus spread from the higher to the lower classes of the population, its legitimating function for the rulers was not yet lost. The new jajmani bonds made by the commoners were only a derivation of the primal bond made by the ruler, while his power and glory were also emphasized by the magnificent buildings he had raised in the centres, reflecting the wealth of his dynasty and also that of his realm. In this way the centres also became places of conspicuous ritual consumption, in which rulers of different states vied with each other in magnificence.

The gradual change in the scale of pilgrimage in North India, as described by Bayly and as reflected in the documentary evidence in the possession of the Ayodhya priests, not only had its effect on the registration maintained by the pandas, but also, in my opinion, on their social organization. Before the nineteenth century there was probably never a clearly demarcated group or caste of Brahmans calling themselves Gangaputras. The documents mention all kinds of Brahmans with a great variety of names who act as pandas for jajmans, but from the fog of history a few lineages gradually emerge as the core of the later group of pandas who call themselves Gangaputra. I would speculate that there have always been families of the Sarayuparin caste of Brahmans, which forms the great majority of Ayodhya's Brahman population, specializing in the pilgrimage trade. They entered the profession and maybe they sometimes left it as well, but there were no clear boundaries between those who did and those who did not. The Gangaputras are therefore not originally an endogamous caste, but an occupational group of Sarayuparin Brahmans who had specialized in the pilgrimage trade. It was only due to some specific constraints in the nineteenth century that this group began to behave like a caste, but this policy lost its force again in the modern period, let us say from the 1950s onwards. Before the nineteenth century pandaship was an open occupational identity for the Sarayuparin Brahmans who lived, as their name designates, 'on the other side of the river Sarayu'. There is a well-known legend which might indicate the early connection of the Sarayuparins in general with pandaship. In the *Rāmāyaṇa* one of the great themes is the struggle between the god Ram and the king of the demons, Ravan, who resides in Lanka. As is typical for the Hindu conception of the demons, Ravan is not entirely bad but has simply become too powerful as a result of his ascetic worship of the god Shiv. His enormous power threatens the harmony in the world, so that Ram must come down to earth to kill him. The problem is, however, that Ravan is a very high and learned Brahman, so that Ram commits the very defiling act of slaying a Brahman (*brahmahatyā*). According to the rules of the world he must, as the model of the virtuous king, submit himself to an expiation ritual which includes, as we have seen, the giving of a gift to a Brahman. No Brahman, however, wanted to accept this gift.

There are now several versions explaining how Ram acquired his Brahman. The first is that he or Hanuman kidnapped a few Brahman children from Rajasthan and made them accept. These children were then no longer accepted in their homes and Ram gave them land on the other side of the Sarayu, and thus they became the Sarayuparins. Another version is that it was simply the Brahmans of Ayodhya who accepted the gift, but there are still families who make it clear that they were among the few who did not. It is interesting that everyone in Ayodhya knows this myth, but it is mostly told by two groups: the other Brahman castes and the Gangaputras. Other Brahman castes like the Kanyakubja Brahmans use the story to stress their own relative superiority *vis-à-vis* the Sarayuparin Brahmans, while the Gangaputras use it to draw attention to the fact that they are in fact no different from the other Sarayuparins in accepting gifts. Sarayuparins, confronted with the story, do not deny it, but often say that their family happened to be among the few who did not accept the gift of Ram. It is clear that the acceptance of gifts has always been important to the status of Brahmans, but the emergence of a specialized caste-like group of Gangaputras seems to have had other causes.

I am able to offer only a dim picture of the Brahmans who worked as pandas before the nineteenth century. There are at least two main reasons for this. The first is that the present-day pandas of Ayodhya are locked in conflicts over the right to work in this profession, to such an extent that every investigation into the positive evidence of the claims has a political value and is therefore regarded with considerable suspicion (cf. Goswamy, 1966). I did not, like Conlon (1977), for example, select a caste for which sufficient documentation in the form of caste journals and genealogies exists and which appeared to be interested in its own positive history. On the contrary, historical questions proved to be important in the political struggle for power and survival among the pandas I had begun to study, and the people involved were only too eager to have their claims endorsed.

In brief, the past is an important resource in the present-day conflicts in Ayodhya, as I will show below. This is not the most favourable starting-point for social historical research on castes. The second impediment for this type of study is that caste in no way proves to be such a clearly defined and unchanging social formation as has long been assumed in the social anthropological literature on Hindu India. As Carnegy, in his extensive *Notes on the Races, Tribes and Castes inhabiting the Province of Awadh* (1868), has remarked: 'It appears to me that there is a glory and a halo surrounding the institution of caste, to which it has no stronger claim than prescription and prejudice ... Caste is at best a social institution, and apparently it can at times be got over in India as easily as in England' (37–8). 'It appears to me that the result forced upon one by a diligent inquiry into the subject treated of in these notes, is that amongst the people we see around us, whether they be Mohammedans or Hindus, the mixed families are the rule, and the pure ones the exceptions. It might indeed perhaps with truth be said that the exceptions necessary to prove the rule are almost, if not altogether, wanting' (77). These remarks are confirmed in recent social historical research on caste histories. Conlon (1977: 6) remarks on the Saraswat Brahmans: 'The separateness of the Saraswats cannot be spoken of as a rigid, unchanging concept, but rather as a tendency of an identity to inhere in certain families, who subsequently joined to form what is known as the Chitrapur Saraswat Brahmin jati.' Much the same can be said of the Ayodhya Gangaputras.[11] Pandaship was an open identity for the Sarayuparin Brahmans of Ayodhya till the nineteenth century and due to specific historical developments these panda families became separate enough to call themselves, and to be called by outsiders, Gangaputras. I will describe this process of identity formation in the following section.

THE GANGAPUTRAS

On 23 January 1889 the rules and regulations (*panchnāmā*) of a group of Brahmans calling themselves Gangaputras were laid down for the first time in an official document. Twenty-nine members signed the document as well as seven witnesses, including such leading personalities in Ayodhya as the raja and several abbots. The members of the group were all, as they say, Brahman by caste, Gangaprasad (= Gangaputra) panda, inhabitants of the ward Svargadvar, city Ayodhya, Tahsil District Faizabad. The document was explicitly drawn up to decide and prevent litigation among the group. It laid down the rights of members with regard to specific 'kings and their subjects', all mentioned by name (the kings and their pandas). Some of the greater rajas were shared by the pandas, and their shares are also explicitly mentioned. Strict rules about difficult cases are given, such as instances where pilgrims are received by one panda and belong to another. The document is a clear attempt to bring unity and order among the pandas who were all living in the oldest ward of Ayodhya, near the river. The attempt was forced upon the Gangaputras by the growing involvement of the British in the settlement of rights on land, tax payment and conflicts among priests.

After a long period of more than fifty years, in which they gradually took over all actual power in the state, the British decided in 1856 to annex the kingdom of Awadh. This meant that they had to become involved in the direct administration on the district and lower levels. In the case of Ayodhya its implication was that they had to interfere in the intricate conflicts between individual pandas and groups of pandas on their relative shares in the pilgrimage system, which, as we have seen, had been expanding rapidly from at least the beginning of the nineteenth century. To take a balanced position regarding the conflicting claims proved excruciatingly difficult. The main conflict the British faced was between two groups of pandas, Bhareriyas and Gangaputras, both claiming to have been working as pandas from time beyond memory or, better still, from the time of Lord Ram. The first thorough investigation was made by the assistant to the deputy commissioner of Faizabad, C. R. Shaw, in a report dated 31 March 1862. Shaw asked three authoritative Brahman pandits (savants) of Ayodhya for their opinion on the relative rights of Bhareriyas and Gangaputras. One of them simply refused to give an opinion. The second, Raja Ramadhin, the elder brother of the famous raja of Ayodhya, Man Singh – they are Sakaldipi Brahmans – argued that nothing in Hindu religion prevents the Bhareriyas from receiving gifts from pilgrims.[12] The third and most important pandit, known as Umapati, was regarded as an unparalleled saint in this period. It was suggested that even the gods Ram, Lakshman and Sita treated him as their spiritual preceptor (*guru*). He answered Shaw's question by citing a cryptic Sanskrit text to the effect that a man who deprives a Brahman of gifts given by himself or by others becomes a demon after death and will live in a jungle without water. It would appear that Umapati avoided making a clear statement so as not to deprive one of the two parties of the right to gifts. Later Shaw tried to get him to clarify his stand in a personal conversation. But all he learned was that Umapati was himself jajman of a Gangaputra and that he would give his opinion only if it were not officially recorded. Nevertheless Shaw was able to reach a clear conclusion with the help of further investigations. According to his opinion, thirty or forty years before, around 1820–1830, there had been no chowkees on the bathing-ghats. Both Gangaputras and Bhareriyas already took gifts (in British parlance 'begged') from pilgrims. The Bhareriyas were, however, considerably weaker than their rivals and were regularly chased from the ghats. At this time the Gangaputras began to put up chowkees, and they continued to do so increasingly during the ten years prior to Shaw's investigation.

Another investigation was made by Patrick Carnegy, officiating commissioner and settlement officer of Faizabad district in the 1870s. I found his notes in the files of the pandas and since they are rich in information, I would like to quote them in full. They are not dated.

Report on the claim to chowkees in Ayodhya at the time of religious festivals. The claimants are 3 in kind: 1. Gangaputras of Ayodhya; 2. Jotishis; 3. Gangaputras of Guptarghat.

The first are shown by their proofs, some of which are very ancient (one being 1907 years old), to have from time immemorial taken at festivals on chowkees and at all other times standing anywhere. On the river bank they keep records of the pilgrims who visit the shrines and thus generation after generation of pilgrims and priests keep up an acquaintance as it were. The pilgrim of the present day finds his father's name recorded in the records of the Gangaputras and records his own to be seen here after by his posterity. This is the custom of other holy places such as Hardwar, Prayag and Benares. The institution of a religious charitable ... [illegible] many generations is a peculiarity of the Gangaputras and their rights are so far defined and respected that they do not interfere with one another's clients and a Gangaputra can and does employ *gomāsthas* to attend on their clients and take fees where they cannot personally attend. In Vilayat Ali's Chakladari's time from 1823 to 1825 the Jotishis raised a dispute but were not able to erect chowkees on the river bank and Vilayat Ali levied a tax of one rupee per chowkee but it only lasted 1 year and some people say it was not carried out for even one year. Mr. Goldney, Commissioner of Fyzabad, in an order of 23th March of 1857 recorded that a fee of Rs 1/- per chowkee had been raised from the time of Molvi Hafizoola who was an authority in Fyzabad and from 1825 to 1850 should have been levied on the cucha [kaccha] ghats, whereas the pukka ghats were untaxed. This is the authority of the customs which prevailed till the auction sale of 1870.

Jotishis. These claim to be more ancient than the Gangaputras, but they have no documentary evidence such as the latter. The want of this evidence shows that they have enjoyed no such presumptions of taking alms. They have a document given by Buxchi Teg Singh of Rawalpindi, who was ... [illegible] in the Oudh Police who affects to have availed himself in 1863 of their services at Ayodhya, but no records involving the taking of alms earlier than 1860 can be shown. It appears that some Jotishis used to act as *gomāsthas* of Gangaputras and also indiscriminately. The Gangaputras withdrew the employment and the Jotishis resented it by opposing the Gangaputras who have always appraised them strangers and actually prevented them in begging in the vicinity of the river. At annexation they enjoyed the general privilege of freedom of alms of the government and began to beg and also got a grant of 100 chowkees alleging their action to be opposed to the Gangaputras. At the time the river's annual changes left a large space of shore for chowkees – some 400 à 500 and in place of 100 they managed to set off 500. Being thus installed in this river bank they take fees from bathers etcetera. They are called Bhadarias in the Panjab and their speciality is to take Parishardan, Balidan and Toladan and to beg indiscriminately. If the Jotishis had a place set apart and were known to the pilgrims, no pilgrim would go to them.

Gangaputras of Guptarghat. Their old records are they say to have been burnt some 40 years which shows that they have a privilege with their Ayodhya fellows as decided by arbitration in March 57. The arbitrators refused right to the Jotishis, but this fact was not recognized by authority, during the closing of the Guptarghat because of the cantonment. The Guptar ganges ... [illegible] have been given 150 chowkees at the time till the chowkees were sold by auction in November 1870. No Jotishis purchased chowkees at the auction of 1870. The Gangaputra Laxmi Saran bought 10 chowkees at the auction, but the majority abstained and made afterwards their own terms with the purchasers who were chiefly residents of Ayodhya. A copy of letters to the collectors of other bathing places and their replies in original for your information are sent. This petition received from you is also returned. Signed: Patrick Carnegy.

It might be useful to clarify some points in these notes, before we start discussing them. The British were clearly interested in two things: to decide who was entitled to erect chowkees on the riverside, and to gain a certain amount of income from pilgrimage, at least at the time of festivals. The Jotishis mentioned by Carnegy are the group nowadays generally known as Bharleriyas and they are regarded by Carnegy as *gomāsthas*, agents in the service of the 'ancient' Gangaputras. There is another group mentioned: the Gangaputras of Guptarghat. This is a bathing-place (Gopratara Ghat) on the outskirts of Faizabad, several miles from Ayodhya, being the place from which Ram went to heaven after his long stay on earth. This ghat was closed in 1866 when a large military cantonment was opened there. The original document of Carnegy was found in the pandas' files, which means it has been taken from the archives of the settlement court. It is unclear to whom these notes were addressed.

What can we make of the notes and reports of the British administration? First of all, we have to ask ourselves what is meant by 'the right to put chowkees on the bank of the river Sarayu'. As we have seen in the report made by Shaw, both Gangaputras and Bharleriyas began erecting chowkees on the bank of the river only in the 1820s. This simple fact supports our contention that pilgrimage to Ayodhya began to expand considerably only at the beginning of that century, and consequently it became worthwhile for pandas to sit on the ghat, at least during the festivals, in order to receive new pilgrims who, being the first in their families to come to Ayodhya, would not have come to their houses. It was also in this period that the first pilgrim registers were drawn up. Shaw continues to emphasize that the erection of chowkees caused conflict between Bharleriyas and Gangaputras. This is quite understandable, since the strategic position of the stalls implied advantages in getting a share in the expanding market. New pilgrims could just as easily be entertained by Bhareriyas as by Gangaputras.

The officer in the Oudh police force, Buxchi Teg Singh, who belonged to a place as far away as Rawalpindi is a case in point. He became jajman of a Bhareriya panda. It is also clear from Shaw's report that the Gangaputras were dominant on the ghats and that they sometimes chased the Bhareriyas away. This is no surprise, since the Gangaputras were Sarayuparin Brahmans, by far the dominant caste in Ayodhya. The only way for the Bhareriyas to acquire a place in the pilgrimage system was by bribing Muslim officials who had to keep law and order in Ayodhya in the time of the nawabs. When the British took power in Awadh they inherited the situation and decided to have an independent judgement on the right to put up chowkees, which had almost become equivalent to the right to pursue the profession of panda. The Brahman savants who were asked to give their opinion were not very helpful in reaching such a decision, since they based their arguments on Hindu tradition. One of them answered straightforwardly that the Bhareriyas had rightful claims as well, while the other two either refused or hesitated to give an answer. This can be understood, when we take a closer look at the so-called 'rights' involved.

When there is a jajmani bond between the patron and his priest, the latter has the right and the obligation to receive gifts from his jajman. This is also the case with the panda who has the right and the obligation to receive the gifts (mostly to the ancestors) given by his jajman on pilgrimage to Ayodhya. In many cases, however, jajmani bonds did not exist. Many pilgrims who came for the first time to Ayodhya there initiated jajmani bonds. As far as custom and tradition were concerned they could enter such a bond with whatever Brahman they liked, as long as the Brahman did not refuse. In fact there were only two constraints on this choice. First, the Sarayuparin Brahmans enjoyed as a caste higher status than the Bhareriyas for a number of reasons, which I will discuss later. This implied that a jajmani bond with a Sarayuparin was considered to be higher than one with a Bhareriya, but this kind of consideration depends critically upon information. It plays a great role in a small-scale world with face-to-face contacts, but a much smaller role in the large-scale world of pilgrimage in which new groups started to participate. The

Bhareriyas therefore had considerable opportunities to make jajmans among the newcomers. The second constraint was formed by the existing jajmani bonds between rajas and Ayodhya pandas, exclusively Sarayuparin Brahmans. The saying 'whose king, whose people' implied that the Gangaputras as well as their jajmans, the rajas, tried to make their jajmani bonds paradigmatic for the new bonds made by pilgrims from these states. When the Gangaputras came into conflict with the Bhareriyas on the right to serve the pilgrims they quite understandably sought the help of their powerful jajmans, the kings, to safeguard their position. This becomes clear, for example, in the occasion for Shaw's inquiry. The raja of Mainpuri had asked the British via his panda, the Gangaputra Hanumanprasad, to prevent the Bhareriyas from putting up chowkees. It is, however, significant that the raja did not intervene himself, but asked the British to do so, since, as he puts it nicely in his request, 'it will not become himself to show an authority in such cases'. In fact he did not have the power, the means of legitimate violence or, as they put it in India, the *daṇḍa* ('the stick') to intervene. The new rulers, having monopolized the means of violence, had to step in and take decisions. Their policy, however, was not related to the traditional interdependence of the kingly patron and his priest. This constraint was still there and remained there till, say, the 1920s and 1930s, but it was losing force, leaving enough space for the Bhareriyas to gain a share in the pilgrimage market.

The right to put chowkees on the bank of the river Sarayu is therefore in no way a 'traditional' right, derived from jajmani bonds. The erection of chowkees was the result of a new situation, the expansion of the pilgrimage market, and the stronger party, the Gangaputras, attempted to remove the weaker party. The British tried to reach a compromise. They decided that the most important bathing-places with solid steps of brick, the so-called *pakkā ghāts* which were built by rich patrons for the benefit of the pilgrims, belonged to the Gangaputras, whereas the Bhareriyas were allowed to put 100 chowkees on the sandy bank, the so-called *kacchā ghāts*. In this way both groups literally got a place in the pilgrimage market which was defined not in terms of jajmani, but of plots on the bank of the river. These rights were finally laid down in a register of all the ghats and chowkees with their 'owners' by the commissioner A. J. Robinson in 1887. In this register we find mostly Gangaputras, but also a few Bhareriyas. It is interesting to see that in general the British were more favourable towards the Gangaputras, who had, as Carnegy writes, very old documents to prove their claims, than towards the Bhareriyas, who did not have such documents. While the Brahman savants interviewed by Shaw were reluctant to deny the Bhareriyas a right to put up chowkees, Carnegy was very straightforward in his idea that the Bhareriyas were only agents of the Gangaputras who tried to operate independently, but would never get any pilgrims if people knew that they were Bhareriyas or Jotishis. Nevertheless the British did not feel that it would be legitimate to deny the Bhareriyas everything and they decided to give them at least a minor share of the spoils.

Another aspect in these British documents is the interest in the tax which could be derived from the pilgrimage. Carnegy tried in 1865 to increase the sum available for police and conservancy expenditure, but only in 1870 did he succeed in putting up for auction all the chowkees which were not acknowledged by the government as belonging to either Gangaputras or Bhareriyas.[13] Only the pakka ghats were considered tax-free (*māfi*), because the British were under the impression that they had been built for the benefit of the Gangaputras and not for the benefit of the pilgrims. The 100 chowkees on the sandy bank were given to the Bhareriyas under the condition that they paid a tax of 17 anna per chowkee. The rest – and how much that was depended on the considerable annual changes in the course of the river – was thus put up for auction in 1870, but there was considerable trouble and, as Carnegy admits, almost no panda bought a chowkee. After a fresh investigation the British decided that the municipal board was entitled to sell by auction all the sites which were not held under old arrangements, but in fact the custom became that the municipal board levied a yearly tax per chowkee on the sandy bank, while the 'owners' of these chowkees were also registered. Only when the tax was not paid did the chowkee come into the possession of the municipal office, which might indeed auction it.

The Brahmanical right of pandaship became in this way a registered right to plots on the bank of the river, in a number of cases tax-free, in others not. This settlement of rights to the bathing-places brought the pandas into a heightened conflict not only with each other, but also with other claimants.[14] A case in point is the litigation between the abbot of the temple of Lakshman Ghat, Shatruhandas, and the Gangaputras, before the settlement court (case 887: 5-4-1905). Shatruhandas expected the Gangaputras to pay him rent for the use of Lakshman Ghat, on which his temple stood. The ghat and the temple were built by Raja Ramdat Pande of Dhanipur (Gonda). The abbot could, however, show only that the temple was given by the raja to his spiritual lineage of Ramanandis. The ghat was altogether something different. Like all the other brick ghats it had been built for the benefit of the pilgrims and of course for the glory of the builder, but it belonged to no one as immovable property. Just as in other cases, however, the Gangaputras showed that they had the right to erect chowkees on this ghat and that this right had been acknowledged by the British as a tax-free one. In short they did not have to pay any rent to the abbot. The settlement was in their favour, so that from then on the abbot lost his claim to the ghat, although he and other abbots continued with their legal battles against the Gangaputras.

There is one other aspect to this case which is of great significance. The settlement officer acknowledged the right of the Gangaputras to mortgage, sublet and sell their chowkees. The right of putting chowkees on the ghats became in this way a marketable commodity. The ghats which were built for the benefit of the pilgrims were thus subdivided into plots of land (*zamīn*) and the pandas became the landowners (*zamīndārs*). This situation was not an exception in the pilgrimage market. Pilgrim registers were another marketable property which could be mortgaged, sublet and sold. In this way one could win a place in the panda community by buying chowkees and registers. As regards the pilgrim registers, the paradoxical situation arose that recorded jajmani relations, generally depicted in the literature as pre-market relations, became *in toto* marketable commodities. The extent to which this situation was totally new is an open question.

The fact that the Gangaputras of the present are not able to clarify their connection with the pandas mentioned in the old documents of the seventeenth and eighteenth centuries might indicate that jajmani relations were already marketable and in each case transferable before the expansion of the pilgrimage system in the nineteenth century. On the other hand, while the situation in the seventeenth and eighteenth centuries was not entirely different, it was no doubt quantitatively so. There is a marked difference between a situation in which single jajmani bonds can be maintained without large recording and accounting and a situation in which pilgrims registers become, together with rights on the ghats, the central items of property for pandas.[15]

To return to the question of the formation of the Gangaputra identity, it seems clear enough that there were a number of considerable forces impinging on those Sarayuparin Brahmans in Ayodhya who had made pandaship their vocation. The expansion of pilgrimage to Ayodhya from at least the beginning of the nineteenth century in terms of the sheer number of pilgrims, but perhaps more significantly in terms of participation of new status groups which had not formerly participated, seems the most important force to be mentioned. It made the pandas put chowkees on the ghats and brought them into growing conflict. The increase of pilgrims to Ayodhya in the second half of the nineteenth century was greatly enhanced by the improvement of communications in the area. Until 1850–60 it was far from easy to reach Ayodhya as a pilgrim. The roads in Awadh were dangerous and troublesome. Only after the mutiny of 1857 did the British, guided mainly by military motives, decide to build a network of roads. At that time there was only one metalled road in the province, namely the one between Lucknow and Kanpur. The British started with the improvement of roads in the district of Faizabad (a core area of the mutiny) and likewise with the road between Faizabad and Lucknow. In this way Ayodhya became relatively easy to reach by road. In the same period the accessibility by waterways improved. Until 1860 a steamer sailed up the river Ghagra only once a month – the same river that flows past Ayodhya and is regarded there as the holy river Sarayu – to the provinces of Bihar and Bengal. After 1860 steamer traffic expanded considerably. Finally in 1872 the Faizabad-Bara Banki railway connection was opened (for details see the *Gazetteer of India*, Faizabad, 1960: 180–1). Thanks to these developments Ayodhya came within easy reach of a growing number of pilgrims and its catchment area expanded accordingly. As a result, more pilgrims came to Ayodhya from more distant places.

This expansion of the pilgrimage system during the nineteenth century, however important, cannot be taken as the sole force impinging on the Ayodhya pandas. Perhaps even more important in the process of identity formation was the British attempt to establish clear definitions of what pandaship was and what their rights were. Old documents proving jajmani relations and the long-time vocation of pandaship were taken as proof of customary rights to put up chowkees on the pakka ghats without paying tax and, rather surreptitiously, the customary right to be a panda as such.

It is interesting to see the ambivalence of the British position. The old configuration, attested to by the old documents, was one dominated by jajmani relations between élite jajmans, preferably rajas, and pandas of Sarayuparin Brahman caste. This configuration did not fall apart when other status groups started to flock to Ayodhya in increasing numbers. The question then became one of the impact these élite jajmani bonds had on the behaviour of the newcomers. It is clear that the élite bonds had a paradigmatic value.

The rival group of Bhareriyas, having no documents to prove existing jajmani bonds with élite patrons, were nevertheless clearly able to get a place in the expanding market. Rajas could not do very much to prevent this since they lived at a distance and lacked the power to force anything upon pilgrims coming from places as far away as Rawalpindi. It was the British who had to enforce the élite conception of Hindu society in the pilgrimage centre. It was no accident that it should be the raja of Mainpuri, Bhawani Singh, who asked the British to intervene. He, even more than most other rajas in Awadh, must have been aware of the fact that after the annexation the sources of power were at the command of the British. While his cousin Tej Singh, as the incumbent raja of Mainpuri, had joined the anti-British forces in the mutiny, Bhawani Singh, as a disappointed claimant to the throne, had thrown in his lot with the government. After the British victory Tej Singh's holdings, together with the title of raja of Mainpuri, were awarded to his loyalist cousin (Metcalf, 1979: 141–3). With the British annexation a new configuration had come about, in which the élite lost its 'kingly' authority and new men and new property relations came to dominate the rural scene (cf. Metcalf, 1979). The change can be summed up in Metcalf's apt phrase 'from rajas to landlords'. Bhawani Singh understood this perfectly well and did not try to exert his own authority, as he put it himself, but asked the real power-holders, the British, to intervene.

The British intervention was ambiguous. On the one hand they acknowledged the 'ancient rights' of the Gangaputras and allowed them the better share in the pilgrimage market, but since they could not get a learned judgement based on Hindu canons of law to the effect that Bhareriyas were simply not allowed to act as pandas, they gave them permission to put their chowkees on the sandy bank – a place of lower esteem, but nevertheless an acknowledged place. The juridical definitions of pandaship and panda rights were used by the British to 'freeze' a previously fluid situation. A clear boundary was created between those who owned pilgrim registers and chowkees and those who did not. Moreover, this was a very valuable property in an expanding pilgrimage market. One could of course try to buy oneself into the market, but who would sell? It is these forces which transformed the 'open' identity of the Ayodhya panda, from being a Sarayuparin Brahman who worked (at least primarily) as panda, into the rather more closed one of Gangaputra. It is in this period that for the first time we find in the documents a clear reference to a Gangaputra group, said to have eight lineages comprising a variable number of households.

The process of identity formation resulted in caste-like behaviour. Marriages were arranged only within the Gangaputra group, and intermarrying and interdining with other Sarayuparin Brahmans came to an end. This is probably the result of forces impinging upon them from within and from without. The endogamous practice, seen from the point of view of the pandas, had the clear advantage of saving the newly acknowledged property rights from dissolution over a much larger group of Sarayuparin Brahmans. The policy was to keep the registers and the chowkees in the lineage. On the other hand this more closed identity resulted from the refusal of other Sarayuparins to marry themselves into this group for fear that they would be totally identified with the panda trade which, while it was financially rewarding, also had its degrading aspects, as we discussed earlier. It is hard to tell which force would have been the more powerful, and the question is not of much interest. To my mind they both belong to a process in which the identity of social actors becomes more closed and defined within clear boundaries. The process finds its clearest expression in the document with which I started this discussion, the rules and regulations of the Gangaputras pandas of Ayodhya of 1889. Rights had to be defended and inner conflicts had to be avoided in the light of the continuous competition with the Bhareriyas and the threatening claims of the abbots of

Ramanandi temples on the ghats. Most of the descendants of the signatories of this document are still in some way involved in pandaship in Ayodhya, so that we may say that a lasting definition of the Gangaputras group was effected at the end of the last century.

We conclude this section with a few remarks on the term 'Gangaputra'. It means 'son of the Ganga' and though *ganga* or Ganges can be used for any sacred river in India it is surprising that the Ayodhya pandas use this generic term and not the term Sarayuputra, 'son of the Sarayu'. Indeed in documents of the beginning of the nineteenth century we sometimes find the designation 'Sarayuputra' used for an Ayodhya panda family which was later to be found among the signatories of the Gangaputra document. My suggestion would be that the Ayodhya Sarayuparin pandas wanted to give more emphasis to their connection with their professional colleagues in other places of pilgrimage rather than to their connection with Ayodhya. In their struggle to be acknowledged by the British, the pandas, like the British themselves, tried to find support in the jurisprudence of Benares, where British power had had its impact on the pilgrimage system much earlier. In the files of the pandas I found many cases dating from the end of the eighteenth and the beginning of the nineteenth centuries from Benares which were used as evidence in their own legal proceedings. It can be readily understood that the Ayodhya Sarayuparin pandas tried to take advantage of the successes of their colleagues in Benares who also called themselves Gangaputras (but more correctly so, since they worked on the Ganges). Important in each case is their reluctance or inability to emulate the localized groups of Brahmans at Gaya or Allahabad, the Gayawals and the Prayagwals, who indeed seem to have been separate endogamous castes for a long period, but preferred to remain a relatively closed professional group of pandas who did not deny that they were Sarayuparins.

THE BHARERIYAS

When I first came to Ayodhya I was told by the group of pandas, known locally as Bhareriyas, that in fact they belonged to the Brahman caste of Shrimalis, Brahmans who are active in Gujarat as priests and pandas.[16] During subsequent conversations they abandoned the idea and instead began to insist that they belonged to the Gaur Brahmans, a regional Brahman caste living in North India. This shift of identification already indicates that we are facing here an even more untraceable group of priests than the Gangaputras who definitely consider themselves as Sarayuparin Brahmans and are seen by others as such. Generally the Bhareriyas are regarded as Brahmans of low status. Only their opponents, the Gangaputras, sometimes try to deny them the status of Brahmans, but this strategy carries little conviction for most people in Ayodhya. Thus they seem to be Brahman priests, and taking that as our point of departure we should ask what it is that sets them apart from other Brahman priests. It might be illuminating to give here a full quotation from Sherring's description of the group he encountered in Benares:

The Bhanreriya [*sic*] is a man of considerable influence in Benares, although in reality holding a very low position among Drahmans. He is by profession a prognosticator of coming events; and it needs scarcely be added that in a large city like Benares, penetrated through and through with superstition, his services are much in request from the highest Hindu to the lowest. To this lucrative occupation he adds another. The multitudes of pilgrims who are constantly visiting the sacred city from all parts of India every month of the year, require a great many guides to direct them to those interesting places in the city, the famous wells, and tanks, and temples, and ghats – to which it is usual for pilgrims to go and there pay their devotions – and initiate them into the duties to be performed at each spot. The Bhanreriyas discharge the functions of guides to such persons, and are well paid for their pains, especially as they do not scruple to take various kinds of presents, which more respectable Brahmans would reject with indignation. The God Saturn, or Sanichar, is mostly worshipped by these people. As Saturday is the day sacred to this deity, on which he receives special adoration, it is customary for the Bhanreriyas to receive presents of oil on this day in honour of the god.
  The Bhanreriya is also called Bhaddali, from following the tenets of Bhaddal. Many of the clan are found at Rudrapur, in the Gorakhpur district; and the village has consequently received the appelation of Bhaddalpur, or town inhabited by Bhaddalis. It is said, and is commonly believed in that neighbourhood, that

Bhaddalpur is the birth-place of the race. The clan is likewise spoken of by the terms Dakaut and Joshi. (Sherring, 1872: 38).

There is much we can learn from this description. The Bhareriya's main profession seems to be what Sherring calls 'prognosticator of coming events'. Even today it appears this is a professional activity of at least some members of the group. According to one of my informants many Bhareriyas live in nearby Bara Banki, where they are known by the dialect term *arapopo*, which means 'people who speak the truth loudly' (i.e. who utter prophesies which come true). The people of Bara Banki are said to be afraid of them and give them gifts to escape their curses. The etymologies of the other terms by which they are known also seem to bear out the same meaning. According to Nesfield (1885: 67) the name Bhareriya means 'gabbler' and has been given to men of this caste on account of the fluent readiness with which they read the fate of a person by examining his hands and face. Elliott (1869: 88) informs us that Dakaut is from the Hindi verb *dakna*, 'to bawl', because they beg aloud in the streets. They are 'a tribe of mendicants of Brahman descent. They are considered to be proficient in astrology. The Bhadariyas are a branch of the same tribe. Both are considered troublesome vagabonds.'

The term 'Joshi' points out another aspect of the Bhareriyas' professional identity. Nesfield (1885: 67) offers the etymological conjecture that this word is a contraction of *Jyotishi*, 'astrologer'. This is quite probable, since the Bhareriya or Joshi is indeed always connected with the planets and most specifically with an inauspicious planet, Saturn or Shanivar. I have already quoted Miller's description of the Dakauts in the village in which he carried out his fieldwork: 'On Saturdays the Dakhot, carrying a brass bucket containing an iron image of Saturn (*sanichār mūrti*), goes from door to door collecting flour, *ghee* and oil' (Miller, 1975: 49). The belief is that the Dakhot takes the inauspiciousness away. The Joshi, Dakhot or Bhareriya is therefore a Brahman priest who is specialized in telling fortunes by reading the stars and palmistry. Nesfield (1885: 67) reports that as such 'each Joshi has a select circle of constituents who live in villages surrounding his own at a distance of about ten or twelve miles, and no other Joshi is allowed to visit him'. This means that the Bhareriyas had their own area of operation in the countryside which had nothing to do with pilgrimage, but everything to do with their primary occupation of fortune-telling.

The art of astrology and to a lesser extent that of palmistry are both held in high esteem as Brahmanical sciences. Knowledge of these branches of science gives a Brahman a high status. Why then is the Bhareriya held in low esteem if he appears to be a specialist in these sciences? We have already remarked that planetary configurations have their effects on the well-being of human beings. Before any important task is undertaken the Hindu consults someone who knows how to work with the intricate astrological manuals (*panchanga*). Certain times are inherently dangerous, such as *sankrantis* (joining of the sun with a new portion of the zodiac), new moon days (*amavas*) and eclipses (*grahana*) (cf. Raheja, n.d.: 18–23; Stanley, 1977). Some planets are seen as inauspicious. To quote Nesfield once again: 'In the Hindu system of astronomy there are said to be nine planets, viz., the five regular planets, the sun and moon and the two demons of eclipse' (1885: 68). He goes on to make a division into three categories of planet: three auspicious (*shubhagraha*), three less auspicious or ambivalent (*pāpagraha*), and three bad (*krūragraha*):

Shubhagraha

Guruwar	Thursday	Jupiter
Somwar	Monday	Moon
Shukrawar	Friday	Venus

Pāpagraha

Bhaumwar	Tuesday	Mars
Budhawar	Wednesday	Mercury
Adityawar	Sunday	Sun

Krūragraha

Shanishchar	Saturday	Saturn
Rahu	both demons of eclipse	
Ketu		

The configuration of these planets at a person's birth, for example, has a definite influence on the rest of his or her life and sometimes marriages have to be avoided or gifts offered to Brahmans because of it. The knowledge of these constellations and their effects as well as the calculation of someone's horoscope is a very specialized matter, but what seems even more important is that it is somehow thought to be possible to influence the future, even though it is pre-established by these conjunctions, by giving gifts to the Brahmans, organizing big sacrifices (*yajnas*) and so forth. In fact is seems that the whole point of making horoscopes and asking about the future is that one can then act upon the prognostication. The main difficulty seems to be, however, finding a Brahman who is willing to accept the gifts offered to a *krūragraha* or to conduct rites at an inauspicious time in order to dispel the inauspiciousness. Formerly the Bhareriya or Joshi seems to have been this kind of Brahman priest, as Nesfield points out:

> With the *kruragraha* is the Joshi in league. The offerings made to these malignant powers and transmitted to them through their appointed priest, the Joshi, consist of oil, the black pulse called urd, pieces of iron, black cloth, etc. The colour black is the appropriate emblem of these deities of darkness, and oil for relieving the darkness is the appropriate offering. It is customary for the Joshi to receive such gifts on the Saturday. (Nesfield 1885: 69)

It seems clear enough from Nesfield's account, as well as from that of Miller, that the connection with the planets, especially with inauspicious ones, constitutes the key feature of the Bhareriya's identity. Living in the countryside, he lives from what the jajmans in his constituency are able to offer him. This indicates a settled life in a village with a clearly defined caste identity. On the other hand, we have evidence that Bhareriyas were and are, in Elliott's unkind words, 'vagabonds' or Brahman 'mendicants'. Some of the older Bhareriya informants in Ayodhya told me that they used to go around the countryside initiating people upon request in a sectarian doctrine by giving them meditation formulas (*mantras*), as if they were spiritual preceptors. This type of activity is still undertaken by a few of the younger Bhareriyas. The case of the Bhareriyas can in this respect be compared with that of the Ramanandi sadhus living a life that constantly oscillates between the two ultimate options of settling down and moving around.

In the nineteenth and twentieth centuries a major tendency

among the Bhareriyas seems to have been to settle down in places of pilgrimage. This clearly appears to have been an effect of the expanding pilgrimage market of this period, which also affected the already settled Sarayuparin Brahmans, as we have seen in the preceding section. From Sherring's description of the Bhareriya's position in Benares we may learn that the Bhareriya had become a man of considerable influence not only because of his main activity of fortune-telling, but also by working as a guide for pilgrims in the ancient city, and by accepting gifts from them. From court cases, found in the files of the Ayodhya Gangàputras, it is clear that in the eighteenth century violent conflicts broke out between Gangaputras and Bhareriyas in Benares in much the same way as they started in Ayodhya almost half a century later. I would therefore suggest that an attractive option for Bhareriyas, besides settling in the country-side, was to settle in places of pilgrimage like Benares, Allahabad and Ayodhya. In these places they were, however, powerfully opposed by those Brahmans who had already settled there and had vested interests in a growing pilgrimage market. This is not to say that there were no Bhareriya families in places like Ayodhya before the expansion of pilgrimage. There is some, admittedly vague, oral testimony that there were two Bhareriya families in Ayodhya 'from time immemorial'. This might be supported by the fact that these families indeed continue to play a dominant role in the Bhareriya community up to the present day. In general, however, everyone in Ayodhya, including most of my Bhareriya informants, were of the opinion that the Bhareriyas had come to Ayodhya in growing numbers only in the course of the nineteenth century.

The Bhareriyas settled in the Ranupalli ward and in the beginning of the twentieth century some of them moved to the Chakratirtha ward when the river Sarayu took a different and more permanent course. These wards were situated near the river, although rather removed from the centre of panda activities, the Svargadvar ward, where the Gangaputras had entrenched positions. Nowadays one can measure the success of a Bhareriya household by seeing where it lives. If it still lives in the Ranupalli or Chakratirtha wards we may conclude that its members are still marginal pandas, but if they have moved to houses near the main road leading to the river or near the station, they are clearly more successful. The common story among Gangaputras is that the Bhareriyas were formerly their agents (*gomāsthas*), and had only later tried to obtain an independent share of the pilgrimage market. This story was also put forward in pamphlets distributed in Ayodhya during my stay in 1982, when there was a violent struggle between the two groups. This is in my opinion, like most other stories, a politically motivated view which is only partly true. I was shown an original document of 1857 which amounted to an agreement of employment between some Gangaputras and some Bhareriyas, so that there can be no doubt that *some* Bhareriyas worked as agents for some Gangaputras. Nevertheless, it is also true that, as we have seen, from 1820 to 1825 Gangaputras and Bhareriyas were fighting each other over the issue of erecting chowkees. Moreover, though the British gave the Gangaputras a superior right on the brick ghats, they also gave the Bhareriyas a right on part of the sandy river bank.

The Gangaputra story about the Bhareriyas therefore seems partly true. With the expansion of the pilgrimage market some of the Bhareriyas were able to set themselves up as pandas, but others were forced to accept a secondary place as gomasthas of the Gangaputras who were able to afford them. However, in their position as agents they did not find themselves alone, since the Gangaputras gradually began to employ people from their own Sarayuparin caste, and from other Brahman castes, such as Sakaldipi and Kanyakubja, as well as – much more recently – from non-Brahman castes.

The Bhareriyas who were able to settle in Ayodhya as pandas had obtained rights to parts of the ghats downstream from Ram Ghat, that is Vasudeva Ghat and Janaki Ghat. To the present day they have never been accepted by the Gangaputras as *partners* in the pilgrimage system, but can only be *servants*. In fact, however, the Bhareriya pandas were very successful in the second part of the nineteenth century and the first part of the twentieth. The steamer that opened a regular service between Ayodhya, Bihar and Bengal after 1860 moored on the sandy part of the bank 'belonging to' the Bhareriyas, so that the Bhareriyas had the first pick of new pilgrims. This situation even improved when the railway to Faizabad was extended to the river Sarayu near the place from which the steamer departed. Since pilgrimage was definitely a growth economy in this period the success of the Bhareriyas did not lead to increasing violence with the Gangaputras, who were also making great profits. The court cases of this period are almost entirely concerned with litigation between

Gangaputras and Ramanandi abbots over the ownership of the stone bathing-ghats. The relative success of the Bhareriya pandas strengthened their belief that they had a legitimate claim to equal partnership in the pilgrimage system, since they felt in no way inferior to the Gangaputras. They make some efforts to live up to this idea. In the first place they refuse to acknowledge that they are Bhareriyas or Joshis or whatever, saying that they are simply pandas, or trying to link themselves with unknown Brahman castes of another area. In the second place all of them refuse to acknowledge that they have ever received any gifts for planets (*grahadān*). They vehemently sought to impress on me the idea that all this was slander by their opponents, the Gangaputras. That they had ever worshipped Saturn on Saturdays was a preposterous idea.

These modern statements can be interpreted as attempts to cover up the past in an endeavour to gain a higher status as well as a legitimation for their panda activities. The great difficulty, however, seems to be the fact that the Bhareriyas always seem to have had an open marriage policy. It is rather difficult to call the Bhareriyas a caste, a *jāti*, according to Mandelbaum's definition: 'a jati is an endogamous, hereditary social group that has a name and a combination of attributes. All members of a jati are expected to act according to their jati attributes, and each member shares his jati's status in the social hierarchy of a village locality in India' (1972: 14–15). Although Mandelbaum allows for some flexibility in the interpretation of caste boundaries, he is of the opinion that marriage is the relation that demarcates each jati most clearly (1972: 16). After observing the actual marriage *behaviour* of many Bhareriya families, I find it impossible to speak of an endogamous, hereditary social group. Within Brahman jatis there are exogamous clan names (*gotras*), but these names were either unknown among the Bhareriyas or invented on the spot. One Bhareriya gave me the clan name Bhardwaj, but I heard later from an elderly key informant that this man, who had begun to feel apprehensive, had come to him and asked whether he had not made a terrible mistake by giving himself such a name, when he did not know whether he had one. In this way I could give here a list of gotra names existent among Bhareriyas which would not have the least practical value. I found cases of Sarayuparins and other Brahmans, but also of a few non-Brahman families which had intermarried with Bhareriyas and in this way had become Bhareriya. It is probable that this is not a modern phenomenon, but has always been the practice.

The Bhareriyas form a relatively open social group engaged in professional priesthood and as such are generically termed Brahman. Their professional identity is primarily focused on a connection with the bad planets, but they showed a great professional mobility when they had the opportunity of becoming pandas on a large scale. Since, generally speaking, they have little to defend, they do not follow a strict marriage policy to safeguard their rights – except for those families who were successful enough to get rights on the sandy ghat and to move to the centre of Ayodhya – but welcome any suitable marriage candidate within certain limits.[17] In this connection it is important to remember that only a few Bhareriya families were able to gain a position on the sandy ghats, whereas a larger part of the 'community' could only attain the secondary rank of agent. This difference, among others, implies great difficulty in controlling the behaviour of the entire group, so that closing ranks by following strict endogamy, for example, could not be enforced. The lack of internal cohesion is also in other respects an important disadvantage in the competition with the Gangaputras.

For the moment it should be clear that the Bhareriyas obtained a place in the pilgrimage system of Ayodhya as pandas and agents, but that they were not able to defend their rights to the extent the Gangaputras have done, partly because of the lower standing of their rights, but mainly because of the particular vagueness of their identity. In these circumstances their statements regarding their pure panda status had to remain merely verbal.

RIGHTS AND PROFESSIONAL IDENTITIES

Gangaputras and, to a much greater extent, Bhareriyas are professional groups which do not seem to have a strictly defined identity. The Gangaputras seem to be different from other Sarayuparin Brahmans only to the extent that they have the specialized profession of pandaship. This is of course not enough to call them a separate endogamous caste or subcaste (*jāti*). This term is only applicable where there are clear boundaries between social groups in terms of marriage, commensality and other interactions. As far as I can see from the historical evidence, there were no such boundaries between pandas and other Sarayuparins before the nineteenth century. These boundaries were erected in that century and it is an open question whether they were imposed on the Sarayuparin pandas or were self-imposed by them. My suggestion would be that both forces – from without and from within – operated simultaneously. During the nineteenth century, therefore, there gradually arose a professional group, calling itself Gangaputras to stress its link with professional brethren in other pilgrimage centres, which started to behave as an endogamous caste. Marriage exchanges took place only within the Gangaputra community, mostly locally, but in a few cases also regionally with Gangaputras in pilgrimage centres like Benares and Chitrakut. This strict caste-like identity, which also implied exclusive interdining, eroded gradually from the 1950s onwards and is no longer upheld in practice. Nowadays Gangaputra sons and daughters are married with other Sarayuparins who are not pandas, as well as within their group. The common explanation is that there are nowadays only a few Gangaputras left, so that they have to marry outside the group.

Why did this group of Ayodhya pandas start to behave as a caste in the nineteenth century and why did they not continue this behavioural policy after the 1950s? An important force in the process leading to the formation of the professional Gangaputra identity was the British desire to arrive at a permanent settlement of rights in the pilgrimage market. The central issue here was not the meaning of jajmani relations, but the right to erect chowkees at the bathing-places. The settlement of these rights made the Gangaputras once again different from other Sarayuparin Brahmans, since they became the owners not only of pilgrimage registers, but also of plots at the bathing-places. This property was so important that the owners tried to keep it undivided within a limited group of families and therefore started to restrict marriage outside the group, besides imposing other restrictions such as the one on interdining. The British expected pandas to belong to a separate and closed caste which from time immemorial had the right to carry out their profession. Although it proved to be difficult to find traditional support for this view of the exclusive rights of Gangaputras, the British wanted to give them their support and protection on the basis of what they thought the tradition to be. The British got what they wanted: the Gangaputras started to behave like an endogamous caste, having exclusive rights to pandaship. This process of identity formation was formalized in the 1889 declaration, in which the families forming the Gangaputra group were mentioned by name with their rights and obligations. Protection of rights which were being settled in this period proved a major incentive for the formation of an occupational identity. The other side of the picture is no doubt that other Sarayuparin Brahmans started to lay more emphasis on the degrading aspects of this professional specialization. The once fluid situation became more rigid on both sides. What happened might be explained as follows. Those families which were in similar circumstances, at the beginning of the nineteenth century, being at least partly engaged in panda activities, due to a number of forces impinging on them, began to form a kin group based upon control of hereditary positions. The Gangaputra 'caste' is a kin group of a few closely related intermarrying families with a professional identity based upon property. The main motivation behind their strategies was in no way to get rid of jajmani relations because these might be seen as degrading according to certain cultural criteria. Quite the contrary, their aim was to protect these relations and to multiply them.

The other professional group engaged in the panda profession was, as we have seen, the Bhareriyas. As far as I can see, they have always been a social group with extremely flexible boundaries, engaged in all kinds of priestly activities. It is interesting to see that they once claimed in an interview to be Gaur Brahmans. Carnegy reports on the Gaur Brahmans of Ayodhya: 'My impression is that the Gors, who are jealous to conceal their origin, are to Brahmans, what the Bais are to Chhattris; viz.: a very elastic gate through which caste pre-eminence is pretty easily attained' (Carnegy, 1868: 34). He observes the 'most strange fact' that the Jain temples in Ayodhya are all tended by Gor Brahman priests who are paid by Jain traders for their services, and adds that 'on questioning one of them about his lax religious views, he told me he would take charge of a Church even if he were paid for it' (1868: 34). This is exactly the impression the group makes nowadays. Bhareriyas, whether they are Gaur Brahmans or not, are a very accretive social group, adaptive to changing occupational opportunities, but primarily focusing on priestly activities which were not hereditarily claimed by settled Brahman groups. When they were not settled in a village, they moved freely through the countryside, begging for gifts, telling fortunes, and initiating illiterate villagers. It was especially this tendency to mobility that made them extremely useful as agents in the pilgrimage system. They collected pilgrims in the countryside and brought them to the unknown places of pilgrimage, guiding them in these religious centres and when possible taking their offerings. On the other hand they also tried to settle in these pilgrimage centres as pandas attempting to get a share in the rights which were conferred by the British. Some of the Bhareriya families succeeded in this attempt, while others did not. The successful acquired rights on the sandy bank and started to keep pilgrim registers. Due to favourable changes in the course of the river and the development of steamer traffic, as well as the establishment of a station near their chowkees, they were well-off by the end of the nineteenth and beginning of the twentieth centuries. These families are still leaders of the community, but they have not been able to make themselves a separate 'caste' in the way the Gangaputras did. Their rights and their property were very minor in comparison with what the Gangaputras had to defend. Some of these property-holding Bhareriya families were working on their own chowkees, others were working as agents for the wealthy Gangaputras.

Although the Bhareriyas have often tried to arrive at a stronger internal cohesion by forming caste councils having jurisdiction on such matters as marriage and general behaviour, they have never been able to close their ranks. The identity of a Bhareriya panda is still open to members of many jatis. At present the group has grown to about 400 households, lacking sufficient internal cohesion for a far-reaching control of behaviour. They behave with less dignity than the Gangaputras in matters of smoking and drinking, a fact which is conspicuous to pilgrims who come to Ayodhya. Most of the Bhareriyas therefore have a secondary place in the pilgrimage system of Ayodhya, working as agents of the Gangaputras without much hope of improving their position. A few of them are relatively wealthy pandas in their own right with a considerable number of jajmani relations. They have been unable, however, either to separate themselves from the rest of their community or to enforce upon the group a more closed identity and appropriate status behaviour. While the Gangaputras gradually established their position in the nineteenth century, the Bhareriyas remained, despite relative successes, the outsiders. This configuration of established and outsiders (cf. Elias, 1965) remained of utmost importance in the twentieth century. How the development of the pilgrimage market influenced the balance of power within this configuration, as well as the relations within both groups separately, is a question to be discussed in the next section.

4. Competition and violence

A CHANGING MARKET

In the previous section we saw how, after the British intervention in the pilgrimage system of Ayodhya, rights and relative positions were settled. The Gangaputras became the established group, while the Bhareriyas, with a few exceptions, remained outsiders. There were at least three points in the pilgrimage system in which crucial interests were vested: the pilgrim registers, the chowkees on the bathing wharves and the jajmani relations with élite pilgrims like rajas. The interesting thing to observe is that all these items were marketable. The registers recording such relations as well as the documents proving an élite jajmani bond could be and indeed were sold for money.[18] The right to put up chowkees at a bathing-place was also marketable – it could be sold and sublet. It is therefore neither irrelevant nor irreverent to speak of the emergence of a pilgrimage market during the nineteenth century. The structure of this market became fixed by the settlement of rights during the latter half of the nineteenth century. The jajmani relations remained of great importance, despite the mass character of the pilgrimage and the possibility for pandas to sell their rights over jajmans. New pilgrims coming to Ayodhya as the first of their families desired to be entered in the pilgrim register, to become jajmans of one of the pandas, while 'old' pilgrims wanted to be shown the register of their panda in order to confirm that they had come to the right man. This has remained the practice to the present day, although, due to reasons I shall discuss below, it has greatly diminished in importance in the course of the twentieth century.

The jajmans, of course, first came to Ayodhya to visit the holy place and to perform their rituals, but the panda also went to the villages and houses of his jajmans. Every year when I was in Ayodhya I met the panda of the Himalayan pilgrimage centre of Badrinath who had come on his tour through North India to collect gifts from his jajmans, which in Ayodhya already amounted to about 200 rupees. In the same way the Ayodhya pandas or their agents went to their jajmans in the slack season. This of course has the advantage that contact between the jajman and the panda is not restricted to a short visit from the jajman and thereby to only one gift. Moreover, often a gift was and is given in the pilgrimage centre in the form of a promise, namely that the panda may come at harvest time to take a part of the grain heap, the traditional form of jajmani payment. In this way the panda may come every year to collect his share. By the 1950s, this practice had assumed enormous proportions. Trains of bullock carts went to the countryside to collect the pandas' shares and bring them back to Ayodhya, where the grain was partly used for feeding the families of the pandas and their agents and partly put on sale. It is interesting that the grain was not sold in the village of the jajman, but had to be brought to the holy place. The gift had to reach Ayodhya, it seems. Besides these profits, there was the fact that the panda could make contact with other potential jajmans and induce them to come to Ayodhya as his clients. In this way the jajmani network was gradually expanded.

It is clear that to manage networks that in some cases encompassed tens of thousands of pilgrims required considerable organization on the part of the pandas. Pandaship could in no way be managed single-handed, and so many of the greater Gangaputra families had some fifty or more agents working for them. These agents could be of any caste, but generally they were Bharariya Brahmans. The head of the household and some members of his family remained at home to receive pilgrims, while the rest went with agents through the countryside to collect gifts as well as recruit new jajmans. The more use the pandas made of agents to maintain contacts with the catchment area, the more of course they came to depend on them. We will see later how some enterprising agents intruded into the pilgrimage system of Ayodhya and became quite wealthy pandas in their own right, but the trend of dependency on agents was general. This trend is also reported by anthropologists working in other centres of pilgrimage (Vidyarthi, 1961; Rösel, 1980). Vidyarthi goes as far as to state that the traditional panda-jajman system was

gradually replaced by a new system which he calls the *rozgāriya-*
panda system. *Rozgāriya* is the name given to those wage-workers
who deal in pilgrims with the Gayawal, the pandas of Gaya (1961:
107). I think that this statement is also correct for Ayodhya. The
central person in the pilgrimage from villages and towns to sacred
centres had been the panda, but he was gradually replaced by an
agent. This is no doubt a logical result of the expansion of the
pilgrimage market, in which the major issue was to get hold of new
jajmans.

The growing importance of agents in the pilgrimage system was
one of the major developments in this century. The second was the
gradual decline of the importance of jajmani relations. Nowadays the
pandas tend to neglect their registers, since 'no one is interested in
them any longer'. Pilgrims are brought by agents on a tour of
pilgrimage centres and the agents are paid at least the costs of their
own travelling by the panda or half of the amount offered by 'his'
pilgrims, from which the travelling costs are deducted. It is indeed
the relation between the panda and the agent which is the key one
here, not the relation between the panda and the jajman. The
pilgrims, moreover, are no longer interested in entering into jajmani
relations with pandas. They are taken on a tour organized by agents
and perform the rituals which are recommended by the agent or the
panda, and the personal contact between panda and pilgrim
diminishes. The pilgrims come by train or by hired buses and their
foremost contact is with the organizer of the tour, the agent, not the
panda. It is a chain of events which has results not planned by any of
the actors in the configuration, but giving benefits to some and
disadvantages to others. To manage the growing inflow of pilgrims
the pandas had to make use of agents, but this development gave
these agents a place in the system which grew in importance. It was
they who had the contacts in the countryside while the pandas could
afford to remain in their palatial buildings in Ayodhya, waiting for
the pilgrims to come. In fact, the larger part of the ritual was
performed by the agents as well, while the pandas restricted
themselves to supervision and indulged in *dolce far niente*. This
situation began, however, to leave a bitter taste, when some of the
pandas and agents began to claim a larger part of or even a monopoly
over the inflow of pilgrims. In the organization of pilgrimage, jajmani
relations had lost their value for pilgrims who only saw agents on

their grand tour. To rely on them was to stick to old ways in a new situation.

The jajmani relations with élite jajmans like rajas have also undergone great changes during the twentieth century. We have seen that these relations were used by the Gangaputras as paradigmatic models for new jajmani bonds to be contracted by the 'subjects' of these rajas and great landowners (*zamīndārs*). The 'subjects', however, were no 'subjects' any more and the awareness of this fact grew in the first decades of this century. The rajas had become landlords and were able to maintain a great deal of their power and influence on their estates under the umbrella of British power. This power, however, gradually weakened, and the extent of the decline is clearly shown by the defeat of the landlords' parties by the Congress in the 1930s (cf. Reeves, 1968). The use of the élite jajmani bonds as paradigmatic models also declined. Pilgrims were free to go their own way. Nevertheless these relations with rajas retained some importance. They gave the pandas status and also a considerable income. Pilgrimage had always been an event of conspicuous gift-giving for these power-holders, but since they no longer had to expend energy and resources on warfare, these rajas seemed to have concentrated on ritual alone.

More and more rajas came to Ayodhya in the latter decades of the nineteenth and the first decades of the twentieth centuries and their gifts were sometimes written on copper plates, a clear attempt at traditionalization. I realized, to my amusement, that the only copper plates to be seen in Ayodhya date from the twentieth century, while I could find no real traditional copper plates from, say, the sixteenth century. The gifts given were often considerable: gold, elephants, houses and so forth. This kind of conspicuous gift-giving is clearly a part of a complex of intensified religious activity on the part of rajas and zamindars in this period. A death blow was dealt to this profitable display of extravagance after the declaration of independence of India in 1947. Despite considerable opposition from rajas and some of the British officials sympathizing with them, the Congress Party did not allow separate status for what in colonial times had been semi-autonomous 'princely states'. Although for a few years at least the former rajas managed to retain some of their old privileges, they lost their political power and much of their income. This development of course only concerned the so-called ruling princes, who had not made the transition from raja to landlord like so many of their petty colleagues at the end of the nineteenth century.

A second and even more serious blow to the economic status of both rajas and landlords alike was dealt to them by the several land reform acts. In 1952 the Zamindari Abolition Act was passed in the state of Uttar Pradesh, the major catchment area for pilgrims to Ayodhya. Although most researchers have grave doubts as to the effects of this land reform, it is widely accepted that the position of great landholders, big zamindars and rajas, was shattered. Only those erstwhile landlords and the relatively better-off of the peasantry who could develop into a class of capitalist farmers seem to have benefited from the reforms. Being a rentier landlord leasing out land to tenants or sharecroppers was no longer a viable way of earning one's livelihood (Joshi, 1978: 473).

Much has been written about these land reforms, but almost nothing of their effects on religious centres which lost the traditional patronage of the former élite groups. The scale of the change is immediately visible in a place like Ayodhya, in which numerous magnificent temples of former rajas and zamindars have been left to decay since the 1950s. The effect on the position of the pandas has also been enormous. Not only did they lose a considerable part of their income due to the disappearance of the rajas from the ritual scene; they also lost their own zamindari property. The interesting thing is that the pandas had received much land as *samkalp*, that is to say as gifts with a religious purpose. Most of these gifts of land, however, were not registered in their names. They only came once a year at harvest time to reap the fruits of the land, a percentage of the total harvest of the landlord-jajman. With the abolition of zamindari the land passed into the hands of the tiller, to those who could prove that they cultivated it. When it was not the cultivator who was the actual jajman, but the absentee landlord, as was more often than not the case, the panda lost his rights to fruits of the land. This loss is still recalled by the pandas with great pain and bitterness. To them it seemed the destruction of the *ancien régime*, the profits of which they had enjoyed for at least a century. It also implied an important change in their relations with the agents. They had always been employers of a large staff of agents who were paid in money and in kind. This service relation gave them at least some power over the agents, to whom they could offer relatively secure employment.

Now, however, they could no longer afford to have so many employees, with the result that many of them became independent entrepreneurs.

So much for the jajmani relations which were still of great importance before India's independence, even though the élite jajmani relations had lost their paradigmatic status, but which declined rapidly in value in the 1940s and 1950s. What about the other crucial interest in the pilgrimage system, the possession of chowkees? In 1887 a final register was signed by District Commissioner A. J. Robinson, listing all the chowkees on the *pakkā ghāṭs*, the brick bathing-steps, which were regarded as tax-free (*mafi*) by the British. It is interesting to see that among the 382 chowkees there were, besides a great majority of Gangaputras owners, also some chowkees owned by Bhareriyas and a few by Muslims. Chowkees were and are marketable, so that outsiders like Bhareriyas and Muslims were able to acquire some – though actually only a few – chowkees on the pakka ghats. The question of ownership, however, remains somewhat problematic despite this final settlement. The ghats were built by rajas and others for the benefit of the pilgrims. Some of the builders, like the raja of Ayodhya, retained some kind of ownership of the ghats they had built, since they asked rent from hawkers who had their stalls on them. Other ghats came into the 'possession' of the endowments office of the municipality (*nazul sarkār*). In this case the municipal office asked for some rent from the hawkers. The pandas, as we have already seen, were not regarded as hawkers with a special religious type of trade. They had the right to put their chowkees on the ghats and this right was also treated as a property right which could be sold, let, or mortgaged. These rights were tax-free and rent-free. The assumption behind this, however, was that these pandas had a right from 'time immemorial' to practise their profession on the ghats. This was not so much a right to practise a profession as a right to a spot on which the profession could be practised. This shift in meaning implied that the rights to the spots, to the places on the ghats, could also be sold to outsiders who might not have the traditional right to practise the profession, such as Muslims. These new 'owners' had therefore acquired a right to sell, let and hypothecate these plots, but not to practise the profession of panda on them. The fascinating element in this was thus that the Gangaputras had acquired the rights to the ghats, on the basis of their 'ancient' pandaship, but that the rights thus acquired were disconnected from their *raison d'être*. The situation became most complex in cases where Bhareriyas had bought chowkees. In this way they not only became owners of spots which had been refused to them at an earlier stage of the settlement, but they also claimed of course the right to sit on the ghats and practise the profession of panda. Because the Gangaputras were careful not to sell more than a few chowkees to Bhareriyas they prevented their opponents from attaining the same level of power in the pilgrimage system which they themselves had reached thanks to the help of the British settlement. It is clear that this shift of meaning in chowkee ownership has caused the judiciary many headaches in the constantly recurring legal battles over the 'ownership' of chowkees, while the very vagueness of the rights involved proved to be an important advantage for the Gangaputras, allowing them to keep the upper hand in the game.

The word *chowkee* also underwent a shift in meaning. Formerly it was used to designate the wooden stalls where a panda could sit when he was working on the ghats, and the right involved was that of being authorized 'to put up chowkees on the ghats'. Gradually, in the last century, the word came to mean a way of measuring the different spots on the ghats. A chowkee on the *pakkā ghāṭs*, the stone ones, meant a spot four feet wide, while a chowkee on the *kacchā ghāṭs*, the sandy ones, meant a spot seven feet wide. In this way the ghats were measured and parts were allotted to the different property-holders. When we compare the present distribution of the space on the ghats with the distribution described in the register of 1887, we see that the majority of the chowkees are still in the hands of the Gangaputras, with the important qualification that most of these are held by only a few households. Some of the chowkees fell into the hands of what the pandas call *Baba-log-mahants*, abbots of Ramanandi institutions, all of them tracing their lineage back to Hanumangarhi, the institution of the nagas or fighting ascetics. We have discussed these naga businessmen in the chapter on the Ramanandis. Some other chowkees have been acquired by Sarayuparin Brahman families who bought themselves into the pilgrimage system. In my interviews with them they said they are merely property-holders, but have *never* gone to the ghats to receive offerings. This latter statement is denied by my Gangaputra informants who say that formerly they actually sat on the ghats themselves, but have abandoned that practice and now only let these chowkees.

Let us consider the story of one such Sarayuparin family. In 1895 Mohanlal Tiwari, son of Kesavaram Tiwari, landlord of an estate near Basi, bought a large house in the Svargadvar ward from Kunjal alias Bikhari (beggar), son of Ramnujavam, Gangaputra panda. In the same year he bought nine chowkees on several ghats from the Gangaputra Ganpathprasad. This property was enlarged by the acquisition of six more chowkees in 1902 and 1925, bought from two different Gangaputras. Mohanlal's son Ram Kumar still lives in the house of his father. He lets the chowkees he owns and has enlarged his property by buying houses and shops in the same area, near the river. At present he is a powerful man in the pilgrimage business with diversified interests. It is interesting that he has not become a Gangaputra by marriage, but he generally takes their side in conflicts.

In some ways these property-holders remind us of absentee landlords. They let their land to tenants who work on it. Every year they decide on a rent and those who are willing to pay it may hire the plot for a year or for some other specific period, such as a festival. Some of the plots are not put on hire, but are occupied by agents of the property-holders. In this latter system they pay their agents a wage for their work. In some cases they sit on the ghats themselves, but it is generally the poorer panda who goes to the ghat to sit on his own chowkee, while the richer one sits at home and receives some pilgrims there, but has many agents or tenants posted at the chowkees. In this way all the richer chowkee-holders are alike whether they are pandas or not: they sit at home and receive the money from the ghats in an indirect way, so that the question of pandaship does not even arise. It is, however, remarkable that there are still relatively few chowkees owned by non-Gangaputras. When we see how these few chowkees came into the hands of non-Gangaputras, it was mostly because a lineage died out and a widow sold her property, or because a minor Gangaputra had great solvency problems which forced him to sell at least one of his chowkees to someone who made a good offer. In general, the Gangaputras as a community have been conservative in selling chowkees to outsiders. When a lineage threatened to die out they adopted male heirs from other Gangaputra lineages inside or outside Ayodhya. Eventually some of the chowkees came into the hands of successful agents, but again very few. It is a pity that, for want of old registers, we cannot follow the development of the property on the sandy bathing-places in the same detail as the property on the pakka ghats. In one of the two copies of the pakka ghat register of 1887 that I was shown, the panda had also recorded his property on the sandy bathing-places, but this was not an official registration. Nowadays the chowkees on the kaccha ghats are numbered and registered in the municipal office, but I have not been able to trace registers older than the one currently in use. The present register gives the same picture as that of the pakka ghats, showing the same proprietors, although there are also 125 chowkees belonging to Bhareriyas which, as we have seen, were allotted to them by the British. Most of the chowkees on the sandy bathing-places, however, have come under the control of the municipal office. This is due to the enormous changes in the course of the river during this century which have made many chowkees completely unprofitable.

The changes in the pilgrimage market during the last century or so can be summarized as follows. The crucial relationship between jajman and panda which had characterized the traditional system was replaced by the crucial relationship between pilgrim and agent on the one hand and panda and agent on the other. The pandas managed the pilgrimage system through agents who went to the pilgrims, brought them to Ayodhya, served them on the ghats and paid them visits if they had promised to give gifts at harvest time. The pandas maintained their control over the pilgrimage system thanks to their proprietary rights with regard to pilgrim registers, documents of rajas, and chowkees. This control weakened considerably, however, when jajmani relations became less important to the pilgrims, élite jajmans lost their power, and property and chowkees could be hired or even in some cases purchased by outsiders. In this way the firm control of the Gangaputras as a group on the pilgrimage system was replaced by increasing control of the system by agents and an inner competition within the Gangaputras themselves, which was eventually won by one Gangaputra panda who has been able to monopolize the greater part of the system from the 1950s onwards. This development will be traced in more detail in the following section.

SACRED BUT VIOLENT ENTREPRENEURS

At the end of the nineteenth century two young boys, Sakadipi Brahmans from Bihar, came to Ayodhya as students. It still is very common for Brahman boys to go to a sacred centre, often Benares, for higher education in traditional subjects such as Sanskrit grammar, the Vedas and astrology. Nowadays there are some twenty *pāthshālās* in existence with a total of about 250 students. Older informants told me that at the beginning of this century there were fifteen genuine schools and some 350 students. Nowadays the degrees obtained in these schools are acknowledged by the government. The students coming to Ayodhya have to arrange for their own board and lodging, which they generally find in temples and in the houses of pandas. The link a student has with Ayodhya as a place of learning was often formed by a sadhu who visited his village or was the guru of his parents, or by a panda whose jajmans live in the village of the student. It always amazed me to see how many young errand-boys there were in temples and in the service of the pandas. Sometimes these boys are poor orphans, but often they are students who do a variety of odd jobs to earn their board and lodging. Some of the students stay in Ayodhya after their study and may become the sadhu inmates of temples or find themselves another religious job, but most of them return home, marry and establish themselves as the village pandit.

Our two boys, Rampal and Shankar, stayed in Ayodhya and lived in the house of one of the greatest pandas of the time, Bihari. The panda saw that they were clever boys and gave them more and more responsibilities in his panda business. Because they had learned to read and write they were given the supervision of that most important property of pandas at the time, the pilgrim registers. The boys were indeed clever, too clever to remain as agents in the service of Bihari. In about 1900 Shankar started to buy up chowkees until he eventually had twelve chowkees on the pakka ghats and seventeen on the kaccha ones. Rampal also acquired a few chowkees on the kaccha ghats, but most of his energy was directed towards the control of the pilgrim flow at the bus and railway stations. From the pandas or the agents of pandas working on the ghats he asked for part of the offerings made by the pilgrims he brought to them. The pilgrims themselves were entertained in his house. He was what the pandas call a houseowner (*makāndār*), rather than a man who sat on the ghat (*ghāṭwāl*). Shankar also tried to get a stake in the pilgrim flow, and the history of the period between 1920 and 1940 is not so much the story of the struggle between the Bharerwyas and the Gangaputras as an account of the rivalry between Rampal and Shankar. The war was fought with an enormous amount of violence, gun-fighting and bribery of the police. It was, of course, not man-to-man fighting between Rampal and Shankar, but rather between their bands of toughs (*goondas*). One can easily imagine what kind of business pilgrimage had become in those days. Pilgrims arriving at the station were taken to the house of a panda, while the retainers of the pandas were fighting each other with sticks and punches. A happy arrival in the birthplace of Lord Ram.

Pilgrims were not only welcomed at the stations in Ayodhya itself, but much earlier at stations and junctions en route. The pandas were forced to organize their catchment of pilgrims long before they reached Ayodhya. The Bharerwyas used their caste linkages with the hinterland of Ayodhya to catch pilgrims while the Gangaputras used the existing jajmani relations to expand their services to other pilgrims from the same and neighbouring villages; but still there was a great number of pilgrims left over who came to Ayodhya without any attachments. The majority of these were received by the well-organized networks of the modern entrepreneurs Rampal and Shankar. Because these pilgrims did not have any previous attachments, they could be won by those who were faster and better organized than their opponents, but the heavy competition virtually implied the use of violence to keep the rivals at bay. It was of course not only Rampal and Shankar who were fighting each other. The pilgrimage market was not neatly categorized into élite jajmans, other jajmans, and unattached pilgrims, each category holding its special token so that no panda might confuse them. On the contrary, the situation was chaotic: there were pilgrims who were actually some panda's jajman, but not clearly aware who he was, jajmans who knew who their panda was, but were easily led astray by the agents, and groups of unattached pilgrims, arriving together at Ayodhya. Moreover, the pilgrims did not usually come in small groups but in great numbers, expecially at festival times, when hundreds of thousands gathered in Ayodhya. These were the occasions when pandas and their small bands of toughs easily came to blows. The two main protagonists of the violence were Rampal and Shankar, newcomers to the pilgrimage scene of Ayodhya, but sometimes Bhareriyas and Gangaputras joined in the holy war.

By the late 1930s and early 1940s Rampal had come to dominate the stations and the flow of unattached pilgrims. Attempts on his life had failed and he was immensely feared by everyone. One might say that he had become the boss of the free pilgrimage market. However, this violent ruler of the stations met his equal in a young Gangaputra panda from Benares. Known as Gangaram, he is the son of a panda in Benares. He married into a respectable Gangaputra family with acknowledged property. It is interesting to see that his wife did not take up residence in Benares, as is usual in the Hindu system which has a clear preference for virilocality. It was Gangaram who moved to his father-in-law's house because he had acquired some chowkees and registers in Ayodhya as a dowry. All my informants came up with the story that after the death of his father-in-law he poisoned the heir to the ancestral property, his brother-in-law, so that he could gain possession of all the property of this family. As the pandas say, he had got hold of an important *gaddi*, a throne from which to rule his pilgrim domain. The house in which he could receive his pilgrims was strategically located in the Svargadvar ward very near to the river and on the main road leading down to it. This proved to be an enormous asset when increasing numbers of pilgrims started to come by hired buses. In a short time, in the 1920s and 1930s, this young outsider had, though by allegedly foul means, usurped a 'traditional' Gangaputra gaddi. This implied that he had his regular income from traditional sources, jajmans and élite jajmans. He recalls that in 1935 he got 13,000 rupees from the maharaja of Cochin (South India), while he was able to enlarge his house enormously by buying and building thanks to a gift of Gangabhai, the wife of Chandalal, one of the members of the powerful Kayasth élite in the realm of the nizam of Hyderabad, described by Karen Leonard (1978).

Gangaram was, however, ambitious enough not to be satisfied with only the traditional income. Maybe he had become aware of the general development of the pilgrimage market before the other Gangaputras in Ayodhya, because he had been brought up in the much larger pilgrimage system of Benares in which similar trends could be discerned much earlier than in the somewhat backward Ayodhya. Anyhow, he had sensed that it was of vital importance to control the flow of pilgrims from their place of origin to Ayodhya and possibly on their complete tour. In his attempts to act upon his idea he came almost immediately into conflict with the man who had been able to become the unofficial ruler of this part of the pilgrimage system, Rampal. After a series of violent incidents between the two men and their bands of toughs, the denouement came in 1944. An informant who lived near the station told me:

> One night in 1944 I was reading a book, when I heard a great outcry at the station. I rushed out to see what was happening. I was, however, soon stopped by police constables who told me to keep away, since the pandas were fighting at the station and outsiders had nothing to do with this kind of internal conflict. The following day I heard that Rampal had been killed by the toughs of Gangaram with *lathis* [long bamboo sticks]. His end must have been horrible, but nobody took pity, since he himself was also a murderer. It is said that Gangaram gave an enormous fee to the police inspector who was put in charge of the murder investigation and he was not even taken into custody.

From that time onwards Gangaram became the ruler of the stations.

Gangaram's position was even better than that of people like Rampal and Shankar. He was a Gangaputra sitting on a traditional gaddi in Ayodhya enjoying its income, while at the same time he was an entrepreneur who managed, by violent means, to get an increasing share of the pilgrim traffic. When, in the early 1950s, the income of traditional jajmani relations began to peter out he could easily shift to more modern methods of pilgrim attendance. By then he had already become the most important panda of Ayodhya. It is quite understandable that this development was looked upon with great jealousy by the other Gangaputras. They did not, however, unite against him for a number of reasons. First of all Gangaram married his sons and daughters strategically into the Gangaputra community. Secondly, and most important, he was able to use the threat of the Bhareriya rivals to his benefit. In the 1950s, when most of the agents had to be dismissed by the Gangaputras, the Bhareriyas were forced to try to get hold of a greater share of the pilgrimage market. Many of the Bhareriyas had been agents, while only some of their brethren had chowkees, registers and houses in which to receive their own pilgrims. In this period the Bhareriyas tried to use the zamindari abolition act to acquire the rights to the chowkees of which they were the tenants. The analogy with the agricultural sphere was clear, but the act of course only concerned the relations between landlords and tenants in that area. Even though the attempt to use the act was abortive, times were turbulent and the Gangaputras felt threatened, which can easily be understood when we consider what a hectic time it was for them. Gangaram manipulated this feeling masterfully by uniting the Gangaputra community under his banner. The violence between Gangaputras and Bhareriyas became even greater in this period, during which many ex-employers and ex-employees felt insecure.

Attempts to stem the conflict from the outside were destined to fail. In 1953 a committee of honourable citizens under the name of *Tirtha Rakshini Sabha*, 'Society for the Preservation of the Place of Pilgrimage', was formed to try to resolve the conflicts which, according to the committee, threatened to damage Ayodhya's reputation as a holy place. The members of the committee suggested distributing tickets of three kinds among the pandas: 1) for guiding pilgrims, 2) for lodging pilgrims in their houses, and 3) for accompanying pilgrims to the river and performing rituals there. Furthermore, they proposed to keep a proper record of all the pilgrims. The Gangaputras protested against this scheme, demanding that there should first be a clear pronouncement from the committee that non-Gangaputras would not be given tickets. When the committee failed to do this they went to the civil court, which declared the entire function of the committee contrary to the law on the grounds that the question of rights should be settled by a judge. The court seems to have forgotten, for the sake of convenience, that for almost a century litigations had been going on, with wavering and unclear judgments on its part.

Gangaram was the leader in this successful campaign of the Gangaputras to frustrate the attempt of the citizens of Ayodhya to interfere in what they considered to be their affairs. He was again the leader of the Gangaputras when plans to build a large bridge over the Sarayu river were finalized at the end of the 1950s; the building was nearing completion in 1964. The bridge is of the utmost importance for an understanding of the present situation of the pandas in Ayodhya. Rivers in India are generally rather badly regulated. They are small streams for most of the year, but during the monsoon they are enormous, wild and fast-flowing masses of water. Moreover, in the monsoon the river may considerably alter its course. Between 1930 and 1980 the Sarayu changed its course by as much as five kilometres in some places. When the river reaches Ayodhya proper it makes an enormous curve and flows past the (brick) bathing-steps which are owned by the Gangaputras and along the sandy bathing-places, of which a considerable share, 125 chowkees, is in the hands of the Bhareriyas. As we have seen, these chowkees were strategically located near the place where the steamer moored and near the railway station. In 1925, however, the old station near the sandy bathing-places of Vasudeva Ghat and Janaki Ghat was replaced by a new one in a different place. Moreover, a bailey bridge was built in the same year near the pakka ghats of the Gangaputras. The ghats of the Bhareriyas therefore declined somewhat in value, although they remained important. The changes of the river did not affect those ghats which remained near the river and continued to be used. Even when the changes affected the ghats on which the pandas had their rights, there was a recognized right to shift to where the river had moved, a principle that was also applied to cultivated lands. This rule, which also deals with the difference between the dry river and the swollen river, is, however, more applicable to cultivation than to the panda business. In the latter the crucial factor is the extent to which the chowkee is within reach of the pilgrim. A new place that is out of reach of the pilgrims has no value, while for a cultivator a move is merely inconvenient. This had happened with many of the chowkees of both Gangaputras and Bhareriyas between the time of settlement of rights and the present, but it did not involve the most important chowkees: those on pakka and kaccha ghats in the centre of Ayodhya, near the road and the bailey bridge. Although the Gangaputras had suffered some setbacks in 1925, their chowkees were still very valuable until the time the bridge was built.

In order for a bridge to be built over the river its course had to be changed. Since the engineers decided that it was impossible to build a bridge that would span the entire width of the river at monsoon time, the course was regulated in such a way that the width was considerably reduced. The result of this regulation was that the ancient brick bathing-places were left high and dry, as well as the sandy bathing-places called Vasudeva Ghat and Janaki Ghat. Of course both groups, Bhareriyas and Gangaputras, applied to the government for replacement of their chowkees. The Gangaputras received other chowkees on the newly built concrete bank of more than a kilometre in length starting from the bridge. In fact their chowkees were allotted in a direct line from the old pakka ghats to the newly built ones, and so the scheme was acceptable to them. The Bhareriyas, however, were not given any replacement for the chowkees on the sandy ghats. A direct line drawn from their old chowkees to the new course of the river would result only in chowkees situated on an almost unreachable bank of the river, far from the main road and therefore of no interest to anybody. The result was that the Gangaputras kept their places, while those few Bhareriyas who had some, lost what they had enjoyed for over a century. How did this happen? The Bhareriyas, though they know that they have been cheated out of their traditional rights, are frustrated, but have no clear idea how this was done. As I have argued earlier, they do not have the social cohesion to exert any political influence on this kind of decision. My Gangaputra informants were totally reticent about what had happened. They said only that at the time they had given most of their old documents, proving the ancient rights of the Gangaputras, to Gangaram, who had made use of them in his negotiations with the government. An interesting detail is that they complained bitterly that none of the documents entrusted to Gangaram had been given back to them. In this way Gangaram had been able to take full advantage of the situation. He had become the leader of the Gangaputras in their conflict with the Bhareriyas, while he had obtained a monopoly over the documentary evidence proving the ancient status of the Gangaputras. In this way the Gangaputras were made dependent on him, while the Bhareriyas were outwitted in the allotment of chowkees after the bridge was built.

It will be sufficiently clear that Gangaram is a brilliant strategist. He has used his power skilfully to enlarge his share in the pilgrimage system of Ayodhya. This can also be seen from the next two examples. The chowkees on the sandy bathing-places are numbered and their exact position is determined annually by officials of the municipal office. By bribing these officials Gangaram manages each year to get the best position on these bathing-places, which is extremely important for attracting a maximum flow of pilgrims. His chowkees are rented out for the highest prices in the whole market, 5,000 rupees per chowkee, while further away from the bridge their value gradually decreases to a mere 100 rupees per chowkee. The other example is that he has been able to acquire complete dossiers on the rights to the ghats from the archives of the Faizabad court. I have worked in these archives and it was amazing to see the monopoly over documents which is the main asset of the clerks working there. Gangaram has not only been able to prevail upon them for photocopies of the important documents, but has even got some original documents from the relevant files. I was only given permission to study part of the documents by employing the services of a new clerk who had not been working there when this transaction had taken place. This was just enough to enable me to see how far Gangaram's influence had reached into the archives, allowing him to acquire the important resource of history in his attempts to gain complete control over the pilgrimage system of Ayodhya. A large number of the unofficial documents which had belonged to other Gangaputras, as well as many of the official documents, were now in his hands. It would be unwise to fight this man in court.

Gangaram, of course, also did not want to explain to me how the new arrangement between the Gangaputras and the government had been made after the building of the bridge. In my interviews with him he was only interested in showing that the courts always confirmed his rights despite all the 'slander' against him which he was aware I must have heard. And indeed, as far as I have been able to observe, he has won all disputes up to the present day. The last violent dispute which I could witness took place in October 1982. What prompted the fight was the fact that Gangaram not only gets a handsome rent for his well-placed chowkees, but also demands 50 per cent of the offerings when *his* pilgrims offer at the ghats. Since he receives a large share of the pilgrims, having, according to his own boast, 32,000 agents who bring pilgrims to him, he tries to get as much from what is given at the ghats as possible. For that reason his agents and toughs roam along the ghats to check whether pilgrims 'belonging to Gangaram' give offerings at chowkees other than those that belong to him, in which case they go to the panda or agent concerned and demand, if necessary by force, 50 per cent of the offerings. These demands are directed against the Bhareriyas who work as tenants on the ghats and who are in this way forced to pay, besides the rent of the chowkees to one of the owners, 50 per cent of what is received as income to Gangaram. In October 1982 a Bhareriya guided a group of pilgrims around some temples in Ayodhya and received part of the pilgrims' offerings in these temples, a practice which incidentally reveals another side to the pilgrimage business, namely that pilgrims are guided to those temples which have agreed to give the pandas a share of the offerings. In this case an agent of Gangaram had followed the group and demanded in his turn half of the panda's share. The Bhareriya, however, answered this demand by giving Gangaram's agent a good hiding. This incident immediately occasioned a violent battle between Gangaram's toughs and the Bhareriyas on the ghats. Subsequently the district magistrate of nearby Faizabad intervened and denied both Gangaputras and Bhareriyas access to the riverside, because he interpreted the struggle between Gangaram and the Bhareriyas as a struggle between Gangaputras and Bhareriyas on which the courts had given judgment in the past and had to give judgment once again. This definition of the conflict in terms of rights to pandaship made it easy for Gangaram to win the case once again. Moreover, he created at the same time dissension in the ranks of the Bhareriyas by coaxing their leader to persuade them to send a letter to the civil judge in which they admitted that they had no rights and declared that they would not cause trouble in the future. This letter was sent in February 1983 and the ghats were again opened for use. Imagine the surprise of the Bhareriyas when they saw at the next festival that their leader was now working as the tenant of Gangaram's chowkees! From that time onwards two committees representing the Bhareriya pandas have existed in Ayodhya.

Besides his clever tactics an important asset of Gangaram is his political influence. He is a major power-broker in local politics. His support is important in local elections, while the propaganda value of pilgrimage centres where enormous crowds gather is also recognized by regional politicians. When Gangaram and his agents support certain candidates they are able to reach a large number of people. When ministers or other high officials visit Ayodhya on pilgrimage, they are certainly entertained by Gangaram, and his connections in Benares bring him into favourable contact with some of the mightiest men of India. I have often seen the white Ambassador cars of chief ministers of Uttar Pradesh and of the president of the All-India

Congress Party Working Committee in front of Gangaram's house. There can be no doubt that all this political influence can be used if necessary, a fact of which his opponents are perfectly aware. Gangaram sits on his throne and rules over the pilgrimage system of Ayodhya. The end of his empire can come only when he dies and if his son is not able to follow his father's example.

5. Conclusion: Values and Existence

'If we concern ourselves with activities as well as with values, with what men do as well as what they think, there are certain advantages to be gained.' This simple statement was part of F. G. Bailey's polemical reaction to the position taken by Dumont and Pocock in their editorial in the first issue of *Contributions to Indian Sociology* (Bailey, 1959: 90). It is surprising that a statement of such simplicity can still be quoted with some benefit more than twenty years later. The reason for this is that the 'sociology of values' presented by Dumont and Pocock has had much more impact on the study of Hinduism than the 'political' approach offered by Bailey. In the case of Hinduism, the implication of this has been that this area of study has been dominated by those who share Dumont and Pocock's belief that 'a Sociology of India lies at the point of confluence of Sociology and Indology'. Accordingly, much attention is given to models derived from texts studied by indologists in the social analysis of the position of the Brahman priest.

Parry holds that the highest goal in life for Brahmans is to renounce the priesthood and the dependence on donations so as to avoid the contradiction inherent in the priesthood. In order to solve this contradiction the 'good' Brahman models himself on the world renouncer. Likewise, Fuller argues that the priests' relative inferiority – within the category of Brahmans – can be defined in terms of a lack of ideal qualities. In North India, he argues, this distance from the ideal appears to be mainly caused by the acceptance of gifts. As we have seen, other anthropologists go even further in reproducing Hindu ideology by depicting the Brahman priest as the acme of purity and Hindu society as a system designed to keep the Brahmans in that high position.

Do the pandas of Ayodhya actually model themselves on the ideal

Brahman, the world renouncer, and do they regard renunciation of priesthood as the highest goal in life? Is the acceptance of gifts the cause of the relative inferiority of Brahman priests in Ayodhya? Following Bailey's advice we should primarily concern ourselves with what the pandas actually do, with their behaviour. In that case we can give a straightforwardly negative answer to both these questions.

The pandas are engaged in a daily struggle for livelihood and their actions and orientations are connected with that struggle. Moreover, this is not a modern phenomenon resulting from a process of secularization, but can already be found in the nineteenth century. When the pilgrimage market expanded and the British startd to define the rights in the system, the actions of the pandas were directed at getting as large a share as possible. It was the positive right to practise the panda profession which was highly valued among the pandas in this period. Its attraction grew with its increasing market value.

One could object that there were (and are) no alternatives to turn to for those pandas who were stigmatized by their caste and forced to stick to their profession. On the contrary, I would suggest that a professional group with caste-like boundaries, called the Gangaputras, was formed only when the pilgrimage system began to expand. Its professional identity had to be defined as a consequence of the British attempt at settling the rights to erect chowkees and controlling the threatening competition of the Bhareriyas. That this process, in which the Gangaputras created boundaries between themselves and other Sarayuparin Brahmans, also evoked stigmatization from the outside, can easily be understood. I would therefore suggest that the panda identity was not the 'cultural given' from which ideas and behaviour could be explained, but that this identity itself was the result of a changing configuration. In recent times this configuration has again experienced a major shift, and that is the reason why the boundaries between the Gangaputras and other Sarayuparins are not as strictly maintained as before. The new conditions of the pilgrimage market have made the 'traditional' rights much less valuable and, as a result, the maintenance of these boundaries has lost much of its importance for the Gangaputras. On the other hand, among the entire Sarayuparin group, other status determinants like education and salary have become deciding factors in contracting marriages. In that way an identity which was maintained for more than a century may dissolve again in the near future. In my opinion it is not ideology but rights in the pilgrimage system and control over resources that determine the 'caste' identity of the Gangaputras.

When we concern ourselves not only with behaviour, but also with the changing values of the Ayodhya pandas, it is not all that easy to give straight answers to our questions. The central problem seems to be the valuation of the gift. Parry presents two diametrically opposed views on the gift in his ethnographical descriptions. In his book on *Caste and Kinship in Kangra* (1979) the gift to the priest (*purohit*) is interpreted as having 'the character of a charitable donation humbly offered to someone of superior status, whose condescension in accepting the gift allows the donor to acquire merit' (65, 66). In an article based upon fieldwork among the Mahabrahmans of Benares he presents a quite different view of the gift by observing that 'as all the Brahman specialists see it, *dān* is bad not just because it subverts their ideal ascetic independence, but more importantly because the acceptance of *dān* involves the acceptance of the sins of the donor' (1980: 103). Contrary to these extreme points of view, which in themselves show the delicacy of the subject, I would propose to consider the gift in its context: the relations between patrons and priests and the nature of the thing given.

The relation between the *jajmān* (patron) and the Brahman priest is what is called a jajmani relation. This kind of relation is ambiguous. It offers protection, a secure income, but on the other hand it is often felt to be the cause of inferiority because it implies a certain dependence of the priest on the resources of the patron. In the Sanskrit literature which propagates the absolute superiority of the Brahman the priest is therefore warned against jajmani relations. The question is, however, what influence this ideology has had on the values of the pandas in the past and in the present. In this connection it is enlightening to see the pandas' view of their relation with the most important patrons, the rajas. They describe most eloquently their relations with the rajas of all parts of India who gave them huge gifts.[19] These are clearly matters of great pride and it is with bitterness that they recall how they attempted to continue these relations after India's Independence, but were rebuffed by the impoverished ex-royal families. In the Brahmanical literature, however, acceptance of gifts from kings is regarded as extremely dangerous. Mauss (1974: 58) gives the following quotation from the *Mahabharata*: 'O king, to receive from kings is honey at first but ends as poison.' It is Mauss's argument that the recipient is in a state of dependence upon the donor and that it is for this reason that the Brahman may not accept and still less solicit from the king. The ideological fear of inferiority seems, however, to be a far cry from the pride clearly expressed by the pandas with regard to their relations with rajas.

Sociologically this configuration can be interpreted as a delicate 'balance of power' in which each party tries to consolidate its own superiority. Viewed in this light, it is not surprising that Brahmanical literature sometimes regards the sacrifice as a contest between two parties. The Brahman tries to show his superiority by accepting the gifts from the king-jajman with as much detachment as possible and by a strategic use of his power, which consists of giving or withholding his blessing and making use of powerful curses. The king does the same by giving or denying his gifts and claiming an independent religious status for his kingship as derived from the cosmic kingship of a great god, be it Ram/Vishnu or Shiv. What is of importance is therefore the *etiquette* obtaining when secular and religious power meet. The Brahman should appear not as a greedy man, but as detached and learned, while the king should honour him without losing sight of the fact that it is only thanks to his gifts that the Brahman *can* appear detached. To a certain extent this is also observed by Mauss: 'Divinity among divinities, he [the Brahman] is superior to the king and would lose his superiority if he did other than simply take from him. On the side of the king his manner of giving is as important as the fact that he gives.' And somewhat later: 'All kinds of precautions are taken. The authors of the Codes and Epics spread themselves as only Hindu authors can on the theme that gifts, donors and things given are to be considered in their context, precisely and scrupulously, so that there may be no mistake about the manner of giving and receiving to fit each particular occasion. There is etiquette at every step' (1974: 58).

It is quite clear from my observations that the panda is worshipped by the jajman. The priest is the representative of the sacred and in this respect he is superior to the jajman. Even when the jajman is a raja, he should behave humbly and respectfully, because he has entered the domain of the sacred. Every jajman, whatever his worldly status, touches the feet of the panda respectfully and asks for his blessing. This is the context in which the gift is offered to the panda as a person who represents 'the sacred'. The acceptance of the gift in itself does not deprive the panda of his awe-inspiring position. The extent to which he is respected, however, depends largely on the way both the panda and the jajman behave. The oral tradition of the Gangaputras records breaches of etiquette, often concerning the rite of *parvatdan* in which the jajman and the panda are seated and gifts are piled up until they cannot see each other any more. Such stories refer to arrogant rajas who heaped up huge gifts without giving due respect to the panda. According to these stories, the panda brings down the raja's pride by distributing the gifts and even more to other pandas without keeping anything himself. In general pandas tend to be seen as inferior and rapacious people when their economic position is such that they are not able to behave in a detached, disinterested manner. The ideal Brahman is therefore economically independent.

Another consideration concerning the valuation of jajmani relations refers to the scale of economic transactions. In a small-scale village economy with little occupational mobility a priest will feel his dependence on landholding jajmans in infinitely subtle ways. It would seem quite understandable for him to try to emancipate himself from the jajmani ties and become an economically independent pandit who has no need to fear economic insecurity. In the large-scale economy of the pilgrimage system jajmani relations are much more impersonal. The names of the jajmans are entered into registers and the priest may see his jajman only once a year, or even once in a lifetime. This may partly explain why jajmani relations are highly valued by the Ayodhya panda. The element of security resulting from them appears to be much more emphasized than the element of inferiority which would be his daily experience in a village owned by his jajmans. It is, however, not only economic security which forces pandas to remain in their profession. Even rich panda families who could afford to take up another profession never seem to have considered leaving it because of an imputed social stigma.

The second question to be answered is that of the nature of the thing given. As I have argued in my discussion of the gift, the Ayodhya pandas make a distinction between 'good' and 'bad' gifts and it will not do to lump them all together. It is simply not true that in all cases the acceptance of a gift involves the absorption of the donor's sins and illnesses. On the contrary, more often than not gifts are given to Brahmans, cows and gods to accumulate merit. Only in the case of certain special rituals is sin or illness removed by giving a gift to a Brahman. In these rituals we find the notion that the Brahman receiver is tainted by the gifts, that indeed the sins or the illness are absorbed by the Brahman, as Parry rightly observes. I would argue that these gifts form a special category and that they are accepted only by Brahmans who are forced to do so by poverty. I regard the Bhareriyas as an open category of *poor Brahmans* who have come to accept dangerous gifts to provide for their livelihood. In fact they seem not to have jajmans as such, but to beg from door to door. Their activities are Brahmanical, since this kind of planetary inauspiciousness is elaborately treated in Brahmanical literature, but they resemble in many ways low caste specialists who deal with ghosts, illness and impurity in a non-Brahmanical way. Gifts of a dangerous and inauspicious character have to be given in the Brahmanical conception of the cosmic order, and there is a category of poor Brahmans at hand to make that possible.

A different and obviously more closed social category is formed by the Mahabrahmans, the funeral priests. With them we do not find jajmani relations, since no one would desire a hereditary bond between himself and the dead or death. The funeral priests provide a necessary service to the community, but they are avoided as much as possible. These specialists represent the dangerous side of the ambivalent sacred. Their position is not desirable and I am not surpised that some of them do indeed try to leave their profession when they get a chance to do so, as noted by Parry (1980). Fear of the dangerous effects of their identification with inauspicious planets and with death and ghosts would seem sufficient explanation for these attempts, and I fail to see what the concept of the ideal Brahman would add to our explanation in such cases.

The position of the Ayodhya pandas in these matters is ambiguous. In the first place, there are a number of borderline cases, gifts which are to some extent dangerous to accept. There is, for example, the gift in the context of an expiation (*prayashchitt*) ritual. The general idea is that when the sins involved are very serious, the gift has to be given to any poor Brahman who is willing to accept it.

When no such Brahman can be found, the gift is given in a symbolic way to sacred *kush* grass which is said to represent a Brahman. The Ayodhya pandas generally deny that they accept such gifts, but they accuse each other of doing so. Sometimes pandas argue that they are not the real recipients of this kind of gift, but that it is the sacred river Sarayu which absorbs all sins. It is clear, however, that this type of gift is not easily accepted and that when it is accepted the pandas will not give much publicity to it. Another borderline case is the *tuladān*: the jajman is weighed against a counterweight of gifts, and the counterweight is given to the panda, with the idea that he absorbs the jajman's illnesses. All pandas I have interviewed make it clear that they would refuse such a gift. Since I have never witnessed this type of ritual in Ayodhya I cannot report their actual behaviour. Maybe it is no longer performed owing to the disappearance of the greatest patrons, the rajas, who could afford to stage such a conspicuous ritual. What I was able to observe, however, was a front stage reservation and high-minded aloofness in these matters, but a back stage scepticism of the dangers involved in accepting such gifts.

The second important observation to be made is that commercialization of the pilgrimage market puts these matters in a different light. According to my informants, what was most important in the aforementioned expiation rituals was for the 'sinner' to get a certificate from the religious authorities of the pilgrimage centre declaring that the ritual had been properly conducted. This certificate can be taken to the caste council (*panchāyat*) which has imposed the punishment, so that the 'sinner' could be readmitted into the network of commensality, marriage and other relations in his caste. The interesting thing is that nowadays it is not only pandas who issue these certificates, but also abbots of Ramanandi temples. They are newcomers to this market and have managed to develop a situation in which they receive pilgrims in their temples in an almost complete pandaship. This fact throws a curious light on the theories we have discussed earlier. The pandas do not seem to be interested in renouncing their priestly profession, but, to the contrary, the so-called renouncers want to intrude on the pilgrimage market.

In fact, our analysis of both the behaviour and mentality of the pandas leads us far from orientalist models to the conditions of existence. The most striking thing in my interviews with many of the pandas was their sceptical, almost cynical attitude towards their own religious activities. When I asked why they had not tried to counteract the bad influence of first Rampal and Shankar and later of Gangaram by magical rituals, of which they no doubt knew quite a number, they dismissed this suggestion out of hand and proclaimed that they would only trust a gunman who was a good shot. Rituals did not have any effect on people like Gangaram. On the question of why they did not pray to Ram and Sita for protection and help, being the traditional priests of Ram's birthplace, one man answered, amid much laughter, that they already had to thank the divine couple for the fact that they had not yet been killed by Gangaram. Another example of their cynicism is the popular story that a panda sometimes used a dog in nocturnal rituals instead of an expensive calf, so that the pilgrims grasped the tail of a dog instead of a cow, being unable to tell the difference in the dark. To my ears this is an almost blasphemous story, but it is often told by the pandas themselves. This was of course merely a joke, but when I walked the *parikrama*, the circumambulation round Ayodhya, at night, I saw pandas performing rituals at places where people normally go to defecate. It was business as usual. The general attitude, with some exceptions of course, is neatly summarized by a Gayawal panda quoted by Vidyarthi (1961: 106):

> In our Gayawal society we find a peculiar situation. Actually only a few practise religion sincerely, most of them are showy. They just pretend to be religious-minded people ... They do not have time to think as how to obtain heaven. They are mad after earning their bread. To them prayer, worship, spiritual merits, meditations and shraddha all have become superfluous and showy – a means for earning their livelihood.

It would, however, be too cynical to say that the pandas of Ayodhya are simply cynics who pretend to be religious, but who are only interested in earning money. Despite having a somewhat cynical attitude towards their 'trade', many of them are strict Brahmans. A good example is Gangaram. He is at one and the same time an unscrupulous entrepreneur, to say the least, *and* a very orthodox Brahman. The domestic rituals which are of great importance to such Brahmans are meticulously performed by him. He lives a rather puritan life. Although he owns an enormous house as well as a car, a television and other luxuries, he is not a big spender. He invests his money in land, in shops and in a flourishing cement dispensary, which is managed by his second son. He reminds one of the Weberian entrepreneur: frugal, religious and rational. His opponents complain of his behaviour in all conceivable terms, but I have never heard anyone objecting against what could be called unbrahmanical or irreligious behaviour by Gangaram. Religious beliefs and attitudes do not prevent one from engaging in sharp practices, as we all know.

Pandaship is a profession and the conditions in which it has to be practised have changed drastically in the course of the last century and a half. The profession has a certain status in the eyes of those who practise it and is given a certain status by Brahmans as well as other people. The acceptance of gifts is certainly a factor in the determination of this status, but a variable factor, since all the elements of gift-giving have changed in this period: the donors, the receivers, the things given and the relations between donors and receivers. It is difficult to see what determined the status of this profession in former times, although we have some indirect information when we look at the behaviour of the pandas concerned. For the present, we can see that circumstances are threatening the position of many pandas and that this situation determines their evaluation of their profession. The former gift relations are highly valued, whereas the present situation, in which impersonal relations dominate, is felt as a threat to their self-esteem and the status of their profession. Although I have not made a systematic inquiry into the views of the visiting pilgrims, it is clear that nowadays the panda profession is held in low repute. I have already reported that people warned me against these dangerous pandas, and this view of pandaship is supported by the evidence that violence is common in the pilgrimage system. It is not really surprising that a pilgrim who arrives at a station to visit a holy place and is almost attacked by the agents of several pandas who fight among themselves for the right to 'guide' his pilgrimage will have a low opinion of the profession. Their haggling to get as much money from him as possible will not help to make this picture any more favourable. As far as I could ascertain, these changed conditions determine the status of the pandas in their own eyes and in those of others. Most of them are fairly poor already and others are living in constant fear of impoverishment. Only a few, like Gangaram, manage to thrive in the present situation, and these are the only ones I have heard boasting about their 'ancient profession' and their enormous pilgrimage organization.

V Conclusion

The Hindus call their religion *sanātan dharm*, the eternal religion. The believers assert that it has neither beginning nor end. Those who wish to study their religion, they argue, would do well to rid themselves of the typical western notions of 'time' and 'history'. Moreover, one should penetrate beyond the plurality of forms to the ultimate oneness of being, since the visible phenomena are mere illusions (*māyā*). This Hindu view is also encountered in the academic community in what I have called the 'orientalist perspective'. Hindu believers assert that one needs an unchanging, transcendent realm of values which serves as a stable and reliable point of orientation. This realm of values is enshrined in the ancient Sanskrit texts. In the same way, a number of anthropologists also seem to derive their sense of direction from such a beacon. Through intense collaboration with their humanist colleagues, who assist them in the correct interpretation of the sacred texts, these anthropologists think they will succeed in constructing a model that will help them to rise above the maya of their fieldwork notes.

Contrary to this point of view, which is basically theological in nature, the argument developed in this book is that the study of textual Hinduism can serve as a tool, but that nothing can replace the direct observation of religious practices, the competition in the various arenas and the shifts in the projection of religious identity, as major sources of anthropological information. Oral tradition and eyewitness reports from observers who lived in earlier periods form another important source for social enquiry. The combination of these two types of information allows us to understand the changing social configurations which inform religious orientations. These points may seem obvious and trite, but still they need to be raised: the position of anthropologists *vis-à-vis* the students of 'ancient civilizations' demands an insistence on principles for the empirical study of religion that elsewhere are accepted without question.

A major complication in the present kind of study is that the history which has to be explored is used strategically, as a resource, in the competition between interest groups. The Ramanandis, for example, are known to have linked themselves with the South Indian Shri-Vaishnavas in the past, while at the beginning of the twentieth century they severed these putative links quite deliberately. Another example is that of the Ayodhya pandas. Gangaram most vigorously asserts his claims over strategically located sites in the pilgrimage centre by emphasizing the fact that, as Gangaputra, he is a 'traditional' panda. At the same time, he controls access to archival documents which may throw light on the development of these 'traditional rights'. In view of the fact that this monopoly on historical information is jealously guarded, and from studying reports from the beginning of the British intervention in the pilgrimage system, one is led to believe that a study of Gangaram's documents would result in a clearer picture of the origin of 'traditional rights' than we have been able to suggest in our analysis.

All groups of religious specialists discussed in this book have at one time or another redefined their identity. What struck me most during my research was the finding that there had been a general development, in which all groups of specialists seem to have participated, from an open and rather flexible identity to a more closed, circumscribed and stable one. The expansion of the colonial state appears to have played a major role in the 'freezing' of status positions. British officials were inclined to take this relative stability, which they themselves had partly created, as the traditional system of 'eternal India', and anthropologists have often followed in their wake.

Religious specialists are, just like other political actors, able to define and redefine the rules of interaction in the arena in accordance with their changing interests (cf. Vincent, 1974: 376). The identities of the Ramanandis and the Ayodhya pandas are not cultural givens, primordial ties, but definitions that are constantly adapted to new realities. Their development is critically dependent on the direction of change of the larger configuration of which they form a part. In the case of the Ramanandis the relevant facts are the development of long-distance trade and military entrepreneurship during the eighteenth century, and the decline of such grand possibilities as a result of the *Pax Britannica* and the concomitant emergence of new networks of trade. In the case of the pandas the expansion of the pilgrimage system at the beginning of the nineteenth century and the later development of a commercialized pilgrimage market had several implications for their professional identity and for their relations with their jajmans. These changes in identities and value orientation can in no way be interpreted along the lines of static cultural models, derived from the elusive concepts of 'caste' and 'sect'.

The religious field (*kshetra*) of Ayodhya itself, in which all these developments took place, also changed considerably during the four centuries under consideration. In the sixteenth and seventeenth centuries the pandas received the pilgrims in Ram's fortress, a collection of ruins. The Ramanandis had not yet settled in Ayodhya on a significant scale. More important were the Shivaite sadhus, probably reflecting the much more prominent place of Shivaism in earlier times. During the eighteenth century Ramanandi sadhus started to settle in this ancient birthplace of their god. Their expansion was greatly enhanced by donations from the successive Muslim governments of Awadh. Hindus played a central role in these governments and were mainly responsible for the patronage of Ramanandi establishments in Ayodhya, but also the Muslim nawabs did not feel above supporting the Ramanandis. Many documents attest to the stimulating influence of the nawabi patronage on Ayodhya, which is contrary to the idea now commonly held that the town could only prosper after the Muslims had left. It was during this period that the Ramanandis began to build their temples in Ayodhya. In fact, this was called 'rebuilding', 'restoration' or 'repair', since the fiction had to be maintained that all the temples built were just replicas of the buildings of Ram's own time, a fiction which was further enforced by the notion of 'timelessness' in Hinduism and the fact that Ayodhya and its buildings were already mentioned in ancient Sanskrit literature, notably of course in the *Rāmāyaṇa*.

In the nineteenth century this building activity began to increase dramatically, especially after the British take-over. Carnegy's report of 1870 mentions an enormous growth of building activity in the period between 1850 and 1870, and from my own research it is clear that it was sustained at a high level until the 1920s. Rajas and large landholders (*zamīndārs*) who aspired to the position of rajas were the builders of temples and pilgrim lodges. They tried to acquire merit (*puṇya*) and fame (*kīrti*). Generally they did not simply hand the temples over to Ramanandis, but appointed their own Brahman priest (*pūjāri*) and other staff to run them. On pilgrimage to Ayodhya they resided in these buildings. Caste associations also started building their own places in the beginning of the twentieth century. Both high status groups, such as merchants and Kayasths (writers, administrators), and low status groups such as untouchable leather-workers and washermen, built their own temples. This further illustrates the increased importance of caste identities in the colonial period.

The great building activities of the rajas and zamindars should also be related to the protection they received from the colonial state. As one of the descendants of a great builder once explained to me: 'We [the rajas] did not have to fight any more. We could devote all our resources and time to religion.' And indeed they did. The position of these élite groups changed drastically during the twentieth century due to the abolition of royal privileges after India's Independence and the abolition of zamindari in the 1950s. New élite groups usurped their position and, by forming religious trusts, became the great builders. Walking through the streets of Ayodhya this change is clearly visible. Next to the decaying ruins of the temples of the former rajas are the new marble edifices of the Marwari and other trusts.

These new élite groups have, however, not taken over the role of their predecessors in the conspicuous ritual gift-giving to pandas. Their activities are to a great extent rational and directed to building and management of their own network of temples. The pandas are the great losers in this changing configuration. They had made great profits in the same period that the old élite started to build. Gift-giving was an integral part of royal status for those who held that rank and probably even more for those who did not have it. From the two great trends in the pilgrimage system, expansion of scale over all status groups and expansion of the scale of gift exchange by the élite groups, only the first proved to be a lasting trend. This had great implications for their position, which can be summarized as a deterioration for most of them and a monopolization of the market in the hands of a few whose position improved considerably.

In all the aspects of pilgrimage to Ayodhya we have thus been able to discover important developments which altered its character in several fundamental ways: Ayodhya itself, the composition of groups of pilgrims and the position of pilgrim-receiving specialists. These developments do not detract from the position of Hinduism as an ancient religion. I also do not wish to suggest that Hinduism is on the wane due to modernization and secularization, but simply that it has a political and historical dimension to be explored by anthropological investigation.

Appendix 1.   Kanak Bhavan, an example of a temple built by a raja

Most of the 100 or so temples built by rajas and zamindars in the British period are now in a pitiful state. The former élite is no longer able to afford the considerable expenditure involved in maintaining a temple, paying its personnel and staging worship in a grand style. Take, for example, the so-called Pali temple, built by the widow of Raja Krishnadatta Singh, *taluqdār* of Pali state in district Sultanpur. The temple was built in 1901 at a cost of 80,000 rupees. An amount of land yielding an annual income of 8,000 rupees was given to the deity. Since the abolition of zamindari the government has paid an annuity of 1,300 rupees to repair damages incurred by the alienation of this property. Bahadur Singh, the grandson of Krishnadatta Singh and present owner of the temple, explained to me that only bare essentials could be paid for from that amount. However, he refused to 'go begging', since he was a Kshatriya who could not ask for financial help. This temple is still in the hands of the family which built it, but many others have surreptitiously fallen into the hands of Ramanandi sadhus or pandas, often with the mute consent of the former gentry which in any case is unable to manage alone. In other cases the rajas are not in a position to do much to oppose the sadhus and pandas who are well entrenched in Ayodhya politics.

Against this background the story of Kanak Bhavan is rather a successful one. The temple and surrounding land were on 23 October 1883 bought from the abbot Lakshmandas for the sum of 3,300 rupees. The temple was in fact a small hut (*kuti*) which was demolished by the new owner, Maharaja Sir Pratap Singh of Orccha in Bundelkhand. The motivating force behind the building and decoration of the new temple was Pratap Singh's wife, Vrishabhanu Kunvari. She bought land and gave it to the temple as well as fixed deposits amounting to 324,000 rupees in the bank. The decoration of the temple, especially the upper storey which contained the so-called apartments of Ram and Sita, must have cost millions of rupees, if we simply take into account the quantity of precious stones used. Vrishabhanu Kunvari died in 1905; in 1908 the temple was given to a private trust named after her.

The trust has a committee of eleven members who come together at the time of great festivals in Ayodhya. The president, a direct descendant of the raja, has a double vote and may veto new members. Five of the members are from Orccha and the rest from Ayodhya. The temple personnel is from Orccha and the manager of the temple is at the same time the raja's guru, who is, interestingly, a South Indian Brahman belonging to the Krishnaite community of the Pustimarg. In the year October 1981–October 1982 the temple had an expenditure of 324,215.55 rupees and an income of 596,878.44 rupees. Interesting income particulars are: *daily offerings* (annual), 65,328.15; *special offerings*, 56,857.85 (this is a very fluctuating income, since in the preceding year it had amounted to 186,000); and *annual gifts*, the largest being from the owner of the Star papermills in Shaharanpur who gives 21,000 rupees annually, but a large number of people give smaller amounts annually or sometimes larger ones irregularly, as for example the raja of Diggi, who sometimes gives 50,000 rupees.

Except for Hanumangarhi, no temple in Ayodhya attracts as many pilgrims as Kanak Bhavan. This is also the key to its success. While the other temples built by rajas remained of parochial interest to the pilgrimage system of Ayodhya, Kanak Bhavan's very splendour gave it an importance which surpassed its connection with the Orccha family. It spread the fame (*kīrti*) of the Orccha family by being in particular Ram's temple and not that of Orccha. In this way it had become independent of the vicissitudes of a royal, landholding family in North India.

Appendix 2. Caste temples

The building of temples by and for particular castes is a phenomenon of the twentieth century. Caste consciousness was greatly enhanced by British administrative policies such as the census operations in which Hindus were asked to declare which caste they belonged to. In this period castes began to organize themselves on a regional or even a national level into associations (*sabha*) to promote the interests of the caste. It is interesting to observe that this modernizing effort on behalf of castes had as its cultural corollary the establishment of caste temples in sacred centres like Ayodhya. Sadhus who originally belonged to a caste were mostly the ones who organized the fund-raising and who became officiating priest (*pūjāri*) and manager in such caste temples. Take, for example, the temple of the Nishad caste (boatmen). In 1917 a Kabirpanthi sadhu of the Nishad caste raised funds among his caste to build a pilgrim lodge in Ayodhya. When the *panchāyat* of his caste decided to build a temple for Ram and Sita next to the lodge, he, as a Kabirpanthi, opposed that plan, but was removed from his post by a court order. A Ramanandi sadhu of Nishad caste took over his position. This man had for a long time been an itinerant tyagi and took the opportunity of spending the rest of his life in Ayodhya with a secure income provided by his caste.

Although most of these temples cater for low castes, some belong to relatively high and upwardly mobile castes, like the Kayasths. A rich caste like the Marwari is also very active in building temples, but its members are rich enough to build temples which are attractive to Hindu pilgrims in general. The typical Ayodhya caste temple is clearly meant only for members of the caste and not for outsiders (who would not even think of visiting them). An interesting aspect of the caste temples is whether they have a Brahman as an officiating priest (*pūjāri*) or not. In general, low and untouchable castes have a member of their own caste as pujari, while middle and higher castes have Brahmans or Ramanandi sadhus who are at least *dvija*, twice-born.

These are the caste temples I observed in Ayodhya:

1. Agarhari Vaishya (shopkeepers)
2. Ayodhyavasi Thater (brassware-sellers)
3. Kalvar (liquor distillers)
4. Kayasth (scribes)
5. Karusha (chair-makers)
6. Kurmi (agriculturalists)
7. Kumhar (potters)
8. Kevat (boatmen)
9. Khatik (fruit-sellers)
10. Garereya (shepherds)
11. Teli (oil-pressers)
12. Dhobi (washermen)
13. Nai (barbers)
14. Nishad Bans (boatmen)
15. Pathar (garland-makers)
16. Pasi (pig-tenders)
17. Barai (betel-sellers)
18. Barhai (carpenters)
19. Beldar (woodcutters)
20. Rajbhar (labourers)
21. Bhuj (grain-roasters)
22. Bhangi (sweepers)
23. Mali (gardeners)
24. Murai (vegetable-growers)
25. Yadav (milk-sellers)
26. Raidas (subcaste of leather-workers)
27. Loniyam (salt-makers)
28. Lohar (blacksmiths)
29. Sonar (goldsmiths)
30. Halvai (sweet-makers)
31. Barvai Kshatriya (pickpockets)
32. Kori (weavers)
33. Dhiman (traders by boat)
34. Kanhar (water-carriers)
35. Jaiswal (traders)
36. Lodhi (labourers)
37. Shin (subcaste of barbers)

Appendix 3. Rules and regulations of Hanumangarhi

In order to give an impression of the basically democratic character of a Ramanandi akhara it might be interesting to quote here some of Hanumangarhi's rules and regulations:

Rule 4: In the eye of law there are three types of math recognized: 1. Hereditary; 2. Panchayati; 3. Haqabi. Hanumangarhi is a panchayati math. The seat of gaddinashin is not hereditary, not based on guru-chelaparampara (succession of guru and disciple), but all the members (*panch*) of the akhara appoint a mahant by majority from a patti. The whole responsibility to manage the akhara goes on the shoulders of the panchayat. The panchayat is the owner and manager of the temple. Each member has equal rights and in his turn he has the right to get a share whatsoever.

Rule 5: When mahants of pattis have earned property for the baithak, this property is managed according to the rules of the akhara.

Rule 8: There are three types of panchayat: that of the patti, that of the akhara, that of the executive panchayat of the akhara. The rights and duties of the members are given below. All the members of all the jamats constitute the panchayat of a patti. They manage the whole movable and immovable property and they decide by majority of vote. The mahant of a patti is elected and turned out according to the decision of the members of the patti. Any sadhu of the patti misusing the property of the patti or avoiding the rules, regulations and traditions or violating the fame and honour of the akhara, can be punished or turned out after a decision taken by the patti-panchayat, called for this very purpose. The decision is strictly imposed and obeyed. The mahant of the patti presides over such meetings and if he is absent a president is chosen out of the members. A sadhu thus found guilty may get punishments like termination of mahantship or membership, monetary fine, stoppage of food, lodging.

The panchayat of the akhara is composed of all the sadhus of all the pattis and jamats. It is responsible for the management of the property belonging to the four pattis and for its supervision. This panchayat initiates the gaddinashin and chooses and appoints members for the executive panchayat. It has supreme power, but if any member of the akhara panchayat has any doubt against any member of the executive panchayat in regard to his working or ambitions, he may raise a question in the akhara panchayat and therein a decision is taken after consideration, which the member has to face and accept. Every year in the month of Karttik an account of the akhara is read before the members, who give their decision. The akhara panchayat is ordinarily presided over by the gaddinashin. If absent, the assembly may appoint a president. This executive body is constituted of 21 members of all four pattis, jamats and toks. They appoint a sarpanch (president). The term of the executive panchayat is two years, which can be extended for one year. The members, including the sarpanch, can be re-elected. The sarpanch presides and calls the meeting of the executive. He makes suggestions to the members present and gives his ruling on the proposals. All the members of the executive panchayat have to be sworn in before the sarpanch and the sarpanch himself before the gaddinashin. An emergency meeting of the executive can be called for at any time by a request signed by ten members of the executive. This executive has a quorum of sixteen members. All the proposals of a patti panchayat or of the akhara panchayat, if not decided, can be taken for consideration in the executive, where it is decided by majority vote. The sarpanch has the right to decide when the votes are fifty-fifty. Before the term of sarpanchship has ended this position will only be vacant if he dies or resigns or is removed by a majority vote. The decision of the executive supersedes all decisions. The decision of this panchayat is like that of the highest court of the government. Why is such authority given to this body? To maintain the dignity of the institution. The executive can take the following decisions: it can expel any member for his misconduct, it can impose fines, and it can decide litigations between pattis. The first monetary punishment may be of 200 rupees, after that it becomes more. A panch or sarpanch may be dismissed if he does not attend three consecutive meetings.

Rule 9: There are some customs regarding the session of an assembly in a baithak. A kotwal gives date and place of the session and makes arrangements for it. The kotwal informs only those members who are present in the asan, because most of the sadhus are wandering in jamat. The decision among the members present is taken to be accepted by all the members of a akhara. If the decision is taken against some member of the akhara a written copy of the decision, signed by the members present at the session, is given into the hands of that member. This paper is called *panchnama* ...

Rule 10: The property is in the name of the mahant, but it is not his property. He is only the executive of the decisions of the assembled sadhus. The system of choosing a mahant gaddinashin is by selection from a patti, one after the other. The three pattis from which no one will be chosen gather to select someone from the fourth patti. This patti absents itself. This old tradition is strictly observed. The gaddinashin, chosen and seated, would never go out of the boundary of Hanumangarhi of his own accord. He may go out on occasions if the akhara panchayat allows him to do so and then he may go with great pomp and show, befitting his position. In matters of attending courts and offices he sends his mukhtar. The gaddinashin is considered to be the chief in matters of management and religious worship (*pūjāpāth*). The gaddinashin has a throne (*gaddi*) before the deity in the verandah facing the deity. After being selected the ceremony of *mahanti* is performed on this very gaddi, where he has to write an agreement in which he pledges himself to obey all the customs, rules, etc. of the akhara. His pledges are the following. 1. He would strictly follow customs and traditions. 2. He would do nothing against religion or against his own pujapath. He would always work with the permission and consultation of all the members of the akhara. 3. During the time of his mahantship any property obtained would be the property of the akhara and will never belong to him or his successor, no matter if it is mentioned in his name. He can never transfer any property to anyone. 4. If any act of his is found to be against religion or against the akhara, he may be turned out of mahantship and a new gaddinashin may be appointed. After taking these pledges before the assembly the gaddinashin is honourably seated on the gaddi and all the members, one by one, come to him and adorn him with a mala, kanthi, tilak, chadar, and his mahantship is announced by ringing the big bell, which hangs before the deity. The duty of the gaddinashin is to prepare the budget of the akhara and produce it before the annual meeting. He is always responsible for the members of th akhara.

[*Rule 11* has much the same to say about the mahant of the patti.]

Rule 15: The sadhus of Hanumangarhi living in or out of Hanumangarhi cannot have any property in their own name. Property attained by such sadhus will be in the name of the gaddinashin or in the name of the mahant of the patti. Their chelas (disciples or shishyas) may remain in this place as long as they are members of the akhara. If they do not become naga due to misbehaviour, they may not stay in the house.

Rule 16: The sadhu of Hanumangarhi is owner of the housing property as long as he lives. After his death it will go in the name of the gaddinashin as the property of the akhara.

Rule 17: Sadhus of Hanumangarhi are *nihamga* (unmarried). According to the customs and traditions, they cannot get themselves married and may not have any connection with women. According to agreement, they would be at once turned out and expelled when any doubt of this nature is raised.

Notes

Prologue

1. In 1971 Ayodhya had 22,790 inhabitants, and in 1981 30,468. It
   is, however, extremely difficult to make a correct estimate of its
   population, which consists in large part of peripatetic sadhus and
   pilgrims who may stay for a week, month, or even a year. Besides
   the relatively fixed population, the Municipal Office therefore
   also has an estimate for the so-called 'floating' (*pravahaman*)
   population, which in 1983 was one million. According to rough
   estimates there are 4,360 houses and 3,000 temples in Ayodhya.
   The place has almost no industry. Its economy is based on
   pilgrimage and agriculture. It is difficult, or, rather, impossible, to
   estimate the number of pilgrims visiting Ayodhya during a year.
   When we add up the pilgrims estimated to visit the large festivals
   of *Rām Naumi*, *Jhūlā* and *Kārttik Parikram*, we arrive at
   something like 1.3 million. The pilgrim tax received in 1983 by
   the Municipal Office was Rs 278,000. This tax is Rs 0.25, levied
   on every pilgrim visiting Ayodhya by public transport. This means
   that at least 1,112,000 pilgrims made use of public transport in
   coming to Ayodhya in 1983.

   Before 1902 the area now known as the province of Uttar
   Pradesh was called the North-Western Provinces and Oudh. From
   1902 until 1947, the name was changed to the United Provinces of
   Agra and Oudh. Since 1947, the official name has been Uttar
   Pradesh (Northern Province). It covers an area of 294,000 km^2 and
   in 1971 had a population of about 85 million. It is an agricultural
   area, only 3 per cent of the population working in industries.

2. Fieldwork was carried out at intervals between 1977 and 1985.
   The first time I worked in Ayodhya was between 1977 and 1978
   with a studentship given by the Indian government under a
   reciprocal Indo-Dutch scholarship scheme. I returned to Ayodhya
   in December 1980 for two months, in December 1983 for three
   months and again in October 1984 for three months.

I Ayodhya: Time and place

1. Although several cases have already been pending more than
thirty years in the High Court, the district and session judge of
Faizabad decided on 14 February 1986, that the gates of the
shrine should be opened immediately. It would not be difficult to
say that this decision was politically motivated, as indeed Muslim
leaders have already done. It seems, however, that the judge
decided upon a petition of a local Hindu lawyer 'seeking the
unlocking of the gates of the disputed shrine on the grounds that
it was only an earlier district administration and not a court which
had ordered its closure' (*India Today*, 28 February 1986). These
developments triggered off great communal disturbances in
many North Indian cities. *India Today* also reports that violent
quarrels over the control of the shrine have already broken out
between several Hindu groups. It is impossible to say what will be
the future of the shrine, since no court has yet decided whether it
is a mosque or a temple.

II Problems and perspectives

1. I use the term 'orientalist perspective' to refer to the way
anthropological interpretations make use of indological constructions of Indian reality. I do not intend to go as far as Said
(1978) and Inden (1986) in attacking a 'western' way of 'knowing'
societies in the east by showing that knowledge and power are
intimately related, though I accept at least part of that argument.

III Devotion and asceticism

1. The conceptual difficulties in dealing with Hinduism have
recently been discussed along similar lines by Cantlie (1984).
She is also of the opinion that the caste–secte dichotomy is not
helpful. Her general argument that Hinduism should be
understood in its own terms, however, involves her in saying, for
example, that renunciation is a religious experience entirely
different from devotion, having been accorded within Hinduism

the status of an independent path (256). This is again a construction of a Hindu conceptual universe, an approach I have already criticized in my discussion of Burghart.

My description follows accepted usage in research into Buddhism. Besides a Buddhist *sangha* or monastic order, there is a Buddhist laity which supports the order. The laity is often equated with 'society' at large in Buddhist countries such as Burma and Sri Lanka. Instead of 'society' we will speak here of 'community', since in Hindu society there are several lay communities which are the followers and supporters of sadhus, organized into different orders. These communities are highly amorphous, since a layman is prone to see himself as a Hindu, following the teachings of a particular *guru*, rather than as a Vishnuite or a Ramanandi. This fact emerges clearly from nineteenth-century census returns in which people were asked to identify themselves as belonging to certain religious communities. See, for example, the returns of Faizabad District in which the Ramanandis are strongly present: 'In Faizabad District no more than 7.7 per cent were returned as Vaishnavites and 5.5 per cent as Ramanandis. In both cases the proportions are high, but still the great mass of the Hindus appear to belong to no particular sect, as is generally the case throughout Oudh' (Faizabad District Gazetteer, 1905: 60).

2. This initiation ritual is very similar to the Shri-Vaishnava initiation, with one notable exception. The fifth ritual act among the Shri-Vaishnavas is the presentation of an image of God for worshipping (cf. Gonda, 1970: 65), while here the tulsi *kanthi* is given, which reminds one of low-caste Sant practices which are still prominent among the Kabirpanthis. It is therefore not surprising that the Shri-Vaishnavas from the south as well as Brahmans in general take issue with this part of the initiation (see the discussion in the second section of this chapter).

3. There is in fact quite a diversity in *tilaks*, in which personal predilections play an important part (cf. Entwistle, 1982). The following types are most common:

lāl shrī: two white lines drawn with clay (*gopīchandan*) with a red line in the middle made with *kumkum* powder. This *tilak* is similar to the Shri-Vaishnava *ūrdhvapundra*, both with or without a line on the bridge of the nose (*āsan*).

laskari or shvet shri: all three lines are white.
bindi: central white dot instead of middle line.
chaturbhuji: only two white lines.
Hanuman devotees often smear some red paste, called *mahabir* (another name for Hanuman), on their left brow.

4. *acyut* means 'infallible, unerring, immutable' according to Chaturvedi & Tiwari (eds), *Practical Hindi–English Dictionary*, Delhi: 1978.

5. The question of a sadhu returning to his own caste is of course important. According to Richard Burghart the Ramanandi sadhus in Janakpur could return to their caste if an urgent request was made; for example, by the parents of a sadhu to the guru (personal communication in letter of 8 July 1983). My information is ambiguous. Some sadhus answered right away that this caused no difficulties, while others were very circumspect or answered that it was impossible. Brahman householders whom I interviewed on the subject made a straightforward denial of the possibility. Remarkably often both, sadhus and laymen who answered negatively referred to adoption customs. When one has been adopted into another *gotra* one cannot return. He who returns is called *samyogi*, he who mingles illegally. Ramanandis change their *gotra* at initiation; Shri-Vaishnavas, for example, do not change it.

6. Pocock describes how Shivaite ascetics visited the village he lived in: 'They were received, initially, with a cautious respect but within forty-eight hours they were beaten up and chased out of the village. What they had done I could not clearly elicit, but it had something to do with women' (1973: 97).

7. There is a telling difference between the ritual of samnyas and that of vairagya. In samnyas the hair is shaved and the yajnopavit removed, while in vairagya the hair is shaved except for the *shikha*, a tuft of hair on the crown of the head, and the yajnopavit is renewed. In samnyas the sadhu clearly departs from the society of householders, while in vairagya the distinguishing marks of high caste are retained.

8. It is extremely difficult to say what is Tantric and what is not in religious methods. Goudriaan proposes the following interpretation of the term Tantrism: 'What is most often called by this term is a systematic quest for salvation or for spiritual excellence

by realizing and fostering the bipolar, bisexual divinity within one's own body. This result is methodically striven after by specific means (kinds of *sādhana*): the recitation of *mantras* or *bijas*; the construction of geometrical cosmic symbols (*maṇḍala*); the making of appropriate gestures (*mudra*); the assignment or "laying down" (*nyāsa*) of powerful sounds or syllables on the body; the meditation on the deity's concrete manifestation (*dhyāna*); the application of these and other elements in special ritual procedures, to wit Tantric worship (*pūjā*), initiation (*dīksā*), etc.; besides, the performance of Kundaliniyoga by means of which the microcosmic form of the Sakti (female divine power) present in the body in the form of a fiery tube or serpent is conducted upwards along the yogic nerves towards Siva's mystic residence at some distance above the head' (1981: 1).

9. Gonda sees a complementary tendency in the worship of stones by both Vishnuites and Shivaites: 'The Vishnuites for instance believe that their god is present in every *sālagrāma* – a black fossil found in the Gandak river – while the adorers of Siva are convinced that this deity resides in every round white pebble found in the Narmada' (1970: 113).

10. What do we mean by a liberal attitude towards caste? It might be illuminating to use here a distinction developed by Mark Holmström (1971) between *religious* universalism and *moral* universalism. In his view, bhakti represents a religious universalism, in which devotees are religiously equal, but socially bound by the values of caste society. Moral universalism would imply on the contrary a real moral attack on these values. In the bhakti movement there seems to be a contradiction between consciousness and existence (Iswaran, 1980: 81, 82). Commonly bhakti is associated with relativization of caste in anthropological and indological literature (see, for example, contributions to Singer, 1966). All this is based on an essentialist interpretation of the 'real' theological and sociological meaning of bhakti. As we will try to show later, bhakti as a religious experience can only be understood in the context of practices conditioned by religious organization. In the case of the Ramanandis there is a clear difference between ascetic and devotional styles which are related to different types of organization. The devotional

worship of images requires an emphasis on caste distinctions, while the peripatetic style of asceticism tends to minimize these distinctions. Historically, there has been an expansion of the devotional style, while peripatetic asceticism has been on the decline. Both processes have led to a greater importance of caste within the Ramanandi order (see Van der Veer, 1987a).

11. The building of the large Shri Rang Nath temple of the Shri-Vaishnavas in Vrindaban was commenced in 1851 and completed in 1854 at a cost of 4,500,000 rupees. The patrons were two merchants who had become the disciples of a great Shri-Vaishnava scholar, Swami Rangacharya (Growse, 1880: 260). Except for a South Indian family which established itself in Ayodhya as Shri-Vaishnava gurus in the course of the nineteenth century, all the so-called Shri-Vaishnava (Ramanuji) sadhus of Ayodhya were affiliated with this institution.

12. One of the 'doors' was founded by Ram Kabir who is said to be unrelated to Kabir the weaver (cf. Sinha, 1957: 329).

13. The obvious text to start with, therefore, is Nabhaji's *Bhaktamāl* in which Ramanand is related to both the Shri-Vaishnava and the Sant traditions. Nabhaji in fact summarizes the historical development neatly: it is an attempt to combine diverse Sant traditions in which Ram is worshipped by regarding them as forming one Vishnuite bhakti tradition deriving from South Indian Shri-Vaishnavism.

14. It is significant that Tulsidas is not mentioned as belonging to the *parampara* of Ramanand which, according to McGregor (1984: 107), strongly suggests that he was not a Ramanandi. It might also suggest that there was not yet a Ramanandi order, but diverse traditions which only later crystallized in the rather vague Ramanandi theology. The work of Tulsidas has clearly had a great influence on the formation of that theology and thus also on the formation of a more definite Ramanandi order.

15. Besides the mandals of the tyagis, which are practically defunct, there is in Ayodhya an institution called *tar* in which both sadhus and laymen can participate. I, for example, was often asked to do so. There are seven tar in Ayodhya: Hanumangarhi, Rajgopal, Janakighat, Ratnasinghasan, Gudar Janmasthan, Qila Dish and Digambar akhara. The functions of a tar are to stimulate social relations and to raise funds. The tar issues shares, called *tokna*.

The owner of a share is called *ek tokna ka mahant*, 'the abbot of one share'. A share can, however, also be divided into halves or quarters. The tar has an abbot who is also the largest shareholder. He is called *taradish*. Shareholders are invited to banquets (*bhandaras*) of the tar and to those banquets to which the taradish is invited. Depending on one's share one may get one or more meals in such a banquet. A shareholder cannot retract his investment. When he dies his share is divided among the survivors, while his son or disciple is enabled to buy a new share. In that case the successor has to give a banquet to the members of the tar. The tars are in general connected with one institution and are thus a way of raising funds for bhandaras, banquets which serve to promote solidarity. Therefore I suppose that it is a successor of the mandal for sedentarized sadhus on a local level. It serves the purpose of maintaining social relations between the several Ramanandi temples in Ayodhya. For example, the tar Janakighat has 32 toknas of 225 rupees each; many of the leading abbots own such a share, and they are invited when the abbot of Janakighat, who is at the same time taradish, decides to give a banquet.

16. In short, ashes are symbolic of the burning of the dead body in the cremation fire, the burning of food for the gods in the sacrificial fire and of the burning of desire (*kāma*) in the fire of asceticism (*tapas*).

17. There is a strong conviction among Hindus that 'you are what you eat'. All kinds of qualities are ascribed to food and often people discuss what one should eat and when. There are, for example, 'cold' fruits which one should never eat in winter. Sadhus particularly avoid 'hot', tamasik food like onions which they consider to be aphrodisiac.

18. The vastradhari Ramanandi sadhus, like other Vishnuite specialists, often wear white or yellow cloth. There are, however, a number of exceptions to this rule. The nagas of Nirvani akhara who are worshippers of Hanuman wear deep red, while many sadhus also wear ochre cloth like the Shivaite ascetics. Ochre is regarded as the colour of the fire.

19. 'Religious madness' due to intoxication or otherwise is highly valued among the tyagis. I met several *pāgal bābās* who acted in a way similar to the behaviour of Aghori ascetics described by

Parry (1982). Also in the rasik section, however, there is a tendency towards extreme 'divine joy' though I have in fact only encountered a rather restrained type of devotion among them.

20. Chandpolia is the name of a bazaar in Jaipur, Rajasthan. The name of Chandpolia for these attendants of the sadhus appears to be a generic name for all those hired in this bazaar. This bears some similarity to the name Baksariya for the migrant-soldiers who were recruited in Baksar (cf. Kolff, 1983).

21. Alsdorf (1962: 603) shows convincingly that the theory that ahimsa originated as a part of Buddhist and Jaina propaganda against the Vedic sacrifice is probably not correct. His own suggestion that its origin lies in pre-Aryan civilization seems, however, to be an example of the common fallacy of pushing the historical search for origins back to an era of which we do not have sufficient documentation. His interpretation (1962: 589) that ahimsa originally had nothing to do with ethics, but everything to do with a magical-ritualistic tabu on life appeals to me. It is still echoed in present-day attitudes towards ahimsa which are admirably described by Pocock (1973: 164–71). As far as I can see, ahimsa implies primarily vegetarianism and 'the protection of Mother Cow' (*go-raksha*). That one sometimes has to injure or even kill another human being for the protection of the cow appears not to be the subject of ethical discussions in India.

22. The crucial notion seems to be that ascetics are dangerous. They have great powers and may use them against others. The bad use of these powers makes an ascetic seem wicked or demonic, but here again the connotation seems to be dangerous rather than ethically bad. There is no doubt a Hindu tradition which attacks the secular power of ascetics, as is attested by the poem of Kabir, but on the other hand there is a strong need felt among worshippers that the sadhu should be powerful. If he has no power in a social or spiritual sense he cannot help, he is without value. I have never heard any objection either against the martial tradition of the nagas or against the opulent life-style of some of the rasik gurus.

23. The word *ani* for 'army' means literally 'tip of a spear'. This spear is called *moti bala*, 'big spear', and is put in the ground at every place where the army stops to camp. The spear's base is

called *ghumgha*. Every army has its own banner. In the Nirmohi army the banner has a silver colour, in the Digambar army five colours (black, red, white, green and yellow), in the Nirvani army a golden colour.

24. What do these akharas stand for? Since I could meet only members of Ramanandi akharas in Ayodhya I have only limited information about the others.

To start with Nirmohi akhara, Vishnuswami Nirmohi is clear. Maladhari Nirmohi is, however, an intriguing puzzle. Maladhari means, of course, 'wearers of malas', and as we have seen there is a distinction between sutradharis, the wearers of the sacred thread, the *yajnopavit*, who are members of the three highest social categories, the dvijas or twice-born, and on the other hand the maladharis, who are non-dvijas or Shudras, the lowest category. Maladharis are accepted in initiation by the Ramanandis, but are given a restricted place, and it seems that once they even had a separate grouping or, as is also quite possible, some of them formed their own akhara. This is, of course, no more than a poorly informed guess, since it is clear from my evidence that maladharis make up a considerable part of all the Ramanandi akharas. The next grouping is that of the Radhavallabhis, a community founded by Hita Harivams. The last group in the Nirmohi akhara is formed by Jhariya Nirmohis. Jhariya means 'bush', which suggests that they are ascetics. According to my information they are Harivyasis, which is another name for Nimbarkis. Knowing that Harivyasis are Nimbarkis we see that the remaining groups in the Nirmohi ani do not pose any problems.

In the Nirvani ani we have only two difficulties: Balabhadri and Tatambari. Balabhadri contains ascetics from the Madhva Gauriya sampradaya; I could not work out who the Tatambari were. In the Digambar ani the situation is simple. A distinction is made between *Rām upāsaks*, devotees of Ram, and *Shyām upāsaks*, devotees of Shyām, another name for Krishna.

25. The fact that the *Rāmdal* is the military arm of the four Vishnuite sampradayas is most clearly borne out by the custom that nagas may stay in any Vishnuite temple whenever and for as long as they want to, and that they get a special gift (*bidai*) when they take leave.

26. In the secondary naga initiation the typically Ramanandi necklace with beads of tulsi (*kanthi*) is given to the neophyte.

27. The extent to which these nagas had become professional soldiers is sufficiently clear from correspondence between Raja Omrao Giri, Anupgiri's brother, and the British government in Bengal (Board's collections F/4/239), dated 1 October 1807 and 18 November 1807. The British Government had given stipends of Rs 2,000 a month to the five sons of Omrao Giri, while Raja Nerinder Giri, the son of Anupgiri, had got a *jagir* of Rs 126,320 per annum. The five sons of Omrao Giri 'uniformly professed distinct interest from their father and a desire of remaining in the service of the British government'. Between Omrao Giri and Hunchun Giri there was a dispute about the succession of Anupgiri after the death of that great naga general, an interesting example of a conflict between brother and spiritual disciple, and so between family and spiritual lineage.

28. In the nineteenth century the rajas were great patrons of rasik practices. One of the best examples is the court of Rewa which stimulated rasik poetry in this period (McGregor, 1984: 168).

29. I am not convinced that the pain of separation (*viraha*) can only be felt in the parakiya condition, as Dimock argues. Classically it can also refer to the attitude of the faithful wife who longs for the return of her husband. The Ramanandi rasik may point out that Sita's abduction to Lanka by the demon Ravan causes viraha. Indeed, in Kalidasa's *Meghadūta*, one of the best-known poems of the classical tradition in which viraha is the central mood, there is a reference to Sita's longing, her viraha (*Meghaduta*, stanza 97, in Nathan 1976: 80, 81).

30. In the *Rāmcharitmānas* Sita represents the ideal woman who is pativratā. This term is glossed by Obeyesekere (1984: 430) as follows: virginity at marriage, chastity as the wifely goal, unassertiveness, submissiveness and unquestioning loyalty to the husband. His psychoanalytically inspired interpretation of this ideal is: 'Since the Hindu female role ideal of pativrata pertains to sex and aggression control, implementing the ideal in the socialization process entails the radical proscription of sexual and aggressive activity, which on the personality level demands the radical and continued repression of sex and aggression drives' (1984: 431). It is no doubt surprising that

Ram and Sita who are paradigmatic for the ideal conservative Hindu couple become the object of rasik devotion.

31. A discussion in Krishnaite theology is pertinent to this problem. The *rāganurāg* devotion implies that one can adopt the bhava of a particular favourite of Krishna and live in the ecstasy of that vicarious enjoyment. The worshippers are therefore considered as females (De, 1961: 176). This, according to De (1961: 208), is a later development, since Jiv and Rup Goswami are considered sakhis as helpers in the erotic sport of Krishna and Radha. This enjoyment is vicarious, consisting of an approval of the enjoyment of the divine couple.

32. Lorenzen (1978: 72–5) interprets the Sanyasi rebellion as the last attempt of the itinerant sadhus of both Hindu and Muslim orders at continuing their life-style, which had come under the pressure of the British endeavour of ousting all competition in the field of tax-levying. This period is extensively documented in Ghosh (1930). Recently, Willem van Schendel (1985) has described a peasant revolt in the same area between 1824 and 1833 in which religious leaders again played a dominant role.

33. Militant asceticism gradually beats a retreat from the public scene. It remains visible in an organized fashion till the end of the nineteenth century in the independent princely states. For example, only in 1875 was the ascetic army of Jaswant Singh of Jodhpur disbanded (Orr, 1940: 95). The Dadu panthi nagas who had entered the service of the Jaipur state in 1797 survived until 1938 in a ceremonial capacity (Orr, 1947: 219–20). The marginalization of militant asceticism is clearly seen in the fact that they have only antique weapons (cf. Ghurye, 1964: 113). Wrestling, however, is still highly popular among the nagas of Ayodhya. To be able to fight is, of course, a considerable asset in contemporary India, where open violence is more often than not the only way to settle a dispute. Nagas can be hired by local *magnati*, so that they still have a violent reputation as toughs.

IV The sacred as a profession

1. At first it was surprising to me that so many Ayodhya pandas were Shivaites, but considering the fact that the riverside has

been and partly still is Shiv's domain it became less so. No Hindu pilgrim of Ramanandi persuasion would object to having a Shivaite panda. Tension is rather to be expected between specialists; for example, between pandas and Ramanandi sadhus. However, it is clear that both have separate niches in the pilgrimage system and are mutually uninterested in competition except for the still marginal cases of sadhus who pose as pandas.

2. Kalpvas is mostly in the month of Karttik which is full of religious activity. Some pilgrims have taken a vow that they will stay in Ayodhya every Karttik for a fixed number of years.

3. An abridged version of the argument in this and the concluding section can be found in Van der Veer, n.d.

4. Parry and Fuller do not see eye to eye on this point. Parry remains convinced that the threatening nature of the gift has a pan-Indian significance (Parry, 1980).

5. In a pamphlet which was distributed in 1983 in the midst of fights between the two main groups of pandas in Ayodhya, the Gangaputras warned the pilgrims that their opponents were *kupatras*, 'unworthy recipients', and that to give *dān*, 'gifts', to them would have bad consequences for the donors.

6. Monier-Williams (1883: 285) also observes that funeral rites are regarded as inauspicious (*amangal*), while the ancestor worship is regarded as auspicious (*mangal*).

7. A remuneration (*dakshiṇā*) is given to the participants in a *brahmbhoj*. A feast for Brahmans (*brahmbhoj*) closely resembles the feast for sadhus (*bhandārā*) described in the preceding chapter. Participants in a bhandara also receive a fee (*dakshiṇā*).

8. The patron in 'the last sacrifice' is, however, called *jajmān* and therefore one could decide to call the relation between the patron and the Mahabrahman a jajmani relation. Enduring relations between the two which are inherited from father to son seem, however, to be lacking here. Instead there are systems which regulate the division of the spoils within the Mahabrahman community itself. Parry (1980) argues that this is the only reason for such systems and that the nature of the Mahabrahman's profession has nothing to do with it.

9. Heesterman (1959: 241) argues that 'it will generally be acknowledged that the *dakshiṇā* or sacrificial gift given by the Vedic sacrificer to the priests cannot, at least not in its original

11. In a book on the social history of the Kayasth caste in Hyderabad Karen Leonard (1978: 4) argues that the most important structural units have been kin groups, based upon control of hereditary positions: 'The kin groups, consisting of a few closely related families, were thus property groups. They distributed not only social but economic and political resources.' The same could be said of the Gangaputra pandas.

12. The right of the pilgrim to give his dan to any priest he chooses was also upheld by the Indian courts since the gift was regarded as voluntary and directed at whosoever acted as officiant (cf. *Calcutta Law Journal*, vol. 13 (1911): Dwarkanath Misier and others versus Rampertab Misier and others).

13. The Faizabad District Gazetteer of 1905, edited by H. R. Nevill, p. 179, makes the mistake of regarding 1865 as the date of institution of the auction system.

14 Much of the discussion here is based on documents found in the files of both Gangaputra and Bhareriya pandas. The larger number of these documents were in the hands of the Gangaputra leader Gangaram, for reasons which we will discuss later.

15. In the courts pandaship came to be seen as a business which, according to practice, could be passed from one family to another via the line of daughters. It was not to be regarded as a religious hereditary office (cf. *Patna Law Journal*, vol. 2 (1917); Lachman Lal versus Baldeo Lal).

16. Shrimali Brahmans who act as family priests (*purohit*) are mentioned in Pocock (1981: 324).

17. A generally accepted story about the Gangaputras and Bhareriyas is that the Gangaputras gradually became a diminishing group in the course of a century, while the Bhareriyas grew considerably in numbers in the same period. It is tempting to connect this with the marriage policies of both groups. The Gangaputras became a closed property group, while the Bhareriyas had to remain a relatively open group of 'poor Brahmans' and others.

18. Again the distinction between *micro* and *macro* seems to be important. Parry (1979: 64) reports that in the village economy of Kangra the rights of Brahman family priests (*purohit*) were heritable and divisible among male heirs, but that the people were shocked at the very idea of them being marketable.

However, the rights of the funeral priests in Kangra, who have a rather anonymous constituency, were marketable.

19. The situation seems to have resembled that of Jagannath Puri described by Rösel (1980). The great temple at Puri has been, however, a ritual-political centre to an extent which is only found in the south, not in the north (cf. Appadurai and Breckenridge, 1976).

Bibliography

Primary sources

Report of R. D. Shaw, assistant to I. Reid, deputy commissioner, Faizabad, 31 March 1862.
Register of 382 tax-free chowkees, their ghats and zamindars, signed by A. J. Robinson, the district commissioner, Faizabad, 1887.
Report on Ayodhya fairs by Patrick Carnegy, n.d.
Case in the court of settlement officer Singh in Faizabad. Shatruhandas against Lalbihari and other Gangaputras. Judgment: 5 April 1905; case no. 887.
Panchnāmā of the Gangaputras, 23 January 1889,
Agreement between a contractor, Dudall Ahir, and Gangaputras for renting all the chowkees, samvat 1955 (AD 1898).
Svami Bhagavadacharya. Alvar: Shri Ramanand Sahitya Mandir 1958.
Shrīvaishnavamatābjabhāskar; Shrīrāmarchanapaddhati published by Ramkrishnanand, mahant on the seat of Balanand, dat.1985 Vi (AD 1928).
Guru Paramparā ('written by Agradas and accepted on the Kumbh at Ujjain 1921'); Ayodhya.
Niyamavali; Hanumangarhi; Ayodhya, n.d.

Secondary sources

Allchin, F. R. (1966), *Tulsi Das: The Petition to Ram. Hindi Devotional Hymns of the 17th Century.* London: Allen & Unwin.
Alsdorf, L. (1962), *Beiträge zur Geschichte von Vegetarismus und Rinderverehrung in Indien.* Wiesbaden: Steiner.
Appadurai, A. (1981a), *Worship and Conflict under Colonial rule: A South Indian Case.* Cambridge: Cambridge University Press.
Appadurai, A. (1981b), 'The Past as a Scarce Resource', *Man* (NS), 18: 201–19.
Appadurai, A. and Breckenridge, C. (1976), 'The South Indian Temple: Authority, Honour and Redistribution', *Contributions to Indian Sociology* (NS), 10 (2): 187–211.
Asad, T. (1983), 'Anthropological Conceptions of Religion: Reflections on Geertz', *Man* (NS), 18: 237–59.
Babb, L. (1975), *The Divine Hierarchy: Popular Hinduism in Central India.* New York: Columbia University Press.
Bailey, F. G. (1959), 'For a Sociology of India?', *Contributions to Indian Sociology*, 3: 88–101.

Bakker, H. T. (1986), *Ayodhya: The History of Ayodhya from the 17th Century BC to the Middle of the 18th Century*. Groningen: Egbert Forsten.

Barnett, R. B. (1980), *North India Between Empires: Awadh, the Mughals and the British, 1720–1801*. Berkeley: University of California Press.

Basham, A. (1975), *The Wonder that was India*. London: Fontana.

Bax, M. (1983), '"Us" Catholics and "Them" Catholics in Dutch Brabant: The Dialectics of a Religious Factional Process', *Anthropological Quarterly*, 56 (4): 167–78.

Bax, M. (1985), 'Popular Devotions, Power and Religious Regimes in Dutch Brabant', *Ethnology*, 24 (3): 215–28.

Bayly, C. A. (1981), 'From Ritual to Ceremony: Death Ritual and Society in Hindu North India since 1600', in J. Whaley (ed.), *Mirrors of Mortality*. London: Europa Publications.

Bayly, C. A. (1983), *Rulers, Townsmen and Bazaars: North Indian Society in the Age of British Expansion, 1770–1870*. Cambridge: Cambridge University Press.

Bhardwaj, S. M. (1973), *Hindu Places of Pilgrimage in India*. Berkeley: University of California Press.

Bhatnagar, G. D. (1968), *Awadh under Wajid Ali Khan*. Benares: Bharatiya Vidya Prakashan.

Biardeau, M. (1981), *L'Hindouisme: Anthropologie d'une Civilisation*. Paris: Flammarion.

Bloch, M. (1977), 'The Past and the Present in the Present', *Man* (NS), 12: 278–92.

Bourdillon, M. F. C. (1978), 'Knowing the World or Hiding It: A Response to Maurice Bloch', *Man* (NS), 13: 591–9.

Briggs, G. W. (1938), *Gorakhnath and the Kanphata Yogis*. Calcutta: YMCA Publishing House.

Burghart, R. (1976)' 'Bairagi Mandals', *Contributions to Nepalese Studies*, 3 (1): 63–104.

Burghart, R. (1978a), 'Hierarchical Models of the Hindu Social System', *Man* (NS), 13: 519–36.

Burghart, R. (1978b), 'The Disappearance and Reappearance of Janakpur', *Kailash: A Journal of Himalayan Studies*, 6 (4): 257–84.

Burghart, R. (1978c), 'The Founding of the Ramanandi Sect', *Ethnohistory*, 25 (2): 121–39.

Burghart, R. (1983a), 'Wandering Ascetics of the Ramanandi Sect', *History of Religions*, 22 (4): 361–80.

Burghart, R. (1983b), 'For a Sociology of Indias: An Intracultural Approach to the Study of "Hindu Society"', *Contributions to Indian Sociology* (NS), 17 (2): 275–99.

Burghart, R. (1983c), 'Renunciation in the Religious Traditions of South Asia', *Man* (NS), 18: 635–53.

Burghart, R. and Cantlie, A. (eds), (1985), *Indian Religion*. London: Curzon Press.

Cantlie, A. (1984), *The Assamese*. London: Curzon Press.

Carnegy, P. (1868), *Notes on the Races, Tribes and Castes inhabiting the Province of Awadh*. Lucknow: Oudh Government Press.

Carnegy, P. (1870), *Historical Sketch of Tahsil Fyzabad, Zillah Fyzabad*. Lucknow: Oudh Government Press.

Carrithers, M. (1979), 'The Modern Ascetics of Lanka and the Pattern of Change in Buddhism', *Man* (NS), 14: 294–310.

Carrithers, M. (1984), 'The Domestication of the *Sangha*', *Man* (NS), 19: 321–2.

Cohen, A. (1974), *Two-Dimensional Man*. London: Routledge & Kegan Paul.

Cohn, B. S. (1964), 'The Role of the Gosains in the Economy of Eighteenth and Nineteenth Century, Upper India', *Indian Economic and Social History Review*, 1: 175–82.

Cohn, B. S. (1968), 'Notes on the History of the Study of Indian Society and Culture', in M. Singer and B. Cohn (eds), *Structure and Change in Indian Society*. Chicago: Aldine.

Commander, S. (1983), 'The *Jajmani* System in North India: An Examination of its Logic and Status across Two Centuries', *Modern Asian Studies*, 17: 283–311.

Conlon, F. (1977), *A Caste in a Changing World*. Berkeley: University of California Press.

Daniélou, A. (1964), *Hindu Polytheism*. London: Routledge & Kegan Paul.

De, S. K. (1961), *Early History of the Vaisnava Faith and Movement in Bengal*. Calcutta: Mukhopadhyay.

Dimock, E. C. (1966), 'Doctrine and Practice among the Vaisnavas of Bengal', in M. Singer (ed.), *Krishna: Myths, Rites and Attitudes*. Honolulu: East-West Center Press.

Dumont, L. (1970), *Religion, Politics and History in India*. The Hague: Mouton.

Dumont, L. (1971), 'On Putative Hierarchy and some Allergies to it', *Contributions to Indian Sociology* (NS), 5: 58–81.

Dumont, L. (1972), *Homo Hierarchicus*. London: Paladin.

Eck, D. (1981), 'India's *Tirthas*: "Crossings" in sacred geography', *History of Religions*, 20: 323–44.

Eck, D. (1982), *Banaras: City of Light*. New York: Knopf.

Eickelman, D. (1976), *Moroccan Islam*. Austin: University of Texas Press.

Eickelman, D. (1982), 'The Study of Islam in Local Contexts', *Contributions to Asian Studies*, 18: 1–17.

Eliade, M. (1973), *Yoga: Immortality and Freedom*. Princeton: Princeton University Press.

Elias, N. and Scotson, J. L. (1965), *The Established and the Outsider*. London: New Sociology Library.

Elliott, H. M. (1869), *Memoirs of the History, Folklore and Distribution of the Races of the North-Western Provinces of India*. London: Trübner.

Ensink, J. (1974), 'Problems of the Study of Pilgrimage in India', *Indologica Taurinensia*, 11: 57–79.

Entwistle, A. W. (1982), 'Vaisnava Tilakas – Sectarian Marks Worn by Worshippers of Visnu', *IAVRI-Bulletin* 11 & 12.

Epstein, A. (1978), *Ethos and Identity*. London: Tavistock.

Eschmann, A., Kulke, H. and Tripathi, G. C. (1978), *The Cult of Jagannath and the Regional Tradition of Orissa*. New Delhi: Manohar.

Foster, W. (ed.) (1921), *Early Travels in India, 1583–1619*. London.

Fuller, C. J. (1984), *Servants of the Goddess: The Priests of a South Indian Temple*. Cambridge: Cambridge University Press.

Gazetteer of India (1960), *Uttar Pradesh: Faizabad*. Allahabad: Government Press.

Geertz, C. (1973), *The Interpretation of Culture*. New York: Basic Books.
Geertz, C. (1980), *Negara: The Theatre State in Nineteenth-Century Bali*. Princeton: Princeton University Press.
Gellner, E. (1969), *Saints of the Atlas*. Chicago: Chicago University Press.
Ghosh, J. (1923), *The Sannyasis of Mymensingh*.
Ghosh, J. (1930), *Sannyasi and Fakir Raiders in Bengal*. Calcutta: Bengal Secretariat Book Department.
Ghurye, G. S. (1964), *Indian Sadhus*. Bombay: Popular Book Depot.
Gonda, J. (1963), *Die Religionen Indiens*, 2 vols. Stuttgart: Kohlhammer.
Gonda, J. (1970), *Visnuism and Sivaism: A Comparison*. London: Athlone Press.
Goody, J. (ed.) (1968), *Literacy in Traditional Societies*. Cambridge: Cambridge University Press.
Goody, J. (1977), *The Domestication of the Savage Mind*. Cambridge: Cambridge University Press.
Goswamy, B. N. and Grewal, J. S. (1969), *The Mughal and Sikh Rulers and the Vaisnavas of Pindori*. Simla: Indian Institute of Advanced Study.
Goswamy, B. N. (1966), 'The Records Kept by Priests at Centres of Pilgrimage as a Source of Social and Economic History', *The Indian Economic and Social History Review*, 3 (2): 174–85.
Goudriaan, T. (1979), 'Introduction, History and Philosophy', in S. Gupta, D. J. Hoens and T. Goudriaan, *Hindu Tantrism*. Leiden: Brill.
Goudriaan, T. (1981), 'Hindu Tantric Literature in Sanskrit', in T. Goudriaan and S. Gupta (eds), *Hindu Tantric and Sakta Literature*. Wiesbaden: Harrassowitz.
Gould, H. (1966), 'Religion and Politics in a U.P. constituency', in D. Smith (ed), *South Asian Politics and Religion*, 51–74. Princeton: Princeton University Press.
Gross, R. L. (1979), *Hindu Asceticism: A Study of the Sadhus of North India*. Ann Arbor: University Microfilms International.
Growse, F. S. (1880), *Mathura: a District Memoir*. Allahabad: Government Press.
Hardy, F. (1983), *Viraha-Bhakti: The Early History of Krishna Devotion in South India*. Delhi: Oxford University Press.
Harper, E. (1964), 'Ritual Pollution as an Integrator of Caste and Religion', *Journal of Asian Studies*, 23: 151–79.
Hawley, J. S. (1983), *Krishna, The Butter-Thief*. Princeton: Princeton University Press.
Heesterman, J. C. 'Reflections on the Significance of the Daksina', *Indo-Iranian Journal*, 4: 241–58.
Heesterman, J. C. (1971), 'Priesthood and the Brahmin'. *Contributions to Indian Sociology* (NS), 5: 43–7.
Heesterman, J. C. (1985), *The Inner Conflict of Tradition*. Chicago: Chicago University Press.
Hill, W. D. P. (tr.) (1952), *The Holy Lake of the Acts of Rama*. London: Oxford University Press.
Hocart, A. M. (1969), *The Life-giving Myth and Other Essays*. London: Oxford University Press.
Holmström, M. (1971), 'Religious Change in an Industrial City in South India', *Journal of the Royal Asiatic Society*: 28–40.

Inden, R. (1986), 'Orientalist Constructions of India', *Modern Asian Studies*, 20 (3): 101–446.

Ishwaran, K. (1980), 'Bhakti Tradition and Modernisation: The Case of Lingayatism', *Journal of Asian and African Studies*, 1–2: 72–83.

Joshi, P. C. (1978), 'Land Reforms in India', in A. R. Desai (ed.), *Rural Sociology in India*. Bombay: Popular Prakashan.

Kakar, S. (1982), *Shamans, Mystics and Doctors*. Boston: Beacon Press.

Kane, P. V. (1953), *History of Dharmasastra*. Poona: Bhandarkar Oriental Research Institute.

Kolff, D. H. A. (1971), 'Sannyasi Trader-Soldiers', *The Indian Economic and Social History Review*, 8: 213–20.

Kolff, D. H. A. (1983), 'An Armed Peasantry and its Allies' (dissertation, Leiden).

Kulke, H. (1979), *Jagannatha-Kult und Gajapati-Königtum*. Wiesbaden: Steiner.

Leach, E. (1954), *Political Systems of Highland Burma*. London: Athlone.

Leonard, K. (1978), *A Social History of an Indian Caste: The Kayasths of Hyderabad*. Berkeley: University of California Press.

Lorenzen, D. N. (1978), 'Warrior Ascetics in Indian History', *Journal of the American Oriental Society*, 98 (1). 61–75.

Malamoud, C. (1976), 'Terminer le sacrifice: Remarques sur les honoraires rituels dans le brahmanisme', in M. Biardeau and C. Malamoud (eds), *Le Sacrifice dans l'Inde Ancienne*. Paris: P.U.F.

Mandelbaum, D. (1972), *Society in India*. Bombay: Popular Prakashan.

Marriott, M. (1955), 'Little Communities in an Indigenous Civilization', in M. Marriott (ed.), *Village India*. Chicago: Chicago University Press.

Marriott, M. and Inden, R. (1975), 'Caste Systems': *Encyclopaedia Britannica*, 'Macropaedia', vol. 3: 982–91.

Marx, E. (1976), 'Communal and Individual Pilgrimage: The Region of Saints' Tombs in South Sinai', in R. Werbner (ed.), *Regional Cults*. London: Academic Press.

Mauss, M. (1974), *The Gift*. London: Routledge & Kegan Paul.

McGregor, R. S. (1984), *Hindi Literature from its Beginnings to the Nineteenth Century*. Wiesbaden: Harrassowitz.

McLeod, W. H. (1976), *The Evolution of the Sikh Community*. Oxford: Clarendon Press.

McLeod, W. H. (1978), 'On the Word *Panth*: A Problem of Terminology and Definition', *Contributions to Indian Sociology* (NS), 12 (2): 287–95.

Metcalf, T. (1979), *Land, Landlords and the British Raj*. Delhi: Oxford University Press.

Miller, D. B. (1975), *From Hierarchy to Stratification*. Delhi: Oxford University Press.

Mital, P. (1968), *Braj ke dharm-sampradaysm ka itihao*. Delhi: National Publishing House.

Monier-Williams, M. (1883), *Religious Thought and Life in India*, Pt I: *Vedism, Brahmanism and Hinduism*. London: Murray.

Monier-Williams, M. (1899), *Sanskrit–English Dictionary*. Oxford: Clarendon Press.

Morinis, E. A. (1984), *Pilgrimage in the Hindu Tradition: A Case Study of West Bengal*. Delhi: Oxford University Press.

Mukherjee, T. (1980), 'Manuscripts and Documents in the Gauriya Temples of Vrindaban and Rajasthan'. *IAVRI Bulletin*, 8: 9–17.

Nathan, L. (1976), *The Transport of Love: The Meghaduta of Kalidasa*. Berkeley: University of California Press.

Nesfield, W. (1885), *Brief View of the Caste System of the N.W. Provinces and Oudh*. Allahabad: Government Press.

Nevill, H. R. (1905), *Faizabad District Gazetteer*. Allahabad: Government Press.

Obeyesekere, G. (1966), 'The Buddhist Pantheon in Ceylon and its Extensions', in Manning Nash (ed.), *Anthropological Studies in Theravada Buddhism*. New Haven: Yale University Press.

Obeyesekere, G. (1984), *The Cult of the Goddess Pattini*. Chicago: Chicago University Press.

O'Flaherty, W. D. (1973), *Asceticism and Eroticism in the Mythology of Shiva*. Oxford: Oxford University Press.

Olivelle, P. (1975), 'A Definition of World Renunciation', *Wiener Zeitschrift für die Kunde SüdAsiens*, 19: 75–84.

Olivelle, P. (1981), 'Contributions to the Semantic History of Samnyasa', *Journal of the American Oriental Society*, 101 (3): 265–74.

O'Malley, L. (1974), *Indian Caste Customs*. London: Curzon Press.

Orr, W. G. (1940), 'Armed Religious Ascetics in North India', *Bulletin of the John Rylands Library*, 24 (1): 81–100.

Orr, W. G. (1947), *A Sixteenth-Century Indian Mystic*. London: Lutterworth Press.

Parry, J. P. (1979), *Caste and Kinship in Kangra*. London: Routledge & Kegan Paul.

Parry, J. P. (1980), 'Ghosts, Greed and Sin: The Occupational Identity of the Benares Funeral Priests', *Man* (NS), 15: 88–111.

Parry, J. P. (1982), 'Sacrificial Death and the Necrophagous Ascetic', in M. Bloch and J. Parry (eds), *Death and the Regeneration of Life*. Cambridge: Cambridge University Press.

Parry, J. P. (1985a), 'Death and Digestion: The Symbolism of Food and Eating in North Indian Mortuary Rites', *Man* (NS), 20: 612–30.

Parry, J. P. (1985b), 'The Brahmanical Tradition and the Technology of the Intellect', in J. Overing (ed.), *Reason and Morality*. London: Tavistock.

Parry, J. P. (1986), '*The Gift*, the Indian Gift and the "Indian Gift"', *Man* (NS), 21: 453–73.

Pocock, D. (1973), *Mind, Body and Wealth*. Oxford: Basil Blackwell.

Pocock, D. (1981) 'The Vocation and Avocations among the Guggali Brahmans of Dvaraka', *Contributions to Indian Sociology* (NS), 15: 321–37.

Preston, J. (1980), *Cult of the Goddess*. New Delhi: Vikas.

Raheja, G. (n.d.), 'Auspiciousness in North Indian Social Life', in M. Moffatt (ed.), *Beyond Purity and Pollution: Studies in Indic Categories and Everyday Experience* (forthcoming).

Rangachari, K. (1931), *The Sri Vaisnava Brahmans*. Madras: Superintendent Government Press.

Redfield, R. (1956), *Peasant Society and Culture*. Chicago: Chicago University Press.

Reeves, P. (1968), 'Landlords and Party Politics in the United Provinces 1934–37' in D. Low (ed.), *Soundings in Modern South Asian History*. London: Weidenfeld & Nicolson.

Renou, L. (1968), *Religions of Ancient India*. New York: Schocken Books.

Rösel, J. (1980), *Der Palast des Herrn der Welt*. München: Weltforum.

Roy, A. (1978), *History of the Jaipur City*. Delhi.

Said, E. (1978), *Orientalism*. New York: Vintage.

Sallnow, M. (1981), 'Communitas Reconsidered: The Sociology of Andean Pilgrimage', *Man* (NS), 16: 163–82.

Sarkar, J. (n.d.), *A History of the Dashanami Naga Sannyasis*. Allahabad: Shri Panchayati Akhara Nirvani.

Sharma, G. (1971), *Sri Ayodhya-ji ka pracin itihas ya Ayodhya-gaid*. Ayodhya.

Sherring, M. A. (1872), *Hindu Tribes and Castes as Represented in Benares*. London.

Singer, M. (1972), *When a Great Tradition Modernizes*. London: Pall Mall.

Sinha, B. P. (1957), *Rambhakti mem Rasik sampradaya*. Balrampur: Avadh Sahitya Mandir.

Sitaram, L. (1930), *Avadh ki jhanki*. Prayag.

Srinivas, M. N. (1967), 'The Cohesive role of Sanskritization', in P. Mason (ed.), *India and Ceylon: Unity and Diversity*. London: Oxford University Press.

Staal, J. F. (1963), 'Sanskrit and Sanskritization', *Journal of Asian Studies*, 22 (3): 261–75.

Stanley, J. M. (1977), 'Special Time, Special Power: The Fluidity of Power in a Popular Hindu Festival', *Journal of Asian Studies*, 38 (1): 27–43.

Stein, B. (1968), 'Social Mobility and Medieval South Indian Hindu Sects', in J. Silverberg (ed.), *Social Mobility in the Caste System in India*. The Hague: Mouton.

Stirrat, R. L. (1984), 'Sacred Models', *Man* (NS), 19: 199–215.

Strenski, J. (1983), 'On Generalized Exchange and the Domestication of the Sangha', *Man* (NS), 18: 463–77.

Thiel-Horstmann, M. (1986), 'Symbiotic Antinomy. The Social Organization of a North Indian Sect', *Sixth Basham Lecture*, Canberra: Faculty of Asian Studies, Australian National University.

Thiel-Horstmann, M. (n.d.), 'Warrior Ascetics in 18th Century Rajasthan and the Religious Policy of Jai Singh II'.

Turner, V. (1974), *Dramas, Fields and Metaphors*. Ithaca: Cornell University Press.

Van Buitenen, J. A. B. (1966), 'On the Archaism of the Bhagavata Purana', in M. Singer (ed.), *Krishna: Myths, Rites and Attitudes*. Honolulu: East-West Center Press.

Van der Veer, P. (1984), 'Structure and Anti-Structure in Hindu Pilgrimage to Ayodhya', in K. Ballhatchet and D. Taylor (eds), *Changing South Asia: Religion and Society*. Hong Kong: Asian Research Service.

Van der Veer, P. (1985), 'Brahmans: Their Purity and their Poverty; On the Changing Values of Brahman Priests in Ayodhya', *Contributions to Indian Sociology* (NS) 19 (2): 305–21.

Van der Veer, P. (1987a), 'Taming the Ascetic: Devotionalism in a Hindu Monastic Order', *Man* (NS) 22: 680–95.

Van der Veer, P. (1987b), 'God Must be Liberated: A Hindu Liberation Movement in Ayodhya', *Modern Asian Studies*, 21 (2): 283–303.

Van der Veer, P. (n.d.), 'The Concept of the Ideal Brahman as an Indological Construct', in G. D. Sontheimer (ed.), Approaches to *Hinduism* (forthcoming).

Van Gennep, A. (1977), *The Rites of Passage*. London: Routledge & Kegan Paul.

Van Schendel, W. (1985), 'Madmen of Mymensingh: Peasant Resistance and the Colonial Process in Eastern India, 1824 to 1833', *The Indian Economic and Social History Review*, 22 (2): 139–73.

Varady, R. (1980), 'North Indian Banjaras: Their Evolution as Transporters', *South Asia* (NS), 1 (1&2): 1–19.

Vaudeville, C. (1974), *Kabir*, vol. I. Oxford: Clarendon Press.

Vaudeville, C. (1976), 'Braj, Lost and Found', *Indo-Iranian Journal*, 18: 195–213.

Vidyarthi, L. P. (1961), *The Sacred Complex in Hindu Gaya*. Delhi: Concept.

Vincent, J. (1974), 'The Structuring of Ethnicity', *Human Organization*, 33 (4): 375–9.

Williams, R. B. (1984), *A New Face of Hinduism*. Cambridge: Cambridge University Press.

Wolf, E. (1985), 'The Virgin of Guadaloupe: A Mexican National Symbol', *Journal of American Folklore*, 71 (1): 34–9.

Glossary

ahiṃsā	non-injury
akhāṛā	division of fighting ascetics
ani	army
ārati	lamp-offering
avatār	incarnation
bhakta	devotee
bhakti	devotion
bhandārā	banquet for sadhus
bhāva	emotional condition
chatuhsampradāy	the four Vishnuite traditions
chaunī	army camp
dakshiṇā	sacrificial fee
dān	gift
darbār	court
darshan	seeing, act of worship
dharma	cosmic order, religion
dhuni	sacred fire
dīwān	chief minister
dvija	twice-born, member of one of the three highest social categories
ghāṭ	bathing-place
gomāstha	agent
gosain	member of a caste of married Shivaite ascetics
gotra	clan
guru	religious preceptor
jajmān	patron of the sacrifice
jajmānī	system of patronage
jamāt	itinerant group of sadhus
jāti	caste
jhāṃkī	vision of the divine
jhūlā	'swing' festival
kacchā	rough, mud, sandy
khālsā	itinerant order of sadhus
kīrti	fame
krishna-paksh	dark fortnight
kumbh mela	great bathing festival
lashkarī	militant sādhu
linga	phallic symbol of Shiv
mahimā	greatness, power
maṇḍal	regional circle
maṅgal	auspicious

mantra	meditation formula
mantra guru	preceptor who initiates
mūrti	idol, religious image
nāgā	fighting ascetic
nirguṇa	transcendent, without attributes
pakkā	refined, made of brick
paṇḍā	pilgrimage priest
parikram	circumambulation
pitṛi	ancestor
prasād	grace, item of worship
pret	ghost of a deceased ancestor
pūjā	worship
pūjāri	priest officiating in worship
puṇya	merit
purohit	Brahman priest
ras	experience of bliss
rasik	Ramanandi sadhu belonging to the devotional current
sādhak guru	preceptor who teaches a method
sādhanā	religious method
sādhu	monk
sakhī	girl-friend
samkalp	declaration of intention
samnyas	renunciation
sampradāya	religious tradition
seli	division of nagas
sevā	service, worship
shālāgràm	black fossil representing Vishnu or Ram
shishya	disciple
shrī mahant	chief abbot
shukla-paksh	bright fortnight
siddha guru	see *sādhak guru*
tapas	magical heat, asceticism
tilak	religious forehead-marking
tīrtha	pilgrimage centre
tyāgi	Ramanandi sadhu belonging to the ascetic current
vairāgya	desirelessness, Vishnuite renunciation
varṇa	social category
vrat	vow, austerity
zamīndār	landholder

Index

Ahiṃsā and vegetarianism, 118, 131, 132, 288
Akhāṛā, 76, 137, 138; in Ayodhya, 142–151; See also Hanumangarhi
Ancestor Ritual, 3, 64, 187, 199

Allchin, 81
Alsdorf, 288
Ārya Samāj, 101, 102
Appadurai: on history, 50, 51, 97, 173; South Indian temples, 65, 98; See also Appadurai and Breckenridge
Appadurai and Breckenridge, 65, 295
Asad, 46
Ashes: on body, 92, 114, 115, 165
Aurangzeb, 16

Babar, 20, 21, 36
Babar's Mosque, 38–39, 40, 41
Babb, 191
Bailey, 259, 260
Bakker: on Ayodhyāmahātmya 9; on early history of Ayodhya 11, 13, 25, 36; on early Vishnuism, 92, 95; on mantra, 81, 91; on Shivaites in Ayodhya, 145
Balanand, 136, 137, 139
Barnett, 144, 151
Basham, 4, 6, 53
Bax, 9
Bayly, 37, 133, 134, 213, 214, 215
Bhagavadachārya, 101–106
Bhaktamal, 95, 98
Bhandārā, 112, 113, 124–126

Bhardwaj, 61, 62
Bhatnagar, 39, 47
Biardeau, 55
Bloch, 49
Bourdillon, 49
Braj, 85
Breckenridge, see Appadurai and Breckenridge
Briggs, 149
British legislation and priestly rights, 219–229
Burghart, 57; on conceptual universes, 68–70; on history of Ramanandis: 86, 87; 100; on 'fallen' sadhus, 284; on tyagis, 109, 111, 113, 114, 117, 127, 128, 142;

Cantlie, 282
Carnegy: on Ayodhyamahatmya 2, on building of temples 39, 270; on caste formation 217, 239; on rights to riverside stalls 219–221, 224
Carrithers: on domestication: 80, 126–130, 174
Caste: and devotion, 93, 94; formation, 217, 228–229, 236–237; temples belonging to, 42, 271, 275–276; and occupation, xiv, 238–241; and renunciation, xiii, 67, 72, 125–126, 176; see also varna
Celibacy, Brahmanical theory of 73, 74, 180; and renunciation, 74–75, 180–182; as vow, 118
Chatuhsampradāy, 95, 103, 136, 140, 141

Chaitanya, 98, 100, 166, 178
Church-Sect dichotomy, 66–67
Cohen, 52
Cohn, 52, 53, 133
Collingwood, 188
Commander: on jajmani, 209–210
Communalism, 40–42
Conlon, 216, 217
Conze, 53

Dakshiṇā, 208–209
Dādupanthi, 134, 291
Dān, see gift
Daniélou, 6
Dashnāmi, xiii, 72, 96, 134, 136,
    141–147, 149, 150, 176, 181
De, 81, 166, 167, 291
Dhuni, 92
Dimock, 98; on ras: 166–167; 170,
    200
Divine play, 69, 164, 168, 170
Domesticated sādhu, vignette of:
    78–80
Domestication, 85, 126–130, 157
Dumézil, 52
Dumont, xiii, xiv; general theory,
    54–57; on renunciation, 66–68;
    108, 132, 195, 196. See also
    Dumont and Pocock
Dumont and Pocock, 54, 259
Durkheim, 49, 55

Eck, 3, 6
Eickelman, 60
Elias, 241
Eliade, 2, 49, 108; on yoga,
    122
Elliott, 150, 231, 233
Ensink, 3
Entwistle, 283
Epstein, 187
Eschmann, 65

Festivals, 28–33, 164, 165, 171
Foster, 210
Fire Worship, 115–117, 124
Finch, 37, 211, 212
Fuller, xiv; on history, 51, 57; on
    South Indian temple priests, 186,
    194–197, 259, 292
Gauriya, 98, 100, 101, 136, 139,
    143, 166, 171, 178
Gaya, 64
Gellner, 7
Geertz, 45–48, 50, 52, 56
Ghurye, 291
Ghosh, 291
Ghats, description of, 9–18
Gift, xiv, 186; auspicious and
    inauspicious, 201–205, 263;
    ritual of, 200–201, 208, 209;
    status and gift exchange 192–
    195, 261–263
Gonda, 80, 209, 283, 285
Gorakhnāth Yogis, xiii, 89, 90, 92,
    117, 146, 147, 175, 176
Goswamy, 133, 216
Goody, 56
Goudriaan, 284, 285
Grewal, 133
Gross, analysis of Rāmcharitmānas:
    83–84; 110, 121
Growse, 286
Guptas, 11
Guru Nanak, 27

Hanumān, 92, 148, 149, 150, 152,
    155, 156, 157, 158, 162, 164,
    173, 175
Hanumāngarhi, 19, 23, 24, Muslim
    attack on, 38–39; organization of,
    151–159, 277–280
Hardy, 97
Harivyāsi, 96
Harper, 191

Hawley, 168, 170
Heesterman, xiv; on dakshina, 292–
    293; on the ideal Brahman, 192–
    194, 209
Hill, 82
Hindu-Muslim Conflict, 12, 21, 22,
    24, 25, 36–42
History: and anthropology, 46–51;
    of Ayodhya, 34–43; Hindu
    perception of, 10–12, 34–36
Hocart, 8
Hokusai, 78
Holstrom, 285
Householders, 68–71

Ishwaran, 285
Inden, 282; See also Marriott and
    Inden

Jai Singh II, 98, 100, 137
Jajmānī, xiv, xv, ambiguity of, 261–
    264; decline of, 242–246, 253;
    209–210; patron-priest, 206,
    207, 213, 214, 222, 223, 240,
    241; as 'system', 209–210
Janakpur, 142, 143, 174
Jones, 52
Joshi, 245

Kabīr, 88, 89, 93, 100, 132, 133,
    178, 286, 288
Kabīrpanthi, 94
Kakar, 49, 87, 111, 160, 161
Kanak Bhavan, 22, 23, 161, 273–
    274
Kane, 4
Kanthi, 72, 73
Khālsā, 112, 113
Kolff, 132, 134, 176, 177, 288
Kulke, 65
Kumbh Mela, 77, 101, 103, 104,
    140, 141, 174

Leach, 50, 56
Leonard, 252, 294
Lorenzen, 132, 133, 291

Mādhvās, 95, 96, 98
Mahābrahmans, 193, 194, 264
Malamoud, 209, 293
Maṇḍal, 113, 114
Mandelbaum, 61, 236
Marriott, 44, 54. See also Marriott
    and Inden
Marriott and Inden: on varna
    ideology, xiv, 189–191
Mauss, 55; on the gift, 192–193,
    196, 262
McGregor, 286, 290
McLeod, on Sikhs: 87, 135
Metcalf, 39, 227
Militant monks, 131–142, 145, 150,
    151, 176, 177, 291
Miller, 203, 206, 208, 231
Mital, 98
Moneylending, 79
Monier-Williams, 199, 200, 292
Morinis, 61
Mortuary rites, 193, 194, 205
Mukherjee, 37
Müller, 52
Muslim patronage: of Hindu
    priests, 213, of Hindu temples,
    37–38, 143–144

Nabhaji, 95, 98, 174, 286
Nāgā, vignette of: 76, 77
Nath Yogis, see Gorakhnath
    Yogis
Nawabs of Awadh, 11, 12, 16, 17,
    21, 23, 37, 38, 144, 145, 150,
    212, 222, 270
Nimbarkis, 95, 96
Nirguṇa, and low caste: 93
Nirguṇa, 80–81, 91, 92, 93, 94, 174

Nesfield, 180, 181, 231, 232, 233
Nevil, 294

Obeyesekere, 60, 290
Olivelle, 115
O'Flaherty, 74, 117
O'Malley, 53
Orientalism, 52–58, 282
Orr, 133, 291

Padmavati, 88
Pancarātra, 91
Pāp, see sin
Parry, xiv, 57, 115, 186, gifts to
    funeral priests 193–194, 200,
    205, 206, 207; on the gift in
    general 259, 261, 264, 292; on
    jajmānī, 210, 294 on tantric yogis,
    288
Pilgrimage: expansion of, 213–214,
    226; Hindu notion of, xiv, 1, 2; as
    market, 241–250; reasons for,
    183–184; ritual, 197, 199, 201;
    theory of, 58–65; and violence,
    250–259
Pitṛi, see Ancestor ritual
Pocock, 64, 176, 205, 284, 288, 294
Preston, 132
Puṣṭimārg, 96, 98, 171

Radhakrishnan, 53
Raheja, 232
Ram: story of 4–5; birthplace of, 19,
    20, 21; expiation of, 215–216
Rāmanand, 86–87
Ramanandis, history of, 86–95;
    initiation of, 71–73; relation to
    Shri Vaishnavas, 85, 95–106,
    173; and trading, 129–130, 134,
    176–177
Ramanuja, 95, 96, 97

Ramanujan, 34
Ramanujis, 27, 69
Rāmcharitmānas, 80–81; analysis
    of: 83–84; 117
Ramkot: description of: 18–24
Ram Nam, 81, 84, 91, 94, 122,
    123
Rangachari, 98
Ras, 166–167
Rasik theology, 166–170
Rasik, vignette of: 77, 78
Ravidas, 88, 93, 100
Redfield, 44, 54
Reeves, 37, 244
Religious method, 108, 109, 160
Renou, 95
Roy, 100, 137
Royal patronage: of pandas, 213–
    214, 223, 227, 244, 261–262; of
    temples, 39–40, 271, 273–274
Rösel, 65, 242, 295

Sādhu: definition of, 7–8; 'fallen',
    72; vignette of domesticated, 78–
    80
Said, 282
Saguṇa, 80–81, 92, 93, 94, 174
Sakhī, 84
Sallnow, 60
Saṃnyās, 75, 107
Sants, 90, 91, 93
Sarkar, 151
Sedentarization, 85, 126–130
Shālāgrām, 93, 124, 285
Shankara, 80, 96
Shankarachārya, 87, 194, 197
Sharma, 9
Shivaite renunciation, 75, 107
Sherring 230, 231, 234
Shri Vaishnava, 85, 88, 95, 96, 98.
    101–16, 173, 179, 269, 283, 286
Sikh, 27, 94, 134, 135

Sitaram, 9, 14, 23, 35, 144
Sin, xiv, 18, 183, 203, 204
Singer, 54, 285
Sinha, 168, 286
Srinivas, 60
Staal, 66
Stanley, 29, 232
Stein, 97
Stirrat, 49, 54
Strenski: on domestication, 126–130, 174
Sādhanā, see religious method
Swami Narayan, 27

Tantra, 88–89, 90, 94
Tapas, 92, 107, 116, 117, 118, 133, 174
Thiel-Horstmann, 100, 136, 137
Tilak, 24, 71, 99, 136, 283–284
Teṇkalai, 97, 102
Tieffenthaler, 134
Turner, 44; on pilgrimage, 58–60, 210
Tulsidas, 4, 80–84, 173, 174
Tyāg, 76, 92, 93, 107
Tyāgi, vignette of, 76, 77

Vairāgya, 75, 284

Vaitarani, 3, 198
Vallabhachārya, 96, 98, 100
Valmiki, 4
Van Buitenen, 56
Van der Veer, 8, 42, 60, 186, 286, 292
Van Gennep, 59
Van Schendel, 291
Varady, 177
Varṇa: ideology of, 189–191; among Ramanandis, 73
Vatakalai, 97, 102, 147
Vaudeville, 89, 90, 91, 92, 95, 143, 166, 176
Vidyarthi, 52, 64, 242, 243, 266
Vikramaditya, 10, 11, 19, 20, 34
Vincent, 187, 269
Vishnuite renunciation, 75, 284
Vishnuswami, 95, 96, 98, 101
Vows, 118–121

Weber, 204
Williams, 27
Wolf, 60
Wrestlers, 78, 7, 131

Zamīndāri Abolition, 245, 271, 273

Printed in Great Britain
by Amazon

74640045R00190